INTERNATIONAL HANDBOOK OF REGULATION

This book is dedicated to the memory of Dieter Bös, who died while this book was being prepared. Dieter made a major contribution to regulatory economics while Professor at the University of Bonn and had agreed to contribute to this volume. He will be sadly missed both as an outstanding scholar and a colleague.

International Handbook on Economic Regulation

Edited by

Michael Crew

Professor of Economics, Director of the Center for Research in Regulated Industries (CRRI) and the CRRI Scholar, Rutgers, The State University of New Jersey, USA

and

David Parker

Research Professor in Privatisation and Regulation, Cranfield School of Management, Cranfield University, and Co-Director of the Regulation Research Programme, Centre on Regulation and Competition, University of Manchester, UK

Edward Elgar
Cheltenham, UK • Northampton, MA, USA

Published by
Edward Elgar Publishing Limited
Glensanda House
Montpellier Parade
Cheltenham
Glos GL50 1UA
UK

Edward Elgar Publishing, Inc.
136 West Street
Suite 202
Northampton
Massachusetts 01060
USA

A catalogue record for this book
is available from the British Library

ISBN-13: 978 1 84376 671 1 (cased)
ISBN-10: 1 84376 671 X (cased)

Typeset by Manton Typesetters, Louth, Lincolnshire, UK
Printed and bound in Great Britain by MPG Books Ltd, Bodmin, Cornwall

Contents

Figures

Tables

Contributors

Tony Ballance is Director of Regulation at Severn Trent Water. He was Chief Economist at the Office of Water Services (Ofwat) from 1997 to 1999 and a consultant specializing in the development of regulatory frameworks in the water sector from 1999 to 2005.

Phil Burns is a Director at Frontier Economics where he specializes in regulatory and competition analysis in a number of sectors, with particular emphasis on the energy and postal markets. He has advised companies and authorities on a large number of regulatory and competition cases and he also serves on the panel of advisers to Postcomm, the Dutch Competition Authority (the NMa) and is a member of the States of Guernsey Utility Appeals Panel.

Ian Byatt is Chairman of the Water Commission for Scotland and advises the Northern Ireland government on the reform of their Water Services. He was Director General of Water Services for England and Wales (OFWAT) from privatization in 1989 to 2000. He is a Senior Associate at Frontier Economics and a Professor at Birmingham University.

Lisa J. Cameron is an economic consultant at Deloitte Financial Advisory Services LLP, where she advises clients involved in litigation and regulatory proceedings. Dr. Cameron specializes in the economics of industry and regulation and has published has published her research in leading academic and professional journals. Before becoming a consultant, she taught economics, antitrust and regulatory policy at Carnegie Mellon University. She obtained her PhD in Economics from Stanford University and her BSc in Applied Economics from Cornell University.

Paul Cook is Professor of Economics and Development Policy and Director of the Centre on Regulation and Competition in the Institute for Development Policy at the University of Manchester. His research interests include public enterprise reform and privatization, regulation and competition, economic policy issues in the transitional economies, macroeconomic and trade policy, and public sector management. He has experience as a policy adviser in a number of developing countries and has published widely in the field of development economics.

Michael A. Crew is the Director of CRRI and the CRRI Scholar, Rutgers University. He has been Editor of the *Journal of Regulatory Economics* since its

ix

founding in 1989. His principal research interests are regulatory economics, peak-load pricing, and the theory of monopoly. His publications include five books, 25 edited books, and articles in journals, including *American Economic Review, Economic Journal, Bell Journal of Economics, Journal of Political Economy* and *Journal of Regulatory Economics.*

Thoralf Dassler is a Research Fellow at Queen Margaret University College, Edinburgh. Earlier in his career Thoralf worked in Project Management at Volkswagen in Germany. His PhD was on performance and regulation in EU telecoms, which is to date the only comparative study including the 15 previous member states of the EU. Thoralf has published in internationally renowned journals such as *Utility Policy.*

Gregory M. Duncan consults and teaches economics, statistics, and network industries. He taught at Northwestern, the University of California, Berkeley, and others. His research appears in top journals. He is Director of Economic Consulting, Deloitte Financial Advisory Services LLP and is an academic at the Fuqua School of Business in Duke University, North Carolina. Formerly, he was Senior Vice President at NERA Consulting and, earlier, Senior Scientist at GTE (VZ) Laboratories. He received an MA in Mathematical Statistics and a PhD in Economics from the University of California, Berkeley.

Dan Elliott is a Director of Frontier Economics. He is a specialist in the economics of networks industries, focusing particularly on telecommunications, transport and water. His work covers the full range of competition, regulatory and pricing issues arising in these sectors and since privatization began in the UK in the 1980s he has advised many companies in proceedings with regulatory bodies and the Competition Commission.

Michael Harker is a member of the ESRC Centre for Competition Policy and a lecturer in Norwich Law School at the University of East Anglia. His main research interests are in the fields of UK utility regulation, competition law and public law, particularly public law litigation concerning regulation.

Anthony Heyes is Professor of Economics at Royal Holloway College, University of London, and was previously a Fellow of Nuffield College, Oxford. He has published and advised extensively in the area of environmental regulation and policy.

Cloda Jenkins is a Consultant at Frontier Economics, working across the regulation, competition and strategy practices. She has provided advice to regulators and companies on key issues affecting the postal, energy, water and transport sectors. Cloda was awarded a PhD from University College London in 2004. Her thesis, entitled *Efficiency Properties of Price Cap Regulation*, examines the performance of RPI – X regulation in the UK water, electricity distribution and electricity transmission sectors.

Tim Jenkinson is Reader in Business Economics at the Said Business School, Oxford University, a Fellow of the Centre for Economic Policy Research, and a director of the economics consultancy OXERA. He has written widely on finance and economics, and his current research focuses on initial public offerings, corporate finance, private equity and the cost of capital.

Colin Kirkpatrick is Hallsworth Professor of Development Economics at the Institute for Development Policy and Management, School of Environment and Development, University of Manchester, UK. He has published widely on privatization and regulation issues in developing countries, and was a co-editor of *Leading Issues in Regulation, Competition and Development*, published by Edward Elgar in 2004.

Paul R. Kleindorfer is Anheuser Busch Professor of Management Science and Professor of Business and Public Policy at the Wharton School of the University of Pennsylvania. He has published extensively on managerial economics and regulation. He is the co-author, with Michael Crew, of several monographs on economic regulation as well as an edited book series on the postal sector.

Catherine Liston is a Reader in Business Economics at Royal Holloway College, University of London. She has wide research experience in environmental management issues and has published academic papers in outlets such as the *Journal of Environmental Economics & Management*, *Public Choice* and *Journal of Public Economics*.

Eileen Marshall worked as a stockbroker in the City before becoming senior lecturer in industrial economics at University of Birmingham, UK. She then worked for 14 years as a regulator – in the Office of Electricity Regulation, the Office of Gas Supply and finally the Office of Gas and Electricity Markets, where she was a Managing Director. She was awarded the CBE in 1998 for her contributions to regulatory policy.

Laurence Mathieu is a Research Associate in the ESRC Centre for Competition Policy at the University of East Anglia, in the UK. She is an economist primarily focusing on the UK energy markets.

David Parker is Research Professor in Privatisation and Regulation at the School of Management, Cranfield University, UK and a member of the UK Competition Commission. He has written extensively on competition and regulation issues and was joint editor of the companion volume to this Handbook, the *International Handbook on Privatization*, published by Edward Elgar in 2003.

Scott Reid is Director, Water Markets at ICF Consulting. He advises regulated water utilities and water sector regulators in the UK on tariff development, business and investment planning, efficiency analysis and cost–benefit analysis. He was Head of Tariffs and Water Resource Economics at the Office of Water Services (Ofwat) from 1997 to 2000.

Martin Ricketts is Professor of Economic Organization and Dean of the School of Humanities at the University of Buckingham. He is author of *The Economics of Business Enterprise* and editor of *Neoclassical Microeconomics*, both published by Edward Elgar. With Alan Peacock he is co-author of the Edinburgh Business School's distance learning MBA course 'Government, Industry and Privatization'.

Colin Robinson is Emeritus Professor of Economics at the University of Surrey where he founded the Economics Department. Before that, he worked for 11 years as a business economist. His writings are mainly in energy economics and policy and regulation of utilities. In 1998 he received the Outstanding Contribution to the Profession and its Literature award from the International Association for Energy Economics.

David S. Saal is Lecturer in Industrial Economics and Deputy Director of the Centre for Performance Measurement and Management at Aston Business School, Aston University, UK. His research focuses on the impact of public policy on performance, including work on the impact of utility privatization and regulation on efficiency and productivity growth. He was joint editor of the companion volume to this Handbook, the *International Handbook on Privatization*, published by Edward Elgar in 2003.

Ian Savage is a member of the faculty of both the Department of Economics and the Transportation Center at Northwestern University, USA. He specializes in the analysis of transport safety regulation and safety performance. He has also published on the economics of urban public transport finances and operations and, more specifically, the impacts of competition and privatization.

Timothy J. Tardiff is Vice President with NERA Economic Consulting and specializes in telecommunications economics, including studies of demand,

competitive trends, and regulation accommodating those trends. He has participated in proceedings in over 25 states on interconnection and other issues
addressed by the 1996 US Telecommunications Act as well as in proceedings
before national regulators in the USA, Peru, and New Zealand.

Peter Vass is Director of the Centre for the Study of Regulated Industries (CRI)
at the University of Bath School of Management, UK, and a senior lecturer in
accounting and finance. He was the specialist adviser to the House of Lords
Constitution Committee for its 2003/4 inquiry into *The Regulatory State: Ensuring its Accountability*, published in May 2004.

Catherine Waddams Price is Director of the ESRC Centre for Competition
Policy and Professor in the School of Management at the University of East
Anglia in the UK. She has published widely on privatization, regulation and the
introduction of competition, especially in energy markets, and is a member of
the UK Competition Commission.

Thomas Weyman-Jones has been Professor of Industrial Economics at Lough-
borough University since 1995. His major research interests are efficiency and
productivity analysis using non-parametric and parametric methods, and the
theory and practice of utility regulation. He has published numerous papers on
data envelopment analysis and stochastic frontier analysis for yardstick competition, and on mechanisms for incentive regulation. He has been specialist adviser
to energy regulators in several European countries.

Preface

The subject of economic regulation has become more important in the study of economics over the last 30 years because of important advances in theory and because of major changes in public policy, which have led to the privatization of a number of state-owned, monopoly industries and the introduction of competition. This has been occurring in both advanced and developing economies and, most strikingly, in the former command economies of Central and Eastern Europe. Growing concerns about 'global warming' have sparked off theoretical and policy initiatives related to environmental regulation; while development economics places emphasis on the importance of regulatory 'institutions' in explaining impediments to sustained economic growth.

This handbook covers and critiques the developments in both regulatory theory and practice. It is intended to be a primary source of information for students, researchers and practitioners in the field of regulatory economics. In putting together this book we wish to thank a number of people including the editorial and publication staff at Edward Elgar and especially Eve Hussey at Cranfield, who has diligently typed and retyped the various drafts. We also thank our families for (once again) their patience and support.

Michael Crew, Rutgers University, New Jersey
David Parker, Cranfield University, Bedfordshire
September 2005

1 Development in the theory and practice of regulatory economics

Michael A. Crew and David Parker

Introduction[1]

This book reflects some of the major developments in the applications of regulatory economics to network industries over the past 20 years or so. This chapter gives a commentary on these developments to provide context and motivation for the chapters that follow. The first part of the chapter reviews the background in which regulatory change has taken place and provides the motivation for the book. This is followed by a brief evaluation of theoretical developments over the period[2] and later by an examination of some of the major events that have occurred in practice in the wave of restructuring and 'deregulation' undertaken in the network industries over the past two decades. While our approach is intended to be general, it is focused, as is most of the content of this book, mainly on the United Kingdom and the United States because of the wealth of experience of economic regulation in these countries, although the theoretical developments reflect contributions from economists around the world. We provide a brief summary and comments in a later part of the chapter. Finally, we conclude by providing some implications for the future of regulation and regulated industries.

The background to regulatory reform

The regulatory scene in the early 1980s differed significantly from what we see today. The change that has taken place in the last 20 years is ostensibly greater than that of the previous 80 years. In the UK during the 1980s and early 1990s the network industries, except for the Post Office, were privatized and a new regulatory apparatus was instituted. In the US change was also major. Take telecommunications as a prime example. In 1982 the world's largest company, American Telephone & Telegraph (AT&T), controlled around 80 per cent of the access lines and over 90 per cent of the long-distance traffic. In addition, it was, through its Western Electric subsidiary, a large manufacturer of telecommunications equipment ranging from handsets to cables to central office equipment. Its research arm, Bell Labs, was one of the premier research and development organizations in the world. However, as Phillips (2002) and Kovacic (2002) explain in detail, trouble was afoot. The Justice Department had waged war on AT&T with a landmark antitrust suit that was settled with the divestiture by

1

AT&T of its local telephone companies. The industry has undergone further dramatic changes since then with the Regional Bell Operating Companies (RBOCs) consolidating into four enterprises, and with one of these, GTE, merging with another, Bell Atlantic, to become Verizon, one of the four surviving RBOCs. SBC and Verizon continue to have aspirations for acquisition. Ironically, with SBC's acquisition of AT&T, what was once the world's largest company disappears into oblivion, like some poor creature in the process of being swallowed by a giant python. MCI, the second largest long-distance carrier has also been acquired by Verizon. Even more ironically, the government, having broken up the industry, has allowed the industry to be reconsolidated with the acquisitions by SBC and Verizon.

In the UK change in telecommunications was initiated by the separation of BT from the Post Office in 1981 and by its privatization in 1984. In the first seven years of private ownership a duopoly existed in fixed-line systems with a new licensed operation, Mercury (which shortly after it was established became wholly owned by the international telecommunications operator Cable and Wireless, itself privatized by the British government in 1981) operating as the only competitor to BT. From 1991 the UK telecommunications market was opened up to further competition, although today BT still accounts for the vast majority of domestic calls, albeit with a smaller share of business and international connections. Paralleling this development has been the introduction of competition in telecommunications markets across the European Union. In each of the EU Member States dedicated regulatory offices have been established, with Oftel in the UK being the oldest and dating back to BT's privatization.

The changes in telecommunications have been dramatic because of the changes in the underlying technology. Technologies that existed only in rudimentary form in 1982 are now ubiquitous – personal computers, optical fibre, the Internet and wireless technology. Fax was considered a big deal in 1982. It is now commonplace, but of much less significance than it was in the early 1990s. Wireless technology has become widespread and a major competitor of wireline technology across the world. Cable, through the voice over Internet protocol (VOIP), has started to become an alternative to landlines for voice calls. Similarly, wireless is also providing competition for traditional landlines. These developments have enabled SBC and Verizon to argue in the US that their major acquisitions are unlikely to increase market power significantly. Both have major holdings in wireless and with their acquisitions in long distance they will have significant control of the Internet backbone, and therefore their potential market power will be enhanced. Similarly, in the UK BT emphasizes the existence of increasing competition from wireless ('mobile') phones and has entered, exited and then re-entered this market. The developments in telecommunications have, indeed, been startling and the resulting changes make the industry of 20 years ago seem but a distant glimmer.

Developments in energy have also been significant but the technological change has been less dramatic. Changes in the natural gas industry over the last 20 years have been major in the US and in the UK. As Leitzinger and Collette (2002) note, the changes have been in institutions, market structure and regulation. The process began in the US in the 1970s with a concern over take-or-pay contracts and with the bundled nature of transportation and production companies that was seen as a barrier to open and non-discriminatory access to pipelines. In the ensuing regulatory changes of the 1980s and early 1990s, traditional long-term contracting was replaced by shorter-term contracts and risk hedging instruments benchmarked on new spot markets. Contracting and spot markets were driven by market intermediaries and brokers and the increasingly real-time information of the digital economy. Enron's demise in December 2001, and the ensuing and ongoing investigation that followed, cast a dark shadow over the energy sector generally and on energy trading in particular. However, trading in natural gas futures has again regained considerable vigour, now with new oversight on both markets and data underlying the derivative instruments traded. Thus the basic institutions of the deregulated natural gas markets appear to have survived Enron's fall, but as Weaver (2004) notes in her treatise on the subject, there will continue to be repercussions from 'Enronitis' for some time to come. In the UK the state owned British Gas Corporation was privatized in 1986 with only large gas users having a choice of supplier. During the 1990s gas supply was gradually opened up to further competition so that by the end of the decade all consumers had a choice of gas supplier. In the face of these market changes, British Gas voluntarily divided into two separate companies, Centrica (mainly concerned with gas retailing and servicing) and British Gas Trading (whose main activity was gas production, storage and distribution, the latter through its subsidiary Transco). In October 2000 a demerger from BG plc resulted in Transco becoming a part of the Lattice Group plc. Two years on, Lattice Group plc had merged with National Grid (the owner of the electricity high-voltage transmission grid) to form National Grid Transco plc – the UK's largest utility. Gas distribution is still regulated, by the Office of Gas and Electricity Markets (which incorporated the separate gas and electricity regulatory offices in 1999). Gas supply to customers is now competitive and retail prices are no longer regulated.

Deregulating the electric utility industry has proved to be exceedingly challenging as Hogan (2002) and Joskow (2003) note in their summary of developments. Major change in the industry has taken place over the last 20 years. The first major change to affect the industry in the US was the Public Utility Regulatory Policies Act of 1978 (PURPA). This set in motion a process whereby generators other than vertically integrated utilities would be allowed to sell power into the grid, *inter alia*, requiring utilities to purchase such power at prices that utilities deemed to be excessive. With PURPA, the independent generation industry was effectively born. This led to dramatic changes in the industry but hardly to a resolution of its problems, as the ensuing chaos in California in 2000–02 dramatically illustrates. During this period, a series of radical changes (enabled by the Energy Policy Act of 1992) were introduced by the Federal Energy Regulatory Commission (FERC), directed at assuring open access to the transmission grid to a now unbundled and competitive generation sector. These regulatory decrees and the associated creation of wholesale power markets have met with mixed success. As we will discuss in more detail below, they are clearly a work in progress.

These trends in the US have been motivated partly by the experience of the UK and indeed the entire process of deregulation is now an international affair, with countries and regions attempting to copy best practice in other systems and avoid the worst mistakes of others. The electricity industry was privatized in England, Wales and Scotland in 1990/91 (Northern Ireland has its own electricity supply industry which remains differently structured to the rest of the UK). As part of the privatization, the industry was unbundled into separate generation, transmission, distribution and supply companies, although recent years have seen a number of mergers that are leading to the creation of new vertically integrated companies.[3] Electricity supply, like gas supply, is now competitive. Currently, Continental Europe is undergoing its own market liberalization journey following the opening of the electricity market in the European Union in 2002. It is hoped that the lessons of the US, especially California, and the UK will be of some value in the EU and elsewhere as these experiments unfold. As Wolak (2004) notes in his review of electricity markets internationally, an ounce of precaution and humility before the fact is worth a pound of cleaning up afterwards.

Other network industries, including airlines, water, railways and afterwards the postal service, have gone through similar changes in a number of countries, as economists have touted the benefits of better pricing, ownership and governance structures. Many of the changes that have taken place have occurred under the umbrella of deregulation. Deregulation was touted in the economics community as the single best approach to reforming utility industries, promising increased production efficiency, lower prices and better service. The results achieved have been, however, much more modest.

A major problem of the deregulation movement is that its foundations were logically weak, especially the many claims that it would improve efficiency. These were typically grounded in self-interest, but this in itself, as Adam Smith noted long ago, is not going to lead to an economically efficient outcome in the absence of competition. In the case of a monopoly that exists because of government policy, abolishing it and going to competition would generally be welfare enhancing as long as no significant scale or scope economies are lost in the process. This is basically the old economic argument of the superiority of perfect competition to pure monopoly. Unfortunately, a choice as simple as this is almost never available in the world of regulated monopoly, as argued in more detail in the chapter by Crew and Kleindorfer in this volume (Chapter 3). The choices that are available are much more complex and it is much more difficult to make efficiency claims about them. The scenarios and choices available all derive from the basic strategy of 'whittling down' rather than total elimination of the monopoly, along the lines of the following scenario.

A basic deregulation scenario
Under this scenario a regulated (possibly multi-product) monopoly is replaced by competition upstream and remains a regulated monopoly downstream, at least for some of its products. To the extent that there are X-efficiency gains upstream and these are passed on downstream, this is welfare enhancing. The expectation is that regulation will continue downstream, but that the more limited monopoly may be easier to regulate in that the information asymmetries between the firm and the regulator may be reduced.

This questioning of regulation was known generally as 'deregulation'. Anyone who objected to regulation could argue his or her point preaching the gospel of deregulation. It did not seem to matter much that the arguments were based on self-interest. Indeed, deregulation seemed to open up new avenues for rent seeking not previously available when the old system was accepted. The potential monopoly rents had always been large for utilities. Regulation had managed to transfer many of these to customers, especially small users. For most small customers regulation was and still remains a rather good deal. As long as the traditional consensus held, consumers retained their share of the rents and the companies, although limited in the profits they could make, were not subject to major pressures to minimize costs. By raising the average cost curve, the system may have dissipated some of the rents in X-inefficiency, a total deadweight loss, in addition to the allocative efficiency of the resulting higher price. These X-inefficiency losses were the subject of significant criticism on the part of economists, whose arguments provided a foundation in debates and regulatory hearings for rent seekers preaching change in the name of deregulation. Deregulation opened the door of the chicken coop and many foxes entered wearing the clothes of deregulation.

Partly because of the lack of transparency of regulation, and its inherent multi-party nature in splitting the rents generated by protected monopolies, the deregulation process has also typically been piecemeal, serving one set of interests after the next in selective implementation of changes and reforms. Large bodies of professional expertise in the legal and economic communities have become dependent on the continuing process of justifying these changes and reforms of reforms. Essentially the approach has been to adopt changes that seem to be the most easily implemented without addressing some of the fundamental underlying problems. This piecemeal approach and the failure to recognize the role of rent seeking have jointly led to a failure to think through the consequences of regulatory changes. At this stage, it is still too early to guess what the outcome of all this will be for the next two decades in the UK and the US and elsewhere. Taking an optimistic perspective, some of the worst decisions of the past on regulatory reform may yet provide instructive guidelines for the future.

Developments in the theory of regulation

Two decades ago regulatory economics had just completed some big strides. In part, this had been as a result of a major investment made in economic research by the Bell System (AT&T). Notable in this was the founding in the spring of 1970 of *The Bell Journal of Economics and Management Science*, which became the *Bell Journal of Economics* in the spring of 1975, which begat the *Rand Journal* in the spring of 1984 immediately following the divestiture of AT&T. AT&T apparently saw no significant benefit in continuing its major effort in regulatory economics, which had ostensibly been a costly failure memorialized in the divestiture. The divestiture of the *Bell Journal* to Rand and the gutting of its premier economics group at Bell Labs might be seen as two casualties in the failure of some outstanding economic brainpower and innovative research to carry the day for Bell. The trend has continued with RBOCs becoming less interested in economic research.

In many ways the research of the 1970s and 1980s was inspired in a significant way by the resources ploughed into microeconomics by AT&T. Take the *Bell Journal*,[4] money appeared to be no object. The *Bell Journal* had no difficulty attracting extremely talented editors and contributors, including already distinguished scholars like William Baumol, Walter Oi, Richard Posner, George Stigler, William Vickrey, Oliver Williamson, and others. Perhaps even more important was that the *Bell Journal* attracted many young economists, including Elizabeth Bailey, John Panzar, Robert Willig, and David Sibley, whose work in the 1970s and 1980s played a major role in the evolution of regulatory economics. Together the visibility of regulated industries and the quality of the researchers involved made regulatory economics the most important subspecialty in the study of industrial organization within economics.

Before the founding of the *Bell Journal* regulatory economics was extremely undeveloped. There was the seminal work of Averch and Johnson (1962),[5] and the marginal cost pricing debate for monopolies of the 1940s and 1950s, which itself became specialized into the peak-load pricing debate through the work of Boiteux (1949), Steiner (1957) and Williamson (1966). Ramsey pricing was given a new lease of life by Baumol and Bradford (1970) and the Bell Labs economists, including Rohlfs (1979). These contributions all provided the context for the research that the *Bell Journal* fostered in the 1970s. They also provided important benchmarks for policies in energy and telecommunications that were intended to emulate the benefits promised by theory in practice.

All of these developments were outgrowths of already established theory. However, the theory of contestable markets, due primarily to Baumol et al. (1982), did not have such roots. This theory was thus original and unconstrained in a way that other developments were not. Perhaps for this reason, the authors of contestability had very high hopes for the impact of their work.[6] Indeed, now, more than two decades on, it is clear that it has become one of the landmarks in regulatory economics. Among other contributions, this work clarified considerably the nature of economies of scale and scope. The authors also provided clear definitions and tests for cross-subsidy in a multi-product firm in the form of the *burden test*.[7] The work of Baumol and his colleagues has been important for both the development of theory as well as for guiding practice.

Principal–agent models and mechanism design theory
Around the mid-1980s a change took place in the theory of regulatory economics, and this involved the incorporation of principal–agent theory, mechanism design theory and information economics. This began with the work of Baron and Myerson (1982). The work was an outgrowth of the work on principal–agent theory in the 1970s (e.g. Ross, 1973 and Groves, 1973), which, indeed, offered major insights into issues of managerial effort and corporate governance. However, as noted in Crew and Kleindorfer (1986) and in Chapter 3, the insights of this rather large (and still growing) stream of literature have had very little to do with designing institutions or mechanisms that can be applied to regulatory problems as they exist in practice, one issue is sometimes summarized as the *commitment problem*.[8]

Lest we are seen to paint too pessimistic a picture about mechanism design theory, we hasten to point out that one of its offshoots, auction theory, has been an important contribution to both regulatory theory and practice. This literature points to both important empirical work, as well as an increasing number of experimental and behavioural contributions with extensive regulatory applications, as illustrated in the two special issues of the *Journal of Regulatory Economics* in May and July 2000 (see e.g. Salant, 2000). But although economists now have a much better understanding of auctions and bidding, the applications have not been without their problems, as the California electricity generation market, discussed further below, illustrates. However, unlike the mechanism design literature, the bidding, auctions and experimental economics literature offers considerable potential in regulatory economics. These innovations do not mean that franchise bidding along the lines of Demsetz (1968) is going to replace traditional regulation or that bidding will result in radical changes in regulation. They do, however, provide regulatory economists with some powerful tools, which have already resulted in a number of promising applications. Besides providing the backbone for spot market and futures exchanges, well-designed auctions are also now providing workable solutions for dealing with the thorny problem of providing default service obligations (e.g. Salant, 2002).

Price-cap and incentive regulation

Allowing more rent seekers to compete for the rents, according to the original Tullock (1967) analysis, is likely to dissipate more of the rents as the rent seekers compete them away. This is likely to be true unless the gain from any reduction in X-inefficiency somehow outweighs the dissipation of the rents. In the 1980s economists offered a new form of regulation, incentive regulation or price-cap regulation (PCR) that seemed to offer just this – improvements in X-efficiency. In addition, it seemed to fit in well with the macroscopic political changes that were taking place. In the UK the election of Margaret Thatcher in 1979 and again in 1983 and 1987 gave her the opportunity to carry out her Party's election platform, which promised the dismantling of most of the economic institutions of democratic socialism. Her programme of privatization of public enterprise was a centrepiece of her vision of a non-socialist, free market economy (Parker, 2004, p. 3). Along with privatization, changes in regulation were required. Stephen Littlechild (1983), a long time critic of rate of return regulation (ROR), proposed PCR for British Telecom, the former Post Office Telephones and PCR spread to other public utilities in the UK as they were privatized in the 1980s and 1990s. PCR and other forms of 'incentive regulation' gave rise to a whole new generation of theory and institutional development in the UK, the US and elsewhere.[9]

All this led in the 1980s to great expectations from incentive regulation. However, by the mid-1990s the façade of incentive regulation started to crack and hybrid systems known as performance-based regulation (PBR) appeared on the scene. What was it that Littlechild and most economists found so problematical about ROR, making it such an easy target and why did regulatory practice partially turn against PCR? The feature of ROR that most offended economists was that it coupled revenue and cost closely together. The firm earned revenue by demonstrating that its costs were at a particular level and its regulators then allowed revenues based on the proof of these costs. Thus revenue directly depended on costs. The greater the costs, the greater the revenue allowed. Given the asymmetry of information about a regulated firm's efficient costs it was very difficult for a regulator to determine whether the firm's costs were minimized. The firm was able to take some of the monopoly rents in the form of higher costs, a result entirely consistent with the much earlier notion of J.R. Hicks (1935) that a 'quiet life' was the 'best of all monopoly profits.' It was this internal inefficiency or X-inefficiency that was at the root of most economists' distaste for ROR, and PCR was an attempt to overcome these inefficiencies (Littlechild, 1983).

By creating a discontinuity in the firm's marginal revenue curve, PCR opened up the prospect of X-efficiency and even a move toward allocative efficiency. Unfortunately, PCR offered no free lunch, as readily became apparent in theory and practice. The theoretical problem was already apparent in the mechanism design literature reviewed above. Under the framework developed by Laffont and Tirole (1993), the firm can be shown to operate in a least-cost manner provided it is able to appropriate the rents attributable to its information advantage and *provided the regulator allows it to continue to retain these rents*. If a regulator cannot be counted on to keep to the regulatory bargain, the firm loses its incentives to operate at least cost. This is dubbed a failure of *commitment*. However, as history has demonstrated, regulators cannot simply promise to leave rents on the table, whether or not this might be theoretically justified. Thus, in practice, under PCR, regulatory commitment and reneging are a significant problem (Gausch, 2004, pp. 80–87). When a regulated firm makes large profits, regulators adjust PCR parameters to appropriate them. When a regulated firm shows signs of approaching financial distress, regulators have relaxed the PCR regime. The required theoretical commitment of the regulator to a stable regime is not evident in practice, with the end result that 'pure PCR' has been difficult to implement in practice.

In the US, PCR was rarely embraced as enthusiastically as it was in Europe. Could it be that years of regulatory practice had bred a concern about the regulator's congenital inability to commit? Put more gently, there was a long established practice in US regulation of pragmatism or 'working things' out as you go along. Goldberg (1976) argued that regulation should be seen as a complicated form of contract for which all eventualities could not be specified, where the regulator acted as the intermediary between consumers and the firm to address problems as unforeseen eventualities arose. The alternative argument, developed from Tullock (1967), would see the regulator as a broker distributing the rents dependent on changes in the political equilibrium, as developed in Crew and Rowley (1988). Either interpretation is consistent with the way practice developed in the US. PBR is a hybrid of PCR and ROR. The firm's ability to make profits is attenuated by a sharing rule, whereby above or below an upper and lower limit, respectively, the firm shares profits or losses according to a pre-specified sharing rule. Either the regulator or the regulated firm has the option of reopening the regulatory process to renegotiate the 'agreement' should significant adverse or positive consequences materialize. These protocols and procedures provide a process for attenuating the regulator's ability to take away what are perceived as excess profits, by agreeing in advance on a process for limiting the scope for excess profits on the upside and limiting the exposure faced by the firm for losses on the downside. Clearly, incentives for X-efficiency are weakened in the process and the distribution of rents is affected less. However, this may be the best that is achievable now given the state of technology in regulatory economics today.

Access pricing and regulated competition

Even 20 years ago, concerns over access pricing were a practical issue in telecommunications. With the divestiture of AT&T in the US and the liberalization of telecommunication markets in Europe and elsewhere, these concerns increased significantly. However, theoretical contributions to address the problem of access pricing came later. Access to an essential or bottleneck facility is the issue. The problem is compounded when the owner of an essential facility is also selling to final consumers in competition with the other firms. An example would be long-distance telephone companies purchasing access from local phone companies to complete their calls. The local companies themselves might be also providing long-distance service. This is the case, for example, with BT in the UK, and in a few jurisdictions in the US for RBOCs. The *efficient component pricing rule* (ECPR), which originated with Willig (1979), was one of the first attempts by economists to address the issue of efficient access pricing. Among the leading exponents of ECPR are Baumol and Sidak (1994). The idea of ECPR can be summarized, as in Baumol and Sidak (1994, p. 178), as follows:

Optimal input price = the input's direct per-unit incremental cost +
the opportunity cost to the input supplied of the sale of a unit of input.

The problem with ECPR arises from the second term on the right-hand side. If this could be determined on the basis of a readily observable price in a competitive market, then ECPR would be an efficient rule, at least for a homogeneous product. However, it is precisely because of the bottleneck facility that such a competitive price cannot be determined. ECPR then comes down to allowing the bottleneck supplier the monopoly rents that he (or she) was earning when he was the only vertical integrated monopolist. As most monopolists are regulated, this presumably comes down to allowing him the regulated return that he would have obtained.

In any event, most access pricing problems encountered in the real world are much more complicated than this. For example, products may be differentiated and entrants may use the incumbent's access product to gain a foothold in the market, and eventually to undercut the incumbent in the monopoly market, thereby undermining the incumbent's financial viability. This is very much the core of the debate on access pricing in the postal arena, where entrants could use the incumbent postal operator's (PO) network to enter the market and deliver in profitable areas leaving the incumbent to serve the high-cost delivery areas. The result of liberalized access policies could well be that entrants deliver end-to-end service in the low-cost urban areas, while leaving to the incumbent PO all other mail for delivery at some published access price. As a number of authors have shown (e.g. Crew and Kleindorfer, 2004a) that great care must be exercised in this instance to define access prices that promote efficient entry without undermining the financial viability of the PO, which retains a default service obligation. In particular, the ECPR approach is not efficient because this is a multi-product environment. Taking the same avoided cost discount off the end-to-end single-piece price of a letter leads to subsidized access in the high-cost areas. Such subsidies not only promote inefficient entry, but they may also lead to the financial demise of the incumbent PO.

As almost every restructuring proposal for network industries foresees some form of competition and entry, access pricing has become a key focus of the debate on deregulation. It effectively allows the gradual entry in network indus-tries, leveraging such entry off the incumbent's existing network and allowing entrants to develop their business based on partial entry rather than on the much more demanding facility-based full entry scenario. Because of the importance of access pricing, a great deal of energy has been devoted in the theory of regu-latory economics to understanding some of the complexities involved and in developing solutions to them. A particularly promising approach seems to be what Laffont and Tirole (1996) have referred to as *global price caps*.[10] The idea is intriguingly simple. Access is treated as a final good rather than as an inter-mediate good and is included in the computation of the price cap. In addition, 'Weights used in the computation of the price cap are exogenously determined and are proportional to the forecast quantities of the associated goods' (Laffont and Tirole, 1996, p. 243). Laffont and Tirole explore the possibilities of forming a hybrid of ECPR and global price caps, which may offer benefits in terms of weight setting and protection against anti-competitive practices. Such a hybrid approach may provide a means of achieving a transition to the global price cap, which has considerable advantages. These are summarized by Laffont and Tirole (1996, p. 254) as follows: 'A global price cap penalizes increases in both access prices and final prices and induces the [regulated firm] to price discriminate very much the way an unregulated firm would do, except that the entire price structure is brought down by the cap.'

While significant progress in the theory of access pricing has been made, a considerable amount of further development is required particularly if it is going to contribute to the practical policy debate, which is the subject of the next sec-tion. Interest continues in access pricing as illustrated by Armstrong's (2002) excellent survey on access pricing and interconnection and the chapter by Tardiff (Chapter 13) in this volume. Many problems remain, some of which are ad-dressed by Armstrong and Tardiff, including two-way interconnection – an important problem for Internet service providers. Other issues include structural separation of access from the rest of the business and divestiture of access mo-nopolies. Finally, access pricing is part of a much larger problem of the role and obligations of incumbent network service providers in industries under deregula-tion, to which we will now turn briefly.

Default service provision
Microeconomic theory over the last 20 years has supported deregulation. However, it has done so in a piecemeal fashion. Consideration of the impact of entry on the obligations of incumbents has left much to be desired. As a regulated monopolist, incumbents have faced default service provider obligations and these have been the vehicle for the propagation of many subsidies. While the understanding of the nature of such obligations has been the subject of some study, for example, the universal service obligation (USO) in the postal sector, as illustrated in Crew and Kleindorfer (2002b, 2005), the bigger picture of the interaction of default service obligations (DSO) with deregulation is still undeveloped.

Consider the case of distribution services for local network services for gas or electricity. A price cap for a distribution utility with a DSO creates a certain dissonance. Is the energy purchased treated as a simple cost pass through, with this component of the bill varying with the purchases in the spot market? Or is the distribution utility required to line up long-term contracts to provide guaranteed prices? In either case difficulties arise. If the default service provider insists on only making purchases in the spot or short-term market and is allowed a straight pass through, the value to consumers of the default service obligation is minimal since they are absorbing all the risks. If the distribution company sets up long-term contracts to guarantee prices and if prices fall, it loses customers and is stuck with high-priced long-term contracts, which will prove costly to it under a price cap. Competition in such markets is very difficult to achieve when distortions like the default service obligation are included. The optimal risk sharing problem, under a DSO, is further complicated when the regulated firm is a for-profit, investor-owned firm because then these contract-based risk sharing decisions must also be integrated with the decision (perhaps co-determined with the regulator) on the capital structure of the regulated firm (see de Fraja and Stones, 2004). The problem is not well understood and awaits a workable solution.

The DSO problem illustrates a deeper underlying problem with deregulation, in that the residual monopoly after deregulation affects classes of consumers very differently. Large industrial and commercial customers are usually not going to face much risk of monopoly exploitation because they have significant alternatives. They can generate their own electricity. They can connect directly to the gas pipeline; they do not need the local gas distribution company. Similarly, they have alternatives to the local phone company and would have no difficulty obtaining mail service in the absence of a postal monopoly. The situation for small customers is, however, very different. They have few alternatives. Indeed, for most of them the reality of natural monopoly is obvious. The only way that they can be economically supplied is by a single producer with the ability to spread large fixed costs across many small customers and the ability to incur and pay for customer-specific sunk costs. Regulation provided rough and ready consumer protection for these small customers. Even if the potential for cross-subsidy that regulation provided could be abandoned, the problem of monopoly exploitation of small customers would remain as a serious issue to be addressed.

The DSO might be considered an extension of the protection from monopoly exploitation that regulation offered to small customers. However, it turns out to be a major obstacle to deregulation. Generally, the default service obligation may be considered the right of any customer, in practice normally only a constraint in the case of small customers, to receive service of some defined quality at a 'reasonable' price. This notion was rather easily achievable under monopoly. In effect the regulator guaranteed that the profitable large customers could not be picked off by entrants, in return for which the monopolist faced the obligation to provide service to customers large and small at the rate set by the regulator. The regulator, in determining 'reasonable' prices, had considerable potential to cross-subsidize and even this did not overly concern the monopolist as long as the regulator barricaded the market against entry. The same result occurred under state ownership of network industries where government guaranteed a universal service supported by endemic cross-subsidies. This all changed under deregulation. The regulator started to allow entry into the profitable parts of the incumbent's business while at the same time continuing to require the incumbent to provide default service. In short, the regulator retained the obligation to serve, while simultaneously removing the wherewithal to finance it.

Deregulation must address these twin issues of residual monopoly and default service. One approach is the Posnerian one. This would essentially say, 'Let 'er rip'. If these residual problems remain as a result of deregulation, so be it. The difficulties of fixing them are just too great. At the other extreme there is tight regulation of the cost of service variety that addresses these twin issues directly. Many economists would find the Posnerian view attractive and, indeed, would find tight regulation reprehensible and against their religion. However, most of them would recognize that the Posnerian approach is not feasible politically. The question that remains then is whether there exists a middle ground, which takes into account the twin problems of residual monopoly and default service and, at the same time, mitigates some of the inefficiencies of traditional tight regulation. Where views are located on this spectrum may, of course, depend on the industry, its technology, its growth potential and its starting condition.

However one proceeds, addressing the twin challenges of curbing monopoly exploitation for the residual monopoly and maintaining default service are critical if deregulation is to succeed. One consequence of all of this might be that the gains from deregulation are likely to be much less than originally anticipated. Also, there may be significant transactions costs of regulation in the face of increased complexity resulting from the interaction of competition, regulation and the characteristics of the DSO itself. In particular, the requirement to provide default service without a regulated monopoly to finance it inevitably leads to major problems that are not easily fixed. These are at the root of many of the ongoing problems of deregulation in specific sectors. A number of these issues are explored further in the chapters that follow, particularly Chapter 10.

Developments in practice
One of the lessons for regulatory economics, which is inherent in many of the chapters of this book, is the importance of the challenge of practical problems. Regulatory economics is an area of economics that is enhanced by practice and most of the important theoretical developments are likely to arise out of practice. Thus in this section we intend not only to evaluate some the developments in practice that have occurred, but some ways in which practical problems may lead to advances in theory. We begin with a general assessment of the interaction of regulatory theory and practice and then turn to a brief review of developments in three specific network industries: telecommunications, electricity and the postal sector.

The growth in regulatory economics over the last 20 years, illustrated by the increasing literature, has led to a change in the role of economists. In the US companies probably employ fewer regulatory economists since the depletion of AT&T's regulatory economics staff in the mid-1980s, but the consulting and academic demand for regulatory economists has continued to grow there and in the UK as economists partake of the feeding frenzy in litigation associated with restructuring.[11] One of the most important elements brought by economists to the restructuring debate has been arguably a conceptual framework to analyse efficiency and notions of cost, and this has been nowhere more in evidence than in the area of pricing. To take two examples, access pricing and peak-load (or its descendant, real-time) pricing, economists have generally led the debate on these innovations in practice.

Access pricing for network industries was in its infancy 20 years ago. In the area of telecommunications, there has been decidedly mixed success in practice in implementing the principles for efficient access pricing and the debate over access pricing and structure continues unabated. Some mixed success has been achieved in access pricing in the gas industry, as indicated by recent developments analysed in Leitzinger and Collette (2002).[12] The postal sector is an unlikely success story. The United States Postal Service (USPS) is often criticized as a moribund public enterprise. Its role and that of its regulator, the United States Postal Rate Commission (PRC), in opening up parts of the postal value chain to access is a major success story. However, postal worksharing – a postal term referring to upstream activities like presorting, bar-coding and drop shipments – has been a major success in the postal sector as illustrated in numerous papers, for example, Mitchell (1999). This seems to be one aspect of the postal sector pricing practices that USPS, large mailers and the PRC all seem to agree is working well, although there are still wide disagreements on how postal worksharing and access pricing should be integrated with the incumbent Postal Operator's Universal Service Obligation (Crew and Kleindorfer, 2004b). Similar debate exists in Europe following the EU's decision to open up postal services to greater competition.

Peak-load and real-time pricing is another mixed success story in terms of practice. Twenty years ago the theory of peak-load pricing was well developed. Since then, it has been successfully applied in many areas, not just in network industries. In some ways, given the head start that peak-load pricing had in network industries, the progress has been disappointing in these industries relative to elsewhere. Peak-load pricing in other industries, notably airlines and hotels, has become successful largely because of advances in computing, telecommunications and the Internet. The airlines, by employing techniques like artificial intelligence and data mining, have successfully combined peak-load pricing with price discrimination. The main device used for price discrimination is flexibility in travel schedules. Business travellers require flexibility in their travel plans. They may need to travel at a moment's notice. Plans may change or the business may be concluded more quickly and they wish to return early. They normally travel during the business week. Thus airlines find means of identifying business travellers. The lower price tickets must be purchased in advance – usually at least seven days – and cannot be changed without penalty. In addition, a Saturday night stay is required. The airlines have found relatively straightforward ways of identifying the travellers with lower demand elasticity, while preventing transfer and arbitrage thus making price discrimination highly successful.

The airlines' successful techniques of price discrimination are combined with peak-load pricing not in the way peak-load pricing is normally employed, namely in real time. Peak-load pricing was traditionally time of day or combined time of day and seasonal pricing. For example, electricity might be charged at a lower price at night and at weekends. For airlines this would appear to translate into last minute fares with people who were prepared to wait at the airport to take up empty seats at low prices. The argument would be that, given that an additional passenger could be put on the aircraft at essentially zero marginal cost, a low (off-peak) price could be offered. With the greater understanding of price discrimination, such last minute cheap fares would not be attractive to the airlines. Because of the tendency of business travellers to change their plans and to be last minute, the airlines may not wish to sell remaining seats to standby passengers. They might prefer to leave them unfilled in case a full fare business traveller shows up. In addition, because of more sophisticated yield management techniques and frequent flyer programmes, standby passengers are of much less importance. In many ways frequent flyer programmes are the ultimate peak-load pricing device. More of them can be made available on flights that have a low load factor. The airlines can estimate weeks and even months ahead how full a given flight is likely to be. If the flight is running light, the airline changes the mix of seats. For example, it can add more frequent flyer seats. The airlines have benefited from deregulation in that they have been able to take into account two of the basic ideas of microeconomic theory, namely price discrimination and peak load pricing, and combine them in a reasonably sophisticated way. Despite the impressive application of these techniques, the structure has recently begun to crack with the onslaught of discount airlines. It may be that it was carrying too heavy a load of bloated labour and other costs and not sufficiently strong barriers to entry, thereby providing fodder for the discounters.

Paradoxically, the success of peak-load pricing in the regulated network industries has been mixed, despite their distinct head. Almost all of the economic theory had been written with regulated network industries in mind. Moreover, the potential benefits from peak-load pricing were significant in electricity and telecommunications. It is interesting why the network industries, especially electricity, failed to capitalize on their head start with peak-load pricing. Several things were in place for success, including innovations in metering that meant that more sophisticated and lower cost time of day meters were now available. These could be employed with smaller customers One problem is that the metering or transactions costs are still high relative to the successful applications in the airline and the hotel industries. In addition, electricity still remained regulated, so limiting its potential profits from innovative pricing and reducing its flexibility in pricing.

As noted in the early part of this chapter, and in Chapters 2 and 3, the essential driver of deregulation in network industries in the US and the UK has been rent seeking. The result has been an unwillingness to give up the benefits of regulation while simultaneously seeking regulatory change. The central question has been a structural one: how far should the initial regulated monopoly be reduced? Once this question is answered, in one way or another, issues of access pricing, market governance and regulation, and the treatment of entrants and incumbents can be addressed. The most likely solution to this question is to pare down the monopoly 'to the bone'. What this means is, of course, different in different sectors, as some of the chapters of this book illustrate.

The question of how to structure network industries will be a continuing issue. Electricity restructuring in the US has resulted in some colossal failures, including the Enron debacle and the California experience, which is itself not unconnected to Enron (see Weaver, 2004, for a discussion of the Byzantine interdependencies of these two histories). Restructuring itself was triggered by early contributions of economists on peak-load pricing (going back to Boiteux, 1949) and detailed assessments of industry structure (in particular, the work of Joskow and Schmalensee, 1984) showing that economies of scale in generation were exhausted at relatively low output levels and were not a barrier to the unbundling of generation from other parts of the electricity supply chain. The basic approach undertaken was in line with that pursued in our question of 'paring down the monopoly', with the understanding that generation would be divested from transmission and distribution, the latter two functions continuing to be treated in a transition phase as regulated monopolies of traditional vintage. Independent power producers were to be on an equal footing with traditional utilities in competing for load. Just as in natural gas, brokers and intermediaries were expected to flourish in linking generation assets to final demand. The transmission system was to operate as an open-access common carrier, providing service to all comers on transparent non-discriminatory terms. In the US with the passage of the Energy Policy Act of 1992, these 'visions' were enshrined in law, and the Federal Energy Regulatory Commission (FERC) began the hard work of drafting regulations that would implement this vision. Similar reforms have occurred in the electricity sectors in many other countries, notably in England and Wales when on privatization in 1990/91 the industry was separated into two main thermal generating companies, a company owning nuclear generation, 12 regional distribution companies and a national transmission company. Since privatization access to the national transmission and local distribution grids has been state regulated (today by the Office of Gas and Electricity Markets).

What has happened in the interim has been a chastening experience in the complexities of inducing economic change when the laws of physics will not cooperate. Whereas in countries such as the UK and Spain, a central authority continued to be in control of transmission, in the US the Energy Policy Act of 1992 is based on the prevailing status in the US in which transmission assets are in the hands of many owners. However, in the emerging competitive markets, instead of vertically integrated monopolies that had previously existed, the externalities and free rider issues that are part of a transmission system surfaced. The result has been confusion, underinvestment in transmission, and general dissatisfaction with the state of electric power markets and their expected evolution going forward.

A central question is why the North American power grid has not kept pace with the growth in generation investments and the demand for electric power. Just to cite one of many statistics reinforcing the issue, electricity demand in the US is expected to grow by 25 per cent over the next ten years, while President Bush's national energy plan predicts an increase in grid capacity of about 4 per cent during the same period.[13] From an economic perspective, the growing gap between existing and required transmission capacity can have huge consequences. Disruptions of supply, such as that on 14 August 2003, obviously have large economic costs in lost production and transactions costs. Beyond disruptions, as the instructive recent report by Huber and Mills (2003) points out, electric power is at the very foundation of the country's critical infrastructure, and growth in electric power has tracked growth in GDP at roughly the same pace. Without reliable electric power, the country stops communicating, stops working, and stops producing.

Given the consensus on the pressing need for additional investment in the grid, why are investors not rushing in to fill this need? The reason: there are large differences in the historical and projected returns for investments in transmission relative to other opportunities, even in the electric power sector. Added to this 'returns disadvantage' is the regulatory uncertainty associated with predicting longer-term revenues that will accrue to existing and new transmission investment. These problems are, in our view, tied up with current models of regulation of transmission and with an inadequate state of knowledge about how to run power markets under distributed ownership of the grid.

The Default Service Obligation (DSO) in electricity is a major issue in electricity regulation. Deregulation, by allowing entry into the profitable parts of a regulated monopoly and by leaving the company with a residual monopoly, which is typically a much smaller base over which to spread such costs, threatens the ability of the company to finance the DSO. In electricity, the local distribution company (Disco) is left with the least profitable customers, the residential and commercial customers, sometimes called 'small' customers. The industrial and large commercial customers have opportunities to bypass under a system with entry. The problem for small customers is that because they are small, there is little at stake to make competition for them worthwhile. The original idea was that the small customers would face regulated distribution rates from the Disco and that energy generators would compete to supply them energy. However, with average residential electric bills even in the Eastern States and in California running at less than a hundred dollars, there is very little incentive to attract competitors. The other aspect of the problem that makes competing for such customers unattractive is the DSO. How this was interpreted in California was especially troubling, but there is no guarantee that regulators elsewhere would view the issue very much differently. The California utilities were forced to maintain a price cap not just on distribution but also on energy when the prices they were paying for power were, for a significant period of time, in excess of their retail rates. In a situation like this the independent energy suppliers quickly dropped out, leaving the utilities with the entire burden of the DSO. In the UK a number of these problems have been averted by effective state regulation. However, the UK has had its own set of problems arising from the manipulation of wholesale electricity prices by generators; for a discussion of the difficulties see Newbery (1999, pp. 207–29) and Chapter 15 in this volume.

Undoubtedly, the failure to run with the ball of peak-load pricing has cost the electric utility industry dearly. Nowhere is this more apparent than in California.

If the companies and the California Public Utilities Commission had begun instituting a major upgrading programme for metering, it is likely that the crisis could have been lessened, if not averted. As Borenstein (2004) notes, peak load pricing would have sent some of the right signals to consumers. Real-time pricing would have sent the precise signals. Moreover, a long-term programme with the sanction of the CPUC would have made reneging on supply contracts much more difficult.

The California electricity crisis and the failure to implement peak load pricing is part of a more general failure of deregulation, namely piecemeal implementation. Some policies have been adopted because they are relatively easy to adopt, while other policies that were necessary for success were not followed. It is this piecemeal approach and failure to understand the larger picture that explains many of the problems with deregulation generally and, in particular, the problems in California. In principle, the California restructuring appeared to be a promising development. It seemed to apply some of the recent theoretical developments and to offer the potential for greater competition and incentives for the California utilities to become more X-efficient. The implementation failed because it was piecemeal, ignored evidence from elsewhere and showed little concern for the nuts and bolts.

Let us see how the California approach made these three serious errors. Starting with the nuts and bolts, California failed to introduce significant amounts of peak-load pricing or smart metering particularly to the smaller customers. This meant that the price signals received in the wholesale market were not transmitted to final consumers. Another area of nuts and bolts was forecasting. California has built little capacity yet at the time of restructuring in 1998 any forecasts of capacity shortages were ignored. This is surprising since the low price elasticities in electricity markets have been common knowledge for many years. In the event of supply shortage, elementary economics says that the price must rise to very high levels. Moreover the experience of the UK with a similar bidding system was that local market power was easily exploited. All these lessons were ignored and the industry went headlong into purchasing all its electricity on the spot or short-term market.

Very little attempt was made to hedge against risk. Indeed, elementary lessons about managing risk were ignored.[14] You can hedge against risk by choosing among different fuels. You can further hedge against risk by entering into contracts of varying duration. A distribution company that is at all concerned about risk would have a portfolio of generation contracted for at various maturities. It might at the one extreme own some generation of its own. In like vein, it might enter into physical bilateral contracts with generators providing for power at a guaranteed price over a number of years. The portfolio would also include forward contracts and options to purchase power months or weeks ahead. Finally, some power would be purchased a few days ahead, or a day ahead, or in the spot market. Unfortunately, the utilities in California concentrated on the very long market, the generation they still owned and the short-term and spot markets, ignoring the options in the middle, particularly physical bilaterals. When demand started to outstrip supply, the spot and short-term markets hit the roof and claims were made about generators exploiting the market power that the bidding system gave them. This should have surprised nobody since the experience of a similar type of power pool in the UK with generators making bids had revealed how easy it was to exploit market power. Since the utilities had agreed to a price cap the result was huge financial deficits and the ultimate declaration of bankruptcy on 7 April 2001 by Pacific Gas and Electric.

The California disaster shows not only a lack of understanding of some basic lessons of economics but also the dangers of piecemeal and ill-conceived deregulation. Although the utilities were no longer provided with a monopoly in the sale of power, almost all the obligations they faced when they had a monopoly still continued. Their monopoly now consisted only of the wires, which effectively meant small and medium-sized customers. Any customer who was willing and able to connect at transmission voltage could bypass their systems. Similarly, any customers worth supplying by others would be taken, leaving the distribution utilities with the least profitable customers because they had default service or carrier of last resort obligation.

The California problem will be with us for a long time. It has already cost the State of California, the utilities and consumers many billions of dollars and the financial outflow will continue. It will correct itself eventually when the State runs out of money – the utilities are already broke – and finally consumers are forced to pay the full cost. This may not prove to be as bad by then as the current policy will have hastened a recession in the State, thus reducing the demand for electricity. Altogether, California is a black eye for deregulation and for economists. As regulatory economists we have to take our lumps over California and learn our lessons. The California deregulation can be interpreted as an attempt to redistribute rents from small to large customers and big business. The California utilities lobbied extensively for change in an attempt to address their 'stranded cost' problem. Unfortunately for the utilities, when push came to shove, the politicians lost their nerve because the redistribution turned out to be much greater and very different from what had been intended. It was not large customers and the California utilities that gained from the process, but the generating companies who became the nouveaux riches overnight. The California utilities began the process with some arguably manageable problems of stranded costs relating to earlier investments. The end result was financial distress for the utilities and for California's consumers, now facing debts for high priced power far in excess of the original stranded cost problem, and acrimonious attempts to determine what are just and reasonable forward looking contract rates.

The problem is that in California 'deregulation' dramatically reduced the potential to tax large customers, who had access to the wholesale market, to fund the cross-subsidies to small customers. It also set up a market that provided no discipline on prices in the event of shortage. The resulting hotchpotch of deregulation required the utilities as default service providers to perform the role of subsidizing smaller customers, a role that the State of California has now taken over at a large cost. The California situation is a gross example of the problems that can result from ill-conceived deregulation. The size, impact and nature of the rent redistribution was badly misunderstood by all, creating a massive windfall for generators and traders, but leaving consumers extremely vulnerable, the default providers (the utilities) facing potential bankruptcy, and the State taking on a huge financial burden for even the greatest State of the Union. The problem was created primarily by the massive redistribution of rents involved and the failure to understand the ramifications of a situation where a supplier faces an obligation without the wherewithal to perform it.

Putting all of this together, it is fair to say that the US electric power industry remains in a state of shock. Enron, California, catastrophic grid failures, and large regulatory uncertainty are the rule of the day. By contrast in the UK and Europe there has been more stability, arguably because more effective regulatory regimes have been created. However, in some parts of Europe deregulation of electricity is still young and the ability to prevent catastrophic supply failures remains largely untested.

Comments on the individual chapters

In the next chapter, Chapter 2, Martin Ricketts provides an overview of economic regulation. Starting with definitions of regulation, he moves quickly to a critical discussion of the notion that regulation is driven by a pursuit of the wider public interest. This is the articulated starting point for most regulatory interventions, but today there is a wide appreciation that regulation can just as easily result from self-interested 'rent seeking' by interest groups. Even when regulators are motivated initially by the public good, they can be 'captured' by self-seeking interests. This approach to regulation equates with the wider 'public choice' view of political activity, which has done much to change perceptions of government from 'what it should be' to 'what it is'. Ricketts also looks at the contribution to regulation theory of New Institutional Economics, with its emphasis on property rights and transaction costs, and then considers how these different approaches affect our understanding of concepts central to debates in the economics of regulation today, namely 'natural monopoly' (how pervasive is it?), the scope for deregulation (when might competition replace regulation?) and what are the appropriate methods of regulation (to what extent do principal–agent relationships affect the methods selected; how do rate of return and price-cap methods of regulating prices differ in reality; and what is the scope for replacing regulation with operating franchises?). A main theme of the chapter is the contrast between regulation as a means of enforcing rules and regulation as a means of attaining collectively determined ends.

As Martin Ricketts emphasizes in his chapter, regulation affects prices and outputs and therefore social welfare. Chapter 3 by Michael Crew and Paul Kleindorfer is concerned with the principles of efficient pricing to maximize social welfare in regulated industries. Theory and practice are compared and contrasted and the role of equity and rents, including information rents, in explaining the differences is examined. Also, they consider some of the future challenges in pricing and welfare analysis in regulated industries and summarize the key principles that have emerged from theory and practice. Three main conclusions follow from their study. First, although economically efficient prices are an important benchmark, problems exist in practice because of the distribution of the resulting benefits. In practice, distribution issues cannot be ignored. Second, prices under regulation in practice are influenced by rent seeking groups. Third, 'information is key to reducing monopoly rents'. Given the asymmetries of information that usually exist between the regulator and the regulated business, the results from the application of economic pricing rules are likely to be modest.

Economic regulation is not simply about controlling prices to protect consumers but is inevitably drawn into controlling quality of service. As Dan Elliott explains in Chapter 4, regulation of prices can lead firms to economize by paring down the quality of the service they provide, including reducing both new investment and expenditure on maintenance of the existing capital stock. To ensure that service quality is not compromised, regulators may have recourse to 'carrots and sticks'. Common methods adopted to incentivize management to maintain or improve service quality include the setting of legally binding targets for specific service levels, the imposition of compensation payments to customers for service failures, the inclusion of special financial incentives via the price-cap formula, and the use of 'peer pressure' to embarrass the management to improve quality, including the publication of quality league tables. All these methods have weaknesses, as Dan Elliott emphasizes. However, using examples from the UK regulatory system, he demonstrates that regulators are managing to improve service delivery.

Regulation involves regulators, directly or indirectly, in determining service prices. Sometimes this is done 'bottom up', by determining revenue needs from a study of a supplier's fixed and variable costs, and sometimes 'top down', by imposing a price or revenue cap. Usually, in practice regulators adopt both practices with some leaning more towards reliance on a 'bottom up' or 'top down' approach. Common to both approaches is establishing some form of performance benchmark, so as to know whether the firm's fixed and variable costs are 'reasonable' or that the 'price cap' is sustainable. No regulator wants to force an efficient firm into bankruptcy through setting a cap that does not permit the firm to finance its activities. Equally, no regulator should be happy if an inefficient firm continues to operate because of slackly regulated prices. Benchmarking performance or what is sometimes called 'yardstick competition' has been promoted as a means of ensuring that firms' prices are set efficiently. In principle, a 'shadow firm' or firms is used against which the regulated firm is compared in terms of its fixed and variable costs and levels of service. In Chapter 6 David Parker, Thoralf Dassler and David Saal review the history of performance benchmarking within economic regulation in the UK since the 1980s, and illustrate the difficulties in operating it effectively drawing on the UK's experience. The UK regulatory offices have used benchmarking to varying degrees but have experienced a number of problems. Some regulators have placed more reliance on benchmarking than others, but in all cases the results of benchmarking exercises have been controversial. The chapter concludes by highlighting the main difficulties that face benchmarking as a tool of economic regulation.

Under both rate of return and price-cap regulation it is important that the regulator allows the regulated firm to earn a return at least equal to its cost of capital, otherwise the firm will be unable to raise finance to fund investment. In Chapter 7 Tim Jenkinson considers how regulators calculate the cost of capital with examples from the UK. He criticizes some of the measures adopted by UK regulators when determining the cost of capital. In particular, he criticizes the way that UK regulators try to influence the level of gearing (leverage) and manipulate the cost of capital and allowed revenues to ensure that certain financial ratios remain within the perceived constraints imposed by financial markets during the price control period. This leads regulators into second-guessing the optimal capital structure for the regulated businesses, something that Tim Jenkinson rightly sees as primarily a matter for the management. The approach adopted by UK regulators to the cost of capital is another example of how what was intended to be 'light handed' regulation in the UK is becoming, seemingly, more and more interventionist.

The nature of regulation and regulatory accountability is the subject of Chapter 9. Drawing from a recent major report by the UK's House of Lords Select Committee on the Constitution, Peter Vass considers how regulatory governance is evolving in the UK, two decades after the first of the 'independent' utility regulators, Oftel, was created. Arguing that effective accountability is necessary for effective regulation, he identifies tensions in the UK between accountability and the associated issue of transparency, and efficient and effective regulatory outcomes. His study confirms that the regulatory state is inevitably a complex system and that communication and consistency between the different components of the regulatory state are endemic problems. He concludes that the nature of regulation in the UK will be dependent on two key developments: first, Parliament taking the opportunity to focus on improved scrutiny of the regulatory system and, second, Parliamentary select committees focusing on Regulatory Impact Assessments to ensure that they are 'fit for purpose'.

Regulation is about protecting the consumer, but in a number of countries governments have been inclined not to leave consumer issues entirely to sector regulators. Instead, dedicated consumer councils and ombudsmen have been established to work alongside the formal regulatory bodies to protect the consumer interest. In Chapter 10 Michael Harker, Laurence Mathieu and Catherine Waddams Price look at the arguments for having separate consumer representation within regulatory regimes and survey practice internationally. Focusing specifically on the UK, they show how consumer representation in utility regulation has evolved since the 1980s as concerns for vulnerable consumer groups have grown. Utility markets in the UK have been opened up to more competition, which therefore means more consumer choice, but at the same time there is evidence that disadvantaged consumer groups may have lost out. The chapter highlights the challenges to traditional economic regulation imposed by consumer representation.

Regulation can provide 'bads' as well as 'goods'; it can distort economic activity to the point where the marginal cost of additional regulation well exceeds the marginal benefit in terms of reducing 'market failure'. With the arrival of the 'regulatory state', increasing attention is being paid to the design and implementation of efficient and effective regulation. Regulatory Impact Assessment (RIA; alternatively known as Regulatory Impact Analysis) is a method recommended for use by governments of the member countries of the OECD. It has also been adopted in some non-OECD states. RIA is a method of policy analysis which is intended to assist policymakers in the design, implementation and monitoring of improvements to regulatory systems. In Chapter 11 Colin Kirkpatrick explains the rationale for RIA and considers its origins within the US government. He reviews the introduction of RIA in North America and the European Union and its more recent spread to the transition economies of Central and Eastern Europe and to developing countries. Good practice guidelines are established, as are the lessons from the experiences of countries that have adopted RIA. Interest in RIA is growing globally. However, the chapter stresses that RIA 'is a tool for decision making, not a decision-making tool'. The hard choices in regulation remain, although through the use of RIA regulators should be better informed.

Environmental costs are now weighing heavily with business, consumers and governments. In Chapter 12 Anthony Heyes and Catherine Liston review the economic issues surrounding environmental regulation, including the different approaches to tackling external costs. Property rights, legal liability, taxation, tradable and non-tradable emission standards and voluntary agreements are all discussed as possible approaches to solving environmental problems. None is found to be problem free. Although over time experience leads to improvements in regulatory instruments, there is clearly no one 'best way' in terms of environmental regulation. Rather, regulation will involve the application of several instruments at once. The authors conclude: 'The way in which sticks and carrots are best combined and managed in a way that delivers the desired environmental outcomes at minimal cost remains a potent academic and policy challenge.'

The content of Chapter 13 covers the important subject of access and interconnection charges. For competition to be effective new entrants into network industries will in certain circumstances require access to the existing wires, pipes and other transmission and distribution facilities. In such circumstances, facilities such as transmission and distribution systems are normally 'natural monopolies' due to pervasive economies of scale and scope. Alternatively, they are sometimes referred to as 'essential facilities' because without access to them new entrants cannot get their services to end consumers. In this chapter Timothy Tardiff discusses the economics of interconnection and access to networks using telecommunications as the example. Current research into interconnection charging is reviewed, as are current difficulties in applying theoretical models. Access in telecommunications raises a number of economic issues that apply more widely to other network industries. However, telecommunications also has some unique properties because of the breadth and complexity of interconnection arrangements in the industry, which makes the study of access in telecommunications so challenging.

In Chapter 14, Gregory Duncan and Lisa Cameron provide an economic analysis of the recent turmoil in the US telecommunications industry and predict how future competition will evolve. Their analysis points out that wireline telephone and cable TV companies have technologies with high start-up and fixed costs and low marginal costs. Their conclusion is that these characteristics limit the survival of competitors using similar technology in the same geographic area unless sufficient product differentiation is possible. In contrast, wireless and satellite communications providers use radio spectrum-based technologies with positive or even increasing incremental costs, which allow a number of competitors to survive in the same geographic area. The authors' model predicts a future telecommunications industry characterized by intermodal competition among companies using different technologies and offering differentiated products. Finally, their model explains the contrasting success in the US of numerous wireless entrants and the wave of consolidation in the wireline and cable industry. In general, the authors' contribution suggests that the current competitive structure of the telecommunications industry will be replaced by one characterized by a few regional wireline carriers, with mutually exclusive serving areas; a few regional cable companies, with mutually exclusive serving areas; and a number of competing wireless and satellite companies that compete with each other as well as competing with the wireline and cable companies. Furthermore, this new competitive environment will require a drastically altered regulatory structure. If Drs Duncan and Cameron are right, their conclusions have profound implications for telecommunications companies and telecommunications regulators alike.

The energy sector is the focus for Chapter 15 by Colin Robinson and Eileen Marshall. Internationally, energy industries are particularly prone to regulation. But as they emphasize, in practice this is not simply a result of 'market failure' but a product of pressure group activity. Nevertheless, they study the general arguments advanced for regulation to remove 'failures' in energy markets, including achieving security of supply, protecting against rising long-run energy costs, safeguarding the environment and caring for future generations (the energy as a finite resource argument). They find none of the arguments compelling, especially when balanced against regulation that is 'implemented by imperfect governments and imperfect regulatory bodies, lacking information and appropriate incentives'. Later in the chapter they draw lessons from the regulation of energy markets in Britain including that 'British experience ... shows that it is possible to deal with the apparently intractable problem of market power in electricity generation through the normal processes of a commodity market'.

The regulation of transport is the subject of Chapter 16. Transport is subject to both economic and safety regulation and is inextricably part of the debate on the regulation of the environment, the subject of Chapter 13. In this chapter Ian Savage focuses on prices, outputs and entry and exit in transport markets. Transport is characterized by huge fixed infrastructure costs, joint costs, multiple users with different valuations of the service, network firms serving different markets geographically and by time of day, and prices that are commonly unrelated to full economic costs. As a consequence, transport remains highly regulated, in spite of relatively recent measures to deregulate some forms of transport, notably air travel and trucking. The privatization of the railways in Britain in the mid-1990s led to disappointing results and a growing regulatory regime. Attempts to make bus markets in Britain competitive have only been partially successful. The chapter sets out a number of the difficulties in achieving competition in transport markets and the challenges for transport regulators.

The last chapter looks at the regulation of water services. Ian Byatt, Tony Ballance and Scott Reid are economists with practical experience of regulating water services. In Chapter 17 they discuss the difficulties facing economic regulation, illustrating their arguments with international evidence and especially the experiences of England and Wales and France. In England and Wales the water industry was privatized in 1989 through the creation of private sector companies which replaced publicly owned regional water authorities. In France, by contrast, private sector provision of water services dates back to the nineteenth century and takes the form of different forms of contractual arrangements (e.g. management contracts, leases/'affermage contracts' and concession agreements). As the authors explain, both methods of private sector supply require some form of ongoing economic regulation. Neither model, they emphasize, should uncritically be exported to other countries – a message of great importance at a time when many lower-income economies are assessing how best to promote private sector participation in water services. The chapter also considers the structure of the water industry and the role of economies of scale and scope in water supply. The conclusion is that the international evidence suggests a 'u-shaped' average cost curve. The authors are cautious about the scope for competition in water services, which implies an ongoing role for economic regulation of industry conduct. The chapter concludes by reviewing recent changes in the regulation of the Scottish water industry, which remains publicly owned. Can economic regulation be as successful where the regulated firm is state owned?

The road ahead

Undoubtedly considerable progress in regulatory economics, both in theory and practice, has been made in the last 20 years and it is important to build on this for the future. Failure to learn the right lessons can set regulation and regulatory economics back. One lesson not to learn as a result of the California experience is that a return to old-style regulation is required, for example, a return to command, control or cost of service regulation and extensive expansion of public ownership. Returning to the old ways will be difficult, if not impossible. New property rights have been created around the world, which will be defended vigorously by the new owners. What we have learned is to respect the complexity of change in network industries, and the huge problems of regulation under the transition to competition. Some old ideas still have great currency, including pricing and incentive alignment. Making use of the new financial instruments and competitive bidding processes should still be part of a reformed system. Such devices have much to offer in terms of efficiency and risk sharing, but their precise structure and design will need to be more carefully thought out than in the past 'rush to markets'. Indeed, the tools exist for more deliberate action; for example, running experiments ex ante; constructing simulations of new designs before they are implemented; encouraging diverse and differentiated solutions rather than a one-size-fits-all approach that may be wrong; watching and learning from others internationally; and most importantly promoting a flexible and evolutionary approach to institutional development and change.

Another lesson is that more must be understood about the deregulatory process. This should start from the public choice insight on rent seeking. The deregulation game is an attempt to secure or redistribute the monopoly rents that exist in regulated industries. The California experience shows how badly things can go wrong if the rent distribution is disturbed too severely. In part, this stemmed from a failure to understand the incompatibility of restructuring with the continuation of an onerous Default Service Obligation. The problem of the DSO and related universal service obligations is that deregulation calls for allowing entry, but the complexity of doing so while assuring that the incumbent responsible for the default service is not towed under in the process is significant. This is a major problem, which is currently unsolved. For now it implies caution; for example in the case of the postal sector, where in most countries major restructuring of the kind that has taken place in telecommunications and electricity is yet to happen. This means deciding what changes to make in the USO before changes in the conditions of entry and other restructuring are allowed.

The final lesson that we draw is that the expectations for deregulation should be revised downward drastically and that further deregulation should be undertaken with caution. Indeed, there may be a return to old style regulation in some areas, for example in transmission ownership in electric power, to achieve sufficient clarity and incentive alignment for long-run sustainability. The willingness of private sector companies to invest in long-life (sunk) assets such as transmission systems and nuclear generating plant remains uncertain and the possibility of inadequate equity to meet the needs of growing economies remains. In other industries, for example, telecommunications, it may be necessary to adopt very different policies, for example, requiring divestiture of the local wires. Local service is dominated by very large companies. If they divested their wires-only operations, all the remaining pieces would still be large enough to take advantage of scale economies.

Regulatory economics in theory and practice has made a lot of important advances in the last 30 years, but much remains to be done. This speaks well to the healthy state of debate in the subject, to which we hope this volume contributes. Regulators, managers in regulated companies, policy makers, pundits and academic researchers have and will continue to have many problems to address in regulatory economics, as the following chapters confirm.

Notes

1. Parts of this chapter draw heavily on Crew and Kleindorfer (2002a). We would like to thank Paul Kleindorfer for his helpful comments and his willingness to allow us to have the benefit of this work.
2. In the second and third sections we attempt to perform essentially the same task as Faulhaber and Baumol (1988), although in a more specialized manner. We are looking for 'practical products of theoretical research' in the field of regulatory economics.
3. The separation of distribution and supply evolved in the years after privatization. Recent mergers have involved the integration of generation and distribution and supply companies; transmission remains under the separate ownership of National Grid Transco Plc.
4. Henceforth we will not distinguish between the two appellations but will use this term to refer to either *The Bell Journal of Economics and Management Science* or the *Bell Journal of Economics*.
5. We intentionally use the word seminal to describe A–J. Although many authors have sought to discredit this paper, it is one of the most highly cited and influential papers in regulatory

economics and includes both insights on single-product regulated firms as well as the distortions that regulation can cause in multi-product firms that may face competition in some of their product lines.

6. This not to say that there has not been controversy about the applicability of contestability theory, e.g. Shepherd (1984, p.572), but the ideas of Baumol and his colleagues on the key role of entry in promoting competition have nonetheless been exceedingly important elements of the ongoing debate on deregulation.

7. According to the *burden test*, a cross-subsidy is not present if the revenue from a product is between its incremental cost and its stand-alone cost. This test and associated procedures for measuring incremental and stand-alone costs are key benchmarks in network industries for monitoring the behavior of regulated, multi-product companies that compete with entrants in some of their lines of business.

8. Interestingly, Littlechild (1983), in proposing price-cap regulation, with characteristic insight showed a clear awareness of the commitment problem.

9. See Schmalensee (1989) and Lyon (1996) for insightful reviews of the literature on incentive regulation.

10. The term is an excellent one. Crew and Kleindorfer (1994) proposed the same basic idea, but unfortunately not the term. Laffont and Tirole (1996) first floated the idea. An interesting recent application in the postal sector is provided in Billette de Villemeur et al. (2003).

11. In some ways consultant economists are at risk of becoming perceived in the same way as lawyers, namely as hired guns. Kovacic (2002) addresses such issues in more detail with the law's treatment of economists as expert witnesses.

12. See also Doane and Spulber (1994).

13. See McNamara (2001). Detailed assessments are available through the Edison Electric Institute and other industry think tanks.

14. Fernando and Kleindorfer (1997) provide an overview of risk management for electric power. For a distribution company, the emphasis is on determining an optimal portfolio of contracts, including forwards, capacity and demand-side options, so as to balance the costs of such instruments against the volatility of spot market purchases and non-performance due to shortages.

References

Armstrong, M. (2002) 'The Theory of Access Pricing and Interconnection', in Martin Cave, Sumit Majumdar and Ingo Vogelsang (eds), *Handbook of Telecommunications Economics*, Amsterdam: North Holland.

Armstrong, M. and Sappington, D.E.M. (2004) 'Toward a Synthesis of Models of Regulatory Policy Design with Limited Information', *Journal of Regulatory Economics*, **26**(1), July, 5–22.

Averch, H. and Johnson, L.L. (1962) 'Behavior of Firm Under Regulatory Constraint', *American Economic Review*, **52**, 1053–69.

Baron, D. and Myerson, R. (1982) 'Regulating a Monopolist with Unknown Costs,' *Econometrica*, **50**, 911–30.

Baumol, W.J. and Bradford, D. (1970) 'Optimal Departures from Marginal Cost Pricing', *American Economic Review*, **60**, June, 265–83.

Baumol, W.J., Panzar, J.C. and Willig, R.D. (1982, revised edition 1988) *Contestable Markets and the Theory of Industry Structure*, New York: Harcourt, Brace, Jovanovich, Publishers.

Baumol, W.J. and Sidak, J.G. (1994) *Toward Competition in Local Telephony*, Cambridge, MA: MIT Press and Washington, AEI.

Boiteux, M. (1949) 'La tarification des demandes en point: application de la theorie de la vente au cout marginal', *Revue Generale de l'Electricite*, **58**, August, 22–40.

Borenstein, S. (2004). 'The Long-run Effects of Real-time Electricity Pricing', CSEM WP 133, University of California Energy Institute, Berkeley, June.

Cohen, R.H. et al. (2002) 'A Comparison of the Burden of Universal Service in Italy and in the United States', in Michael A. Crew and Paul R. Kleindorfer (eds), *Postal and Delivery Services: Pricing, Productivity, Regulation and Strategy*, Boston, MA: Kluwer Academic Publishers.

Crew, M.A. and Kleindorfer, P.R. (1986) *The Economics of Public Utility Regulation*, Cambridge: MIT Press.

Crew, M.A. and Kleindorfer, P.R. (1994) 'Pricing, Entry, Service Quality, and Innovation under a Commercialized Postal Service', in J. Gregory Sidak (ed.), *Governing the Postal Service*, Washington, DC: The AEI Press.

Crew, M.A. and Kleindorfer, P.R. (1996) 'Incentive Regulation in the United Kingdom and the United States: Some Lessons', *Journal of Regulatory Economics*, **9**(3), May, 211–25.

Crew, M.A. and Kleindorfer P.R. (eds) (1999) *Emerging Competition in Postal and Delivery Services*, Boston, MA: Kluwer Academic Publishers.

Crew, M.A. and Kleindorfer, P.R. (eds) (2000) *Current Directions in Postal Reform*, Boston, MA: Kluwer Academic Publishers.

Crew, M.A. and Kleindorfer, P.R. (2002a) 'Regulatory Economics: Twenty Years of Progress?', *Journal of Regulatory Economics*, January, **21**(1), 5–22.

Crew, M.A. and Kleindorfer, P.R. (2002b) 'Balancing Access and the Universal Service Obligation', in M.A. Crew and P.R. Kleindorfer, *Postal and Delivery Services: Delivering on the Competition*, Boston, MA: Kluwer Academic Publishers.

Crew, A. and Kleindorfer, P.R. (2003) 'Regulation Redux', in M.A. Crew and J.C. Schuh (eds), *Markets, Pricing and Deregulation of Utilities*, Boston, MA: Kluwer Academic Publishers.

Crew, M.A. and Kleindorfer, P.R. (2004a) 'Access and the USO for Letters and Parcels', in Michael A. Crew and Paul R. Kleindorfer (eds), *Competitive Transformation of the Postal and Delivery Sector*, Boston, MA: Kluwer Academic Publishers.

Crew, M.A. and Kleindorfer, P.R. (2004b) 'Developing Policies for the Future of the U.S. Postal Service', in Michael A. Crew and Paul R. Kleindorfer (eds), *Competitive Transformation of the Postal and Delivery Sector*, Boston, MA: Kluwer Academic Publishers.

Crew, M.A. and Kleindorfer, P.A. (2005) 'Competition, Universal Service and the Graveyard Spiral', in Michael A. Crew and Paul R. Kleindorfer (eds), *Regulatory and Economic Changes in the Postal and Delivery Sector*, Boston, MA: Kluwer Academic Publishers.

Crew, M.A. and Rowley, C.K. (1988) 'Toward a Public Choice Theory of Monopoly Regulation', *Public Choice*, **57**(1), March, 49–67.

Crew, M.A., Kleindorfer, P.R. and Spiegel, M. (2004) 'Reliability, Regulation and Transmission Investment', mimeo, Wharton Risk Management and Decision Processes Center, University of Pennsylvania, Philadelphia, May.

Crew, M.A., Kleindorfer, P.R. and Sumpter, J. (2004) 'Bringing Competition to Telecommunications by Divesting the RBOCs', in Michael A. Crew and Menahem Spiegel (eds), *Obtaining the Best from Regulation and Competition*, Boston, MA: Kluwer Academic Publishers.

de Fraja, G. and Stones, C. (2004) 'Risk and Capital Structure in the Regulated Firm', *Journal of Regulatory Economics*, **26**(1), July, 69–84.

de Villemeur, B., Helmut, E., Cremer, Roy B. and Toledano, J. (2003) 'Optimal Pricing and Global Price Caps in the Postal Sector', *Journal of Regulatory Economics*, **24**(1), 49–62.

Demsetz, H. (1968). 'Why Regulate Utilities?', *Journal of Law and Economics*, **11**, April, 55–65.

Doane, M. and Spulber, D. (1994) 'Open Access and the Evolution of the U.S. Spot Market for Natural Gas', *Journal of Law and Economics*, **37**(2), October, 477–517.

Economides, N. (1988) 'The Incentive for Non-price Discrimination by an Input Monopolist', *Journal of Industrial Organization*, **16**(3), May, 272–84.

Faulhaber, G.R. and Baumol, W.J.B. (1988) 'Economists as Innovators: Practical Products of Theoretical Research', *Journal of Economic Literature*, **26**(2), June, 577–600.

Fernando, C.S. and Kleindorfer, P.R. (1997) 'Integrating Financial and Physical Contracting in Electric Power Markets', in Shimon Awerbuch (ed.), *The Virtual Utility*, Boston, MA: Kluwer Academic Publishers.

Goldberg, V.P. (1976) 'Regulation and Administered Contracts', *The Bell Journal of Economics*, **7**(2), Autumn, 426–48.

Groves, T. (1973) 'Incentives in Teams', *Econometrica*, **41**(4), 617–31.

Hicks, J.R. (1935) 'Annual Survey of Economic Theory', *Econometrica*, **3**, January, 1–20.

Hogan, W.W. (2002) 'Electricity Market Restructuring: Reform of Reforms', *Journal of Regulatory Economics*, January, **21**(1), 103–32.

Hogan, W.W. (2003) 'Transmission Market Design', J.F. Kennedy School of Government, Harvard University, Paper presented at 'Electricity Deregulation: Where to From Here?' Conference at Bush Presidential Center, Texas A&M University, 4 April.

Huber, P. and Mills, M.P. (2003) 'Critical Power: A White Paper', Digital Power Group, Washington, DC.

Joskow, P.L. (2003) 'The Difficult Transition to Competitive Electricity Markets in the U.S.', Paper presented at 'Electricity Deregulation: Where to From Here?' Conference at Bush Presidential Center, Texas A&M University, 4 April.

Joskow, P.L. and Schmalensee, R. (1984) *Markets for Power*, Cambridge, MA: MIT Press.

Kovacic, W. (2002) 'Economic Regulation and the Courts 1982 to 2001: Ten Cases that Made a Difference', *Journal of Regulatory Economics*, January, **21**(1), 23–34.

Laffont, J.-J. and Tirole, J. (1993) *Theory of Incentives in Procurement and Regulation*, Cambridge, MA: MIT Press.

Laffont, J.-J. and Tirole, J. (1996) 'Creating Competition through Interconnection: Theory and Practice', *Journal of Regulatory Economics*, **10**(3), November, 227–56.

Leitzinger, J. and Collette, M. (2002). 'A Retrospective Look at Wholesale Gas: Industry Restructuring', *Journal of Regulatory Economics*, January, **21**(1), 79–102.

Littlechild, S.C. (1983) *Regulation of British Telecommunications' Profitability*, London: Department of Trade and Industry.

Loeb, M. and Magat, W.A. (1974) 'A Decentralized Method of Utility Regulation', *Journal of Law and Economics*, **22**, October, 58–73.

Lyon, T.P. (1996) 'Evaluating the Performance of Non-Bayesian Regulatory Mechanisms', *Journal of Regulatory Economics*, **9**(1), January, 41–60.

Mandy, D.M. (2000) 'Killing the Goose that May Have Laid the Golden Egg: Only the Data Know Whether Sabotage Pays', *Journal of Regulatory Economics*, **17**(2), March, 157–72.

McNamara, K. (2001) 'Grid Locked: U.S. Transmission Lines Were Built for a Whole Different Era', *Wall Street Journal*, 17 September.

Mitchell, R.W. (1999) 'Postal Worksharing: Welfare, Technical Efficiency and Pareto

Optimality', in Michael A. Crew and Paul R. Kleindorfer (eds), *Emerging Competition in Postal and Delivery Services*, Boston, MA: Kluwer Academic Publishers.

Newbery, D.M. (1999) *Privatization, Restructuring, and Regulation of Network Industries*, Cambridge, MA: MIT Press.

Parker, D. (2004) 'The UK's Privatisation Experiment: The Passage of Time Permits a Sober Assessment', *CESifo Working Paper No. 1126*, Munich: Center for Economic Studies & Ifo Institute for Economic Research.

Phillips, A. (2002) 'What It Was Like, What Happened, and What It's Like Now: Developments in Telecommunications over Recent Decades', *Journal of Regulatory Economics*, January, **21**(1), 57–78.

Posner, R.A. (1969) 'Natural Monopoly and its Regulation', *Stanford Law Review*, **21**, February, 548–643.

Posner, R.A. (1974) 'Theories of Economic Regulation', *Bell Journal of Economics*, **5**, Autumn, 335–58.

Robinson, A. (2002) 'Managing Decline in a Marketing Depression', unpublished manuscript, Direct Communications Group, Silver Spring, MD, March.

Robinson, A. and Rawnsley, D. (2002) 'USPS Finances: Is there a Financially Viable Future?', in Michael A, Crew and Paul R. Kleindorfer (eds), *Postal and Delivery Services: Pricing, Productivity, Regulation and Strategy*, Boston, MA: Kluwer Academic Publishers.

Rohlfs, J. (1979) 'Economically Efficient Bell System Prices', *Bell Laboratories Discussion Paper*, no. 138.

Ross, S.A. (1973) 'The Economic Theory of Agency: The Principal's Problem', *American Economic Review*, **63**(2), May, 209–14.

Salant, D. (2000) 'Auctions and Regulation: Reengineering of Regulatory Mechanisms', *Journal of Regulatory Economics*, **17**(3), May, 195–204.

Salant, D. (2002) 'Default Service Auctions', in Michael A. Crew and Joseph C. Schuh (eds), *Markets, Pricing and Deregulation of Utilities*, Boston, MA: Kluwer Academic Publishers.

Schmalensee, R. (1989) 'Good Regulatory Regimes', *The RAND Journal of Economics*, **6**, December, 339–62.

Shepherd, W.G. (1984) 'Contestability vs. Competition', *American Economic Review*, **74**(4), September, 572–87.

Steiner, P.O. (1957) 'Peak Loads and Efficient Pricing', *Quarterly Journal of Economics*, **71**, November, 585–610.

Tullock, G. (1967) 'The Welfare Costs of Tariffs, Monopolies and Theft', *Western Economic Journal*, **5**, June, 224–32.

Vogelsang, I. and Finsinger, J. (1979) 'A Regulatory Adjustment Process for Optimal Pricing by Multiproduct Monopoly Firms', *The Bell Journal of Economics*, **10** (Spring), 157–71.

Wachter, M.L., Hirsch, B.T. and Gillula, J.W. (2001) 'Difficulties of Deregulation When Wage Costs are the Major Cost', in Michael A. Crew and Paul R. Kleindorfer (eds), *Future Directions in Postal Reform*, Boston, MA: Kluwer Academic Publishers.

Weaver, J.L. (2004) 'Can Energy Markets Be Trusted? The Effect of the Rise and Fall of Enron on Energy Markets', *Houston Business and Tax Law Journal*, **IV**, 1–150.

Weisman, D. and Kang, J. (2001) 'Incentives for Discrimination when Upstream Monopolists Participate in Downstream Markets', *Journal of Regulatory Economics*, **20**(2), September, 125–39.

Williamson, O.E. (1966) 'Peak Load Pricing and Optimal Capacity under Indivisibility Constraints', *American Economic Review*, **56**, September, 810–27.

Willig, R.D. (1979) 'The Theory of Network Access Pricing', in Harry Trebing (ed.), *Issues in Public Utility Regulation*, East Lansing, MI: Michigan State University Press.

Wolak, F.A. (1997) 'Changes in the Household-level Demand for Postal Delivery Services from 1986 to 1994', in Michael A. Crew and Paul R. Kleindorfer (eds), *Managing Change in the Postal and Delivery Industries*, Boston, MA: Kluwer Academic Publishers.

Wolak, F.A. (2004) 'Lessons from International Experience with Electricity Market Monitoring', CSEM Working Paper 134, University of California Energy Institute, Berkeley, CA, June.

Yang, C., Crockett, R.O. and Gow, B. (2004) 'Telecom: The Day After', *Business Week*, 28 June, 98–100.

2 Economic regulation: principles, history and methods

Martin Ricketts

Introduction

Economic regulation is an important instrument of government policy in market economies. We do not talk of regulating planned systems. To regulate implies the exercise of some influence on an activity that is different from total 'control'. It is no accident therefore that the economics of regulation has become increasingly important in recent years as direct state ownership has declined. The perceived failure of central planning has not in itself discredited all government attempts to improve economic performance. Indeed, the idea that the provision of certain limited but crucial regulatory functions by the state is necessary for economic advance is a well-established part of classical liberal (as distinct from libertarian) economic and political theory.

Regulation is not, however, a very precise term. Some forms of regulation are concerned with setting a framework of rules for people to follow in their dealings with each other. In this sense the law of contract or property would comprise part of the regulatory base of the economy. A financial 'regulation'; for example, that all companies must disclose price sensitive information to the market by means of a public announcement within a specified time period, would be of this 'rule setting' type. The regulation applies to all market participants and is 'end independent' in the sense that no one could possibly know exactly what would actually happen in every case as a result of introducing it. Although the detailed outcomes are not known, the regulation could be defended as a means of making the market process more efficient over the long term.[1]

Other regulations are more prescriptive in form. They instruct people to achieve particular ends, often by the implementation of specified means. An example would be a regulation instructing a firm to install certain machinery in order to reduce pollution or improve safety. Measures of this type do not merely establish the rules governing the behaviour of transactors in the market; they attempt to determine the results or to confine them within 'acceptable' limits. Regulations that forbid transactions below a specified price (for example a minimum wage) or that impose restrictions on hours worked may still leave some room for agreement, but they directly rule out contracts with 'unacceptable' characteristics.

34

This distinction between regulation as the 'planning' of collectively determined desired ends and regulation as the 'governance' of a continuing decentralized market process is important. At the conceptual level it seems clear enough – as clear as the distinction between a referee who fixes the outcome of a game and a referee who simply enforces the rules. In practice, of course, it is sometimes difficult to tell them apart. All referees find themselves accused of rigging the rules or interpreting their provisions to the advantage or disadvantage of particular interests. Nevertheless, the conceptual distinction is at the heart of many of the disputes concerning the role of the state in a market economy. Nee (2002) for example supports Polanyi's (1944, p. 140) thesis that a market economy requires administrators to be 'constantly on the watch to ensure the free workings of the system'. He argues that there is a causal link between the emergence of a 'legal-rational bureaucracy' (Weber, 1947) and the support of market institutions, and applies this idea to the transition of modern-day China. Others are more sceptical about the role of bureaucratic agents because they regard them not as abstract rule enforcers but as direct decision-makers with a high potential to distort rather than to assist the allocation of resources.[2]

The following sections discuss in more detail the tension between these two broad traditions in the economics of regulation. The chapter starts by contrasting the standard economic theory of regulation with alternative schools of thought. Later sections investigate the problem of 'natural monopoly' and the various methods used in the regulation of the public utilities.

The public interest theory of regulation

One of the most important consequences of the 'marginal revolution' of the 1870s was the development of a far more rigorous and formal welfare economics than was provided by the preceding classical analysis of economic policy.[3] The new theory was associated with theorists such as Walras, Pareto and Pigou (e.g. 1938). At its heart was an investigation of the properties of a general competitive equilibrium. In this Walrasian equilibrium all economic agents chose the amount of labour and other factors of production to supply and the basket of goods to consume by maximizing their utility at the prevailing perfectly competitive prices. These equilibrium prices were such that no aggregate excess supplies or demands existed in the market for any traded good or service. All markets cleared.

To demonstrate the existence of a general competitive equilibrium was a great intellectual achievement in itself but it was the normative properties of this equilibrium that came to form the basis for economic thinking about public policy to the present day. It could be shown that provided all goods and services were traded and that private benefits and costs were the same as social benefits and costs (there were no externalities or 'spill-overs') a perfectly competitive equilibrium was Pareto efficient. No one could be made better off without making someone else worse off. The gains to trade were exhausted. Maximizing social welfare required the marginal social benefits of each and every activity to equal the relevant marginal social costs. Given that a condition for utility maximization on the part of each consumer was that the marginal benefit of a good or service should be brought into equality with its market price; and given that a condition for profit maximization on the part of each producer was that the marginal cost of a good or service should be brought into equality with its market price; and given that all consumers and producers faced the same market prices; it is possible to see quite intuitively how this theorem was derived. Equilibrium prices represented marginal benefits to consumers and marginal costs to producers.

The 'First Theorem of Welfare Economics' had very complex repercussions for public policy. It was capable of leading in two very different directions depending on how it was interpreted. One response to the 'first theorem' was to argue that since perfect competition had such desirable properties, public policy should concentrate on removing impediments to competition. To the objection that competition might result in a very unequal distribution of income a 'Second Theorem of Welfare Economics' could be used to show that any desired distributional result could be achieved through appropriate lump sum taxes and transfers. Thus the recommended policy package was to achieve efficiency through competitive markets and equity through 'non-distortionary' taxes and transfers. In so far as economic regulation appears at all in this system it takes the form of competition policy.[4]

An alternative response to the first theorem was to emphasize the austerity of the formal conditions. No matter how competitive the real economy seemed to those embroiled in its day-to-day tumult, it was obvious that it would never satisfy the requirements of perfect competition. Indeed almost all competitive behaviour paradoxically could be shown to be incompatible with perfect competition. Price shading, for example, immediately contravenes the formal requirement that all contractors are 'price takers'. The introduction of new products or processes confers monopoly power for short periods. Advertising would be redundant in a world of perfect information. If this were not enough, it was also clear that increasing returns to scale prevailed in some industries, markets were incomplete and the assumption of no external benefits or costs was unwarranted.

Viewed from this second perspective, the role of economic regulation was potentially very extensive. Markets did not have the characteristics of the perfectly competitive model and therefore could not be expected to achieve economic efficiency. Regulators were required to correct for 'market failure'. Industries subject to declining costs required a subsidy since the marginal cost of extra output would be below the break-even price. Polluting activities should be taxed according to the external damage inflicted. Monopolies should be instructed to set prices equal to marginal costs. Jointly consumed or 'public goods', such as environmental quality and public information required the intervention of regulators to ensure an efficient level of provision.

In this tradition, therefore, regulators were seen as technicians acting in the public interest and correcting for the failures of the market. It was implicitly assumed that they had both the information on which to act and the appropriate motivation. This idea of the professional public servant was also a requirement for the macroeconomic regulation that came out of the 'Keynesian revolution' of the 1940s and 1950s. The economy was understood as a system of equations, the public objectives were well defined, and the technical task was simply to control the values of a set of policy instruments so as to bring about the best possible result, social welfare maximization. Regulators were in the Platonic tradition of philosopher kings. Later criticism was to refer to these somewhat elitist assumptions of Keynes as 'the presuppositions of Harvey Road' – the Cambridge road in which Keynes was brought up. Whether based on general equilibrium theory or Keynesian macroeconomics, however, the role of the regulator is better described as Hobbesian. The sovereign authority is used to impose a solution where the social outcome would otherwise be disadvantageous because individuals are unable to come to enforceable agreements. The law is structured so as to 'minimise the harm caused by failures in private agreements'.[5]

Public choice and the theory of regulation
From the 1960s onwards the 'public interest' approach to economic regulation was subjected to increasing criticism. This was to some extent explained by events. Keynesian macroeconomic regulation had not produced stability, although a depression of pre-war intensity was not experienced and it was inflation rather than unemployment that became the problem of the day. Similarly the microeconomic regulation of markets in the United States and the performance of those industries nationalized by the post-war Labour government in the UK did not seem to result in clearly observable efficiency gains. Stigler and Friedland (1962), for example, could find no evidence that electricity prices differed during the inter-war years between those states with regulation and those without, while according to Stigler (1964) the Securities and Exchange Commission had been similarly unable to produce measurable results. When clear effects of regulation were observed, they did not always accord with the expectations of normative economic theory. The regulation of rents, for example, led to investigations of its efficiency costs rather than its benefits (Olsen, 1972). Regulation was sometimes used to keep prices below marginal costs for some groups by setting prices above marginal costs for others, thus using the price system as a redistributive tool in direct opposition to the second theorem of welfare economics (see for example, Posner, 1971).

One response to these observations was to depart from the assumption of a disinterested public official and to model the behaviour of regulators and politicians using the same type of analysis as might be used in the private sector. If managers of public limited companies could be viewed not as traditional profit maximizers but as maximizing firm size or revenue,[6] it was a small additional step to assume that bureaucrats were budget maximizers (Niskanen, 1968, 1971) or that politicians were vote maximizers (Downs, 1957; Buchanan and Tullock, 1962; Breton, 1974). If entrepreneurs in conventional theory were profit seekers they would be expected to lobby for a favourable regulatory environment once they understood that regulators and politicians were open to influence. Producer groups were expected to be particularly powerful because they were in a better position than were consumers to overcome the 'collective action' or 'free rider' problem (Olson, 1965). Stigler (1971) used this framework to advance the so-called 'capture theory' of regulation with its startling conclusion that the regulatory system comes to be operated in the interest of the regulated firms rather than the more general public interest. This theory was criticized by Peltzman (1976) for not taking into account the incentive for other groups to resist as they experienced increasing marginal costs of regulation.

The investment of resources in attempts to divert income from other people through the political and regulatory process became known as 'rent seeking', a term coined by Krueger (1974). Rents arise when sellers receive more than the minimum they are prepared to accept or buyers pay less than the maximum they are prepared to offer. It is a feature of a perfectly competitive equilibrium that the sum total of such rents is maximized and that therefore there is no rent on the marginal transaction. The maximum that a buyer is prepared to offer for additional output (its marginal benefit) is equal in a competitive equilibrium to the minimum a supplier is prepared to accept (its marginal cost). Voluntary trading activity that results in mutual gain is therefore a form of rent seeking that creates rents and increases efficiency. The gains to trade take the form of additional rents accruing to the various trading parties. Political pressure that results in the redistribution of rents through the political and regulatory system, however, is a form of rent seeking that is entirely wasteful. It represents a process of rent dissipation rather than rent creation because the aggregate resources invested in laying claim to rents might equal or even exceed the rents available (Tullock, 1980). Buchanan et al. (1980) have made the analysis of rent seeking a significant component of public choice theory.

This public choice perspective on the regulatory system led to a reappraisal of the history of regulatory growth especially in the United States. Even major historical events such as the establishment of the Inter State Commerce Commission (ICC) in 1887, long seen as a means of curbing the monopoly power of the railroad companies, could be reinterpreted as a means by which these same companies could avoid increasingly cut-throat competition on long hauls (e.g. Kolko, 1965). The Bell Telephone Company during the first decade of the twentieth century supported regulation to restrict new entry after the expiry of patents had made it more vulnerable. Airline interests were prominent in supporting the establishment of the Civil Aeronautics Board (CAB) in 1938. Between 1950 and 1974 no application to start a new inter-state airline was granted by the CAB.[7] For many years the Federal Communications Commission (FCC), established in 1934, restricted the development of cable companies in order to protect the advertising revenue of local television stations. In trucking regulation, Stigler (1971) explained restrictions on the weight of trucks by reference to the average length of haul on the railroads and the strength of the farming interest. Railroads with a long average length of haul would be less threatened by the advent of motor trucks on farms and would therefore tolerate a higher weight limit.

From the point of view of positive economics and as a means of explaining regulatory outcomes, public choice theory had advantages over the public interest theory of regulation. From a normative point of view the effect was to move attention away from the identification of ideal 'ends' to a discussion of what institutional mechanisms would be relatively good at achieving them. The public interest theory of regulation was a branch of what Demsetz (1969) labelled 'nirvana economics'. Actual institutions should not be compared with the nirvana of a perfect regulatory system achieving a Pareto efficient allocation of resources. They should be compared with achievable alternatives that did not depend on unexplained changes in human motivation (the 'people could be different' fallacy) or on unexplained and costless changes in the availability of information (the 'fallacy of the free lunch'). Attention was thus redirected towards the comparative analysis of institutions or alternative governance arrangements. What rules of the game are likely to produce the best results over time that can be achieved in practice? This is the fundamental problem of regulatory economics and forces us to consider 'constitutional' issues about the effects of property rights, procedural rules and individual incentives in regulatory processes.

The New Institutional Economics and economic regulation
Transacting is a process by which people come to mutually beneficial agreements. This fundamental observation greatly influences the way we look at economic life. Agreements do not really feature in the theory of competitive equilibrium. In a perfectly competitive world people adjust their own behaviour to a given set of prices through anonymous 'arm's length' trades. They buy and sell but do not search and bargain. There is nothing left to search for and nothing to bargain about. By following the tradition of Edgeworth (1891) rather than Walras (1954), however, and by investigating the way that people contract and then recontract to their mutual advantage, a different light is thrown on the ul-

timate meaning of 'market failure'. If there were unexploited gains to trade, why would free transactors not come to an agreement to secure them?

By framing the question in this way we are led to look for the forces that stand in the way of exchange. Transactors might not be aware of the potential gains to trade; they might not have secure legal title to the rights over which they wish to transact; they might be unable to police or enforce any agreements arrived at; and they might face a protracted and difficult process of bargaining. In other words, exchange is a process that involves costs and requires supporting legal institutions. Where transactions costs are low and property rights well defined and enforceable, however, private agreements would be expected to achieve most of the gains to trade. Coase (1960) was the first to look at instances of 'market failure' from this perspective. He pointed out that the Common Law already furnished many cases that illustrated this basic idea. In cases of nuisance, the Courts would grant injunctions and then permit private bargaining to achieve an efficient outcome if continuation of the offending activity were of sufficient social value. The proposition that with clearly assigned property rights and zero costs of transacting people will bargain to an efficient allocation of resources is known as the 'Coase Theorem'.

The Coase Theorem applies in conditions that are as rarefied as those underlying a Walrasian general equilibrium. Its implications for the theory of economic regulation are, however, rather different from those derived from static competitive analysis. The normative version of the theorem states that the law should be structured 'so as to remove the impediments to private agreements' (Cooter and Ulen, 1997, pp. 89–90). In other words, the role of the regulator is to clarify property rights and reduce the costs of trading them. The Coasian regulator is the facilitator of the trading process and the provider of transactions cost reducing institutions rather than the achiever of ideal end states. However, in a world where transactions costs will always be significant and can never be removed entirely, Hobbesian judgements cannot be avoided and the regulatory process will not be entirely end-independent. The initial assignment of property rights, for example, will have no efficiency consequences where transactions costs are zero. But where trading is costly, it can matter to whom property rights are assigned. If, for example, airport landing rights were allocated collectively to local residents, the transactions costs of reassigning them to airlines would be formidable. The reverse process might be equally costly, so that the rights would tend to stay where they were assigned and ex ante judgements about desirable outcomes would be an unavoidable element in the design of a suitable trading system for the allocation of congested air space.

The New Institutional Economics has resulted in more than a simple recognition of the existence and importance of transactions costs in economic organisation (for a review, see Kasper and Streit, 1998). By interpreting observed institutions as contributing to the reduction of transactions costs, attention is drawn to the means by which these institutions develop. Institutions such as money or property can be seen as 'internal' – that is, developed by the repeated interaction of transactors over time in a quasi-evolutionary process rather than 'external' and imposed by a powerful sovereign. Repeated coordination games result in the establishment of conventions of behaviour, conventions with which each participant has an incentive to comply and which only later may be codified into formal law (Sugden, 1986). Regulatory arrangements, broadly conceived, are not therefore confined to those introduced by the legislation of the modern state and, indeed, where the state acts it will often be as a substitute for existing private methods.[8] In the sections that follow, however, it is the regulatory activities of the state that are of central concern.

Natural monopoly

Where a single supplier is technically able to serve the entire market at lower total cost than any feasible combination of two or more suppliers, the market is said to be a 'natural monopoly'. Theoretically the condition for natural monopoly is that cost functions are 'sub-additive'.[9] Empirically this means that natural monopoly is associated with industries that require the input of large indivisible amounts of fixed (and usually sunk) capital. Historically, the sectors most subject to natural monopoly have been the 'public utilities', such as gas, electricity, water and telecommunications as well as various forms of transport. At the core of these industries are 'indivisible' assets such as pipes, cables, wires, satellites, rail and road links, waterways and so forth. Even classical liberal economists such as Smith, Mill and (in more recent times) Baumol and Buchanan recognized the desirability of some form of government regulation in the presence of natural monopoly or 'extreme jointness efficiencies' (see Baumol, 1965 and Buchanan, 1975, p. 97). Smith argued for regulation of the toll roads and Mill discussed the case of canals. We have already noted how the regulation of railroads began in the United States in the nineteenth century and was extended in the twentieth century to telecommunications, broadcasting and electricity.

In more recent times, greater attention has been given to network economies in consumption compared with the older focus on simple economies of scale in production. The more users a communications network attracts, for example, the more valuable its services become and, up to some capacity limit, the lower become the costs per unit of service delivered. Economies of scope are also often associated with modern public utilities. These exist where it is less costly to produce different products together rather than in separate firms. These will again ultimately derive from some joint input that can be used simultaneously in the production of several different products. At the retail level, for example, there are economies in metering and billing if consumers deal with a single company for gas, electricity and water. Economies of scope thus favour the growth of diversified rather than specialized firms.

From a Coasian point of view the problem of natural monopoly is the unfeasibility of putting together the contracts that are required for efficient provision. A natural monopolist who could negotiate costlessly and individually with all users for services to be rendered in all future time periods would not require regulation, on standard efficiency grounds. A monopolist who must sink substantial amounts of capital in advance of any such agreements and who has limited ability to discriminate in price, however, will maximize profit by inefficiently restricting access and charging a price in excess of marginal cost. Some form of collective process is required to overcome this problem. The development of cooperative arrangements in which consumers become 'owners' of the natural monopoly enterprise, for example, can occur quite spontaneously (Hansmann, 1996). If consumers collectively hold control rights to the assets they can, subject to the inevitable costs and inefficiencies of collective choice processes, ensure that the monopoly operates in a way that serves their interests.

A 'club' is one organizational response to the problem of natural monopoly. It does not have to take the form of 'the state', but over much of the twentieth century the nationalization of natural monopolies was common nevertheless. In the UK, for example, the gas, electricity, water, rail and telecommunications industries were all under state control by the 1950s.[10] This represented the ultimate Hobbesian solution. Failures in private agreements would be fixed by managers appointed by the state. Managers were specifically required 'to further the public interest in all respects'.[11] This rather vague injunction was refined by technical advice over time to include setting prices related to marginal social costs and undertaking investment projects with positive net present values calculated using a test discount rate.[12] If efficient pricing would lead to financial losses, two part tariffs involving overhead charges were recommended.[13] Effectively the managers were being asked to bring about the efficient outcomes in the natural monopoly sectors that a perfect market might conceptually achieve for the other sectors.

The criticisms levelled during the 1960s and 1970s at the regulatory agencies in the US, mentioned above, were mirrored in the UK by a similar critical response to the performance of the nationalized industries. By the late 1970s official reports and academic studies were questioning the performance of UK public enterprises (e.g. NEDO, 1976; Pryke, 1981). In spite of their legal status as 'public corporations'[14] independent of government, managers of the nationalized industries were subject to political pressure from ministers as well as from labour unions and other pressure groups. Prices, cross-subsidies, employment levels and investment plans were often intensely controversial. Where financial losses occurred it was impossible to tell whether these were a result of efficient pricing or inefficient operations. In response to this problem, specific financial and productivity targets were introduced by the late 1970s.[15]

Innovations of this type only served, however, to throw into sharper relief the contracting problems faced by politicians and managers. What incentives did politicians have to determine appropriate targets, to make them explicit and to stick to them over time? What incentive did managers have to provide target-setters with appropriate information or to achieve the targets once set? Were some of the relevant targets inherently non-verifiable and therefore not contractible? These questions implicitly concerned the best response to agency problems and raised the possibility that public enterprise was inherently likely to be less productively efficient than other forms of enterprise.[16] In particular, if the government wished to purchase certain goods and services on behalf of the public, it was unclear why contracting with managers of privately owned assets should be any more difficult than contracting with managers of publicly owned assets.[17] The absence of privately exchangeable control rights in the public sector constrained the type of incentives that could be arranged. The take-over threat, the bankruptcy constraint, the direct intervention of shareholders with a significant personal stake, and the granting of stock options were all ruled out by state ownership. Many studies during the 1970s and early 1980s attempted to investigate the relative performance of public compared with private enterprise from this property rights perspective.[18]

In cases where public and private concerns could be observed in competition with each other, the latter were usually found to have the edge in terms of factor productivity. This has been confirmed by work in the post-privatization era that investigates the relative performance of public and private enterprise over a whole range of countries and industries.[19] General conclusions about the organization of natural monopolies, however, were more difficult to draw because the alternative to monopolistic public enterprise was monopolistic private enterprise. Any advantages of the latter with respect to cost efficiency might not be very great in the absence of competition and might be counterbalanced by the greater exploitation of monopoly power. In other words any improvements in *technical* and *cost efficiency* deriving from privatization were quite compatible with an overall deterioration in *allocative efficiency*.[20] The important question was whether the advantages derivable from the existence of exchangeable control rights and the value maximizing incentives that accompanied them could be combined with some protection against restrictions in output. This protection would have to come from a regulatory system acting as a substitute for public ownership.

In the natural monopoly industries, therefore, the case for privatization was concerned as much with the incentives faced by politicians, regulators and other interests (and hence about public choice) as it was about managerial incentives. If politicians and industry managers had failed to achieve 'public interest' objectives under nationalization, what reasons were there for expecting politicians and regulators to do better in the context of privatization? Politicians would presumably still be pursuing votes and still be subject to political pressure, while regulators could be 'captured' and would have their own as well as the public interest to consider. The difference between nationalized and privatized utilities from a public choice point of view, however, is in the rules that govern possible political intervention. Under state ownership political pressure on managers could be direct but hidden from public view. Under privatization, managers have fiduciary duties to shareholders, the price of the company's stock acts as a continuing signal concerning financial performance, accounts must be drawn up to meet certain accounting standards, price-sensitive information must be divulged to the market and regulatory intervention must itself accord with procedural rules. These factors might be anticipated to increase the cost and reduce the expected benefit to politicians from trying to influence management decisions. Privatization will therefore tend to be associated with 'de-politicization' (Boycko et al., 1996).

Regulation and competition
One very significant characteristic of the regulatory system that accompanied privatization in the UK was the duty placed on the regulator to encourage competition. This reflected the judgement that privatization would confer far greater social benefits if it were accompanied by a move towards competitive markets than if monopoly power remained intact. It also had important general consequences for the nature of the regulatory regime. The regulator could be seen not as the enforcer of particular outcomes but as the provider of 'governance' for a market process. This is closer to the Coasian approach to 'market failure' than the Hobbesian one. By encouraging or 'facilitating' competition the regulator is permitting the widest possible scope for the striking of new private agreements. The idea of the regulator as a rule provider for market processes is reflected in the recent merger of the offices for gas and electricity regulation into a single office, the Office of Gas and Electricity Markets (OFGEM).

Although regulators can be portrayed as market facilitators the more directly interventionist elements are never far from the surface. The problem is the tension that exists between two distinct views of competition. One emphasizes an evolutionary trial and error process of discovery in which contractors are always searching for a decisive advantage over their opponents. This is the 'Austrian' view associated with Hayek (1949, 1978) and Schumpeter (1936, 1943). If regulation is limited to the classic requirements of preventing force or fraud the result is a 'competitive order'. The other view sees competition more in terms of an athletic contest in which closely matched people try to achieve identical ends in identical conditions constrained by highly formal and often extensive sets of rules. Regulation is required to prevent cheating and the resulting system is one of 'ordered competition'.

Intervention in the competitive order puts the regulator in a position analogous to that of the warden of a game reserve who monitors the natural environment and occasionally takes action to maintain the necessary habitat or cull animals that are becoming too dominant. Intervention in a system of ordered competition, on the other hand, puts the regulator in a position nearer to that of an administrator of the Olympic Games who monitors compliance with the rules on performance enhancing drugs. Clearly these are rather different conceptions of the regulatory process. One is overseeing the competition of predator versus prey and occasionally 'playing God' to bring about desired changes in the balance of forces. The other is trying to produce an ideal of procedural 'fairness'.

In the case of natural monopoly the whole idea of encouraging competition seems paradoxical since a single producer would appear, by definition, to have a decisive cost advantage. There are, however, several ways in which the aim can be interpreted. The first and simplest is for the regulator to make sure that if, as technology advances and market size grows, activities change from being 'natural' monopolies to becoming potentially competitive, new entry is not impeded by artificial restrictions. This would represent a clearly Coasian policy of removing impediments to trade. Even if natural monopoly conditions continue to exist, the removal of entry barriers can make the market more 'contestable' assuming that the problem of sunk capital is not too serious. Where there are potential entrants able to take the market from an incumbent as soon as the latter tries to exploit a monopoly position by raising prices, the market is contestable. Regulatory changes in the airline and bus industries in the late 1970s and 1980s were based on this idea (Baumol et al., 1982).

The second way in which competition has been facilitated in the natural monopolies is by a policy of vertical disintegration. As already noted, the natural monopoly element of most public utilities lies in the provision of network assets. In electricity, for example, it is transmission and distribution that are naturally monopolistic rather than generation. Similarly in telecommunications, the provision of wires from the local telephone exchanges to domestic and business premises may be a natural monopoly, but this certainly would not apply to the manufacture of equipment or the delivery of various telephone services using the wires. The duty to encourage competition can therefore be interpreted as a policy of isolating the natural monopoly element from the surrounding potentially competitive activities. Regulation can then be confined, in principle, to the core natural monopoly assets, and this usually entails trying to ensure access on equal terms to all competing users. The 'common carrier' is required to post regulated prices at which access to the network will be granted. This separation between the provision of network assets and their use in delivering services to consumers might be effected without breaking up the business into its component parts and running them as separate concerns. Regulating a common carrier is more straightforward, however, if the carrier is not itself involved in using its own network. The suspicion that vertically integrated utilities will favour their own 'internal' customers over external users is costly to overcome by regulatory means. This would be especially true if there were real scope economies associated with the integration of network operators and network users.

In trying to achieve equal or 'fair' terms of access of suppliers to a common carrier's network the regulator is approaching most closely the view of competition associated with sporting activities – ordered competition. The problem, however, is that to produce competition of this ordered type at certain points, the regulator interferes in the whole structure of contractual relations. The degree of vertical integration is determined by regulation rather than by 'the competitive order'. It was Coase (1937) who first demonstrated that the scope of the firm could be explained by the existence of transactions costs. The process of contracting within a firm was different from the process of contracting across markets. Sometimes an activity would be more profitably managed within the firm and sometimes the use of an outside supplier using market contracts would be preferred. At the boundary of the firm the cost of undertaking an activity within the firm would be the same as contracting with an outside supplier. Observed forms of business organisation, therefore, were the outcome of a competitive process driven by attempts to economize on transactions costs. The vertical disintegration of the public utilities by regulatory intervention reflects judgements not only about the desirability of ordered competition in network access but also concerning the transactional efficiency of the resulting organizational structure.

Because of the large sunk costs associated with most public utilities, reliance on competitive processes to undermine monopoly power through innovation and new entry has conventionally been regarded as unrealistic in these sectors. Competition, as has been seen above, has had to be artificially contrived. The benefits of this ordered competition are widely seen as outweighing any adverse effects on transactional efficiency. In a few areas, however, transactional issues have featured prominently. In the rail industry, for example, the separation of track and signalling infrastructure from the train operating companies in the UK has been controversial, mainly because of safety concerns and the perceived difficulty of assuring proper track maintenance by the use of contract. This case is interesting because the separation of track and train companies has not resulted in much direct competition between train operators over the same routes, so that the conventional justification for functional disintegration does not apply. The potential importance of transactional considerations is reflected in the decision in October 2003 to suspend the contracting-out of track maintenance by the track operator (Network Rail) and to transfer the work to internal units in order to re-establish greater control.

If transactions costs are an impediment to the introduction of ordered competition in some areas, the appropriate regulatory response to the existence of 'Schumpeterian competition' is a significant problem in others. The telecommunications sector, for example, has been transformed since the 1970s by technological developments in mobile telephony, computer technolog optic cable and satellite communications. In dynamic technological cor like this the regulator either stands aside entirely or, when trying to 'order' the competition, intervenes in ways more reminiscent of the role of the game warden than that of the referee. Until 1998, for example, in the UK BT was forbidden from offering entertainment services in competition with cable companies, although cable companies after 1991 were able to offer telephony services. The idea was to encourage new entry by restricting the ability of BT to respond in a predatory manner. Although justified in terms of encouraging competition, the policy was not based on the Coasian objective of reducing the impediments to private agreements and allowing the market to operate. Instead, it was a Hobbesian policy of trying to bring about particular results.

Methods of regulation

Principal and agent[21]
In the absence of contestability, competition cannot finally solve the natural monopoly problem and the regulation of the core assets remains to be considered. We have already noted the objections to the public interest theory of regulation, which abstracts from information and incentive problems and assumes a well-informed and benevolent regulator able to enforce optimal policies on the regulated firm. An alternative approach sees regulation in terms of a principal–agent relationship and focuses on the problem of moral hazard. Here information asymmetry (the fact that information is not equally available to all interested parties) is assumed to constrain the activities of the regulator. Information about the behaviour of the regulated firm, for example, might not be available or only available at very high cost. The regulator (principal) is still assumed to be pursuing public interest objectives but now does not know the firm's costs, which depend on its effort as well as random factors. A regulatory 'contract' must be drawn up which elicits compliance with the objectives of the regulator.

Where firms (agents) are risk neutral the classic theoretical answer to the 'unobservability' of an agent's effort is for the agent to receive the entire additional benefit from extra effort. If, for example, a farmer received the value of the harvest, he would, unlike an employed labourer, have no reason to shirk. He would, of course, bear the risk associated with vagaries in the weather and other chance factors, but if he were risk neutral or if there existed well-developed insurance markets in the relevant contingent claims, a contract assigning the 'outcome' or harvest to the farmer would be optimal. The principal (in this case the farmer's landlord) would receive a fee or rent that would be independent of the outcome. In certain circumstances, therefore, the unobservability of effort does not matter. A contract representing a pure 'franchise' arrangement, whereby the agent pays a franchise fee to the principal and then keeps the net result, would give 'high powered' effort incentives.

In the case of a regulator (principal) wishing to achieve allocative efficiency and negotiating with a monopoly supplier (agent), the equivalent solution is for the firm to receive the full social value of its output while paying a fixed fee to the government for the right to undertake the business (Loeb and Magat, 1979; Baron and Myerson, 1982). If the firm wishes to maximize its profit it will operate in a cost efficient way without being closely monitored. It will also set the efficient output because, assuming that such a thing can be contrived, its marginal revenue will equal marginal social benefit and profit maximization requires that this is set equal to the firm's marginal cost. Essentially this scheme aligns the firm's marginal revenue with the social marginal benefit of output and avoids risk bearing costs because the firm is assumed to be a risk-neutral party. The firm therefore behaves like a perfectly discriminating monopolist and its expected profit maximizing choices will be socially efficient.

The difficulties with this scheme are not hard to see. It economizes on the need for information about the firm's costs of production and effort, but it requires the regulator to pay the firm sums representing the consumers' surplus generated on its output. Clearly if the firm simply receives revenue from its sales to consumers it will behave like a normal monopolist. If it is to behave optimally, its marginal revenue must reflect the full marginal social value of its output and this requires that subsidies should be paid equal to the consumers' surplus generated. Thus the regulator is assumed to know a great deal about the marginal social value schedule for the firm's product and the whole approach is thus still in the tradition of the 'public interest' theory of regulation. The scheme also requires the regulator and the firm to bargain over the fixed fee. The regulator might try to arrange the fee such that the firm eventually achieves a competitive return on its assets, but the information to calculate this is unlikely to be available. A competitive award of the franchise to the highest bidder would be one way of proceeding but this also involves transactions costs (discussed further below) and implies that all the bidders have the same understanding of the social marginal benefit of output as the regulator. The size of the fixed fee will determine the firm's eventual profit but not the efficiency of its operations under this scheme. If distributional considerations are important to the regulator and not just efficiency, however, the negotiated size of the fee will be important.[22]

Rate of return regulation
Actual regulatory systems have evolved over time and have been influenced only gradually by the theoretical literature on optimal contracting. The original model for the regulation of public utilities was established in the United States and was based on control of the rate of return on capital. Where information about costs is hidden from the regulator, the disadvantages of this system are

substantial from a contracting point of view. The regulatory 'contract' has incentive effects similar to a commercial 'cost-plus' agreement. Unlike the principal–agent model outlined above, which made the firm's return dependent on its own actions, rate of return regulation offers the firm the opportunity to earn an 'acceptable' return and thus undermines the incentive to operate in a cost efficient way. In particular, an unacceptable rate of return can as easily be made acceptable by increasing the use of capital as by reducing prices and profits. It is the cost-plus nature of rate of return regulation or cost of service regulation that creates these incentives which detract from cost economy. The tendency of regulated companies to adopt highly capital-intensive production methods and generally to 'inflate the rate base' is known as the Averch–Johnson effect.[23]

Finding out about costs in a regulated company becomes a central problem for rate of return regulation and draws the regulator into detailed discussions about production methods. In these circumstances the danger of 'capture' is increased and this has figured prominently in the US literature. More indirect methods of generating information and providing incentives include the use of 'yardstick competition'. Here the regulator compares information on costs and performance between firms operating in different regions. Attempts to mislead the regulator about cost conditions would then require all firms to coordinate their responses. In the UK water industry, for example, the existence of sufficient comparators has been an important factor underlying regulatory opposition to mergers between regional water companies (for a fuller discussion, see Chapter 17).

RPI minus X regulation

The post-privatization method of regulation introduced in the UK took the form of a price cap rather than a rate of return cap. The system emerged from an official report by Littlechild (1983) into the regulation of British Telecom (BT). A regulated price is set for a specified service or weighted average basket of services for a given period of time (usually five years). The regulated firm is then permitted to increase this price by the rate of increase in the retail price index (RPI) minus a negotiated factor X to represent anticipated productivity improvements in excess of the national average.[24] Occasionally, as in the case of gas, the formula would be extended to allow for changes in the prices of specified inputs that represented a large component of the regulated firm's costs and that were outside its control.

As a form of contract the RPI minus X system is similar to a fixed price arrangement in which the buyer is assured of the result while the supplier takes the risk and receives the rewards from additional effort or from the discovery of cost reducing innovations. It is therefore closer in its incentive properties to the principal–agent contract discussed earlier and avoids the inefficient Averch–

Johnson effects that are associated with rate of return regulation. It would not be expected to achieve a fully efficient result, however, because, unlike the Loeb and Magat (1979) case, the firm receives the regulated price for its output and not (except by a fluke) a sum equal to the marginal social value.

Littlechild (1983) originally conceived the RPI minus X system as a means of preventing the privatized utilities from exploiting their monopoly positions in the short to medium term, while competition was encouraged in the longer term. As a long-term means of regulating natural monopoly, however, there is a danger that the incentive properties of RPI minus X are weakened. The problems relate to the process of 'renegotiating' the contract at the end of each regulatory period. If the new price cap and the new value of X are related to existing profits and to rates of productivity improvement achieved in the past, incentives are compromised. As the end of the regulatory period approaches, firms will prefer to delay productivity improvements that might adversely affect the coming regulatory bargain.[25] More generally they will use their information advantage over the regulator to try to exaggerate their costs. Changes in the nature of the product or in the contents of the regulated 'basket' of services imply that a central negotiating problem will be to define the 'output' to which the price cap applies.

Beesley and Littlechild (1988) argue that because of the fixed regulatory period, and the fact that each bargain is forward looking rather than merely adjusting to past events, RPI minus X regulation gives greater scope for bargaining than does rate of return regulation. In this bargaining environment capital investment in very long-lived and specific assets becomes a particular problem if price reviews occur too frequently. Firms may worry that, after the investments have been made, future prices will be set at levels that do not yield a sufficient return – the reverse of the 'capture' problem. Political pressure on regulators to keep prices low or to 'claw back' past profits make the firm vulnerable. This can lead to firms financing investment using higher levels of debt rather than equity because regulators cannot ignore obligations to bondholders, at least (as in the UK) where they are required to permit the regulated firms to finance their proper activities. The regulator may promise not to behave in an opportunistic way towards shareholders, but the inability of governments (and hence regulators) credibly to commit very far into the future is widely recognized as a significant problem. Indeed, it is not even clear that a promise not to intervene *within* a regulatory period can be relied on.[26]

Profit sharing regulation

RPI minus X regulation is in principle designed to give high-powered incentives and to encourage profit-seeking behaviour. In practice, however, profits in excess of some limit are subject to heavy popular criticism and this has led to suggestions for incorporating an explicit element of profit sharing into regulatory contracts. A simple tax on the profits of otherwise unregulated utilities would transfer some monopoly profits to the government but would do nothing to change pricing and output decisions. More complex 'sliding scale' profits taxes, in which the tax rate falls as the output of the monopolist rises, can be devised to induce firms to lower prices and increase output.[27] Alternatively a system of price regulation might be modified to incorporate profit sharing with consumers through automatic price adjustments. Such schemes are in the tradition of 'public interest' regulation in the sense that efficiency and distributional objectives are explicitly being pursued by the designers, but the work of public choice and institutional economists is recognized by the introduction of political and other constraints on the policy process.

Franchising

By seeing regulation as a form of contracting over a specified period of time between an agent of government and a private supplier of monopoly services, the close connection between certain types of regulation and franchising is apparent. It was Demsetz (1968), updating the work of Chadwick (1859), who suggested that 'competition for the field' could substitute for 'competition within the field' and that this would reduce the requirement for detailed rate of return style regulation of utilities. In a Demsetz auction, bidders compete with each other to supply the entire market at a certain price for a given franchise term. The franchise is awarded to the bidder offering the lowest price. From the point of view of incentives the outcome of a Demsetz auction is similar to price-cap regulation, but with the cap set by a competitive process rather than by bilateral bargaining. It could also be seen as a way of making the market 'contestable' at specified intervals even if sunk costs prevent the market being contestable on a more continuous basis.

The organizational choice between rate of return regulation and the Demsetz franchise auction involves many of the considerations raised by Coase (1937) in his discussion of the transactional features of firms versus markets. Regulation has firm-like features, such as long-term associations, a continuous process of information gathering, monitoring of behaviour, and a susceptibility to managerial moral hazard. Franchise arrangements are characterized by more arm's length relations, significant transactions costs, but also higher powered effort incentives. An analogy might be between a managed chain of shops (monitored and regulated by the centre) and a franchise chain (with contracts negotiated with the centre but with more local discretion). Franchising is primarily therefore a means of addressing the problem of moral hazard. The marginal profits from extra effort go to the franchisee and this provides strong incentives to find cost-reducing methods and to operate existing facilities efficiently. Awarding a franchise competitively by asking for price quotations also has the advantage of revealing to the regulatory authorities information about cost conditions in the industry.

Franchise auctions are, however, themselves subject to hazards and costs. Where, for example, the nature of the service to be provided is complex, subject to technical change and difficult to measure, it may not be possible to specify in a contract precisely what is required of the franchisee. Bidders may be asked to specify themselves the nature and standard of the service that they can supply along with the prices they would charge were they to win the contest. In these conditions the possibility of opportunistic behaviour is always present. If the true quality of bidders is hidden from the franchisor ex ante the danger of adverse selection – the use of low quality suppliers because higher quality ones have been driven from the market – is always present.[28] A further possibility is that bidders might shade prices below cost in order to win the contract but plan to renegotiate more favourable terms later. This is more likely to occur when non-transferable capital is accumulated so that 'first-mover advantages' accrue to the incumbent. Forcing a franchisee into bankruptcy and changing to a new one might be more costly than simply renegotiating terms. The incumbent challenges the franchisor to 'waste' the firm specific capital already in existence.

In general, long-term franchise agreements involving the use of large amounts of durable, specific and possibly non-transferable capital in unpredictable market conditions are costly to negotiate and enforce. Agreements will often require renegotiation as circumstances change and unforeseen contingencies arise. As a result, the franchising solution to natural monopoly can begin to look very similar to rate of return regulation as time advances. As Williamson (1985, p. 350) noted, franchise bidding can lead to an administrative apparatus little different from the one associated with the regulation for which it was an intended substitute.

Conclusions

A major theme running through this chapter has been the contrast between regulation as a means of enforcing rules and regulation as a means of attaining collectively determined ends. There is increasing recognition that institutional as distinct from purely technological factors play an important role in economic development (North 1990, 1991). In particular the rule of law, the existence of an uncorrupt and competent bureaucracy, an independent judiciary, along with political stability and accountability are all significant elements. These are closely related to the first (rule enforcing) concept of regulation. Where regulation turns into state planning, however, economic development is adversely affected. Jalilian et al. (2003), for example, use a measure of regulatory quality which includes 'quantitative regulations, price controls and other interventions in the economy' (p. 11). Higher quality regulatory governance is associated with a lower incidence of these types of direct intervention. In econometric tests, higher quality regulatory governance was shown positively to affect the growth performance of an economy.

A second major theme has been the political and interest group pressure leading to an expanding regulatory state and to increasingly detailed intervention. In the field of the public utilities emphasis on the promotion of competition has helped to establish regulators as rule enforcers or 'game wardens' rather than planners, but even here it is often difficult to distinguish disinterested adjudication from the fixing of a result.

A final theme has been the development of regulation as a form of contracting. This is an extension of the old public interest approach that allows for imperfect information and the resulting transactional hazards. In the absence of public ownership, intervention to provide public goods or to control natural monopoly requires the implementation of some form of contracting. The extension of state 'contracting' to an ever-wider range of activities, however, is simply to impose collective judgements about resource allocation by means of contract with private suppliers instead of by state ownership and administration. The negotiator of contracts on behalf of the state and the regulator of decentralized market processes are undertaking conceptually quite distinct activities.

Appendix

The following are brief explanations of a number of concepts introduced in this chapter and which feature, explicitly or implicitly, in a number of the chapters that follow. They may be omitted by readers already familiar with basic welfare economics and the economics of regulation.

The first fundamental theorem of welfare economics

This theorem states that in the absence of externalities, or equivalently with a complete set of markets, a perfectly competitive equilibrium is Pareto efficient. In a perfectly competitive market, all contractors face the same set of prices for goods, services and factors of production and all prices are taken as parametric – that is they are not influenced by the behaviour of any individual participant in the market. An equilibrium set of prices is one at which utility and profit maximizing behaviour on the part of all contractors results in universal market clearing. There is no excess demand or supply at these equilibrium prices in any market. A Pareto efficient allocation of resources is one in which it is impossible to make one person better off without making another person worse off. This is equivalent to saying that there are no mutually advantageous exchanges, agreements or 'deals' available.

An intuitive discussion of the theorem is provided in the text. Gains to trade derive from divergences between consumers in relative valuations of goods and services. If, for a given allocation of resources, person A values (i.e. is prepared to pay for) additional units of a particular good more than person B values the same good, there will be mutual gains available from transferring some of the good from B to A at a price somewhere between their two valuations. At such a price, person B will receive more than his valuation of the good he is supplying while person A will pay less than her valuation of the good she is demanding. Both will be better off as a result of the trade. The efficiency properties of a perfectly competitive equilibrium ultimately derive from the fact that individual maximizing behaviour leads people to equate their marginal willingness to pay for each good to its market price. Since all contractors face the same set of prices, the competitive equilibrium must imply that all contractors have the same marginal willingness to pay and that no scope for Pareto improvements based on diverging marginal valuations can exist.

The second fundamental theorem of welfare economics

Many different allocations of resources will have the property of being Pareto efficient. In particular, highly unequal allocations as well as highly egalitarian ones may be in the Pareto set of socially efficient allocations. The second theorem states that each and every one of these allocations can be supported as a competitive equilibrium, given certain technical assumptions about preferences. This theorem is a central pillar of the standard 'first-best' approach to public policy. Ideally, lump sum taxes and transfers that do not interfere with the efficiency properties of competitive markets should be used to pursue redistributional aims. Equity and efficiency can be separated as policy objectives with suitable tools aimed at each target. Measures that distort prices and interfere with the operation of the competitive market should not, according to this view, be introduced in the interests of achieving redistributional objectives. Whatever the desired distributional objectives, their achievement will not require the destruction of the competitive market providing that suitable non-distortionary policy instruments can be found.

Natural monopoly and sub-additivity

A cost function is sub-additive if $C(Q) < \Sigma_i C(q_i)$ for all q_i such that $\Sigma_i q_i = Q$. This simply expresses the essential attribute of 'natural' monopoly that it is less costly to produce output Q using a single firm than by allocating the same output between a set of two or more firms. A production process that is subject to pervasive economies of scale will give rise to a sub-additive cost function. In these circumstances it is possible to double output by using less than double the inputs and there is always a potential cost advantage to concentrating production in a single unit. Even after economies of scale have been exhausted and average costs begin to rise there will still be a range of output over which a single firm will be a lower cost producer than two or more separate firms. Note, however, that this theory is based on the assumption of cost minimization and pays no attention to matters such as managerial slack, rent seeking, or 'X'-inefficiency (Leibenstein, 1978), that might be associated with monopoly. A cost function is also sub-additive where there are economies of scope or cost reductions resulting from producing different goods or services together.

The theory of principal and agent

Contracting would not be a problem if information were costlessly available to all parties. In fact, however, much information is costly to collect and may be distributed unequally (or asymmetrically) across the contractors. A particular difficulty arises if the actions or 'effort' of one party to a contract (the agent) is unobservable to the other party (the principal).

Clearly it is not always necessary for effort to be observable. If, for example, both parties know the results of the agent's effort, and if the connection between effort and result is a simple causal one, a contract specifying the required results or 'outcome' will be efficient. Either the agent successfully achieves the specified results or he (or she) does not. If he achieves the results he gets paid an agreed fee. If he does not achieve the results, he does not get paid. If I agree to pay a gardener for mowing the lawn, it is not necessary for me to observe his actions providing the result is verifiable at low cost.

Greater difficulties arise when the simple causal connection between effort and outcome is broken. Outcomes might to some extent reflect chance factors outside the control of the agent. In this case it would be necessary to draw up a 'state-contingent contract' in which the outcomes promised by the agent were dependent on the occurrence or non-occurrence of certain chance factors. In this way the risks and rewards could be suitably distributed between the principal and agent. The gardener promises to mow the lawn if it is fine but is otherwise free to contract elsewhere. I promise to pay a fee, even if it is wet, for any costs incurred by the gardener in committing to mow my lawn. Clearly these arrangements require that the 'state of the world' (wet or fine) is verifiable at low cost. I will be unhappy about paying a fee to an absent gardener if (in my opinion) it is fine.

The classic analysis of principal and agent concerns the case where both the state of the world and the effort of the agent are unobservable – or at least unverifiable at low cost by a court of law. In this case the contract can only mention the actual results, which will be the outcome of both the agent's effort and pure chance. Consider the case of a risk-neutral principal and a risk-averse agent. A contract that specifies a given payment or fee to the agent irrespective of the result will mean that the principal takes the entire risk. From a risk-sharing point of view this is efficient. The principal is risk neutral and is therefore the efficient risk bearer. The problem is that the agent has no incentive to exert effort. He or she gets paid the same whatever happens. This is the traditional 'wage' or 'time rate' arrangement. At the other extreme we might envisage a contract in which the principal receives a given payment independent of the actual result. This is the pure franchise contract by which the agent pays a fixed fee to the principal and keeps whatever remains of the actual result. From a risk sharing point of view this is inefficient. The agent takes the entire risk although, by assumption, he or she is the risk-averse party. On the other hand, the contract induces a high level of effort because any additional output resulting from higher effort accrues to the person exerting it (the agent).

An optimal contract will share the result between the principal and the agent and will represent a compromise between the two extreme positions described in the previous paragraph. Starting from the position where the agent receives a 'wage' there will be advantages to 'higher powered effort incentives'. These are provided by tying the agent's reward more closely to the actual results. The wage element is reduced and a share in the result is introduced. Risk sharing losses are incurred but, at first, greater effort incentives outweigh them. At a certain point, however, the gains from moving to yet higher powered effort incentives will just be counter-balanced by the losses incurred by transferring risk from a risk-neutral to a risk-averse party. This will be the optimal contract.[29]

If the agent is assumed to be risk neutral, the 'franchise' arrangement turns out to be fully efficient. This is because there are no risk sharing losses incurred by loading risk onto the agent, while effort incentives will also be efficient – the agent will work up to the point at which his or her marginal expected return equals the marginal cost of effort. This is the case discussed in the text.

The Averch–Johnson (A–J) effect
The A–J effect is an increase in the capital intensity of production methods that is predicted to result from the introduction of rate of return regulation.

In Figure 2A.1 an unregulated monopolist producing output q_m and facing competitive factor markets for labour and capital will use L_m units of labour and K_m units of capital.

This is the cost-minimizing technology to adopt. Total costs are equal to C_m. If the firm were to use a different technology it would incur higher costs and hence its profit would fall. If profit is measured on the vertical axis below the origin, a curve can be traced showing profit for each technology adopted by the firm as indicated by the associated input of capital. The curve is drawn on the assumption that output remains constant at q_m. Thus, the unregulated firm will achieve maximum profit of π_m.

The effect of rate of return regulation can be seen by noting that it introduces a regulatory constraint linking profit to the quantity of capital used. In the figure, the area $\pi \leq RK$ represents this constraint, which will presumably be binding as an equality if the firm maximizes its profit. R represents the maximum acceptable rate of return on capital expressed as a 'rental rate' per unit. Under this regulatory constraint the firm will operate with K_R units of capital and L_R units of labour. Its costs will rise to C_R and its profits will fall to π_R. Notice, however, that maintaining the old factor proportions would have caused profits to decline much further to π^*.

Rate of return regulation is thus expected to result in cost inefficiency. Regulated firms will no longer have an incentive to use cost minimizing production

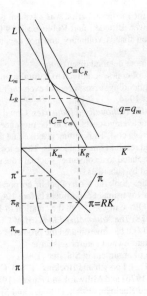

Figure 2.1   The Averch–Johnson effect

methods even when they are assumed to have the objective of profit
maximization.

The analysis in Figure 2.1 focuses on the substitution of capital for labour
and takes output as constant. Clearly the greater the elasticity of substitution
between capital and labour (the more gentle the curvature of the isoquant) the
larger will be the effect of rate of return regulation on the technology used and
the smaller will be the reduction in the monopolist's profit. With a zero elasticity
of substitution (L-shaped isoquants) rate of return regulation could not induce
the substitution of capital for labour.

Notes

1. The regulation might also be attacked on the grounds that it forces firms to divulge sensitive plans to competitors earlier than would otherwise be the case and that this might reduce the dynamic efficiency of the market over the long term. It is not the desirability of this regulation, however, but its character that is the point at issue.
2. Ricketts (2002) elaborates on these points in the context of Nee's paper.
3. See Robbins (1952) for a discussion of classical ideas on economic policy.
4. A more extended description of the first and second theorems of Welfare Economics is provided in the Appendix at the end of this chapter.
5. This is sometimes called the 'Normative Hobbes Theorem'. See, for example, Cooter and Ulen (1997) pp. 89–90.
6. Baumol (1967) and Williamson (1964). Baumol was the originator of sales revenue maximization although Williamson's theory is more appealing in that it deals with the concept of managerial slack and the appropriation of rents.
7. For these and other examples see Wilson (1980).

8.   The 'lex mercatoria' of the medieval period was a system of rules governing trading that did not depend on state power. Blundell and Robinson (1999) discuss the possibilities in the modern era of regulation that is voluntary and not dependent on the intervention of the state.
9.   See the Appendix for a more detailed discussion.
10. Nationalization was not, of course, confined to natural monopolies but in the UK eventually included steel, coal, shipbuilding, aerospace and even car manufacture.
11. Coal Nationalisation Act 1944.
12. See the White Paper (1967) *Nationalised Industries,* Cmnd. 3437.
13. In conditions of declining average costs – as in the presence of economies of scale, marginal cost will be less than average cost. Thus setting prices equal to marginal cost, as recommended by textbook theory, would result in financial losses. These losses could be covered by overhead or 'standing' charges unrelated to a consumer's actual consumption. Alternatively the losses would have to be covered by subsidies.
14. Not all 'natural monopolies' took the form of public corporations. The Post Office (which included telephones) was a government department before 1961. Telecommunications was only separated from the Post Office in 1981 with the creation of BT.
15. See the White Paper (1978) *The Nationalised Industries,* Cmnd. 7131.
16. More recently Shirley (2000) has investigated the problems of introducing performance contracts into the Chinese state-owned enterprise sector.
17. This is an important line of argument in Shleifer (1998).
18. Examples are Davies (1971), Forsyth and Hocking (1980), Caves and Christensen (1980), De Alessi (1974), Lindsay (1976) and Millward and Parker (1983).
19. See for example, Picot and Kaulman (1989), D'Souza and Megginson (1999) and Shirley and Walsh (2000).
20. *Technical efficiency* requires that output is maximized for any given level of inputs. *Cost efficiency* requires that any given output is produced at minimum cost given the prevailing factor prices. Clearly technical efficiency is a necessary condition for cost efficiency but is not sufficient unless there is no choice between different possible methods of production or technologies. *Allocative efficiency* requires that it is impossible to make someone better off by some reallocation of resources without making anyone worse off. Economists sometimes refer to this as *Pareto efficiency.* Cost efficiency is a necessary condition for Pareto efficiency but is not sufficient. As explained in the text, a monopolist could in theory be cost efficient but, if the price set by the monopolist is above the marginal cost of output, potential social gains are available from higher levels of production.
21. See Appendix for further discussion of principal–agent theory.
22. For further discussion see Ricketts (1998).
23. See Averch and Johnson (1962). Further explanation of this effect is provided in the Appendix. The disincentive to operate in a cost efficient way is mitigated to some degree by the existence of regulatory lags. If it takes some time for regulators to notice and respond to unacceptably high rates of return, the firm can take advantage of this period to profit from more efficient operations.
24. National average productivity growth is, of course, reflected in the inflation rate and therefore the RPI.
25. The disadvantages of fixed review periods have been countered in the UK by the use of 'glidepaths' and (in the water sector) a rolling five-year window so that firms benefit from efficiency gains for a time.
26. Helm (2001, p. 478) comments that government is 'not a very credible fixed-price/fixed period contractor', while Stiglitz (1998, pp. 8–11) argues that 'limitations on the ability to make commitments' are often responsible for the difficulty of implementing reforms that seem close to Pareto improvements.
27. See for example, Burns et al. (1998).
28. Laffont and Tirole (1986) derive optimal contracts under conditions of hidden information concerning the efficiency of firms but where ex post costs are observable. Their results suggest a contract in which the supplier announces an expected cost and is reimbursed for a proportion

of cost overruns. By offering a 'menu' of such contracts, firms will self-select such that the most efficient opt for the fixed-price end of the spectrum.
29.   For a fuller explanation see Ricketts (1986).

References

Averch, H. and Johnson, L.L. (1962) 'Behaviour of the Firm under Regulatory Constraint', *American Economic Review*, **52**, 1052–69.

Baron, D.P. and Myerson, R.B. (1982) 'Regulating a Monopolist with Unknown Costs', *Econometrica*, **50**, 911–30.

Bartle, I. (ed.) (2003) 'The UK Model of Utility Regulation', *Centre for the Study of Regulated Industries Proceedings 31*, Bath: University of Bath.

Baumol, W.J. (1965) *Welfare Economics and the Theory of the State*, London: Bell & Sons.

Baumol, W.J. (1967) *Business Behavior, Value and Growth*, New York: Harcourt, Brace and World.

Baumol, W.J., Panzar, J.C. and Willig, R.D. (1982) *Contestable Markets and the Theory of Industry Structure*, New York: Harcourt Brace Jovanovich.

Beesley, M.E. and Littlechild, S.C. (1988) 'The Regulation of Privatized Monopolies in the United Kingdom', *RAND Journal of Economics*, **20**, 454–72.

Blundell, J. and Robinson, C. (1999) *Regulation without the State*, London: Institute of Economic Affairs.

Boycko, M., Shleifer, A. and Vishny, R.W. (1996) 'A Theory of Privatisation', *Economic Journal*, **106** (435), 309–19.

Breton, A. (1974) *The Economic Theory of Representative Government*, Chicago: Aldine.

Buchanan, J. (1975) *The Limits of Liberty*, Chicago: University of Chicago Press.

Buchanan, J. and Tullock, G. (1962) *The Calculus of Consent*, Ann Arbor: University of Michigan Press.

Buchanan, J., Tollison, R.D. and Tullock, G. (eds) (1980) *Toward a Theory of the Rent Seeking Society*, College Station: Texas A and M University Press.

Burns, P., Turvey, R. and Weyman-Jones, T.G. (1998) 'The Behaviour of the Firm under Alternative Regulatory Constraints', *Scottish Journal of Political Economy*, **45** (2), 133–57.

Caves, D.W. and Christensen, L.R. (1980) 'The Relative Efficiency of Public and Private Firms in a Competitive Environment: The Case of the Canadian Railroads', *Journal of Political Economy*, **88** (5), 958–76.

Chadwick, E. (1859) 'Results of Different Principles of Legislation and Administration in Europe: Of Competition for the Field, as Compared with the Competition within the Field of Service', *Journal of the Royal Statistical Society*, **22**, 381.

Coase, R. (1937) 'The Nature of the Firm', *Economica*, **4** (16), 386–405.

Coase, R. (1960) 'The Problem of Social Cost', *Journal of Law and Economics*, **3** (1), 1–44.

Cooter, R. and Ulen, T. (1997) *Law and Economics*, New York: Addison-Wesley.

Davies, D.G. (1971) 'The Efficiency of Public versus Private Firms: The Case of Australia's Two Airlines', *Journal of Law and Economics*, **14** (1), 149–65.

De Alessi, L. (1974) 'An Economic Analysis of Government Ownership and Regulation: Theory and Evidence from the Electric Power Industry', *Public Choice*, **19** (1), 1–42.

Demsetz, H. (1968) 'Why Regulate Utilities?', *Journal of Law and Economics*, **11** (1), 55–65.

Demsetz, H. (1969) 'Information and Efficiency: Another Viewpoint', *Journal of Law and Economics*, **12** (1), 1–22.

Downs, A. (1957) *An Economic Theory of Democracy*, New York: Harper & Row.

D'Souza, J. and Megginson, W.L. (1999) 'The Financial and Operating Performance of Privatised Firms during the 1990s', *Journal of Finance*, **54** (4), 1397–438.

Edgeworth, F.Y. (1891) 'On the Determinateness of Economic Equilibrium', reprinted in Edgeworth, F.Y. (1925) *Papers Relating to Political Economy*, London: Macmillan.

Forsyth, P.J. and Hocking, R.D. (1980) 'Property Rights and Efficiency in a Regulated Environment: The Case of Australian Airlines', *Economic Record*, June, 182–5.

Hansmann, H. (1996) *The Ownership of Enterprise*, Cambridge, MA: Harvard University Press.

Hayek, F. (1949) *Individualism and Economic Order*, London: Routledge and Kegan Paul.

Hayek, F. (1978) 'Competition as a Discovery Procedure', in *New Studies in Philosophy, Politics and the History of Ideas*, London: Routledge and Kegan Paul.

Helm, D. (2001) 'Making Britain More Competitive: Regulation and Competition Policy', *Scottish Journal of Political Economy*, **48** (5), 471–87.

Jalilian, H., Kirkpatrick, C. and Parker, D. (2003) 'Creating the Conditions for International Business Expansion: The Impact of Regulation on Economic Growth in Developing Countries – A Cross-country Analysis', Working Paper 54, Manchester: Centre on Regulation and Competition, University of Manchester.

Kasper, W. and Streit, M.E. (1998) *Institutional Economics: Social Order and Public Policy*, Cheltenham, UK and Lyme, USA: Edward Elgar.

Kolko, G. (1965) *Railroads and Regulation 1877–1916*, New Jersey: Princeton University Press.

Krueger, A. (1974) 'The Political Economy of the Rent Seeking Society', *American Economic Review*, **64**, 291–303.

Laffont, J.-J. and Tirole, J. (1986) 'Using Cost Observation to Regulate Firms', *Journal of Political Economy*, **94** (3, Part 1), 614–41.

Leibenstein, H. (1978) *General X-Efficiency Theory and Economic Development*, New York: Oxford University Press.

Lindsay, C. (1976) 'A Theory of Government Enterprise', *Journal of Political Economy*, **84** (5), 1061–77.

Littlechild, S. (1983) 'Regulation of British Telecommunications' Profitability', *Report to the Secretary of State, Department of Industry*, London. Reprinted in Bartle (2003).

Loeb, M. and Magat, W. (1979) 'A Decentralised Method for Utility Regulation', *Journal of Law and Economics*, **22**, 399–404.

Millward, R. and Parker, D.M. (1983) 'Public and Private Enterprise: Comparative Behaviour and Relative Efficiency', in R. Millward et al. (eds), *Public Sector Economics*, London: Longman.

National Economic Development Office (NEDO) (1976) *A Study of UK Nationalised Industries*, London: HMSO.

Nee, V. (2002) 'The Role of the State in Making a Market Economy', *Journal of Institutional and Theoretical Economics*, **156** (1), 64–88.

Niskanen, W. (1968) 'Non-market Decision-making: The Peculiar Economics of Bureaucracy', *American Economic Review*, **58** (2, Papers and Proceedings), 293–305.

Niskanen, W. (1971) *Bureaucracy and Representative Government*, Chicago: Aldine.

North, D. (1990) *Institutions, Institutional Change and Economic Performance*, Cambridge: Cambridge University Press.

North, D. (1991) 'Institutions', *Journal of Economic Perspectives*, **5** (1), 97–112.

Olsen, E.O. (1972) 'An Econometric Analysis of Rent Control', *Journal of Political Economy*, **80** (6), 1081–200.

Olson, M. (1965) *The Logic of Collective Action*, Cambridge, MA: Harvard University Press.

Peltzman, S. (1976) 'Toward a More General Theory of Regulation', *Journal of Law and Economics*, **19** (2), 211–40.

Picot, A. and Kaulmann, T. (1989) 'Comparative Performance of Government-owned and Privately Owned Industrial Corporations – Empirical Results from Six Countries', *Journal of Institutional and Theoretical Economics*, **145** (2), 298–316.

Pigou, A.C. (1938) *The Economics of Welfare*, 4th edn, London: Macmillan.

Polanyi, K. (1944), *The Great Transformation: The Political and Economic Origins of Our Time*, Boston, MA: Beacon Press.

Posner, R.A. (1971) 'Taxation by Regulation', *Bell Journal of Economics and Management Science*, **2** (1), 22–50.

Pryke, R. (1981) *The Nationalised Industries: Policies and Performance Since 1968*, Oxford: Martin Robertson.

Ricketts, M. (1986) 'The Geometry of Principal and Agent: Yet Another Use for the Edgeworth Box', *Scottish Journal of Political Economy*, **33** (3), 228–48.

Ricketts, M. (1998) 'Bargaining with Regulators', in P. Newman (ed.), *The New Palgrave Dictionary of Economics and the Law*, London: Macmillan Reference.

Ricketts, M. (2002) 'The Role of the State in Making a Market Economy: Comment on a Paper by Victor Nee (2000)', *Journal of Institutional and Theoretical Economics*, **156** (1), 95–8.

Robbins, L. (1952) *The Theory of Economic Policy in English Classical Political Economy*, 2nd edn, London: Macmillan.

Schumpeter, J.A. (1936) *The Theory of Economic Development*, Cambridge, MA: Harvard University Press.

Schumpeter, J.A. (1943) *Capitalism, Socialism and Democracy*, London: Unwin University Books.

Shirley, M. (2000) 'Why Performance Contracts for State-Owned Enterprises Haven't Worked', OECD, Beijing, 18–19 January.

Shirley, M. and Walsh, P. (2000) 'Public versus Private Ownership: The Current State of the Debate', *Policy Research Working Paper No. 2420*, Washington, DC: The World Bank Group.

Shleifer, A. (1998) 'State versus Private Ownership', *Journal of Economic Perspectives*, **12** (4), 133–50.

Stigler, G.J. (1964) 'Public Regulation of the Securities Market', *Journal of Business of the University of Chicago*, **37** (2), reprinted in Stigler (1975), 78–100.

Stigler, G.J. (1971) 'The Theory of Economic Regulation', *Bell Journal of Economics and Management Science*, **2** (1), 3–21.

Stigler, G.J. (1975) *The Citizen and the State*, Chicago: University of Chicago Press.

Stigler, G.J. and Friedland, C. (1962) 'What Can Regulators Regulate? The Case of Electricity', *Journal of Law and Economics*, **5** (1), 1–16.

Stiglitz, J. (1998) 'The Private Uses of Public Interests: Incentives and Institutions', *Journal of Economic Perspectives*, **12** (2), 3–22.

Sugden, R. (1986) *The Economics of Rights, Co-operation and Welfare*, Oxford: Basil Blackwell.

Tullock, G. (1980) 'Rent Seeking as a Negative Sum Game', in J. Buchanan et al. (eds), *Toward a Theory of the Rent Seeking Society*, College Station, Texas: A and M University Press.

Walras, L. (1954) *Elements of Pure Economics*, W. Jaffé (trans.), London: Allen and Unwin.

Weber, M. (1947) *The Theory of Social and Economic Organization*, New York: Free Press.

Williamson, O.E. (1964) *The Economics of Discretionary Behaviour: Managerial Objectives in a Theory of the Firm*, London and Englewood Cliffs, NJ: Prentice-Hall.

Williamson, O.E. (1985) *The Economic Institutions of Capitalism: Firms, Markets, Relational Contracting*, London: Collier Macmillan.

Wilson, J.Q. (ed.) (1980) *The Politics of Regulation*, New York: Basic Books.

3 Regulation, pricing and social welfare

Michael A. Crew and Paul R. Kleindorfer

Introduction[1]
For many years applied microeconomic theory has developed clear prescriptions for efficient pricing for a regulated or public enterprise monopoly. These prescriptions balanced consumer and producer interests and accounted for a number of important elements of public enterprise, such as breakeven requirements, service quality and cost tradeoffs, and peak loads. Interest in the topic goes back many years, including the early work of Coase (1946), Lewis (1941) and Ramsey (1927). However, the well developed prescriptions of the theory stand out in contrast to the practice in public enterprise monopoly and even more so with regulated monopoly. In this chapter we review the theory and examine the divergence between it and practice. Despite the elegance and simplicity of the theory, with its obvious appeal to economists, its adoption in practice has been disappointing. While we show the stark contrast between theory and practice, we also point to some unifying principles by which to approach pricing of regulated or public enterprise monopolies. These principles are in the spirit of our now more modest expectations about realistic objectives for regulation.

Our ability to derive unifying principles derives from advances that have been made in the last 20 years or so in the understanding of information in economics, the role of rents and rent seeking and information rents. First, we review the theory, including some of its origins and antecedents, but in the interests of readability and accessibility derivations and proofs are confined to the Technical Appendix at the end of the chapter. Second, we examine the divergence between the theory and practice. The role of equity and rents, including information rents, in explaining the differences is examined. The impact of deregulation, the emergence of mixed competitive models that derive from rent seeking, and information rent issues clearly have limited the application of the theory in the current situation. Third, we consider some of the challenges in pricing and welfare analysis of regulated enterprises going forward, and we summarize key principles for pricing in regulated industries that we believe have emerged from theory and practice to date.

Efficient pricing in regulated monopolies: a neoclassical synthesis
Elementary neoclassical economic theory shows that a monopoly left to its own devices will restrict output and maximize profit by equating marginal revenue and marginal cost. As a result it will normally earn monopoly profits, henceforth

referred to as rents. The consumer will pay a higher price than would be the case in a competitive industry where price is equal to marginal cost. The loss from the reduced output of monopoly is known as the deadweight loss or the welfare loss from monopoly. The triangle ABC in Figure 3.1 represents this loss. Economic theory and practice were both in agreement that action should be taken to reduce this efficiency loss by moving toward the competitive benchmark of competition. Two devices had traditionally been employed to achieve this. Antitrust law employed primarily structural instruments to address the problem of monopoly, notably divestiture that involved the breakup of the monopoly into several units. Regulation, the subject of this chapter, did not change the structure of a monopoly but instead regulated its conduct on a continuing basis. True antitrust also allowed for remedies involving conduct. The difference between regulation and antitrust is that antitrust might impose traditional 'once-and-for-all' or one-time remedies, for example, restraining orders, while regulation imposes continuing supervision and revisions through a specialized regulatory commission. The choice as to whether to employ regulation over antitrust as an instrument for addressing the welfare loss from monopoly normally hinges on the presence of natural monopoly. Indeed, public utility regulation originates from the problem of natural monopoly. Where there are overwhelming scale economies as in the case of public utilities, traditionally, electricity, gas, water and telephone, the cost to society is arguably minimized by having one supplier. The problem with one supplier is that it allows for monopoly exploitation with the resulting efficiency losses from monopoly. The Marshallian Triangle ABC in Figure 3.1 is the efficiency loss and the rectangle EAB′F represents the losses in consumer surplus resulting from monopoly exploitation. The latter is also the monopoly profit and constitutes a transfer from consumers to the monopolist. As such it is not an efficiency loss. However, following Tullock's (1967) insight on rent seeking, this rectangle is much more important to the process of natural monopoly regulation. It consists of the rents from monopoly and, in fact, will normally be much larger than the triangle. Indeed, it becomes the principal bone of contention in the regulatory process. The quest for these monopoly rents is the main driver of the regulatory process and is critical to understanding it, as we will demonstrate later.

The traditional approach to price regulation or price control was one of maximizing efficiency. As shown in the Appendix, under the assumption that consumer and producer benefits count equally, the sum of these is maximized under marginal cost pricing, which occurs in Figure 3.1 at C where the allocative efficiency losses ABC are entirely eliminated. The problem with this solution is that the firm would not cover its fixed costs and would either have to go out of business or recover them by some form of lump-sum subsidy. Regulation has to find a way for the firm to cover its costs. It would traditionally do this by moving to the second best optimum of C′, which provides an efficiency gain of

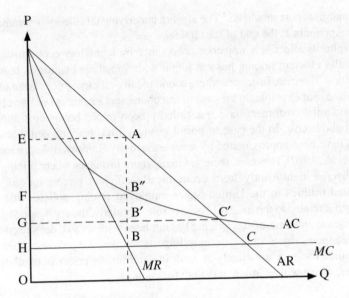

Figure 3.1   Regulation of monopoly and welfare

AB'C' and the monopoly rents are all taken by consumers. This second-best optimum effectively recognizes that the maximum gain of ABC is not attainable. As we show in the Appendix, price is not set at marginal cost ($P = MC$), OH in Figure 3.1, as under competition in the first best case, nor is it set equal to the monopoly level ($P = MC/(1 - 1/\eta)$), OE in Figure 3.1, but rather what is known as the Ramsey level ($P = MC/(1 - k/\eta)$), OG in Figure 3.1, where k is the Ramsey number. If $k = 0$, price is equal to marginal cost. If $k = 1$ the monopoly price at $MR = MC$ results. The greater the level of k the greater is the departure from the allocative efficiency norm.

While this economically efficient pricing result has been known since Ramsey (1927), it was not applied to the pricing of regulated monopolies until the 1970s.[2] The first generalized treatment of Ramsey pricing, extending the theory to interdependent demands, was by Rohlfs (1979). Ramsey pricing was extended further to situations involving peak loads and during the 1980s effectively became commonplace in the regulatory economist's toolbox.[3] Some of the insights gained as a result of extension to interdependent demands were counter-intuitive, the most important probably being the impact of complementary demands. With strongly complementary demands, first-best pricing would still be to set price equal to marginal cost but economically efficient pricing could require one price to be below marginal cost. So in the case of extreme complementarity, namely the case of an 'access good', the price of the access good should be priced below marginal cost, and the greater the monopoly power the greater this divergence from marginal cost should be.[4] The algebra underlying this theory is summarized in the Appendix at the end of the chapter.

Despite its effectively universal acceptance by regulatory economists, economically efficient pricing has not found widespread application in regulated industries. There are instances where economically efficient prices seem to have been used. For example, in the case of telephone service, access or line charges for residential customers have traditionally been priced below cost and calls priced above cost. In the case of postal service, it has been argued that actual prices have been approximated by inverse elasticity Ramsey style pricing (see Crew et al., 1990). However, there are many more instances where pricing policies diverge significantly from economically efficient prices. Indeed, most regulated utilities in the United States employed pricing policies that were clearly not related to the inverse elasticity rule. Similarly, the application of peak load pricing and time-of-day pricing has not been widespread, despite continuing statements by economists extolling its virtues. Objectives other than economic efficiency are clearly at work in determining prices in regulated industries, as we will examine in the next section.

Regulated monopoly in practice: the effects of rent seeking and information rents

Attaining the ideal of second-best or economically efficient, breakeven pricing has proved difficult in practice. What appears to be a rather simple problem in theory, namely to set economically efficient prices that eliminate the allocative inefficiency of monopoly prices and eliminate the rents going to the monopolist, turns out to be difficult in practice. The problem is that the underlying rents from the natural monopoly do not just disappear in the face of efficient pricing proposals; rather these rents are contested. What happens is that the monopoly rents, the rectangle EAB'F in Figure 3.1, are redistributed. This redistribution turns out to be far from a frictionless process. The understanding of this process has increased significantly through the study of rent seeking following Tullock's (1967) insight. Another development that has led to the understanding of the problem arising from attempts to redistribute monopoly rents by regulation is the study of information economics, which in the 1970s and 1980s was in its early stages. The nature and role of information and how rents may arise from asymmetric information were only just beginning to be understood, let alone applied to the problem of monopoly regulation. However, the theories of rent seeking and information economics, which had two highly divergent origins, both seemed to offer the greatest insight into understanding why the quest for economically efficient prices was, is and will continue to be difficult.

Economically efficient pricing for a regulated or public enterprise monopoly assuming a breakeven constraint would require that price be reduced from OE to OG in Figure 3.1, with the consequent transfer of rents to consumers of

AEB'G. In addition, consumers gain the surplus AB'C'. Consumers strongly welcome the change, but the monopolist clearly does not. The neoclassical approach, by focusing on efficiency and ignoring distribution, effectively only identifies the solution. The fallacy in the approach was to conclude that the efficient solution that had been identified would be attained. The reality is that it might not even be attainable because of the frictions caused by rent redistribution issues, and this is why economically efficient prices may be rare in practice.

One of the safeguards required for a market economy to function is the sanctity of private property. Without this, there is a deleterious effect on incentives to accumulate wealth. The market system is driven by profits, or claims to the residual after revenues have been received, expenses paid and a normal return on capital earned. It is the quest for this residual, economic profit, which drives the system. Without a right to retain the residual, it would be pointless seeking it. So a 100 per cent tax on ex post profits would kill any incentives to earn economic profits. Hence, a capitalist system must safeguard ex post residual claims. In the usual model of the competitive case, property rights and residual claimants are at the foundation of firms seeking profits, leading to internal efficiency and marginal-cost pricing. Under monopoly, seeking profits and the sanctity of private property combine together to produce inefficiency, but attempts to remedy this inefficiency are not going to be successful. Effectively, economically efficient prices cannot be attained.

The attempt to reduce prices from OE to OG is going to meet resistance because it implies that the firm's income and therefore its value will be reduced. To do so involves an attack on the firm's property. The firm is therefore going to argue that price reductions, although they increase allocative efficiency, confiscate its property and give it to consumers. In a capitalist system where private property is protected this is a legitimate argument. It does not matter that the private property concerned is composed of rents. If the law recognizes a property right, the owner has the protection of the law. In this case the property right is contested but the owner still will use law to defend the (contested) right. So any attempt to make a monopolist charge less than the monopoly price is going to be contested legally, whether it is through a regulatory or a judicial monopoly process. This addition to costs gnaws at the efficiency benefits. This process of rent preservation on the part of the firm and rent seeking by consumers eats up the rents. Indeed, it is conceivable that all the rents, EAB"F, could be consumed by vigorous rent protection and rent seeking, reducing efficiency to below the monopoly level.

Regulation has taken generally two approaches to controlling monopoly prices, rate-of-return regulation (ROR) and price-cap regulation (PCR). The effectiveness of both is reduced because of the problems arising from rent redistribution and asymmetric information. Both are concerned with obtaining the efficiency ideal of the competitive market or the economically efficient prices that occur under second best. ROR attempts to address the problem of monopoly regulation by what is ostensibly a feasible approach. Under competition price is driven to costs. ROR attempts to replicate this by computing costs and then setting prices equal to costs, thereby regulating profits. PCR proceeds in a different direction. It tries to replicate the competitive market by setting price and allowing the firm to achieve its lowest level of costs thereby maximizing profits. ROR attenuates the ability of residual claimants to obtain economic rents, while PCR attempts to use residual claimants to achieve efficiency in the same manner as the competitive market. As we shall see, both approaches have had very limited success in achieving their objectives.

Regulation cannot operate in the same manner as a competitive market. The regulator does not have the information to set cost as in ROR or the price cap under PCR to achieve the desired competitive result. A competitive market, unlike the regulator, is impersonal and does not require the information that a regulator does to achieve the efficiency objective. ROR proceeds by determining the cost of service – hence it is also called 'cost-of-service regulation' – and then setting prices to produce 'revenue requirements' equal to the total variable expenses plus a 'fair' return on capital. The prices set to achieve these revenue requirements ideally will result in economically efficient prices of OG in Figure 3.1, provided that the fair return is set equal to the opportunity cost of capital. Setting the return so that, taking into account the risk faced by the business, it is equal to a normal or competitive return has proved to be no trivial task. The process designed to safeguard property at best could only result in an approximation and can involve significant transactions costs in the form of hearings to determine the rate of return that the regulator deems appropriate, known as the allowed rate of return.

Unfortunately, the reality in the US has turned out to be somewhat different, not just because of problems in determining the opportunity cost of capital. While prices were set at the cost of service, the problem was that the cost of service was not minimized. With its costs effectively covered then the pressure on the part of the firm to keep costs down is reduced. The problem is exacerbated by a drastic attenuation of the profit incentive. If the firm makes more than its allowed profits the regulator would lower its rates. While this does not amount to a 100 per cent tax on profits, it amounts to a very high effective tax with severe effects on the firm's incentives to minimize costs. Regulators and not just economists, of course, became aware of this problem. However, addressing it was quite difficult because of asymmetries in information on costs between the firm and the regulator. The firm knows considerably more about its operations than the regulator and therefore considerably more about how costs arise, making it quite difficult for a regulator to contest whether certain expenses are reasonable.

It is because of the weak incentives for cost economy that economists criticized ROR. For example, Averch and Johnson (1962) with the famous A–J effect argued that ROR regulation encouraged excessive investment in capital. This accorded with regulatory practice, which sought to avoid such problems by monitoring the rate base – effectively the capital invested – to ensure that it was 'used and useful'. For many years, without the basis of economic theory provided by the A–J effect regulators had sought ways to prevent firms from padding the rate base and had attempted to get the firm to keep variable expenses in check. However, because of the information asymmetries the regulator's efforts were at best limited and even counterproductive.

Other instances where economists criticized ROR involved the distribution of rents. It proved exceedingly difficult for regulators to prevent rents going to organized labour in regulated industries. Since the firm has an attenuated incentive to minimize costs generally, it has a similar attenuated incentive to reduce the rents going to labour. If the firm saved reduced expenses by driving a hard bargain it would stand to gain little or nothing. Unlike the case of strong residual claimants, which is the case for unregulated firms, where reduced labour costs would go the bottom line, the regulated firm would find its revenue requirement and therefore its prices reduced by the amount of the cost savings resulting from the lower labour costs. Similarly, a contract with higher wages would just mean higher (regulated) prices because expenses, in this case labour costs, were higher. Unless labour attempted to raise wages so much that the monopoly price was exceeded, there was little incentive to reduce the rents going to labour.

Economists were highly critical of ROR and as a result sought to develop regulatory schemes that had better incentives for cost economy and were more likely to achieve economically efficient prices. Price-cap regulation (PCR) was the primary alternative. Its practical application was first employed in an extensive way in the United Kingdom as a result of privatization and implementation of Littlechild's (1983, 1986) proposals for PCR. Economic theorists, particularly Laffont and Tirole (1993), put together an elegant theory showing the conditions under which PCR would lead to efficiency. PCR attempted to employ the notion of residual claimants to achieve cost economy and allocative efficiency as achieved under competition. The idea was simple: ROR amounts to regulating profit; PCR does not regulate profits but instead regulates price. The regulator sets price and lets the firm make as much profit as it can. It attempts to mimic the competitive market by making the firm a price taker as in the competitive market.[5] In contrast to ROR where the regulator adopts a central planning type solution and attempts to impose the prices that a competitive market would give, PCR adopts a more market-oriented solution, in that it sets the price and lets the residual claimants proceed from there. Unfortunately, as in the case of ROR, achieving the benefits of a competitive market still elude the regulator under PCR, and for the same reason: the regulator lacks the information to achieve the desired result. Research over the last 20 years has increased considerably the understanding of the problem of information asymmetries facing the regulator. Around the mid-1980s a change took place in the theory of regulatory economics, and this was the incorporation of principal–agent theory, mechanism design theory and information economics into regulatory economics. This began with the work of Baron and Myerson (1982). The work was an outgrowth of the work on principal–agent theory in the 1970s (e.g. Ross, 1973 and Groves, 1973), which, indeed, offered major insights into issues of managerial effort and corporate governance. However, as we noted in Crew and Kleindorfer (1986), the insights of this rather large (and still growing) stream of literature have had very little to do with designing institutions or mechanisms that can be applied to regulatory problems as they exist in practice.

Theorists employing this 'new' approach were highly critical of the earlier theory, which they perceived as having little value as it missed the critical problem of incentives. While we accept that these criticisms have some validity, we argue that the contributions that replaced them were at least as limited in their applicability and fell far short of the expectations created by their authors. Ironically, a principal reason for this is precisely the reason raised above by Laffont and Tirole in ushering in the new theory, namely a heavy reliance by such schemes on information that is not available to regulators. Indeed, the entire mechanism design literature, beginning with Baron and Myerson (1982) and ably summarized by Laffont and Tirole (1993), is based in one way or another on assumptions like common knowledge that endow the regulator with information that he or she cannot have without a contested discovery process. In practice, the regulator is left in a state far short of the level of information assumed in these theories. Common knowledge is the Achilles heel of mechanism design theory.[6]

Why is it that extending the traditional principal–agent theory to regulatory economics is so problematical? When a principal and an agent are involved in a private transaction, there is not a fundamental problem with the principal designing incentive systems for the agent based on assumed 'common knowledge' by the principal about the agent's costs or preferences. In private transactions, the principal bears the costs of any error in his or her assumptions.[7] Contrast this with a regulator with responsibility for the price and quality of an essential good. If the regulator is wrong in his or her common knowledge assumptions about the agent (the regulated firm), it is either consumers or the regulated firm that bear the consequences. The anticipation of these consequences will clearly give rise to strategic interactions, both in theory and in practice, which may have fundamental effects on what common knowledge assumptions are legitimate, and on the ultimate consequences of these for the outcomes of regulation. Theories that fail to address these strategic interactions leave a gaping hole in interpreting the results of any such theory. In particular, lifting the common knowledge assumption from a private principal–agent framework to the regulatory context leads to major problems because it leaves open how this common knowledge distribution will be determined. Note that in the traditional principal–agent theory, the contracting agent is free to take or leave the principal's offer (which must therefore satisfy an individual rationality constraint), but under regulation this does not apply in the case of the firm, which may have considerable sunk costs at risk and cannot simply pull up stakes if the firm does not find the regulator's assumptions acceptable.[8]

The promise of these mechanism-design-style theories was ostensibly considerable. They promised none other than the holy grail of X-efficiency, something previous regulation had manifestly failed to deliver. X-efficiency, however, was only achieved if two conditions – aside from the basic assumptions criticized above – were met. The first condition was that achievement of the promised X-efficiency required that the regulator concede some information rents to the firm.[9] The second condition was what is referred to in mechanism design theory as 'commitment'. This is the notion that the presence of information rents would not present a problem to the regulator and that, as a result, the regulator was committed to his or her original agreement with the firm. In other words, the ex post appearance of excess profits (or financial distress) would not cause the regulator to renege on his or her commitment to the original incentive scheme. Why this would not be a fatal flaw in the whole scheme was never considered. The new theory promised efficiency as long as the regulator was prepared to allow information rents.[10] Theorists, however, never understood the impossibility of this in practice. No regulator can even admit that it allows the firm to retain information rents let alone commit to such a practice. For the regulator, this is a congenital problem of far greater magnitude than has been recognized in economic theory.[11] How do these rents differ so much from the old style monopoly rents that would make them acceptable to the regulator when it was monopoly rents that were the principal motivation of regulation in the first place? Thus the promise of X-efficiency was hedged with conditions, which, we argue, make the theory of little significance for real-world regulation, as subsequent events have shown. In particular, neither commitment nor its associated information rents are reasonable assumptions.

These criticisms of mechanism design theory should not be taken to imply that it has not provided insights into understanding monopoly regulation. Its principal insight is that it provides, in effect, an impossibility theorem. If the concerns of the problems of rent redistribution that arise from the rent seeking literature were not enough to cast doubt on the ability of regulators to attain economically efficient prices, the contribution of mechanism design leaves us in no doubt. The existence of asymmetric information and the resultant information rents mean that regulators are unlikely to be able to achieve economically efficient prices using PCR any more effectively than they were under ROR. So it seems that attaining the economically efficient prices by monopoly regulation is effectively impossible. However, there are some actions that can be taken to mitigate the efficiency losses that result, to which we now turn.

Some unifying principles for approaching pricing and regulation
Based on the discussions above, it is not surprising that monopoly regulation does not normally result in the economically efficient prices that are derived from the application of welfare economic theory. Indeed, we have argued that achieving economically efficient prices through regulatory fiat is not possible. Together, the rent seeking literature and the mechanism design literature amount to an impossibility theorem for the existence of efficient prices in regulated monopoly.[12] However, this does not mean that the message of this chapter for regulation of monopoly and efficiency is completely negative. Indeed, our principal message is that the insights provided by rent seeking into the constraints under which regulation operates lead to a greater understanding of the role of regulation and potentially better policy decisions. As soon as the infeasibility of economically efficient prices is understood, it becomes possible to understand better the third-best alternatives available.

As we saw earlier, both PCR and ROR have little hope of improving efficiency because of problems of rent redistribution, information asymmetries and the resulting incentives. Because of a better understanding of these problems not just by economists but, more importantly, by regulators and firms, it is possible to devise approaches that improve efficiency even though they may fall short of the second-best economically efficient benchmark provided by Ramsey pricing. These involve changing the scope of regulation and redesigning regulatory mechanisms to balance what can be achieved (reductions in X-inefficiency and some degree of price stability) against what cannot be achieved (elimination of rent seeking and excess profits for the regulated firm).

Changing the scope of regulation involves analysing what parts of traditionally regulated monopoly can be provided by competition and what is left as an unavoidable natural monopoly. Under this approach, the amount of the monopoly that is regulated is whittled down to the residual monopoly and the rest of the value chain is supplied by unregulated or much less regulated markets. A successful example of this approach is gas.[13]

Traditionally, gas distribution was regulated as a natural monopoly, as were pipelines. Wellhead gas prices were gradually deregulated during the 1980s and pipelines were unbundled as common carriers from producers. Brokers and other intermediaries emerged to link distribution and production through flexible contracting, including new trading instruments based on spot markets at regional hubs. The overall result was a significant increase in competition, and arguably also an increase in the transparency of the value added of each of the respective elements of the value chain for natural gas.

A more complicated example is electricity, which traditionally has been supplied by vertically integrated electric utilities. Generation, in principle, can be supplied competitively but transmission and distribution are natural monopolies. Distribution is a relatively straightforward natural monopoly and would be subject to regulation. Transmission is also a natural monopoly but because of bottlenecks and externalities it interacts with generation and may create opportunities for the exploitation of market power. The restructuring of ownership of generation has certainly met a number of bumps in the road, notably the crisis in California in 2000–01, and with the blackout in the northeastern US on 14 August 2003. As a result there has been a rethinking of restructuring with a planned increase in vertical integration by electric utilities in California. The restructuring process has proved to be more difficult to apply in practice but it is evolving as a result of the lessons learned.

A better understanding of the shortcomings of ROR and PCR has also led to the development of new regulatory institutions. Instead of ROR and PCR, hybrids of the two have developed. The PBR or 'performance-based regulation' that has supplanted ROR and PCR in the US is really nothing but a hybrid of the two. Its principal feature is dead bands and sharing. The regulator still sets an allowed rate of return. For a small dead band plus or minus, say, a hundred basis points no change in rates is triggered. Amounts in excess of this result in sharing the excess between ratepayers and the company. If the rate of return falls drastically the company can always call for a rate hearing, as can the regulator if it increases too much. This process provides, albeit attenuated, incentives for efficiency and at the same time provides both parties with outcomes that they can both accommodate. It offers greater incentives for cost economy than ROR and avoids the pitfalls to which PCR exposes both parties. PCR offers cost economy at the risk of too large a share of the pie going to the firm, which is unacceptable to the regulator. PCR also carries the downside for the firm that cost economy and other success through good management will be punished through a cut in rates. For the firm, PBR offers protection from the serious downside risk of this type of action by the regulator. By employing PBR both the firm and the regulator recognize the reality that it is impossible for the regulator to make the commitment required in pure PCR. In short, PBR has the potential for increased efficiency, while accommodating both sides of the process.

While the operation of regulation may be better understood as a result of theory and practice over the last quarter century and more efficient regulatory mechanisms have been devised, it does not mean that we will see more Ramsey pricing. At best Ramsey prices, while not completely feasible in practice, still provide a useful benchmark to which regulated monopoly can aspire. However, the increased understanding of the regulatory process, as a result of both theoretical and applied welfare economics, has gone some way to improve the way prices are set, although the economically efficient prices are still elusive and are likely to remain so.

Conclusions

In this chapter we have shown what we see as the role of economically efficient prices given some of the developments in regulatory economics in theory and practice over the last 30 years. By way of summary three conclusions are worth emphasizing.

1. While economically efficient prices provide an important benchmark, applying them in practice faces problems that arise from the inherent simplifying assumption of economic efficiency in maximizing the size of the pie irrespective of the distribution of the resulting benefits. Maximizing net social benefits in the traditional fashion implies that benefits count equally, irrespective of who receives them. This traditional assumption could be modified, but it is central to the usual conclusions on the structure of economically efficient prices.
2. In contrast to the equal weighting assumption that underlies the traditional Ramsey pricing benchmarks, the rent seeking literature and the literature of law and economics have made it increasingly evident that the distribution of the pie is at least as important as the size of the pie. This has made us acutely aware of the challenge of designing policies that improve efficiency when rent seeking and distributional issues are central aspects of the problem. In practice, these policies can play out to advantage one or another of the stakeholders in the regulatory process. The pricing outcomes of regulation in practice must be understood against the pressures of rent seeking and stakeholder distributional issues.
3. Given the asymmetries of information between the regulator and monopolist, expectations from Ramsey pricing and incentive regulations intended to move firms toward efficient operations and pricing should be somewhat modest. One implication of the better understanding of the role of asymmetric information and information rents is that information is key to reducing monopoly rents. One prescription that may arise from this it that the extent of regulation should be limited to the minimal residual monopoly in each sector.

Technical appendix: economically efficient prices[14]

The early literature on efficient pricing for public enterprises and regulated monopolies, notably Bye (1926, 1929), Lewis (1941), Boiteux (1949, 1956), Houthakker (1951), Steiner (1957), and Hirshleifer (1958), linked public utility pricing to economic efficiency and marginal cost and to the growing field of applied welfare economics. Early accounts of these relationships are given in

Drèze (1964). Williamson (1966) expanded this framework to include indivisible capacity increments. Building on the work of Steiner (1957), the approach evolved toward deriving efficient prices from the maximization of an explicit social welfare function of the following form:

$$W = TR + S - TC \tag{3A.1}$$

where W = net social benefit, TR = total revenue, S = consumers' surplus, and TC = total costs.

In the case of a single product, the net benefits in (3A.1) accruing at a given output level X may be expressed as:

$$W = \int_0^X (Px)\mathrm{d}x - C(X) \tag{3A.2}$$

where $P(X)$ is the (inverse) demand function and $C(X)$ is the total cost function. The integral in (3A.2) is referred to as 'gross surplus' and encompasses both total revenue, $TR(X) = XP(X)$ as well as consumers' surplus S. Note that benefits to the producer(s) $(TR - TC)$ and the consumer(s) are valued equally in the social-welfare function (3A.1). The reader can easily compute from (3A.2) that $dW/dX = 0$ implies $P(X) = dC/dX$, so that maximizing W in (3A.2) leads to the standard efficiency result: price = marginal cost.

Since the cost function $C(X)$ may exhibit decreasing average costs leading to deficits under marginal cost pricing, the above first-best result is typically further constrained by a breakeven constraint. We now formulate this constrained problem, following the standard approach identified with Ramsey (1927), as developed by Boiteux (1956) and synthesized by Baumol and Bradford (1970).

Assume consumers are of various types $\theta \in \Theta$, where $f(\theta)$ is the number of consumers of type θ. The preferences of consumers are assumed to be of the separable form:

$$U(x,m,\theta) = V(x,\theta) + m, \theta \in \Theta, \tag{3A.3}$$

where $\mathbf{x} = (x_1, ..., x_n)$ is the vector of goods supplied by the regulated sector and m is a numeraire commodity. Let the prices for $\mathbf{x}$ be denoted $\mathbf{P} = (P_1, ..., P_n)$, so that consumer θ's demand vector, $\mathbf{x}(\mathbf{P}, \theta)$ is the solution to:

$$\underset{x \geq 0}{\text{Max}} \left[V(x,\theta) + M(\theta) - \sum_N P_i x_i \right], \tag{3A.4}$$

where $M(\theta)$ is disposable income of consumer θ and $N = \{1, ..., n\}$. Assuming that purchases of **x** do not exhaust the consumer's budget, $M(\theta)$, implying that expenditures m on other goods are strictly positive, it follows from (3A.4) that an interior solution obtains where $\partial V(x, \theta)/\partial x_i = P_i$ for all i, θ.

Suppose the products **X** are supplied by a monopolist with cost function $C(\mathbf{X})$, where $\mathbf{X} = (X_1, ..., X_n)$ is total demand, i.e.

$$X_i(P) = \int_\Theta x_i(P,\theta)f(\theta)d\theta, \quad i \in N. \tag{3A.5}$$

The Ramsey problem can then be stated as:

$$\underset{P \geq 0}{\text{Max}}\ W(P) = \int_\Theta \left[V(x(P,\theta),\theta) - \sum_N P_i x_i(P,\theta) \right] f(\theta)d\theta + \Pi(P) \tag{3A.6}$$

subject to:

$$\Pi(\mathbf{P}) = \sum_N P_i X_i(P) - C(X) \geq \Pi_0, \tag{3A.7}$$

where $\Pi(\mathbf{P})$ is profit and Π_0 is some desired profit level (e.g. 0). Clearly in the first term in (3A.6), the aggregate excess of willingness-to-pay over price is just consumer's surplus.

When coupled with appropriate lump-sum transfers among consumers and the firm, the Ramsey solution to (3A.6)–(3A.7) can Pareto dominate every other price schedule and lump-sum transfer schedule satisfying (3A.7). This strong Pareto efficiency property depends, of course, on the quasi-linearity of preferences (3A.6) (the 'no income effects' hypothesis). For more general preferences, the same result can be argued to hold approximately when the regulated sector is small (i.e. when $\sum_i P_i x_i(\mathbf{P}, \theta) << M(\theta)$ is small for the preponderance of θ), as Willig (1976) has shown.

The Ramsey solution is obtained from the first-order conditions for the Lagrangian $L(\mathbf{P}) = W(\mathbf{P}) + v\Pi(\mathbf{P})$, corresponding to (3A.6)–(3A.7), i.e.

$$\frac{\partial L}{\partial P_i} = \int_\Theta \left(\sum_{j \in N} \left[-x_i(P,t) + \left(\frac{\partial V(x,t)}{\partial x_j} - P_j \right) \frac{\partial x_j(P,\theta)}{\partial P_i} \right] \right) f(\theta)d\theta$$

$$+ (1+v)\left(X_i(P) + \sum_{j \in N} (P_j, C_j) + \frac{\partial X_j}{\partial P_i} \right), \quad i \in N, \tag{3A.8}$$

where $v \geq 0$ and $C_j = \delta C_j/\delta X_j$. Using $P_i = \delta V/\delta x_i$ and (3A.5), and assuming an interior solution ($P_i > 0$, $i \in N$), setting $\delta L/\delta P_i = 0$ in (3A.8) yields

$$\sum_{j \in N} \frac{(P_j - C_j)}{X_i} \frac{\partial X_j}{\partial P_i} = -\frac{v}{1+v}, \quad i \in N \tag{3A.9}$$

which we rewrite in the form:

$$\sum_{j \in N} \frac{R_j}{R_i} \frac{(P_j - C_j)}{P_j} \eta_{ji} = -\kappa, \quad i \in N \tag{3A.10}$$

where $\eta_{ji} = (\delta X_j/\delta P_i)(P_i/X_j)$ is (cross-)elasticity, $R_i = P_i X_i$ is revenue from product i, and where $\kappa = v/(1 + v)$ is the so-called Ramsey number which is positive except at the welfare optimum (where (3A.7) is not binding) where $\kappa = 0$. The conditions for the profit-maximizing solution are identical to (3A.10) with $\kappa = 1$.

As noted by Phillips and Roberts (1985), it can be shown from (3A.4) that $\delta x_j(\mathbf{P}, \theta)/\delta P_i = \delta x_i(\mathbf{P}, \theta)/\delta P_j$ for all i, j, θ, so that, from (3A.5), $\delta X_j/\delta P_i = \delta X_i/\delta P_j$. We can therefore rewrite (3A.10) as:

$$\sum_{j \in N} \frac{(P_j - C_j)}{P_j} \eta_{ij} = -\kappa, \quad i \in N \tag{3A.11}$$

When there are only two products in the regulated sector, we can solve (3A.11) explicitly to obtain

$$\frac{P_i - C_i}{P_i} = -\frac{\kappa}{\Delta}\left(\eta_{jj} - \frac{R_j}{R_i}\eta_{ji}\right), \quad i = 1, 2 \quad j \neq i, \tag{3A.12}$$

where $\Delta = \eta_{11}\eta_{22} - \eta_{12}\eta_{21}$. If own-price effects dominate ($|\eta_{ii}| > |\eta_{ij}|$ for $i \neq j$), then $\Delta > 0$. We note that (3A.11) reduces to the standard inverse elasticity rule when $\eta_{ij} = 0$ for all $j \neq i$, and that (for both the Ramsey problem and the profit-maximizing problem):

1. If products 1 and 2 are substitutes ($\eta_{ij} > 0$ for $i \neq j$), then $P_i \geq C_i$ with $P_i > C_i$, $i = 1, 2$, except at the unconstrained welfare optimum.
2. If products 1 and 2 are complements ($\eta_{ij} < 0$ for all i, j), then $P_i < C_i$ is possible at optimum for one of the two products.

In the peak-load pricing problem, products are differentiated only by the time of consumption and are therefore typically substitutes, so that the above results imply that price will always exceed marginal cost in all periods except when the profit constraint is not binding (i.e. at the welfare optimum), at which point one price equal to marginal cost obtains. Complements usually arise in this context only when one of the goods is an 'access good' such as connection to the network. This good could be priced below marginal cost, depending on relative elasticity and revenue conditions (see e.g. Crew and Kleindorfer, 1986, Chapters 2, 9).

The above represents only efficiency benchmarks under deterministic conditions. The treatment of pricing under uncertainty would take us well beyond the space available here. Suffice it to say that similar marginal cost pricing benchmarks obtain, but these are now conditioned by issues of rationing (in case of excess demand) for example, Crew and Kleindorfer (1976, 1978), Chao (1983) and Wilson (1993). In addition, the question of efficient capacity rules (to balance capacity costs against avoided losses in consumer surplus at times of excess demand) must be coordinated with the optimal pricing rules. The details are summarized in Crew and Kleindorfer (1986, Chapters 3–6).

An alternative to the breakeven pricing rules formulated above is the use of two-part or other nonlinear tariffs (e.g. Lewis, 1941; Oi, 1971). The simplest such tariff would collect a fixed cost F for connection to the service and a per unit charge P for each unit consumed. Thus, for a single product whose demand is $x(\theta)$, consumer θ's bill under such a two-part tariff would be $B(x(\theta)) = F + Px(\theta)$ for $x(\theta) > 0$. By setting P equal to marginal cost and F appropriately, the firm can both break even and charge efficient, marginal-cost prices. This otherwise efficient approach may run into problems if the required F to cover costs is higher (at least for certain consumers) than their surplus at price $P = MC$. Such consumers would clearly consume nothing. These complexities have been examined in detail in the literature (Brown and Sibley, 1986) and will not be of concern to us here, although the welfare-optimal results characterized above are clearly an important input to two-part tariffs.

Notes

1. The authors are pleased to acknowledge the contribution of Chitru S. Fernando to this chapter, and his understanding of our use of material from Crew et al. (1995). The would like to thank Cliff Rochlin and Jan van Lierop, the Discussants at the Rutgers University, Center for Research in Regulated Industries, 18th Annual Western Conference, San Diego, California, 22–24 June 2005, for helpful comments.
2. Baumol and Bradford (1970) is probably the paper that should get most credit for reviving interest in Ramsey pricing, although Boiteux (1956) was clearly several years ahead. As Boiteux (1956) was in French, it had little impact until translated by Baumol in 1971.
3. Numerous applications and extensions exist. For a typical survey see Crew and Kleindorfer (1986) or Crew et al. (1995).
4. Such pricing has long been practised in the for-profit world. So King Gillette priced his safety razors below marginal costs and his blades above cost. Similarly, Ted Vail, the founder of AT&T, priced telephone lines to the customer premises (access) low and calls high.
5. To be precise it creates a discontinuity in the marginal revenue curve as the firm is allowed to charge less than the price cap.
6. By 'common knowledge', we are referring to the standard assumption of much of the mecha-

nism design literature that the regulated firm actively reveals its type (e.g. its cost or other key parameters), knowing that the regulator will set regulatory parameters (e.g. the allowed rate of return in cost of service regulation or the X factor in price-cap regulation) based on the revealed type of the firm. The common knowledge assumption presumes that the regulator and the firm take as incontestable knowledge the probability distribution of possible revealed types, with regulatory design contingent on this common knowledge distribution. We include in our broad criticism of this assumption also weaker forms of this that allow the regulator to simply declare ex ante the distribution of revealed types, whether or not the regulated firm agrees to it. Any such declaration, unless agreed to by the regulated firm, can and would be contested, since different assumptions about this distribution naturally lead to different regulatory incentive systems under the standard Bayesian Incentive Bargaining approaches used in this literature. To put it plainly, the regulated firm definitely cares about what the regulator claims to be the actual distribution of potential types and would attempt to influence the accepted definition of this distribution if it were a central aspect of regulatory design. If such a distribution is a central feature of a design problem, a theory that simply takes it as a given, without modelling the process that would accompany its adversarial determination, is fundamentally flawed.

7.   In particular, the models and applications in Laffont and Tirole (1993) that deal with private procurement contracts remain significant contributions to the literature of contracting.
8.   In practice all sorts of compromises between regulators and regulated companies take place in the application of incentive regulation, as noted in Crew and Kleindorfer (1996).
9.   These rents arose from the information advantages of the firm relative to the regulator.
10.   It should be noted that theorists have now discovered several cases of the standard regulatory problem under asymmetric information in which information rents are not required to achieve socially efficient outcomes. For a recent synthesis of the issue of information rents and efficiency, see Armstrong and Sappington (2003).
11.   Loeb and Magat (1974), and Vogelsang and Finsinger (1979) implicitly rely on this same notion of commitment.
12.   Although we do not analyse the case of public enterprise monopoly the implications of our arguments would apply in the case of public enterprise, where economically efficient prices are also likely to be infeasible.
13.   Leitzinger and Collette (2002) provide a critical history of gas deregulation in the United States.
14.   This material is based on part of Crew et al. (1995).

References

Armstrong, M. and Sappington, D.M. (2003) 'Recent Developments in the Theory of Regulation', in M. Armstrong and R. Porter (eds), *The Handbook of Industrial Organization*, Oxford: Elsevier Science Publishers.

Averch, H. and Johnson, L.L. (1962) 'Behavior of the Firm Under Regulatory Constraint,' *American Economic Review*, **52**(5), 1052–69.

Baron, D. and Myerson, R. (1982) 'Regulating a Monopolist with Unknown Cost', *Econometrica*, **50**, 911–30.

Baumol, W.J. and Bradford, D.F. (1970) 'Optimal Departures from Marginal Cost Pricing', *American Economic Review*, **60** (3, June), 265–83.

Boiteux, M. (1949) 'La Tarification des demandes en point: application de la theorie de la vente au cout marginal', *Revue Generale de l'Electricité*, **58** (August); translated (1960) as 'Peak Load Pricing', *Journal of Business*, **33** (2), 157–79.

Boiteux, M. (1956) 'Sur la gestion des monopoles publics astreints á l'équilibre budgétaire', *Econometrica*, **24** (January), 22–40; translated (1971) by W.J. Baumol as 'On the Management of Public Monopolies Subject to Budgetary Constraints', *Journal of Economic Theory*, **3** (September), 219–40.

Brown, S.J. and Sibley, D.S. (1986) *The Theory of Public Utility Pricing*, Cambridge: Cambridge University Press.

Bye, R.T. (1926) 'The Nature of Fundamental Elements of Costs', *Quarterly Journal of Economics*, November, 30–63.

Bye, R.T. (1929) 'Composite Demand and Joint Supply in Relation to Public Utility Rates', *Quarterly Journal of Economics*, November, 40–62.

Chao, H.-P. (1983) 'Peak-load Pricing and Capacity Planning with Demand and Supply Uncertainty', *Bell Journal of Economics*, **14** (Spring), 170–90.

Coase, R.H. (1946) 'The Marginal Cost Controversy', *Economica*, **13**, 169–82.

Crew, M.A. and Kleindorfer, P.R. (1976) 'Peak Load Pricing with Diversity Technology', *Bell Journal of Economics*, **7**, 207–31.

Crew, M.A. and Kleindorfer, P.R. (1978) 'Reliability and Public Utility Pricing', *American Economic Review*, **68** (l), 36–40.

Crew, M.A. and Kleindorfer, P.R. (1986) *The Economics of Public Utility Regulation*, Cambridge, MA: MIT Press.

Crew, M.A. and Kleindorfer, P.R. (1996) 'Incentive Regulation in the United Kingdom and the United States: Some Lessons', *Journal of Regulatory Economics*, **9** (May), 211–26.

Crew, M.A., Fernando, C.S. and Kleindorfer, P.R. (1995) 'The Theory of Peak-load Pricing: A Survey', *Journal of Regulatory Economics*, **8** (3, November), 215–48.

Crew, M.A., Kleindorfer, P.R. and Smith, M.A. (1990) 'Peak-load Pricing in Postal Services', *Economic Journal*, **3** (September), 793–807.

Drèze, J. (1964), 'Some Postwar Contributions of French Economists to Theory and Public Policy, with Special Emphasis on Problems of Resource Allocation', *American Economic Review*, **54** (Supplement, June), 1–64.

Groves, T. (1973) 'Incentives in Teams', *Econometrica*, **41** (4), 617–31.

Hirshleifer, J. (1958) 'Peak Loads and Efficient Pricing: Comment', *Quarterly Journal of Economics*, **72** (August), 451–62.

Houthakker, H.S. (1951) 'Electricity Tariffs in Theory and Practice', *Economic Journal*, **61** (March), 1–25.

Laffont, J.-J. and Tirole, J. (1993) *A Theory of Incentives in Procurement and Regulation*, Cambridge: MIT Press.

Leitzinger, J. and Collette, M. (2002) 'A Retrospective Look at Wholesale Gas: Industry Restructuring', *Journal of Regulatory Economics*, **21** (1, January), 79–101.

Lewis, W.A. (1941) 'The Two-part Tariff', *Economica*, **8** (August), 249–70.

Littlechild, S.C. (1983) *Regulation of British Telecom's Profitability*, London: Department of Industry.

Littlechild, S.C. (1986) *Economic Regulation of Privatized Water Authorities. Report Submitted to the UK Department of the Environment*, London: HMSO.

Loeb, M. and Magat, W.A. (1974) 'A Decentralized Method of Utility Regulation', *Journal of Law and Economics*, **22** (October), 58–73.

Phillips, A. and Roberts, G.L. (1985) 'Borrowing from Peter to Pay Paul: More on Departures from Marginal Cost', in F.M. Fisher (ed.), *Antitrust and Regulation: Essays in Honor of John McGowan*, Cambridge, MA: MIT Press.

Oi, W.Y. (1971) 'A Disneyland Dilemma: Two-part Tariffs for a Mickey Mouse Monopoly', *Quarterly Journal of Economics*, **85** (1, February), 77–96.

Ramsey, F.P. (1927) 'A Contribution to the Theory of Taxation', *Economic Journal*, **37**, 47–61.

Rohlfs, J. (1979) 'Economically Efficient Bell System Prices', Bell Laboratories, Discussion Paper No. 138, Murray Hill, New Jersey.

Ross, S.A. (1973) 'The Economic Theory of Agency: The Principal's Problem', *American Economic Review*, **63** (2), 209–14.

Steiner, P.O. (1957) 'Peak Loads and Efficient Pricing', *Quarterly Journal of Economics*, **71** (November), 585–610.

Tullock, G. (1967) 'The Welfare Costs of Tariffs, Monopolies and Theft', *Western Economic Journal*, 5 (June), 224–32.

Vogelsang, I. and Finsinger, J. (1979) 'A Regulatory Adjustment Process for Optimal Pricing by Multiproduct Monopoly Firms', *Bell Journal of Economics*, **10**, 157–71.

Williamson, O.E. (1966) 'Peak-load Pricing and Optimal Capacity under Indivisibility Constraints', *American Economic Review*, **56** (4, September), 810–27.

Willig, R.D. (1976) 'Consumer Surplus Without Apology', *American Economic Review*, **66** (4, September), 587–97.

Wilson, R. (1993) *Nonlinear Pricing*, New York: Oxford University Press.

4 Regulating prices and service quality
Dan Elliott

This chapter considers the issues faced by regulators in attempting to establish appropriate standards for the quality of service provided by network companies subject to price regulation. It begins by considering why the separate regulation of service quality arises as an important issue in price-cap regulation. It then considers the options available to regulators in attempting to address this problem. In each case practical applications of how regulators have addressed these problems are described, drawing examples from the water, electricity, rail, telecommunications and postal sectors.

The problem of service quality when regulating prices
Stephen Littlechild's original conception of price-cap (RPI − X) regulation for BT was that it provides a simple mechanism that creates incentives for the regulated company to become more efficient, because by reducing costs the firm is able to increase its profits and retain this increase, at least until prices are re-set at a subsequent review (Littlechild, 1983). This may be adequate in simple textbook examples, but when applied in reality regulators must also take into consideration the potential impact of price regulation on the quality of service provided.

Competitive markets create incentives to reduce costs, because firms are price takers and cannot pass on excessive costs to their customers. In addition, competition provides incentives for companies to supply the *quality* of service that customers desire, because customers can choose to switch supplier if they are not satisfied with what they get. Different firms may choose different trade-offs between price and quality, and in this way segment the market they are serving. So provided there is no significant asymmetry of information between buyers and sellers there is every reason to expect competition adequately to address quality issues.

In contrast, while price-cap regulation alone can create strong incentives for companies to reduce costs, it may not send the right signals to the regulated company regarding the quality of service it provides. In general, when unregulated firms have market power, they may not have the appropriate incentives to set an efficient level of service quality (a useful review of the literature in this area is provided by Sappington, 2005). Depending on the relationship between the marginal customer's valuation of service quality and that of the inframarginal customer, it is possible for an unregulated monopoly to choose either too low or too high a level of service quality. This is because, in the absence of any additional attention to service quality the regulated company can increase its profits not merely by increased efficiency, but also by cutting back on the quality of service it provides.

There are many aspects of service quality which could potentially suffer in a regulated environment. Of most common concern is the impact of price regulation on the reliability of the service provided. For example, the frequency with which the service is interrupted is a key aspect of the value of the service to end users in all network industries. There is every reason to expect that there is a link between the regulated company's level of investment in network assets and its long-term ability to maintain a reliable service. Furthermore, reductions in operating costs may also impact on reliability or reduce the regulated company's ability to react to failures or unforeseen events, thus extending the duration of interruptions even if the initial cause of the interruptions may be outside the company's control (such as adverse weather bringing down power lines or a freeze–thaw causing pipe bursts and supply interruptions).

In some cases, for instance water supply and airport services, the quality of the product itself may be affected by the company's efforts to reduce costs. The latter case presents particular difficulties because of the multi-faceted nature of the service being offered and difficulties in creating objective measures of quality.

In addition, the impact of price regulation on the way in which the regulated company deals with its customers is a material concern; in particular how the regulated company interacts with its customers across a wide range issues, including its handling of queries or complaints.

What are the options for addressing the quality issue?
The issue for regulators in choosing the appropriate instruments for promoting quality standards is to strike the right balance between the costs and benefits of intervention. Furthermore, it is necessary to ensure that any incentives put in place to improve service quality are neither so weak that they are ignored, nor so strong that they encourage the regulated company to 'gold plate' its service.

Under price-cap regulation there may be some incentive to maintain service quality depending on the way in which investment expenditure is capitalized into the company's regulatory asset base (RAB). Rather than cut investment to make higher profits in the short term, a company may choose to maintain (or increase) capital investment with the aim of earning higher profits in the long run.[1] How effective this mechanism is will depend on the ability of the regulated company to pass these investment costs into its RAB and the trade-off between the profit thus generated and the profits created by cutting costs in the short term.

Analysis of the trade-off between the incentive to cut costs and the gain from 'over capitalizing' has tended to suggest that the overcapitalization incentive cannot be relied on by itself to ensure adequate standards of service quality. For instance, Laffont and Tirole (1993) note that in the US 'there has been concern that "incentive regulation" ... conflicts with the safe operation of nuclear power plants by forcing management to hurry work, take short-cuts, and delay safety investments'. In the UK an analysis of BT's performance after privatization suggests that the incentive to reduce costs outweighed the incentive to overcapitalize.[2]

Assuming that the incentive to raise investment in search of higher long-run profits is insufficient to ensure adequate service quality standards, there are a number of ways in which incentives to achieve particular service levels can be added to a price control regime, including:

1.   The setting of legally binding targets for specific service levels, with the potential for legal action being taken against company directors in the event that the company fails to comply.
2.   The imposition of customer compensation payments for service failure, intended to make the regulated company internalize the impact of service failures on its customers.
3.   The inclusion of specific financial incentives in the price-cap formula, to encourage improvement performance by rewarding successful companies with higher profits.
4.   The use of 'peer pressure' to encourage improvement, by publishing league tables of company performance against particular targets.

In designing the optimum regulatory regime, a regulator needs to take into consideration how effective each of the above options is likely to be in the relevant circumstances *and* the potential cost of falling short of (or exceeding) the desired quality standard (Rovizzi and Thompson, 1995).

In all cases, there are significant practical problems to be faced regarding the quantification and measurement of service quality and the relationship between the actions of the regulated company and the impact these actions have on service levels. This latter point is particularly important in the context of four- or five-yearly periodic price reviews. The National Audit Office (2002) noted that pipe and wire networks have an underlying resilience and it could take some time for inadequate or inefficient expenditure on maintaining them to be reflected in declining performance against output measures. Hence regulators may be justifiably concerned that focusing on *current* service performance may miss the longer term picture as investment decisions in the present may be needed in order to secure service quality in the future, at a time long after the end of the regulatory price control period in question. How in these circumstances can the regulated company be given the incentive to invest sufficiently for long-term quality issues?

Binding targets

The first category, that of binding legal standards, is more akin to command-and-control rather than economic regulation. It is most an approach often reserved for that category of standards where the cost of failure to meet the necessary quality is unacceptable. Obvious examples include drinking water quality and safety standards that apply in transport sectors like aviation and rail.

In most cases these standards will be defined by national (or EU) legislation and enforced by government agencies that are separate from the economic regulator.[3] However, there is a feedback from this type of quality regulation into the activities of the economic regulator in two ways. First and most simply, these enforceable quality standards provide a framework that the economic regulator has to work towards in determining prices and spending limits. Second, and more contentiously, it falls to the economic regulator to decide what allowance in costs should be made for meeting the standards imposed by government. Taking the England and Wales water industry as an example, drinking water standards are enforced by the Drinking Water Inspectorate (DWI), which can prosecute water companies for failing to comply with its instructions on water quality. On the other hand, price limits are set by the Office of Water Services (Ofwat), but DWI's rulings are not legally binding on Ofwat. Ofwat takes the view that it will make allowance in price limits for 'New Statutory Obligations', but will not fund compliance with existing standards. To do so might encourage water companies to let standards slip in the knowledge that Ofwat would allow the funding of additional compliance work in the future.

In practice, however, this division of responsibilities from time to time leads to a conflict in approach between DWI and Ofwat. One grey area arises when the DWI changes its view on the steps a water company needs to take to address a particular problem. In these cases, the DWI may order enforcement of quality standards that involves the water company in significant additional expense, but because the problem is a longstanding one, Ofwat will not recognize these costs in price limits because it is not a *new* obligation.

The second conflict of regulatory approach arises when Ofwat takes the view that the company's plan to deal with the enforcement order is not justified on cost–benefit grounds. For instance, the company may be required to solve a water quality problem, but the costs of doing so are uncertain. The regulator may agree to recognize the cost of a pilot study to assess the total cost of compliance, but not the costs of actually complying, because those costs are as yet uncertain. This can leave a company in a regulatory no-man's land as regards how to fund a legally binding obligation.[4]

Compensation payments

Customer compensation payments have been extensively used as a method of inducing regulated companies to meet specific desired levels of service. Examples exist in the UK electricity and water sectors, fixed line telephony (for BT) and postal services. In passenger rail, Train Operating Companies (TOCs) are obliged to pay compensation to ticket holders if individual trains are excessively delayed and also compensation to season ticket holders if the average standard of the service, in terms of punctuality and train cancellations, does not meet government set targets.

The underlying logic of compensation payments is that they cause the regulated company to internalize the social cost of poor quality service (in particular supply interruptions) into its planning. If the payment levels are set at the correct level then, in theory, the regulated company would have the correct incentives to provide an efficient quality of service.

There are, however, several problems with such an approach. First it may be extremely difficult, if not impossible to identify the 'efficient' level of compensation. In principle it would be as much a fault to set the compensation level too high and encourage excessive expenditure by the company to avoid the need for compensation as it would be to set it too low. Second, it may be difficult to get customers to be aware of the compensation they are entitled to, or to get them to go to the trouble of claiming, as the amounts involved may be relatively small.

Third, compensation payments are only really feasible in the context of clearly identifiable events that can be attributed to particular customers, like supply interruptions. In the context of rail travel, compensation for late arrival is difficult as most rail tickets are sold on a 'turn up and go' basis, without seat reservations, which makes it difficult to prove whether a given individual was on a particular train.

In general, the UK experience is that compensation payments tend to be set at low levels and that the uptake of these payments is poor. Both of these factors tend to suggest that in practice compensation payments to customers have little impact on making regulated companies improve their quality standards. For example, in the electricity sector Frontier Economics (2003a, p. 31) found that 'in a typical year the sums involved are not large in comparison to total price control revenue – tens to hundreds of thousands of pounds (price control revenue is typically £100–200 million per year)'. In the water sector Markou and Waddams Price (1999) note that, in the early years after privatization, the uptake of payments under the regulator's Guaranteed Standards Schemes was poor. Indeed, the regulator is quoted as believing that those who made claims represented 'only 1–2% of all the justifiable claims, and attributed the difference to customer ignorance (only 15% know of the scheme) and/or a belief that the compensation involved (£5 for most claims) was not worth it' (Markou and Waddams Price, 1999, p. 387).

One issue that distinguishes compensation schemes is whether they are calibrated to compensate consumers from the loss of value resulting from a failure of supply, or merely to refund sums paid by customers for services that were not delivered. There can be a significant gap between these two figures. We would expect the value most customers to place on utility services to be substantially in excess of the price paid. Hence compensation intended to reflect the social cost of a service failure should be significantly greater than the price of the service itself.

If compensation payments are small because they only reflect refunds of the sums paid by customers for short periods then this will exacerbate both the problems identified here: that payments are too small to make the utility change its behaviour and too small for customers to bother with claiming.

Examples of compensation payments

Water   In 1989 the statutory Guaranteed Standards Scheme (GSS) was introduced, offering financial protection to customers suffering from poor service.[5] This initially involved fixed payments, which in 1993 was changed into an automatic compensation scheme, together with higher penalties and tighter targets.[6]

The current penalties under the scheme are summarized as follows:

- failing to keep an appointment: £20;
- failing to make a timely response to an account query: £20;
- failing to respond to a complaint within 10 working days: £20 for domestic customers and £50 for businesses;
- insufficient notice of a planned interruption: £20 for domestic customers and £50 for businesses, plus £10 (£25 for businesses) for each 24 hour period the supply remains interrupted;
- failure to restore supply in a timely manner after an unplanned interruption: £20 plus a further £10 for each 24-hour period the supply remains unrestored for domestic customers; £50 plus a further £25 for each 24-hour period the supply remains unrestored for businesses;
- sewer flooding: customers may be entitled to receive a refund of their sewerage charges for the year up to a maximum of £1000 for each flooding incident;
- low pressure: if a customer is affected by low pressure on two occasions, with each lasting an hour or more in a period of 28 consecutive days, then the company must pay the customer, or credit their account, to the sum of £25.

Electricity   As will be made clear in the discussion below, Ofgem has placed more emphasis on incentives in the price-cap formula than on customer compensation as a mechanism of incentivizing improved service quality.

However, electricity customers do receive compensation for supply interruptions, which amount to £50 for domestic customers for a supply interruption of 18 hours and an additional £25 for each subsequent 12 hour period.

Fixed telephony/BT   A formal customer compensation scheme was first introduced in 1989 by BT, which offered financial compensation whenever the specified standards of service in terms of line installations and repairs were not met. It has been subsequently extended and now makes up the Customer Service Guarantee, which specifies target response times for orders and repairs, as well as the speed of connection. In addition, it also guarantees compensation when a financial loss is incurred by a customer due to a failure of service quality. An example of the penalties paid under the Customer Service Guarantee following a line interruption and failure of repair is given in Table 4.1. This quality measure provides an integral part of the annual reports published by Ofcom on telephone service.

Table 4.1   Compensation related to delay in repairing a line fault

Delay	Financial compensation
1–3 days	One month line rental
4–6 days	Two months line rental
7–9 days	Three months line rental
10 days plus	Four months line rental

Source: BT Customer Service.

Post   Under its operating licence outlined in the Postal Services Act 2000, in the UK the Royal Mail is responsible for service quality defined by the geographical density of the postal service provided and by its standard in terms of delivery of post within a specified timeframe. Sixteen such delivery targets have been defined, examples being first class mail of which 93 per cent has to be delivered on the next working day, and second class mail which has to arrive within three working days. In addition a 'tail of mail' target has been set out such that all post has to be delivered within three days of the expiry of the required standard.[7]

There are mechanisms to provide incentives so that these targets are met:[8] these cover both formal adjustments to Royal Mail's allowed revenue and a compensation scheme established in 2003 for retail and bulk users relating to delay, but not to loss or damage of items. Retail users are entitled to free stamps or monetary payments if post is subjected to serious delay. Compensation for bulk users is based on the extent to which Royal Mail fails to achieve the quality of service target for each service. Customers of any service which has failed its quality target by 1 per cent or more automatically get a refund of 0.1 per cent of their expenditure on that product that year for each 0.1 per cent failure. Compensation is capped at 5 per cent of spend. This cap is justified by the regulator by the need to ensure the financial viability of the universal service function.[9] Unlike in the cases of electricity and water, the compensation payment for poor postal service reflects the price paid by customers rather than any estimate of the loss of value suffered by the customer.

Regulatory formula

In 1999 both the water and electricity regulators decided to extend their regulatory regimes by linking quality of service directly to the price cap. The intention was to increase the incentives for companies to achieve better standards of service.

As with the issue of compensation payments, calibrating the allowance is extremely difficult. As previously discussed, there are no guarantees that the targets against which companies are assessed are efficient and hence the scheme, even if it works, may not achieve an efficient level of service quality. Given the uncertainties, there is a suspicion that the amounts involved may be arbitrary. Thus, while companies may be rewarded for good performance, and this may be positive in itself, it is not clear to what extent the policy actively encourages companies to *improve* their quality of service.

We have seen that both regulators changed the approach to performance bonuses in their 2004 reviews. The lack of stability in such schemes and the inability of regulators to commit to such schemes over the long term have the effect of undermining any incentive properties they might have. If companies cannot rely on the magnitude of benefits for good performance, or even which aspects of good performance will be rewarded, they are unlikely to invest significantly in the hope of gaining that reward.[10] Furthermore, the lag between underinvestment and service problems becoming apparent will often be sufficient that problems resulting from neglect do not become apparent by the time of the next price review, while the benefits of remedial action may also not be fully visible until it is too late to reflect in the price cap. This problem of lags makes it extremely difficult credibly to build incentive mechanisms into the price-cap formula itself.

Finally, quality of service performance is also affected by factors that are genuinely outside company control. Climate has a significant impact on the performance of both water and electricity distribution companies. Ideally, price-cap adjustments should distinguish quality of service problems resulting from company action from those resulting from external factors that could not have been anticipated or prevented. This increases the complexity of the ideal adjustment mechanism.

Examples of the application of regulatory formulae to service quality issues

Water   At the 1999 Periodic Review Ofwat introduced a 'Service Performance Adjustment' to reflect the overall standard of service provided to customers. Ofwat stated that this would 'provide an incentive to improve services and a disincentive to companies to cut costs by reducing the standard of service provided' (Ofwat, 1999b, p. 99). The adjustment was based on an assessment of a wide range of services in the period 1996–97 to 1998–99, which was refined over time to incorporate a broader assessment of water quality published by the DWI. Results of the assessment were then combined with equal weighting to give a single score.

Where the standard of service was assessed as being significantly better than that provided by the industry generally, a one-off increase in price limits of 0.5 per cent was made; and where service was judged to be particularly poor relative to the industry, a one-off reduction of 0.5 per cent was proposed. In principle Ofwat reserved the right to reduce a company's prices by 1 per cent if it found that its performance was particularly poor, but in practice no company fell into that category.

In the event five companies were given an upward price adjustment of 0.5 per cent, while five were given a downward adjustment by the same amount. After the 1999 review Ofwat continued to monitor company performance against its consolidated performance measure and found that company performance improved significantly and variation between companies was also reduced. This is illustrated in Figure 4.1.

Whereas in 1996–99 some companies achieved as little as 50 per cent of the maximum achievable score, by 2002–04 all firms were bunched tightly around a level greater than 80 per cent.

Given the high absolute level and low variance in service quality between companies, Ofwat subsequently decided that for the 2004 price review *relative* comparison measures were no longer appropriate. First, because basing financial incentives on relative rankings provides difficulties when company performance is evenly matched. Second, to avoid the problem of perverse incentives that might lead companies to overinvest in improving service provision, so as to leapfrog their rivals and gain the performance uplift.

In its 2004 price review, Ofwat consequently revised its mechanism so that the price cap is determined on company performance relative to a 100 per cent benchmark (Ofwat, 2004). The bands that were introduced were as follows:

- 90 per cent to 100 per cent score: potential price adjustments of 0.1 per cent to 0.5 per cent;
- 90 per cent to 70 per cent score: potential price adjustments of 0 to –0.5 per cent;

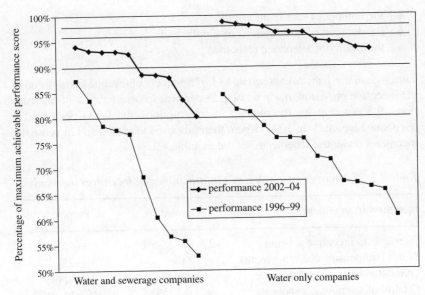

Source: Ofwat (2004) 'Future water and sewerage charges 2005–10: Final determinations', *Periodic Review*.

Figure 4.1   *Comparison of performance as a percentage of maximum achievable score*

- Below 70 per cent score: potential adjustments of –0.5 per cent to –1.0 per cent.

In the end, the adjustments applied ranged from +0.4 per cent to –0.1 per cent with two companies each falling into the highest and lowest band. It should also be noted that 17 of the 22 companies received some *upward* adjustment to prices. Hence, the relative discrimination between companies created by this incentive mechanism was substantially reduced in comparison to the previous periodic review.

Electricity   Ofgem developed the Information and Incentives Mechanism (IIP) following the conclusion of its price control review in 1999, and this was introduced in 2002. This scheme is intended to provide incentives to the electricity distribution companies (DNOs) to improve their level of service by linking certain quality measures to the revenue they may retain. Under the IIP both financial rewards and penalties depend on the quality of supply performance in three key areas:

- the number of supply interruptions;
- the duration of interruptions to supply; and
- the quality of telephone responses.

The original mechanism exposed up to 1.875 per cent of revenue to risk through the incentive provision, made up of 1.25 per cent for the duration of interruptions, 0.5 per cent for the number of interruptions and 0.125 per cent for telephone responses. In 2004 Ofgem then proposed to extend and increase the incentives under the scheme, as set out in Table 4.2.

Table 4.2   Incentives under Ofgem's Information and Incentives mechanism

Incentive arrangement	Current	Proposal
Interruption incentive scheme	+2% to –1.75%	+/– 3%
Storm compensation arrangements	–1%	–2%
Other standards of performance	Uncapped	Uncapped
Quality of telephone response	+/– 0.125%	+0.05% to –0.25%
Quality of telephone response in storm conditions	Not applicable	0 initially; +/–0.25% for 3 yrs
Discretionary reward scheme	Not applicable	Up to +£1m
Overall cap/total	+2% to –2.875%	4% on downside; no overall cap on the upside

Source: Ofgem (2004).

An integral part of the price control review set by Ofgem is its Interruption Incentive Scheme. Under the revised mechanism, companies face symmetrical incentives with regard to their revenue (+/–3 per cent). Service quality targets are defined both in terms of the number of customers interrupted per 100 customers (the CI measure) and the number of customer minutes lost (the CML measure). The actual incentive amount is calculated as a formula based on actual and target performance for each company.

The IIP also includes a measure of the quality of telephone response. It is based on customer surveys carried out on behalf of Ofgem, the results of which are published on Ofgem's website. The quality of telephone response is defined by:

- total calls on the specified lines;
- total calls answered by an automated message providing fault details;
- total calls answered by an agent;

- mean time taken for response by an agent;
- total number of unsuccessful calls, comprising:
  - total calls not reaching the specified lines
  - total calls terminated by the DNO
  - total calls not allowed into the queue or flushed from the queue
  - total calls abandoned by the customer in the queue.

Customer satisfaction is measured on a scale of 1 to 5 and the incentive scheme is implemented using a sliding-scale penalty if the score falls below 4.1. If performance below 3.6 is realized, a full penalty of 0.25 per cent of revenue may be incurred. The mechanism exhibits an asymmetric reward schedule as its upside is limited to 0.05 per cent of revenue, which is granted whenever annual mean scores above 4.5 are achieved.

Finally, Ofgem has also introduced an additional discretionary remuneration. This is meant to encourage best practice in areas that cannot easily be measured or incentivized through more mechanistic incentive schemes. The reward is designed especially to cover priority customer care initiatives, communication strategies implemented by the companies, such as relationships with local health authorities, and initiatives relating to corporate social responsibility. It is interesting to note that the relative magnitude of the adjustments envisaged under Ofgem's incentive scheme is significantly larger than those contained in the Ofwat out-performance adjustments.

Peer pressure

The final method of encouraging improved service quality from regulated companies has come in the form of applying 'peer pressure' to companies. This usually takes the form of the publication of 'league tables' of performance of the regulated companies against a selection of relevant criteria. These allow customers and the public to judge the relative performance of companies. Even if most customers do not realistically have the option to switch suppliers themselves (which would be the case for domestic water customers and most train passengers, but possibly not for electricity and gas customers). The theory goes that the mere publication of league tables will act as a spur to make private companies improve their performance because management and shareholders dislike being compared unfavourably with their peers, even if they are not direct commercial rivals.

The use of this type of peer pressure can be criticized for a number of reasons. First, comparison cannot be calibrated to ensure an efficient level of effort by the regulated company into improving service quality. Depending on whether the reaction to reputation effects is great or small, the company's reaction could be negligible or excessive. Second, league tables are often criticized for being misleading as they may not reflect the legitimate reasons outside the control of management why one company may perform worse than another on a particular measure.

The counter-argument to these points is that at least league tables have the virtue of being easy to create, relatively simple to interpret, and push all companies in the right direction, even if it is difficult to determine how hard or how far. In terms of the effect, Waddams Price et al. (2002, p. 24) found that 'companies are clearly sensitive to the standards set, but the direct financial penalty is often less important than reputation effects'. Moreover there is good reason to consider that private companies may be responsive to this sort of pressure for strictly rational reasons. In particular there may be two sources of long-term advantage that regulated companies may gain from good performance in league tables. First, reputation effects may be particularly important for firms seeking to develop their non-regulated businesses in overseas markets. The firm's reputation for service quality in its home markets may be an important factor in determining its chances of success or failure in winning foreign contracts. Second, good performance in league tables may signal that the regulator will look more favourably on that company at future price reviews, which would have a positive value to shareholders. Finally, the idea that good performance in league tables may be reflected in favourable regulatory treatment in the future may make the company more attractive to investors and hence reduce its cost of finance in the present.

In the UK we see the use of peer pressure techniques in a variety of industries. Obviously regulators will have difficulty in applying this technique if it does not have a number of broadly similar firms that it regulates. If the regulator does not have a number of firms to compare it could make use of international comparisons, but as with problems of more complex benchmarking (see Chapter 6) this is complicated by the problems of data collection and comparability. The alternative is to publish time series of performance figures from the regulated company, which has the effect of putting an emphasis on trends in performance over time.

Thus peer pressure is relatively easily applicable in the case of the water, electricity distribution and rail industries; whereas in other sectors such as gas distribution or postal services comparison between companies may be more difficult, although regulators can still publish trends in data to highlight changes in company performance.

Examples of the use of peer pressure

Water   In the UK Ofwat has been the most vigorous exponent of this sort of peer pressure, producing an extensive range of comparative data about the companies that it regulates. Ofwat's various publications present companies' relative performance on almost every possible dimension, including operating

Table 4.3 *Water company performance against DG measures*

Company	Sewer flooding (overloaded sewers) DG5	Sewer flooding (other causes) DG5	Poor pressure DG2	Unplanned interruptions to supply DG3	Billing contacts DG6	Written complaints DG7	Bills for metered custs DG8
Anglian	★	★	●	●	★	★	★
Dŵr Cymru	▶	●	★	★	★	★	★
Northumbrian	▶	●	★	★	★	★	★
Severn Trent	★	▶	★	★	★	★	★
South West	●	●	★	★	★	★	★
Southern	★	●	●	★	★	★	★
Thames	★	●	●	▶	★	★	★
United Utilities	▶	★	★	★	★	★	★
Wessex	★	▶	●	●	★	★	★
Yorkshire	▶	★	★	★	★	★	★

Key DG5: ★ Above average ● Average ▼ Below Average ▼ Needs Improvement

Source: Ofwat: *Levels of Service for the Water Industry in England and Wales; 2003–2004 report.*

95

costs, capital costs and levels of service. In the field of levels of service, Ofwat has defined a series of measures (known as DG measures) against which the companies are considered and publicly ranked. An illustration of this ranking is presented in Table 4.3.

Electricity   Ofgem's primary focus on service quality is based on incentive mechanisms (see above). However, as part of the process of deriving the performance measures used for this mechanism, Ofgem publishes comparative tables of performance which make the relative performance of the companies clear to customers and the public. Ofgem's process, therefore, has the joint effect

Table 4.4   Electricity – customer supply interruptions

	2001/2002	2002/2003	2003/2004
CN Midlands	120.1	99.8	113.1
CN East Midlands	77.0	74.7	–
United Utilities	55.5	65.7	–
CE NEDL	82.2	–	
CE YEDL	77.4	–	
WPD South West	100.7		
WPD South Wales	–		
EDF LPN	–		
EDF SPN			

Source: Ofgem.

Table 4.5   Customer minutes lost

	2001/2002	2002/2003	2003/2004
CN Midlands	116.9	100.9	100.3
CN East Midlands	87.0	78.5	–
United Utilities	61.7	65.6	–
CE NEDL	83.9	–	
CE YEDL	72.6	–	
WPD South West	78.6		
WPD South Wales	–		
EDF LPN	–		
EDF SPN			

Source: Ofgem.

	2004–05 Q4	2003–04 Q4	Year to 31 March 2005	Year to 31 December 2004
Long distance operators				
First Great Western	79.6	83.0	79.6	80.5
Great North Eastern Railway	79.2	76.9	77.5	76.9
Midland Mainline	92.9	80.4	88.3	85.3
ONE* (InterCity)	83.3	79.5	84.3	83.5
Virgin CrossCountry	82.7	80.7	77.8	77.2
Virgin West Coast	74.7	81.5	72.1	73.7
Sector level	**81.3**	**80.7**	**79.1**	**78.9**
London and SE operators – all day				
c2c	94.0	88.0	93.2	91.7
Chiltern Railways	93.9	91.5	92.5	91.9
First Great Western Link†	84.2	85.5	82.9	83.2
ONE*	90.8	–	89.0	–
Silverlink	89.7	81.8	84.2	82.2
South Eastern Trains	84.5	82.4	84.2	83.6
South West Trains	90.0	74.0	81.4	77.4
Southern	84.8	80.4	81.8	80.7
Thameslink	89.6	77.8	83.9	81.0
WAGN*	90.0	86.2	89.3	87.6
Sector level	**88.0**	**82.1**	**84.7**	**83.2**
London and SE operators – peak				
c2c	94.3	85.8	92.7	90.5
Chiltern Railways	91.3	86.6	90.3	89.1
First Great Western Link†	70.1	81.0	73.9	76.7
ONE*	88.9	–	86.7	–
Silverlink	90.2	85.8	86.1	85.0
South Eastern Trains	78.9	73.0	80.1	78.5
South West Trains	85.8	69.6	78.3	74.2
Southern	78.4	75.2	77.9	77.1
Thameslink	85.0	70.8	78.5	75.0
WAGN*	87.9	83.2	87.2	85.1
Sector level	**83.9**	**77.3**	**81.8**	**80.2**
Regional operators				
Arriva Trains Wales	83.0	84.6	80.8	81.2
Central Trains	74.6	78.2	73.1	74.1
First ScotRail	83.7	86.2	83.1	83.7
Gatwick Express	87.1	80.4	84.7	83.1
Island Line	98.3	98.7	97.3	97.4
Merseyrail	94.7	94.5	94.2	94.1
Northern Rail	87.3	–	–	–
TPE	78.5	–	74.6	–
Wessex Trains	86.6	87.1	85.4	85.6
Sector level	**84.6**	**84.6**	**82.7**	**82.7**
National level	**86.2**	**83.1**	**83.6**	**82.8**

Source: SRA (2005), *National Rail Treands Year Book 2004–2005*.

Figure 4.2 Percentage of trains arriving on time

Operator	2004–05 Q1	2004–05 Q2	2004–05 Q3	2004–05 Q4	2004–05 Total	2003–04
Long distance operators						
First Great Western	100%	100%	89%	99%	96%	100%
GNER	88%	61%	58%	69%	68%	74%
Midland Mainline	83%	54%	71%	72%	69%	89%
Virgin CrossCountry	100%	99%	98%	100%	99%	95%
Virgin West Coast	100%	100%	100%	100%	100%	96%
London and South East operators						
c2c	98%	99%	100%	100%	99%	98%
Chiltern Railways	100%	99%	62%	67%	76%	99%
First Great Western Link†	99%	99%	99%	87%	96%	74%
ONE*	99%	100%	93%	96%	96%	–
Silverlink	96%	99%	100%	100%	99%	98%
South Eastern Trains	100%	100%	100%	100%	100%	100%
South West Trains	99%	100%	100%	99%	99%	98%
Southern	100%	100%	100%	99%	100%	98%
Thameslink	98%	99%	99%	100%	99%	98%
WAGN*	97%	100%	100%	100%	99%	94%
Regional operators						
Arriva Trains Wales	100%	100%	100%	100%	100%	100%
Central Trains	90%	98%	93%	96%	94%	93%
First ScotRail*	89%	91%	85%	91%	89%	86%
Gatwick Express	76%	90%	75%	85%	82%	82%
Island Line	100%	100%	100%	100%	100%	100%
Merseyrail	100%	100%	100%	100%	100%	100%
Northern Rail*	100%	99%	100%	100%	100%	–
TPE	99%	93%	97%	99%	97%	100%
Wessex Trains	100%	100%	100%	100%	100%	100%

Source: SRA (2005), *National Rail Trends Year Book 2004–2005.*

Figure 4.3   Percentage of complaints answered within 20 working days

of creating direct incentives through the price cap and indirect incentives through the use of league tables.

An example of the data that Ofgem publishes is shown in Table 4.4 and Table 4.5. However, Ofgem's publication of comparative data is much less comprehensive than Ofwat's. Hence its value in creating pure peer pressure effects on companies is likely to be much less.

Train operating companies   In the UK rail industry, in recent years the Strategic Rail Authority[11] has been the regulatory body responsible for the performance of the train operating companies (TOCs). In addition to penalty schemes built into each of the TOCs' franchise agreements for delays, cancellations and short-formation trains, the SRA also publishes comparative data in its yearbook on the relative performance of TOCs as regards delays, overcrowding and how well

Properties at risk of low pressure

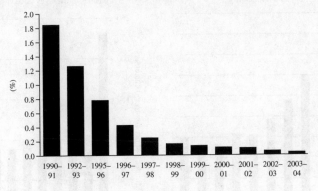

Properties subject to unplanned supply interruptions

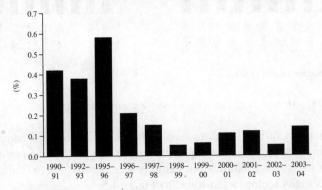

Source: Ofwat: *Levels of Service for the Water Industry in England and Wales*; 2003–2004 report.

Figure 4.4   Reliability of the water network

they deal with customer complaints. Two examples are shown in Figures 4.2 and Figure 4.3.

Conclusions

Regulators have adopted a variety of different strategies to induce companies to maintain and improve quality of service under price-cap regulation. The key question, however, is whether there is evidence to prove that these approaches have been effective, and if possible to identify which are more effective than others.

In practice, despite concerns arising from the possibility that the regulation of profit through price caps would lead to deterioration in the quality of service

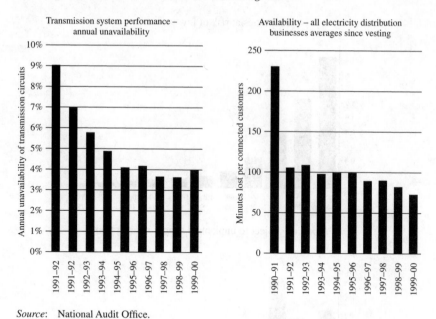

Source: National Audit Office.

Figure 4.5   Measures of electricity service change over time

there is actually little evidence to support the idea that this has occurred in the UK. Figure 4.4 illustrates the improvement that is typical of the performance measures in the water industry. Similar improvements have been demonstrated in the electricity sector, as illustrated by Figure 4.5.

However, the pattern is not uniform across all regulated sectors. Since the introduction of the performance delivery standards, Royal Mail has never simultaneously fulfilled more than eight out of its 16 targets. As shown in the last two columns of Table 4.6 all standards were breached in 2003–04. Also, the rail network has failed to maintain standards of pre-privatization perform-ance, although many complex factors are at work in the industry, which are outside the scope of this chapter – including a substantial increase in the volume of traffic carried on the network. Nevertheless, there is little doubt service qual-ity and reliability issues were neglected to some extent, under the now defunct Railtrack which was responsible for the rail infrastructure during the years im-mediately after privatization.

There is however some evidence from that the performance on service quality of the UK utilities since privatization that firms are motivated by factors other than simply short-term profit maximization and that reputation effects may be remarkably important in determining companies' behaviour. According to Waddams Price et al. (2002, p. 21), 'The performance of the water and sewerage

Table 4.6   Royal Mail performance against benchmarks

	Apr 2001– March 2002	Apr 2002– March 2003	Apr 2003– March 2004	Targets Apr 2003– March 2004
First Class: % delivered next day				
Stamped & Metered	89.9	91.8	90.1	92.5
Postage Paid Impression	81.4	83.9	83.5	90.6
1st class Response Services	78.1	80.3	81.7	90.3
Mailsort 1	90.0	90.8	89.2	91.0
Presstream 1	89.2	90.8	88.1	90.5
First Class: Postcode Performance				
All mail	60.2	91.5	55.9	100.0
Local mail	71.9	90.9	80.2	100.0
Second Class: % delivered with 3 days				
Stamped & Metered	98.3	98.6	97.8	98.5
Postage Paid Impression	94.4	96.9	94.6	97.4
2nd class Response Services	93.7	93.7	92.2	97.5
Mailsort 2	95.5	96.5	95.7	97.5
Presstream 2	96.2	96.8	95.1	97.5
Other				
Special Delivery (% next day)	98.5	98.6	97.9	99.0
Standard Parcel (% within 3 days)	81.0	88.5	88.9	90.0
Mailsort 3 (within 7 days)	97.9	98.0	97.4	97.5

Source: Postcomm.

companies against the various DG measures shows a pattern of consistent improvement across all companies and measures.' Similarly, in the electricity distribution sector (ibid., p. 22), 'There are steady and consistent improvements.' This across the board improvement contradicts the idea that companies may be reacting in particularly calculating and profit maximizing ways to specific incentive signals.

The National Audit Office (2002, p. 25) also supported the idea that, more than anything, reputation effects have the strongest impact on the behaviour of regulated companies: 'the publication of league tables by the regulator acted as an incentive for companies to maintain and improve service performance in order to maintain their reputation'. This does not mean, however, that regulators should be complacent about the use of league tables as the best or indeed sole method of creating incentives for regulated companies to improve service quality. While this approach may often lead to improvement against the measures chosen, the quality of service targets set by the regulators may still not be efficient.[12] The regulator considers the trade-off between increased prices and increased quality of service, but a regulator does not have explicit information on consumer willingness-to-pay, particularly at the individual firm level. In addition, as emphasized by Markou and Waddams Price (1999), the regulator's decision on the appropriate target is based on duties that are often not clearly specified. The regulatory standards pursued therefore reflect, at best, the regulators' judgement on what the trade-off should be between price and quality not that of consumers.

Notes

1. The importance of 'overcapitalization incentives' is discussed in Waddams Price et al. (2002).
2. See Armstrong and Vickers (1995), Rovizzi and Thompson (1995) and Markou and Waddams Price (1999) for discussions of the quality of service issues following from the introduction of price-cap regulation for British Telecom and British Gas.
3. An exception in the UK is the Civil Aviation Authority, which is responsible both for the economic regulation of designated airports and for the enforcement of safety standards in UK aviation. However, even in this case, these functions are performed by completely district parts of the organization.
4. See the Competition Commission (2000) report on Sutton & East Surrey Water for an example of where a company argued that it had been caught between the inconsistent approaches of an economic regulator and its enforcement agencies.
5. Statutory Instrument 1989 No 1159, *The Water Supply and Sewerage Services (Customer Service Standards) Regulations 1989*.
6. Statutory Instrument 1993 No 500, *The Water Supply and Sewerage Services (Customer Service Standards) (Amendment) Regulations 1993* and Statutory Instrument 2000 No 2301, *The Water Supply and Sewerage Services (Customer Service Standards) (Amendment) Regulation 2000*.
7. Postcomm (2000): *Postal Services Act 2000, Section 11, Amended Licence*.
8. Postcomm: (2005): *2006 Royal Mail Price and Service Quality Review, Initial Proposals*.
9. See Balogh et al. (2006) for more details on postal compensation schemes.
10. See Laffont and Tirole (1993).

11. Merged into the Department for Transport in 2005.
12. A similar point is made by Forsyth (1999) with respect to price cap regimes in Australia. He notes that 'The quality monitoring approach supposes that the initial level of quality is optimal; this may or may not be the case'.

Bibliography

Armstrong, M., Cowan, S. and Vickers, J. (1994) *Regulatory Reform: Economic Analysis and British Experience*, Cambridge, MA: MIT Press.

Armstrong, M., Rees, R. and Vickers, J. (1995) 'Optimal Regulatory Lag Under Price Cap Regulation', *Revista Espanola de Economia*, **12**, 93–116.

Armstrong, M. and Sappington, D. (2002) 'Recent Developments in the Theory of Regulation', in *Handbook of Industrial Organisation* (Volume III), Amsterdam: Elsevier Science Publications.

Armstrong, M. and Vickers, J. (1995) 'Competition and Regulation in Telecommunications', in M. Bishop, J. Kay. and C. Mayer (eds), *The Regulatory Challenge*, Oxford: Oxford University Press.

Armstrong, M. and Vickers, J. (2000) 'Multiproduct Price Regulation Under Asymmetric Information', *Journal of Industrial Economics*, **48**, 137–60.

Arocena, P. and Waddams Price, C. (2001) 'Generating Efficiency: Economic and Environmental Regulation of Public and Private Electricity Generators in Spain', *International Journal of Industrial Organization*, **20**, 41–69.

Averch, H. and Johnson, L. (1962) 'Behaviour of the Firm Under Regulatory Constraint', *The American Economic Review*, **52**, 1052–69.

Balogh, T., Moriaty, R. and Smith, P. (2006) in M.A. Crew and P.R. Kleindorfer (eds), *Progress Toward Liberalization in the Postal and Delivery Sector*, Springer (forthcoming).

Banerjee, A. and Dasgupta, K. (2001) 'Does Incentive Regulation "Cause" Degradation of Retail Telephone Service Quality?', Presentation at the Rutgers University Advanced Workshop in Competition, 20th Annual Conference.

Baron (1989) 'Design of Regulatory Mechanisms and Institutions', in R. Schmalensee and R. Willig (eds), *Handbook of Industrial Organization, Volume II*, Oxford: Elsevier Science Publishers, pp. 1347–447.

Baumol, W. (1995) 'Modified Regulation of Telecommunications and the Public Interest Standard', in M. Bishop, J. Kay and C. Mayer (eds), *The Regulatory Challenge*, Oxford: Oxford University Press.

Beesley, M.E. and Littlechild, S.C. (1983) 'Privatization: Principles, Problems and Priorities', *Lloyds Bank Review*. Reproduced in Beesley, M.E. (1997) *Privatization, Regulation and Deregulation*, 2nd edn, London: Routledge.

Beesley, M.C. and Littlechild, S.C. (1989) 'The Regulation of Privatized Monopolies in the United Kingdom', *RAND Journal of Economics*, **20**. Reproduced in Beesley, M.E. (1997) *Privatization, Regulation and Deregulation*, 2nd edn, London: Routledge.

Bennett, M. and Waddams Price, C. (2002) 'Incentive Contracts in Utility Regulation', in E. Brousseau and J. Glachant (eds), *The Economics of Contracts: Theories and Applications*, Cambridge: Cambridge University Press.

Competition Commission (2000) *Sutton & East Surrey Water plc: A Report on the References Under Sections 12 and 14 of the Water Industry Act 1991*, London: HMSO.

Competition Commission (2002) *Vodafone, O2, Orange and T-Mobile: Reports on References Under Section 13 of the Telecommunications Act 1984 on the Charges Made by Vodafone, O2, Orange and T-Mobile for Terminating Calls from Fixed and Mobile Networks*, London: HMSO.

Cowan, S. (1997) 'Tight Average Revenue Regulation Can Be Worse than No Regulation', *Journal of Industrial Economics*, **XLV**, 75–88.

Drinking Water Inspectorate (various years) *Drinking Water Report by the Chief Inspector*, London: HMSO.

Forsyth, P. (1999) 'Monopoly Price Regulation in Australia: Assessing Regulation So Far', Paper presented at the 1999 Industry Economics Conference, Melbourne, 12–13 July.

Frontier Economics (2003a) *Developing Network Monopoly Price Controls: Workstream A. Regulatory Mechanisms for Dealing with Uncertainty. A Final Report Prepared for Ofgem*, London: Frontier Economics, March.

Frontier Economics (2003b) *Developing Network Monopoly Price Controls: Workstream B. Balancing Incentives. A Final Report Prepared for Ofgem*, London: Frontier Economics, March.

Helm, D. (1995) 'British Utility Regulation: Theory, Practice and Reform', in D. Helm (ed.), *British Utility Regulation: Principles, Experience and Reform*, Oxford: OXERA Press.

Laffont, J.J. and Tirole, J. (1993) *A Theory of Incentives in Procurement and Regulation*, Cambridge, MA: MIT Press.

Lewis, T. and Sappington, D. (1992) 'Incentives for Conservation and Quality Improvement by Public Utilities', *American Economic Review*, **82**, 1321–40.

Littlechild, S.C. (1983) *Regulation of British Telecom's Profitability*, London: Department of Industry.

Mariñoso, B.G., Hviid, M. and Waddams Price, C. (2002) 'The Quality and Quantity of Regulatory Information', *CCR Working Paper CCR 02-5*, Centre for Competition & Regulation, UEA, Norwich.

Markou, E. and Waddams Price, C. (1999) 'UK Utilities: Past Reform and Current Proposals', *Annals of Public and Co-operative Economics*, **70**, 371–416.

National Audit Office (2002) *Pipes and Wires: Report by the Comptroller and Auditor General*, London: HMSO.

Ofgem (1999) *Review of Public Electricity Suppliers 1998 to 2000: Distribution Price Control – Final Proposals*, London: Ofgem, December.

Ofgem (2000) *Information and Incentives Project: Defining Output Measures and Incentive Regimes for PES Distribution Businesses: Update*, London: Ofgem, March.

Ofgem (2004) *Final Proposal for Electricity Distribution Price Control Review for 2005–2010*, London: Ofgem.

Ofwat (1993) *Paying for Quality: The Political Perspective*, Birmingham: Ofwat, July.

Ofwat (1994) *Future Charges for Water and Sewerage Services: The Outcome of the Periodic Review*, Birmingham: Ofwat, July.

Ofwat (1998a) *A Proposed Approach to Assessing Overall Service to Customers: A Technical Paper*, Birmingham: Ofwat, March.

Ofwat (1998b) *Open Letter from the Director General of Water Services to the Secretary of State for the Environment, Transport and the Regions and the Secretary of State for Wales and accompanying paper: Setting the Quality Framework – An Analysis of the Main Quality Costings Submission 2000–05*, Birmingham: Ofwat, April.

Ofwat (1999a) *Informing the Final Decisions on Raising the Quality 2000-2005: An Open Letter to the Secretary of State for the Environment, Transport and the Regions and the Secretary of State for Wales*, Birmingham: Ofwat, January.

Ofwat (1999b) *Final Determinations: Future Water and Sewerage Charges 2000–05*, Birmingham: Ofwat, November

Ofwat (2004) *Future Water and Sewerage Charges 2005–10, Final Determinations*, Birmingham: Ofwat.

Ofwat (various years) *Report on Company Performance*, Birmingham: Ofwat.

Ofwat (various years) *Report on Financial Performance and Capital Investment of the Water Companies in England and Wales*, Birmingham: Ofwat.

Ofwat (various years) *Report on Levels of Service for the Water Industry in England and Wales*, Birmingham: Ofwat.

Postcomm (2000) *Postal Services Act 2000, Section 11, Amended Licence*, London: Postcomm.

Postcomm (2005) *2006 Royal Mail Price and Service Quality Review, Initial Proposals*, London: Postcomm.

Rovizzi, L. and Thompson, D. (1995) 'The Regulation of Product Quality in the Public Utilities', in M. Bishop, J. Kay and C. Mayer (eds), *The Regulatory Challenge*, Oxford: Oxford University Press.

Sappington, D.E.M. (2005) 'Regulating Service Quality: A Survey', *Journal of Regulatory Economics*, **27** (2), 123–54.

SRA (2005) *National Rail Trends Year Book 2004–05*, London: Strategic Rail Authority.

Statutory Instrument 1989 No. 1159 *The Water Supply and Sewerage Services (Customer Service Standards) Regulations 1989*, London: HMSO.

Statutory Instrument 1993 No. 500 *The Water Supply and Sewerage Services (Customer Service Standards) (Amendment) Regulations 1993* and Statutory Instrument 2000 No. 2301, *The Water Supply and Sewerage Services (Customer Service Standards) (Amendment) Regulation 2000*, London: HMSO.

Waddams Price, C. (1997) 'Regulating for Fairness', *New Economy*, **4**, 117–22.

Waddams Price, C. (2000a) 'Efficiency and Productivity Studies in Incentive Regulation of UK Utilities', *Revista de Economia del Rosario*, **3**, 11–24.

Waddams Price, C. (2000b) 'Gas: Regulatory Response to Social Needs', in C. Robinson (ed.), *Regulating Utilities: New Issues, New Solutions*, Institute of Economic Affairs in association with the London Business School, Cheltenham, UK and Northampton, MA, USA: Edward Elgar.

Waddams Price, C. (2003) 'Yardstick Competition and Comparative Performance Measures in Practice', in L. Hunt (ed.), *Book in Honour of Colin Robinson*, London: Routledge.

Waddams Price, C., Brigham, B. and Fitzgerald, L. (2002) 'Service Quality in Regulated Monopolies', *CCR Working Paper CCR 02-4*, Centre for Competition & Regulation, UEA, Norwich.

Waddams Price, C. and Hancock, R. (1997) 'UK Privatization: Effects on Households', in G. Palma and M. Sawyer (eds), *Frontiers of Political Economy, Volume 7*, London: Routledge.

5 Utility regulation and competition in developing countries

Paul Cook

Introduction

Defined as the transfer of productive assets from public to private ownership and control, privatization has continued to grow, particularly in developing and transitional economies. A significant proportion of privatization transactions in the developing economies have entailed sales of public utilities. This chapter will concentrate on regulation and competition in developing countries though many of the arguments apply equally to the transition economies of Central and Eastern Europe and to some developed economies.

In general, private participation in economic infrastructure in developing countries has been concentrated in the telecommunications and the electricity sectors. According to the World Bank (2003), between 1990 and 2001 privatization accounted for 41 per cent of total private participation in infrastructure projects in developing countries. The percentage share for cumulative investment in infrastructure with private participation over the same period was 44 per cent for telecommunications and 28 per cent for electricity. The water, gas and transport sectors accounted for a smaller share (World Bank, 2003).

Privatization was central to the expenditure reducing and resource switching policies of structural adjustment introduced by the World Bank and the IMF in the early 1980s and pursued vigorously up to the mid-1990s (Cook, 1988; Cook and Kirkpatrick, 1995). The reduction in government expenditure achieved through privatization was viewed as a policy that would improve productive efficiency in the public and private sectors. Liberalization that accompanied privatization was meant to ensure that relative price signals worked and would promote welfare-enhancing resource allocation (Cook, 1997). In practice, policy-makers had often set a broader agenda for privatization than the efficiency and resource allocation objectives that had been implicit in adjustment programmes. The motives for privatization had encompassed improved fiscal, equity and distributional performance (UNCTAD, 1996). The importance attached to each varied between and within countries over time, and the contribution of privatization to one objective may have made it difficult to achieve others.

However, privatization did not necessarily mean more competition. As a consequence, the regulation of monopoly utilities became a major policy issue.

New regulatory structures and institutions were required to protect consumers from monopoly abuse and to provide incentives to management and investor interests to maintain profitability, efficiency and investment. Regulation for utilities did not necessarily emerge in a systematic way. In part, particularly in Europe, it resulted from the game being played out in the pre-privatization period between the management of public enterprises and the government. When governments signalled their intention to privatize in a given period, the shaping of the post-privatization environment involved a dynamic game between government, new owners of utilities and the various interested parties such as consumer and producer groups. In Europe, for example, when governments had announced privatization, they did not initially appoint a regulator until public enterprises had agreed to a form of regulatory regime. In these circumstances public enterprise management had been able to exert pressure on government to extract relatively lenient regulatory environments. In the UK the regulatory environment has evolved from the privatization programme, with each experience contributing to the development of subsequent systems of utility regulation. The gas industry, privatized in 1986, preceded a parliamentary election and proceeds had been required to fund a budgetary deficit. This resulted in the natural gas industry being able to secure a regulatory system that was under-resourced. The system of regulation that emerged was lenient and was unable to permit effective competition, at least until a decade had elapsed.

In contrast, privatization has often been used in some countries as a shock to the economic system, and this has resulted either in severe regulatory systems being imposed or at the other extreme, no system at all. This was the case that emerged in many of the transitional economies in the post-communist era (Nellis, 2000).

This chapter discusses aspects of regulation and competition in relation to the utility sector in developing countries. The chapter is divided into four sections. Following the introduction, the second section focuses on the critical issues relating to regulation and competition in the formerly public sector natural monopolies such as telecommunications, electricity, gas and transport. The third section discusses the issues involved in introducing a greater degree of competition. The final section draws conclusions.

Privatization, regulation and competition

The nature of the national regulatory framework that has developed for privatized utilities in developing countries has been influenced by a country's capacity to implement a system of regulation and by the type of markets within which enterprises have functioned. The processes of regulation that have developed have differed widely in both form and scope. Some regulatory systems have established price caps that have aimed to limit the price that can be charged for a particular service. This form of regulation is intended to provide incentives to reduce costs because savings can be achieved that are used to increase profitability for the owners of the utilities. Other forms of regulation have commonly consisted of profit regulation, which imposes ceilings on the permitted rate of return, or cost of service regulation, which approves profit mark-ups on an agreed cost of providing a service (Martin and Parker, 1997).

A recent study reveals that some form of the price-cap system of regulation has been widely adopted in developing countries, despite having a number of disadvantages given the context in which it is being applied (Kirkpatrick et al., 2004). Under price-cap regulation a price ceiling is established and the profitability of the enterprise then depends on the extent to which it is able to keep its costs below the determined maximum revenue under the cap. Cost pass-through may also be permitted for any increase in the costs of production that are outside the control of the regulated enterprise. It has been observed that this may present problems in many developing countries, where inflation rates tend to be high and fluctuate more than in developed economies (Kirkpatrick et al., 2004). In some industries, such as the energy sector, where oil is an important input to electricity generation, then costs are sensitive to changes in the world price of oil, and electricity cost may have an effect on the domestic level of inflation. In this case the formula for incentive regulation under a price cap becomes more complex and may end up providing distorted signals to the market incumbent. Also, as part of creating conditions for surrogate competition, the establishment of a price cap is often based on a reference to the most efficient performance. The idea behind this is to reduce the reliance on an enterprise's own costs and revenues, in order to build in incentives to reduce costs (for a fuller discussion see Chapter 6). This may be difficult to apply in developing countries which have newly established regulatory agencies because they usually lack data on efficiency and have weak enforcement systems to collect such data.

Similarly, there have been difficulties in the institutional arrangements for regulation across developing countries. It has been quite common to establish a dedicated regulatory authority for each of the main utility sectors, following the UK pattern. In other cases, regulation of all utilities has fallen under the umbrella of a single institution. Some have attained a high degree of autonomy, while others have been tightly controlled by government authorities. The scope for regulation has also varied. In some cases, such as the telecommunications sector, regulation has generally been comprehensive and has consisted of controls on market entry, rules for permissible pricing and business earnings, monitoring equality, and oversight of investment programmes (Sappington, 1994). Alternatively, regulation has been more partial, affecting only some of the activities of an enterprise or sector.

Issues of capacity and the institutions that can be developed for regulation, and the methods they will use, have been viewed as critical factors that affect the performance of a regulatory system (Kirkpatrick and Parker, 2004). Both the methods and the design of regulatory policy are largely derived from theories developed in an industrialized country context and their transfer to developing countries, with different institutional structures and legal systems, critically affects practice (Minogue, 2002; Ogus, 2004). Further, actual implementation and design of regulation is not necessarily in line with theory. This is a feature of regulation that applies in developed countries too but is particularly likely to be found in developing economies (Crew and Kleindorfer, 1996). Indeed, as Parker (2002) points out, even where developing country governments purport to have particular methods of regulation, such as a price cap, in practice implementation may produce various hybrids.

Besides the evident weaknesses in the institutional environment for regulation, there is both the problem of what approach to competition sector regulators ought to adopt for the various utility industries, and how this might conflict or be complemented by whatever competition law or policy that exists. In most developing countries, as also in a wide range of developed economies, the introduction of competition law is a relatively recent event. Only a handful of developing countries had what would constitute an effective competition framework, backed up by competition law, in the late 1980s (Gray and Davis, 1993). More recently, however, most developing countries have introduced or are in the process of preparing new competition legislation (UNCTAD, 2004).

The privatization of utilities in developing countries, in such sectors as water, energy and telecommunications, has meant that competition is usually limited, since these industries include natural monopoly elements arising from economies of scale and scope. Even though technological change has eroded some of the natural monopoly characteristics in these utilities, particularly in the telecommunications sector, and has permitted a greater degree of competition in various areas of service delivery, developing countries still have high levels of concentration in these fields. As well as the risk that monopolies will be established following privatization, there is the additional risk that incumbent monopolies will exploit their monopoly power by seeking excessive profits that can harm consumers. The risk is particularly high in the context of developing countries because, irrespective of the economic rationale for a limited number of participants in the market, privatization as a monopoly may be integrally related to political motives and the expediency of attracting scarce buyers. Yarrow (1999) has pointed to the strong fiscal motivation to privatize, with many developing countries requiring revenue to supplement that raised through weak and highly skewed fiscal systems. In other words the fiscal benefits from changing management and ownership through privatization may override consideration of the efficiency gains that could potentially be made by introducing greater competition (Shirley and Walsh, 2000).

Given the various motives for privatization and the newness of competition policy in most developing countries (and the absence of it in a few prominent countries that have undertaken widespread privatization), regulation in a large number of cases becomes a surrogate for competition. As such, the performance of regulatory bodies is critical for both economic efficiency and consumer protection.

The aim of surrogate competition is to police the revenues and costs of production, while providing the incentive framework that is absent when the environment is not competitive. However, the role of regulation in relation to the utilities is broader than this since there is also the environment to be considered, which compares the monopolistic situation prior to privatization, with utilities under government ownership, and the post-privatized situation, with a privately-owned regulated monopoly (Kirkpatrick and Parker, 2004). This is especially relevant since managerial slack, often observed in state-owned monopolies, has to be balanced against the possibility of private monopolists pursuing a quiet life and exploiting opportunities for cost padding, given the information asymmetry associated with private ownership coupled with state regulation.

Indeed, one argument in favour of privatization in relation to regulation, and therefore of surrogate competition, is that it forces a government to be more explicit about objectives and to be more transparent about the costs involved in meeting these objectives (Armstrong, 2003). How seriously this is taken can be seen in the regulator's terms of reference and powers. In a country with strong legal traditions and institutions, contracts and licences can be used to limit opportunistic behaviour or what is sometimes termed a lack of regulatory 'commitment' by governments. However, in developing countries, as already observed, these institutions may be weak and contract enforcement poor. Moreover, not all aspects of an enterprise's performance and the government's behaviour can be written into various forms of licences, and therefore, these incomplete contracts become crucial for determining the outcome and effectiveness of privatization and regulation (Newbery, 2000). In developing countries a private utility monopolist will be in a position to manipulate the quality and extent of its service if these considerations cannot easily be embodied in a form of contract or if the regulator's contract places too much emphasis on cost reductions. Similarly, regulatory contracts may be difficult to prescribe when a government may have raised prices prior to privatization, to ensure that future investors would have high enough returns on their intended investment, and be faced with the prospect of pruning them after under public pressure. Nevertheless, despite the contractual complexities, a large number of developing countries have introduced new, dedicated regulatory bodies for both their state-owned and their privatized utilities. In general, these new regulatory offices have attempted to have a degree of independence, at least from day-to-day political control. In practice this has been difficult to achieve (Cook, 1999).

How effective surrogate competition through regulation is depends critically on the effectiveness of the regulatory agency. Regulation itself may result in regulatory inefficiency and regulatory failure (Bradburd and Ross, 1991). Regulatory inefficiency can be defined in terms of the market inefficiency that regulation was supposed to remove. Regulation aims to remove the tendency for a monopolist utility to produce at output levels where prices are set above marginal costs and bring prices in line with costs leading to allocative efficiency. If regulation leads to efficient costs of production then productive efficiency is also achieved. Regulatory inefficiency represents a departure from this optimal economic outcome. Another way of looking at regulatory inefficiency is to consider the optimal level of regulation that should be imposed. In principle, this optimum will be where the marginal costs of the remaining market inefficiency are equal to the marginal social costs that would be imposed by the imposition of regulation to overcome that market inefficiency. In this sense regulation can be economically inefficient because it is at the wrong level, there is too little or too much of it, or it is not operating in a cost effective manner. Extensive regulatory inefficiency can be viewed as regulatory failure. This occurs when regulation simply makes the situation worse than it would have been in the absence of regulation. This outcome cannot be ruled out in developing countries where regulatory capacity is very low and the threat of 'regulatory capture' high.

Regulatory capture occurs where the regulators adopt the objectives of special interests, including the regulated utilities, as their own (Peltzman, 1976). This can occur at the beginning of regulation where utility interests influence the design of the regulation and may be referred to as 'top level' or 'political' capture. Lower level capture results from regulations that were established at the outset truly to promote the public interest but which become skewed in favour of special interests over time. The regulations become detrimental to other interests, notably consumers. Regulatory capture is likely to be a particular problem in developing countries because utilities wield considerable political power, and a lack of expert skills within government may mean that staffing in regulatory agencies has to be largely drawn from the industry that is being regulated.

Regulatory capture may be an extreme situation and regulation may simply not be operating as originally conceived. Utilities may be attempting to circumvent regulation through their control of information. Information asymmetries that exist between regulators and the regulated are central to the regulation problem. Regulatory inefficiency and effectiveness may also be closely linked to the degree to which regulators are able to learn by doing. Initially, regulators may know little about the regulatory environment they occupy. New institutions may have been created, with the regulatory rules embodied via legislation in the regulatory contract. The specification of the contract might be a key determinant of the efficiency with which learning can take place (Parker, 1999). Regulatory contracts that permit a reasonable degree of discretion but avoid uncertainty over regulatory decisions are more likely to increase the scope for learning. Clearly, where learning opportunities can be taken, then regulatory efficiency and effectiveness will improve over time.

While it is possible that regulation becomes more efficient over time as learning takes place, it is also likely that the risk of lower level regulatory capture increases. The scope for learning will be strongly influenced by the type of regulatory contract, the degree of discretionary powers given to the regulator and the level of funding for regulatory activities. As regulatory efficiency increases information asymmetries are reduced, with the consequence that utilities cannot so easily pad or over-inflate their costs at each price or profit review in order to influence the setting of prices in their favour. But at this point the incentive to capture regulation is at its greatest. It is also at this point that the regulator has a greater need to adopt pro-competitive regulation, to counteract the tendency for capture and information distortion by the regulated industry.

Failing to learn from past experiences is not the only reason why regulatory institutions may not work effectively. Others include the failure of regulatory institutions to adapt to changing external conditions, the tendency for regulation to escalate over time in response to fire-fighting and the pursuit of self-interest by regulators, which may result in self-preservation and the avoidance of monitoring mechanisms that have been established by government. All these difficulties are likely to be present in developing countries (as elsewhere).

Competition in utilities

Judging the appropriate degree of competition is difficult for a sector regulator in a developing country. If the government privatizes a former state monopoly enterprise but permits a limited degree of competition, there remains the question of how much discretion is to be used actively to promote rivalry. Some degree of competition is likely to yield benefits because, although in principle a monopoly can be regulated in ways that approximate the constraints imposed by effective competition, competition remains superior for several reasons. First, the regulator faces considerable information asymmetries in the absence of competition. The regulator is dependent, to a large extent, on information obtained from the monopoly enterprise being regulated. Second, competition may be able to achieve an efficient outcome more quickly than regulation, which experience tells us often entails a lengthy trial and error process with the ever present threat of capture, as already discussed.

Several factors, however, impede the development of competition in developing countries. The argument for economies of scale may simply be more pervasive in lower income and small market economies. Taxation systems are generally less efficient than those found in developed economies and this affects regulation, according to Armstrong (2003), in at least two ways. First, the government may place a greater weight on revenue collection from privatization than on the social benefits that accrue from greater competition. Second, with an inefficient taxation system, the pricing of essential services, such as water, may play an important role in the policy for income redistribution. Hence, any rebalancing of tariffs to more closely reflect changes in underlying costs is less likely to be favoured. The development of competition may also impose an additional burden on regulators and add to the complexity of regulation. Armstrong (2003) points out that rebalancing of tariffs may need to be a prerequisite for enhanced competition since the conditions relating to the operation of an existing service may preclude new entrants to the market. For example, a fixed line telephone service that in some localities is subsidized may not meet competition from other operators who would face a price disadvantage.

Beato and Laffont (2002) also reinforce the importance of the marginal cost of public funds argument and the ability to audit costs as elements in determining the viability of sector-regulated competition policy, or indeed, of competition policy as a whole. The marginal cost of public funds is defined as the social cost of raising a unit of funds, and is estimated to be high in developing countries owing to the inefficiency of the tax system and weak capital markets. Despite efforts to reform their taxation and auditing systems, in developing countries the cost of public funds is likely to remain high for some time. As a consequence, many of the important problems relating to the resourcing of regulation and competition agencies stem from the difficulties in obtaining funds, and on the supply side in attracting needed foreign investment.

Beato and Laffont (2002) review the options available with respect to competition policy and utilities. First, there may be general reliance on competition law on an industry-wide basis, such as employed in New Zealand. In this respect regulation of a particular sector is akin to or embodies an element of self-regulation. Of course, it is recognized that reliance on competition law requires a well developed enforcement and detection mechanism, particularly where sector regulation is considered to be tightly reined or passive.

Second, integrated competition and sector regulatory agencies have been considered in some countries and it is argued that they are particularly attractive to developing countries facing severe regulatory capacity constraints. According to Beato and Laffont (2002) the argument appears to be stronger for combining regulatory functions across different utilities rather than for combining regulatory and general competition policies. The roles of sector regulators and competition agencies may conflict where social objectives are embodied. Competition policy may favour more competition and the promotion of smaller enterprises, as in the case of South Africa, while utility regulators may restrict the number of competitors, at least in the immediate period following privatization.

Third is the case discussed earlier, where a dedicated form of economic regulation also acts as a surrogate for competition, and determines at some point in time when the competitiveness of the market is increased. Inevitably, such an approach ought to entail coordination with whatever competition regime exists or is established.

Of course, the approach to competition in relation to utilities will be influenced by the industrial structure that emerges or is allowed to emerge from privatization. Three types have occurred, namely vertical disintegration ('unbundling'), vertical integration and competition. Beato and Laffont (2002) argue that the high cost of public funds makes it more expensive to duplicate fixed costs. Vertical disintegration may also be an unwise policy choice, as it may slow down the eventual emergence of competition if the enterprise that controls the natural monopoly facility, such as a local loop in the telecommunications sector, uses it as an input to compete in providing services. It may also be the case that competition law is not able to deal with the complex issues relating to utilities with varying market structures. This may be particularly the case when the type of competition policy recommended for developing countries is based on a structural rather than a behavioural approach due to a lack of regulatory skills and the need for simple competition rules in a country (Cook, 2002, 2005). It can be argued that a structural approach, because it relies on mechanistically applied rules and draws heavily on the application of rigidly based measures of market concentration to assess the degree of competitiveness in markets, may overly encourage industry restructuring and a too cautious approach to mergers. In contrast, a behavioural approach is considered to be more resource intensive, as it requires an assessment of how enterprises are acting uncompetitively and with what consequences. There may also be a tendency for regulatory agencies to persist with monopolies in order to attract foreign investment in sectors where there are large sunk costs and a scarcity of capital and technology. Competition agencies may view things differently and argue that in situations that require large sunk costs, it is all the more important to create the conditions for new entrants by improving the 'competitive infrastructure', in the form of institutions and legal frameworks (Carlin and Seabright, 2000).

Whatever the institutional arrangements for competition, there are significant issues that need to be tackled regarding the effects of monopoly abuse and harmful collusive behaviour that occur in markets with limited competition. Also the experience of Latin America has shown there is a need to develop stronger merger and acquisition rules, following bouts of privatization associated with significantly increased levels of foreign capital (Amman and DePaula, 2004).

Conclusions

The relationship between regulation and competition policy is complex. In many developing economies economic regulation only developed after privatization and without the framework provided by a more general competition policy. Interest in the two is now developing side by side in developing countries and this is bringing to the forefront of the policy debate the potential conflicts that can exist between them.

Governments in developing countries continue to face pressures to widen access to basic services through pricing policies and expansionary investment that may result in some regulators favouring incumbents over new market entrants. Alternatively, favouring new entrants may mean that less efficient entrants are encouraged. Similarly, poorly thought-out entry promotion policies to stimulate competition might provide the wrong market signals and weaken the incentive for market incumbents to invest in and expand utility networks and services.

Despite the growth in utility sector regulatory agencies and the spread of competition authorities, the availability of skilled resources for these institutions remains low in many developing countries. This is compounded by the need to improve access to information as a major ingredient for assessing competitive conditions. Data continue to be lacking to assess market conditions and claims of market dominance and strategic behaviour by enterprises. Given the lack of information and legal and institutional weaknesses in low-income countries, private monopolies are more likely to exploit their position by influencing or evading regulation. Weak regulation of competition is then likely to undermine the benefits expected of both privatization and deregulation in utility sectors.

References

Amman, E. and De Paula, G. (2004) 'Ownership Structure in the Post-privatised Brazilian Steel Industry: Complexity, Instability and the Lingering Role of the State', Centre on Regulation and Competition, Working Paper No. 75, University of Manchester.

Armstrong, M. (2003) 'Privatisation, Regulation and Competition', paper prepared for the conference Competition and Development, Competition Commission and the Competition Tribunal, Cape Town, March.

Beato, P. and Laffont, J. (2002) 'Competition in Public Utilities in Developing Countries', Sustainable Developing Department Technical Papers Series, Inter-American Development Bank, Washington, DC.

Bradburd, R. and Ross, D. (1991) 'Regulation and Deregulation in Industrial Countries: Some Lessons for LDCs', Policy, Research and External Affairs Working Paper No. 699, World Bank, Washington, DC.

Carlin, W. and Seabright, P. (2001) 'The Importance of Competition in Developing Countries for Productivity and Innovation', background paper for *World Development Report*.

Cook, P. (1988) 'Recent Trends in Multilateral Development Bank Lending to the Private Sector in LDCs: Policy and Practice', *Development Policy Review*, **6** (2), 165–82.

Cook, P. (1997) 'Privatisation, Public Enterprise Reform and the World Bank: Has "Bureaucrats in Business" Got it Right?', *Journal of International Development*, **9** (16), 887–97.

Cook, P. (1999) 'Privatisation and Utility Regulation in Developing Countries: The Lessons So Far', *Annals of Public and Cooperative Economics*, **70** (4), 549–87.

Cook, P. (2002) 'Competition and its Regulation: Key Issues', *Annals of Public and Cooperative Economics*, **73** (4), 541–58.

Cook, P. (2005) 'Competition Policy, Market Power and Collusion in Developing Countries', in P. Cook, C. Kirkpatrick, M. Minogue and D. Parker (eds), *Leading Issues in Competition, Regulation and Development*, Cheltenham, UK and Northampton, MA, USA: Edward Elgar.

Cook, P. and Kirkpatrick, C. (1995) *Privatisation Policy and Performance: International Perspectives*, Hemel Hempstead: Prentice Hall.

Crew, M. and Kleindorfer, P. (1996) 'Incentive Regulation in the United Kingdom and the United States: Some Lessons', *Journal of Regulatory Economics*, **9**, 211–25.

Gray, C. and Davis, A. (1993) 'Competition Policy in Developing Countries Pursuing Structural Adjustment', *The Antitrust Bulletin*, Summer, 425–67.

Kirkpatrick, C. and Parker, D. (2004) 'Infrastructure Regulation: Models for Developing Asia', ADB Institute Research Paper 60, Asian Development Bank Institute, Tokyo.

Kirkpatrick, C., Parker, D. and Zhang, Y. (2004) 'Price and Profit Regulation in Developing and Transition Economies, Methods Used and Problems Faced: A Survey of the Regulators', Centre on Regulation and Competition, Working Paper No. 88, University of Manchester.

Martin, S. and Parker, D. (1997) *The Impact of Privatisation, Ownership and Corporate Performance in the UK*, London: Routledge.

Minogue (2002) 'Public Management and Regulatory Governance: Problems of Policy Transfer to Developing Countries', Centre on Regulation and Competition, Working Paper No. 32, University of Manchester.

Nellis, J. (2000) 'Privatisation in Transition Economies: What Happened? What's Next?', World Bank, Washington, DC, mimeo.

Newbery, D. (2000) *Privatisation, Restructuring, and Regulation of Network Utilities*, Cambridge, MA: MIT Press.

Ogus, A. (2004) 'The Importance of Legal Infrastructure for Regulation (and Deregulation) in Developing Countries', Centre on Regulation and Competition, Working Paper No. 65, University of Manchester.

Parker, D. (1999) 'Price Cap Regulation, Profitability and Returns to Investors in the UK Regulated Industries', *Utilities Policy*, **6** (4), 303–15.

Parker, D. (2002) 'Economic Regulation: A Review of Issues', *Annals of Public and Cooperative Economics*, **73** (4), 493–519.

Peltzman, S. (1976) 'Towards a More General Theory of Regulation', *Journal of Law and Economics*, **19**: 211–40.

Sappington, D. (1994) 'Principles of Regulatory Policy Design', Policy Research Working Paper No. 1239, World Bank, Washington, DC.

Shirley, M. and Walsh, P. (2000) 'Public versus Private Ownership: The Current State of the Debate', World Bank, Washington, DC, mimeo.

UNCTAD (1996) 'Comparative Experiences with Privatisation: Policy Insights and Lessons Learned', United Nations, New York.

UNCTAD (2004) 'Competitiveness and Development: Lessons from Developing Countries', United Nations, Geneva.

World Bank (2003) 'Private Participation in Infrastructure: Trends in Developing Countries, 1990–2001', World Bank, Washington, DC.

Yarrow, G. (1999) 'Theory of Privatisation, or why Bureaucrats are still in Business', *World Development*, **27** (1), 157–68.

6 Performance benchmarking in utility regulation: principles and the UK's experience

David Parker, Thoralf Dassler and David S. Saal

Introduction[1]

In the UK, the privatization of utility industries has led to the development of regulatory regimes to prevent monopoly abuse. There are two main methods of economic regulation, namely cost of service, alternatively known as rate of return regulation, and price-cap regulation. In very broad terms, whereas cost of service regulation sets prices based on operating expenditure (OPEX) and capital expenditure (CAPEX) figures with an allowance for a normal profit, price-cap regulation places a ceiling on prices or revenues. As is now recognized, price-cap regulation provides incentives for management to economize on OPEX and CAPEX. As a result, all privatized utilities in the UK have been subject to price-cap regulation.

An approach to determining the revenue required to meet efficient costs would be to base future revenue on the costs achieved by the firm in previous years, adjusted for any known exceptional items or expected cost changes. The problem with this approach, which is essentially identical to the method adopted under cost of service regulation, is that incentives for cost efficiency are reduced. Where management expects that cost increases can be passed through to consumers, there is little incentive to reduce them. Moreover, if future OPEX and CAPEX funding is based on the firm's forecasts of its own costs, there will be an incentive for management to pad these costs.

The objective of incentive based utility regulation is, therefore, to establish an incentive compatible set of cost comparisons that can be used to determine an *efficient* firm's revenue needs. Benchmarking or 'yardstick competition' as it is sometimes described involves comparing the performance of a regulated firm with some comparator. In a seminal paper, Shleifer argued that a regulated firm's revenue needs should be assessed by looking at costs in comparable firms or industries (Shleifer, 1985). Benchmarking costs reduces the effects of the company's own costs on prices; in extremis, if a firm's costs have no effect on its own revenues, the incentives for management to reduce costs will be maximized. This chapter therefore considers the arguments for yardstick competition and highlight difficulties in achieving efficient and effective benchmarking, focusing on the UK's experience of implementing price-cap regimes in

117

telecommunications, gas, electricity, and water and sewerage.[2] The chapter begins by reviewing the case for benchmarking.

The case for benchmarking

Benchmarking or yardstick competition (we use the terms interchangeably[3]) can provide regulators with information about efficient OPEX and CAPEX requirements, thereby reducing the regulated firm's informational rents. Benchmarking is now used extensively: for example in Costa Rica for transport tariff setting, in telecommunications regulation in Hungary (Rossi and Ruzzier, 2000, p. 82), in Dutch electricity and telecommunications (DTe, 1999), and for electricity regulation in Norway and New South Wales, Australia. It is also a component of some price-cap setting in the UK.

The price-cap regime for privatized utilities was first developed in the UK in the early to mid-1980s. Under RPI-X price cap regulation, a factor, X, is introduced, which effectively increases or reduces real prices relative to the retail price index (RPI) over the price-cap period (often five years). However, in Littlechild's 1983 proposals to the government for the regulation of British Telecom, which was the first privatized utility in the UK, there was almost no reference to how price caps should be set.[4] At privatization, BT's initial X factor was set behind closed doors in discussion between the government, its bankers and City investors, so as to ensure a successful share flotation. Littlechild stated in his proposals that 'X is a number to be negotiated' (Littlechild, 1983, para. 13.17) and he appears to have expected competition to develop quickly in telecoms. Therefore, Littlechild (1983) provides virtually no guidance as to how price caps should be reset after the completion of a regulatory period. However given that effective competition did not quickly develop in telecoms, and the privatization of other network industries with varying degrees of monopoly power necessitated the development of more permanent price-cap regimes, the attention of regulators quickly turned to the process of setting appropriate price caps for the industries (Saal, 2003).

Arguably, regulatory regimes should set out to mimic the discipline imposed by a competitive market. In a highly competitive market, prices are external to the costs of any individual firm and the prices facing any firm in the industry change at the same rate as the growth in the industry's, not the firm's, unit costs. Broadly, there are two approaches to setting a price cap. The first is 'bottom up', under which the regulator starts by taking the firm's forecast operating expenditures, asset base, depreciation rate and capital expenditures, and computes the necessary revenue requirement taking into account demand changes. The alternative is a 'top down' approach, where a revenue ceiling is imposed (based on forecasts of the firm's costs – as similar to the bottom up approach – or through some form of benchmarking performance) and both OPEX and CAPEX requirements are managed within this cap. A pure price-cap regime approximates the latter. In the UK the price-cap regime is not pure and is based on a combination of both 'bottom up' and 'top down' approaches. The process generally involves a truncated future cash flow model including estimates of OPEX and CAPEX over the life time of the price cap (Vass, 1999) and an expected rate of return set by reference to the estimated cost to the firm of raising capital.[5]

Achieving reasonably correct cost estimates is demanding in terms of the information that the regulator requires. In particular, the regulator needs information about the firm's *efficient* levels of OPEX and CAPEX, but regulated firms will have an incentive not to search out these costs given that cost minimization requires management effort. In 1985 Shleifer set out to tackle the inherent information asymmetry in economic regulation by arguing that the firm's revenue requirement to cover its OPEX and CAPEX should not be based on its own costs. Instead it should be based on benchmarked costs or a *relative* efficiency measurement. As he comments at the outset of his paper, the objective should be to find 'some relatively simple benchmark, other than the firm's present or past performance, against which to evaluate the firm's potential' (Shleifer, 1985, p. 319). Shleifer's solution was to identify 'comparable firms to infer a firm's attainable cost level' (p. 312). Provided that the regulator has two or more firms under its jurisdiction, then yardstick competition can overcome information asymmetry. Each regulated firm, i, is assigned a 'shadow firm'. The shadow firm becomes the benchmark for setting the revenue requirement. The efficient outcome for each firm is to select cost, $c_i = c^*$, where c^* is the cost consistent with the minimum feasible cost for any given output. As long as the information provided by the benchmarking exercise leads the regulator to impose c^*, the regulated firm sets price (P) according to efficient costs:

$$P_i = c_i = c^*.$$

This is best achieved when 'a firm's choice of c_i has no effect on the price it gets' (Shleifer, 1985, p. 322).

Shleifer recognized, however, that certain requirements were necessary for this approach to regulation to work satisfactorily. In particular, he was at pains to emphasize (1985, p. 323):

> It is essential for the regulator to commit to not paying attention to firms' complaints and to be prepared to let the firms go bankrupt if they choose inefficient cost levels. Unless the regulator can credibly threaten to make inefficient firms lose money ... cost reduction cannot be enforced.[6]

Shleifer was also aware that this form of yardstick competition required a 'shadow firm' comparable in terms of its cost structure. If the firms scrutinized for benchmarking purposes by the regulator were heterogeneous in terms of efficient cost structures, the result would be unreliable. The result would also be unreliable if the firms faced different demand functions, although for simplicity Shleifer assumes a common demand function for much of his analysis. To overcome the lack of a perfect 'shadow firm', Shleifer recognized that multivariate regression models would need to be developed to reflect characteristics that could account for cost differences between firms that are not within the control of management (e.g. topography, customer density, regional wage costs, etc.).

Shleifer was aware that the use of multivariate regression as the basis for yardstick competition is demanding in terms of modelling. If some significant environmental or 'exogenous' variables are omitted from the model, and these impact on any particular firm's costs differently from the way they impact on the costs of other firms, the outcome will not be optimal due to omitted variable bias. It is also difficult for the regulator to know what variables are truly exogenous to the firm and which are at least partially under its control. However, Shleifer also notes that applying more and more detailed models can lead to additional complexity that outweighs any useful economic gain, thereby anticipating the potential for OPEX and CAPEX modelling to employ more and more regulatory resources for less and less marginal benefit. Thus he warns against the marginal cost of the exercise overwhelming its marginal benefit in terms of more accurate price setting. Finally, Shleifer makes reference to the dangers of 'collusive manipulation' of yardstick competition by participating firms (1985, p. 327). Yardstick competition requires managerial independence across the firms used as comparators; otherwise the results will be biased.[7] Shleifer's (1985) paper has made an important contribution to the economics of regulation literature. Today yardstick competition is widely used by regulators internationally and has led to various methods of modelling relative efficiency. The four main approaches to comparative performance measurement are as follows:

1. *Productivity indices*, and particularly nonparametric index approaches to productivity measurement such as labour productivity and total factor productivity (TFP) indicators based on, for example, Törnqvist indices.[8]
2. *Stochastic analysis of production and cost functions*,[9] such as translog cost functions, which are a second order approximation to any arbitrary functional form. The standard OLS (ordinary least squares) econometric method assumes that the residual term is normally distributed around zero. An alternative is to use COLS (corrected ordinary least squares) where the regression equation is estimated using OLS and then, for cost functions, shifted to the efficient frontier by adjusting the constant term by subtracting the value of the largest positive residual. As a result, the function passes through the most efficient firm and bounds the other firms. An extension where there are multiple inputs and outputs is to estimate distance functions (Shephard, 1970).[10] More recently, regulators have been experimenting with

stochastic frontier analysis (SFA). This is based on the assumption that part of the error term results from inefficiency.[11] Stochastic methods allow for diagnostic tests that are lacking in mathematical methods (discussed next) and therefore allow an analysis of the probability that the results are inaccurate.[12] However, a problem with stochastic approaches is that a functional structure is imposed on both the data and the error term.

3. *Mathematical modelling*, especially the use of DEA (data envelopment analysis). Bogetoft (1994, 1997) has demonstrated that yardstick competition based on DEA may be optimal in regulatory environments with technological uncertainty.[13] But being non-stochastic, arguably DEA is less satisfactory for dealing with the uncertainties that surround the data that enter into benchmarking exercises.[14] Also, unlike in econometric analysis standard statistical tests cannot be readily applied to test for the significance of the variables included in the model. Norway has experimented with the use of DEA (Weyman-Jones, 2003), as has the Netherlands electricity regulator (DTe, 2000). But in New South Wales the regulator, IPART, switched from using DEA to a more basic engineering-based approach to benchmarking because of concerns about the reliability of DEA results. In the Dutch electricity sector, DEA was later abandoned.

4. *Engineering models*. An alternative approach is to calculate theoretical production functions based on engineering data. Farrell (1957) argued against theoretical functions in favour of empirical efficient frontiers based on best-observed practice because of the difficulty of estimating theoretical frontiers accurately: 'the theoretical function is likely to be wildly optimistic' (1957, p. 255). Nevertheless, some utility regulators in Latin America rely on theoretical functions (Fischer and Serra, 2000).[15] Although not widely used in the UK, engineering analysis has entered into the regulatory process through commissioned work on issues such as telecoms interconnection, network reliability and serviceability, and efficient capital project costs, for instance in the water industry. Process analysis, under which consultants compare how firms do common tasks, including how many staff they use, has some similarities to this approach to performance measurement, though it may not involve the use of sophisticated engineering models.

In practice, these different performance measures can be used on their own, but can also be used as part of a more complex process for setting prices and profits based on a range of yardsticks. Bauer et al. (1998) have proposed a set of consistency conditions when different measures are adopted by regulators, if they are to be relied on, namely that the different methods used should provide consistent efficiency levels and rankings and identification of best and worst performers, and also be consistent in their results over time. Coelli and Perelman

(1999) have suggested combining the results from alternative modelling exercises by using the geometric means of the performance scores for each data point in order to reduce potential bias. However, regardless of the precise process adopted, the modelling of efficient costs is unlikely to produce an outcome that completely replaces 'negotiation' in price-cap setting.[16] Indeed, as the UK's experience demonstrates, yardstick measures are best seen as a tool for regulators to boost their negotiating position *vis-à-vis* regulated companies.

Figure 6.1 illustrates benchmarking methods by focusing on OPEX as an example and assuming, for simplicity, a linear frontier. OLS regression analysis establishes an estimated average relationship between OPEX and output in the industry. Subsequently, this average cost function is shifted down (to B) using COLS techniques, which effectively assume that the firm with the largest negative OLS residual is on the efficient frontier.[17] The inefficiency of all firms not on the frontier is then measured as the distance between their actual OPEX and that which is predicted by the frontier. This distance can be interpreted as a measure of the potential efficiency 'catch-up' that an inefficient firm could achieve if it became efficient. Figure 6.1 also shows the potential effect of a 'frontier shift', perhaps caused by positive technological change or experience curve effects. A frontier shift reflects the impact of technological change and changes in working practices on efficient best practice performance across the industry, over time.

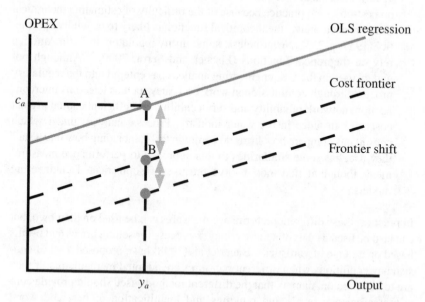

Figure 6.1   Comparisons of efficiency benchmarking

An important distinction must be drawn between 'catch-up' and 'frontier shift' effects when setting prices with benchmarking techniques. Catch-up or what is sometimes referred to as the 'stretch' factor refers to the efficiency gap that needs to be closed between the firm and the efficient frontier. For example, the US FCC (Federal Communications Commission) approved a price-indexing plan for AT&T in 1988 with a stretch factor of 0.5 per cent, equivalent to 20 per cent of the company's estimated TFP growth. Similar catch-up factors have been introduced for the interstate services of local exchange telecom carriers in the US and for North American electricity utilities. They are also applied by UK regulators, as discussed below. By contrast, frontier shift represents an estimate of the actual or potential productivity improvement achieved by a firm that is already on the frontier, and is therefore already efficient. The actual decomposition of efficiency change and technical change is typically derived using COLS, DEA or SFA techniques, but could alternatively be estimated using engineering models.

While any shortfall from the estimated frontier is usually interpreted as inefficiency, there is always the possibility that the estimated frontier and hence the resulting efficiency scores are biased because of measurement errors or model misspecification. For this reason, regulators may be reluctant to put complete reliance on frontier estimates. Moreover, leaving aside the theoretical extreme of 'perfect competition', expecting all firms to be on the efficient frontier is inconsistent with the usual operation of competitive markets, whose outcomes some economists see economic regulation as attempting to emulate. In real-life competitive markets the *average* performer, not the best performer, can determine prices and firms with above average performance then earn super-normal returns. If regulators were to determine their view of the expected performance in the industry based on the most efficient firm, then this would penalize firms earning average returns. These firms would not necessarily be penalized in a normal competitive market accommodating a number of suppliers with different costs.

Bernstein and Sappington (1999) demonstrate that when modelling the average X factor, which includes the total frontier shift and efficiency gains that a regulated industry can be expected to achieve over the regulatory period, the relative change of TFP in the regulated industry (TFP_r) compared to the competitive economy as a whole (TFP_c) becomes important. Also relevant are changes and differences in input prices in the economy (W_c) relative to those in the regulated industry (W_r). Thus they demonstrate that the X factor can be expressed as the difference between the total factor productivity growth potential in the regulated sector and that in the remainder of the competitive economy, plus the difference in the rate of growth of input prices in the two sectors:

$$X = \Delta(TFP_r - TFP_c) + \Delta(W_c - W_r)$$

However, Bernstein and Sappington (1999) also emphasize that this approach to setting X depends on a number of assumptions, including that the regulated sector is small in comparison to the economy as a whole, otherwise its performance will materially affect economy-wide TFP and input prices. Nevertheless, average TFP growth in the economy often serves as a starting point for determining X factors. For instance, in US telecommunications the average rate of productivity growth is used as a benchmark (DTe, 1999; Jamasb and Pollitt, 2001).

The UK experience

In the UK, benchmarking performance is now part of resetting regulatory price caps and is used to help determine appropriate X factors (Jamasb and Pollitt, 2001).[18] Over time there appears to have been movement towards a more common approach to benchmarking across the regulatory offices, see below, no doubt as the result of increasing experience, Monopolies and Mergers Commission (now Competition Commission) investigations,[19] demonstration effects and government policy that favours more consistency in regulation across the different regulatory bodies (DTI, 1998, para. 80). Nevertheless, some important differences remain. The regulatory offices undertake their own productivity and cost analyses and from time to time use research produced by different outside consultancy firms. Expert judgement also plays a part in efficiency assessment by the regulatory offices and the experts come from diverse backgrounds including industry and academia. There is, therefore, some heterogeneity in the approaches adopted by UK regulatory offices when setting price caps.

Telecommunications

It is appropriate to start with telecommunications regulation because the first privatized, regulated utility in the UK was BT. In 1984 just over a half of the equity of BT was sold by the government and a dedicated regulatory body, OFTEL (the Office of Telecommunications) was established. OFTEL became the model for the regulatory offices that were created during the later privatizations of the gas, water and electricity industries. In January 2004 OFCOM (the Office of Communications) replaced OFTEL, when a number of control bodies covering broadcasting, radio communications, and spectrum management were merged with telecommunications regulation.

As mentioned above, immediately after privatization BT's price cap was based on discussion between the government, the company and the City. When OFTEL came to reset the price cap from the late 1980s, it began to experiment with benchmarking (OFTEL, 1987). Service baskets were constructed for the UK, France, Italy and West Germany, which are the four largest telecoms markets in Europe. The baskets included the number of calls by distance, time of day, day of week and duration. However, OFTEL acknowledged the difficulties involved in making useful comparisons, especially because pricing differed substantially between countries. OFTEL continued to experiment with international benchmarking in the following years, because within the UK there was no available comparator to BT (OFTEL, 1989, 1991, 1992a).

Despite the existence of international benchmarking, it is unclear how it influenced the setting of BT's X factor and its service targets, if at all, in the early years. In a 1988 consultative document, OFTEL invited views on how productivity analysis and international performance data should be used in the regulation of BT (OFTEL, 1988). This was further pursued in a 1992 consultative document (OFTEL, 1992b) and in a regulatory statement in the same year (OFTEL, 1992c). However, it appears that at this time the main influence on price-cap setting was BT's own past and forecast cost performance. This, of course, rules out the establishment of an efficient frontier and the application of catch-up efficiency targets determined by such a frontier (e.g. OFTEL, 2001). Forecasts of BT's future costs were also made, although the precise forecasting methods used are unclear. In general, BT's X factors in the early post-privatization period appear to have been based on OFTEL's judgement of what was fair after weighing historic and forecasting evidence and after discussion with BT and its advisers.

The use of benchmarking was more evident after 1995, when an international benchmarking exercise was commissioned from NERA (National Economic Research Associates) (NERA, 2000; OFTEL, 1996a, 1996b). In this study BT's OPEX and CAPEX levels were separately compared to those of Local Exchange Carriers in the US (NAO, 2002, para. 2.5).[20] BT's interconnection charges were also benchmarked against those of domestic mobile networks and international ISDN charges (OFTEL, 1996b). The NERA study was later complemented by an international comparison of corporate telecommunication costs (OFTEL, 1997a) and by an international comparison of BT's interconnection charges (OFTEL, 1997b).

In the run-up to the most recent price control review for BT, in June 2003, OFTEL again used international comparisons, for the Internet, fixed line and mobile markets (OFTEL, 2002a, 2002b, 2002c). The range of prices within these markets in a number of countries was compared, alongside indicators of service quality. An important comparison in these studies appears to have been an index of average package prices. The lowest priced packages offered by two different service providers were determined for each country, and then averaged and indexed. The index was then used to make cross-country comparisons. Other benchmarking studies also influenced OFTEL's price review (NERA, 2000), in which BT's performance was compared with US local exchange carriers. NERA applied OLS, SFA and DEA methods to derive comparative measures. The results from these exercises were complemented by OFTEL's own performance estimates, including figures for market shares and domestic market growth within the UK (OFTEL, 2000a, 2000b). An interesting result of the exercise was the conclusion that UK interconnection charges and call tariffs were uncompetitive.

Gas and electricity

From privatization in 1986, the UK gas industry was regulated by the Office of Gas Supply (OFGAS), while the English, Welsh and Scottish electricity sectors were regulated by the Office of Electricity Regulation (OFFER) after their privatization in 1990/91. Since 1999 both gas and electricity have been regulated by the Office of Gas and Electricity Markets (OFGEM).

Gas　British Gas (BG) was the second utility to be privatized and regulated in the UK. BG was overwhelmingly dominant in retail gas supply and to a lesser extent in industrial gas well into the 1990s, and for the regulator finding national comparators was therefore difficult. Moreover, the national gas transmission and storage system was initially part of BG, although it was later separated into an independent company, Transco, which still had no domestic comparators. The nearest potential comparator was the electricity transmission grid which had been privatized as the National Grid Company (NGC). But, as the two systems are technologically very different, direct comparison was not possible. Nevertheless, from time to time there were experiments to compare the performance of these two networks. In 2002 Transco's owner, the Lattice Group, merged with the electricity transmission company, NGC, to form National Grid Transco plc. This has further limited the potential usefulness of comparing the performance of NGC and Transco.[21]

In early price control reviews, OFGAS appears to have relied heavily on BG's forecasts for costs and gas volumes (e.g. OFGAS, 1994a, 1994b). During the run-up to the 1996 price review, consultants were appointed to analyse BG Transco's OPEX and CAPEX figures and to identify possible cost savings (OFGAS, 1996a). A similar approach was adopted in arriving at the final retail price-cap proposals (OFGAS, 1996b). Given the vertical separation of both gas and electricity supply, in the late 1990s the regulator discussed benchmarking BG Trading (the company established to supply gas to final consumers) against PESs (Public Electricity Suppliers). The basis of the comparison would be the ratio of supply costs per customer (OFGAS, 1998, 1999). This method of benchmarking was applied in the final price cap proposals (OFGEM, 2001a). However, after April 2002 BG's gas supply to final consumers ceased to be capped because OFGEM deemed that sufficient competition had developed in gas supply. In contrast, Transco, as the sole gas network operator, remained price regulated.

In 2000 to 2001 OFGEM considered using benchmarking in the gas transmission sector. Initially, the possibility of benchmarking cost domestically or internationally was discussed (OFGEM, 2000a). This discussion was complemented by an investigation into whether it would be useful to compare the performance of Transco's LDZs (Local Distribution Zones) against each other (OFGEM, 2000a). OFGEM also commissioned an analysis of Transco's OPEX and CAPEX figures by consultants. For OPEX, for example, pay and staff ratios and vehicle leasing and pipeline costs across the company were considered and labour and total factor productivity calculations were made to supplement the expenditure benchmarking based on an inter-LDZ benchmark (MNR, 2001; OFGEM, 2001b). OFGEM also commissioned an international benchmarking study. Capital expenditure in the UK national transmission system was compared with US performance using data from FERC (Federal Energy Regulatory Commission).

Based on OLS regressions, consultants determined upper and lower cost levels of OPEX for each LDZ, from which median efficiency points were identified and used for comparison. The consultants suggested a way to compare CAPEX costs in the UK national transmission system domestically and internationally (MNR, 2001).Transco's costs for its national transmission pipelines were first compared with the costs for large diameter (> 600 mm) pipelines of the UK local transmission system. Then FERC data on US inter-state gas pipelines were employed to benchmark Transco's costs. To further inform the benchmarking exercise, the same consultants compared labour and total factor productivity figures in other UK sectors, including electricity, gas, transport and communications, and water. However, turning to the latest price review for Transco in 2002–2003, relating to regional charges, OFGEM does not appear to have relied on benchmarking to any appreciable extent (OFGEM, 2003a).

Electricity   At privatization in England and Wales in 1990/91, 12 regional electricity companies were established and were given primary responsible for the distribution and supply of electricity. Two large thermal and one nuclear electricity generating enterprise were created, and the high-voltage transmission grid (along with responsibility for balancing demand and supply on the system) became the responsibility of the NGC.[22] In Scotland, by contrast, two vertically integrated electricity utilities remained, one serving the south of Scotland and the other the north.[23]

During the 1990s competition developed in electricity generation and supply and today only the non-competitive parts of the market, namely transmission and distribution, are subject to price capping. When undertaking benchmarking, OFFER and later OFGEM used statistical comparisons, expert judgements (for example, OFFER established an advisory panel composed of senior industrialists for the transmission price review in 1996/97 and for the electricity distribution price review in 1998/99) and econometric analyses of data trends, with OPEX and CAPEX considered separately. Before 2000, cost trends in electricity distribution were analysed using COLS regression and average performance in the industry was identified. Since 2000, OFGEM has experimented with other forms of statistical modelling.

Electricity distribution   OPEX benchmarking in the first price control review was undertaken using cost regressions and data from the 12 regional electricity companies (OFFER, 1994, 1995), with controllable OPEX as the dependent variable and a 'composite variable' for the independent variable. To create the composite variable different weights were placed on a number of explanatory variables including system peak demand, units sold and number of consumers. Different regressions were run and from the results the residuals were used to identify possible inefficiencies between the companies (MMC, 1995, paras 6.5–6.12). However, for CAPEX econometric analysis was not used. The regulator relied mainly on comparative figures within the industry. OFFER (1995) also took into account a cost analysis of the UK electricity distribution sector undertaken by the Monopolies and Mergers Commission (MMC, 1995).

For the 1999 distribution price control review, OFFER and later OFGEM used COLS regressions of controllable OPEX, complemented by a frontier group determined by consultants (OFFER, 1999a). An efficiency study for OFFER in 1997 had looked in detail at past cost reductions, engineering studies that benchmarked performance, human resource costs, organizational structure and IT costs, and had placed two companies, Eastern Electricity and Southern Electricity, on the 'efficient frontier'. This study was complemented by OFFER's own econometric analysis, which regressed the base costs of each company on a composite variable consisting of the number of customers, units of electricity distributed and network length. Adjustments were made to account for agreed differences in operating environments including regional variations, and a constrained constant was included to reflect the regulator's assessment of required fixed costs in distribution. This analysis was then supplemented by a bottom up analysis of company costs, which were compared across companies (OFFER, 1999a). Regarding CAPEX, consultants undertook some modelling of costs for OFGEM and benchmarks were applied in the regulator's final price-cap proposals (OFFER, 1999a). The efficient level of CAPEX was set midway between the domestic industry median and the upper quartile of the sample.

For the 2004 distribution price control review the same principal approach to modelling efficiency was used and the same composite variable as in the 1999 review was used (e.g. OFGEM, 2003b). However, OFGEM also adopted regression models involving total costs and combined operating expenditure data as the dependent variables.[24] In setting the efficiency targets either the score from the first of these regressions was used or the average efficiency score across the three models, depending on which was the highest. Also, as part of the process the regulator commissioned research from external consultants (CEPA, 2003) into the potential for the use of frontier analysis, based on panel data (OFGEM, 2003b, 2004a). But an attempt to include international data in the frontier analysis, to increase the number of observations and to facilitate the application of SFA, was later abandoned due to the limited number of suitable comparators. In electricity distribution the number of observations is restricted because there are only 14 distribution companies in England, Wales and Scotland and some are commonly owned. In fact, only eight corporations now control electricity distribution in England, Wales and Scotland.

Electricity transmission   In the mid-1990s there appears to have been some discussion within OFFER as to whether the NGC's transmission business could be usefully benchmarked against the performance of BG's transmission and gas storage activities. However, difficulties in making sound comparisons were recognized because of differences in production technologies. OFFER (1996) experimented with the use of DEA analysis to determine cost efficiency in transmission using 40 overseas network operators. However, there were strong reservations within the regulatory office about these results because of differences in the size and nature of the transmission networks – most of the observations came from the US, Canada and Australia. Therefore, in later years more reliance seems to have been placed on benchmarking of NGC's OPEX against domestic comparators, namely three public electricity suppliers and the Scottish electricity transmission businesses – both overall OPEX and elements of OPEX were compared (OFGEM, 2000b). For example, the exercise included comparisons of NGC's staffing and pay levels against the market median (OFGEM, 2000b, 2000c).[25]

Between 1999 and 2000 the regulator again experimented with benchmarking transmission OPEX internationally. This time 20 European transmission businesses were chosen for comparison. But the benchmark was eventually dropped because of the continuing difficulty in obtaining meaningful comparisons (OFGEM, 2000b).

Electricity supply   The last price control review for electricity supply was undertaken between 1998 and 2000 (OFFER, 1996b). In general, the approach to setting the price cap involved comparisons of costs across the electricity supply companies with allowances made for certain cost differences. However, it is not clear that formal benchmarking played a critical role in the final price caps established, which applied from 1 April 2000 to 31 March 2002 (OFGEM, 1999, 2000d).

Recent electricity regulation   Work began on the 2005 distribution price review in August 2002 and the first consultation document was issued in July 2003. During the review, in all OFGEM issued seven main documents, held joint working groups with the distribution network operators, and held two public workshops in order to elicit views. Consultants were employed to work on benchmarking and productivity analysis (Cambridge Economic Policy Associates Ltd.), cost efficiency and tax (Ernst & Young), pensions (Ernst & Young and Deloitte and Touche) and CAPEX modelling (PB Power). A senior business adviser (Duncan Whyte) was employed to advise across the cost assessment work (OFGEM, 2005b, para. 2.16). OFGEM's final proposals for the 2005–10 distribution price caps were therefore, as in the past, based on a combination of econometric analysis, performance ratios, including quality of service measures, the companies' own cost projections, other financial data, past efficiency gains and discussion.[26] Formal benchmarking was applied only to OPEX and was but one of a number of inputs into the decision on price caps.[27] It also seems that benchmarking has not played much of a role in the setting of the price caps from 2005 for electricity transmission (OFGEM, 2003c, 2004b, 2004c). With retail electricity supply now competitive in Britain, consumer prices are no longer regulated.

Water and sewerage

The water and sewerage industry in England and Wales was fully privatized in 1989.[28] OFWAT (the Office of Water Services) was established at privatization to administer economic regulation of the industry and environmental regulation was placed in a separate government body, which later became the Environment Agency. Ten regional water and sewerage companies (WaSCs) were privatized in 1989 and they operated alongside 29 (today 15) water only companies (WoCs), which were already in the private sector. The WoCs serve relatively small geographic areas, where sewerage services are provided by one of the WaSCs. From the outset OFWAT placed considerable emphasis on yardstick competition in price-cap setting. Indeed, its use is legislated for in section 34(3) of the Water Act 1991. As the scope for competition in water and especially sewerage services is limited because of the technology of water services and the nature of the product, it was believed that the water sector was likely to continue to consist of geographical monopolies after privatization. Moreover, given the relatively large number of companies in the water sector benchmarking performance through econometric means was perceived to be a viable option at privatization. The water industry is the only regulated industry in the UK where the use of benchmarking in setting price caps is mandated by legislation.

The first review of water and sewerage charges came in 1994. In the run up to this review OFWAT maintained that there were practical difficulties in calculating total expenditure for water and sewerage services. These arose particularly in terms of data collection and making comparisons between companies serving different geographical areas and with different inherited capital stocks (NAO, 2002, Appx. 5, para. 53). Therefore, OPEX and CAPEX were modelled separately, as were water supply and sewerage services.[29] To arrive at the OPEX benchmark for water supply, OFWAT developed OLS models to identify the frontier firm. DEA was then used to check the econometric results (OFWAT, 1994a, 1994b; Stewart, 1993). Differences between a company's actual expenditure and that predicted by the model were assessed and the residual was used as a measure of efficiency, as in COLS modelling discussed above. Catch-up factors were computed based on the distance of each firm from the frontier.[30] However, to reflect the likelihood that the resulting efficiency estimates were imperfect, companies were set efficiency targets for catch-up to be achieved over a five-year period. Also, the catch-up was set modestly, at around 25 per cent to 35 per cent of the difference from the predicted costs.

A different form of benchmarking was used for OPEX in the sewerage sector, and for capital maintenance expenditures in water and sewerage. Based on comparative statistics, unit cost models were relied on and each company was asked to provide estimated costs for a number of illustrative projects, which OFWAT could then challenge based on figures supplied by the other firms in the industry. As part of CAPEX estimation, a report from external consultants formed the basis of OFWAT's assessment of the possible frontier shift. Given the existence of only 10 domestic sewerage service suppliers, econometric modelling is problematic for sewerage services and reliance was placed on what can be most closely described as engineering models.

In the 1999 price review OFWAT used a panel of senior industrialists as advisers and detailed comments on the price caps to be set were published in April 1998, to allow time for challenge (OFWAT, 1998a). Also, as in other price reviews, consumer interests were represented. As part of the price review process, unit cost comparisons were again used for capital enhancement projects in CAPEX. But for the first time a new capital maintenance model was adopted. The capital maintenance figures in CAPEX were based on a combination of unit cost measures and econometric analysis (OFWAT, 1998b, 1998c, 1998d, 1998e).

In the mid- to late 1990s OFWAT seems to have abandoned the use of DEA entirely and relied on econometric modelling. Water supply CAPEX was treated separately and again water and sewerage were considered independently. The 1999 price review used four models for water OPEX and these were similar to (though not the same as) those used in 1994. A water resources and treatment model was adopted with two independent variables (number of water sources divided by distribution input, and proportion of supplies derived from river sources), a water distribution model (consisting of an independent variable representing the proportion of mains above a given size), a water services power model (with distribution input multiplied by average pumping head as the independent variable) and a water service business activities model (consisting

of business activities expenditure regressed against the number of billed properties).[31] The results from the different econometric models were summed to
create efficiency bands, after making adjustments for company-specific costs
considered to be outside the control of management (e.g. regional salaries, requirements for additional water treatment and where there are large numbers of
small water sources). An allowance was also made where companies were assessed as efficient in OPEX and inefficient in CAPEX, or vice versa. This was
undertaken to address criticism from the industry that modelling OPEX and
CAPEX separately risked inappropriate efficiency scores. New in 1999 was the
application of a price-cap adjustment to reward or penalize service quality.
OFWAT then set the price caps for 2000 to 2005 on the basis that 60 per cent
of the OPEX gap would be closed over the five years (OFWAT, 1998a, 1998b,
1999a, 1999b).

Using the efficiency bands, OFWAT determined CAPEX in terms of catch-up
and frontier efficiency movements for capital maintenance and capital enhancement schemes. For both the companies' own cost assumptions formed a starting
point, again based on their unit costs for a range of specimen projects. These
figures were then subjected to expert assessment by consulting engineers
(OFWAT, 1998c). They were then compared and adjusted for each company to
reflect OFWAT's judgement of the efficiency of each company's costs relative
to the industry as a whole. For capital maintenance, four econometric models
covering resources and treatment, distribution infrastructure, distribution non-
infrastructure, and management and general expenses were also used. The data
in the models were expenditures over the five years from 1993/4 to 1997/8, to
even out year to year spending fluctuations.

Over time, based on its modelling exercises, OFWAT appears to have determined the efficient frontier in different ways. In 1994 the benchmark for capital
schemes was the lower quartile of the cost population for each standard cost. In
1998 this was changed to the lowest reported standard costs for groups of standard costs meeting certain criteria. In 1994 catch-up was calculated based on 50
per cent of the difference between each company's reported standard cost and
the benchmark cost. In 1999 this was set at 50 per cent for capital maintenance
and 75 per cent for capital enhancement, and now the catch-up was to be
achieved in the first year of the price-cap period and not over its full five years
as previously. During the review process, outside consultants were commissioned by one of the water and sewerage companies to assess OFWAT's capital
maintenance modelling. Their report set out a number of criticisms including
the omission of key economic and engineering cost drivers, something OFWAT
contested (Competition Commission, 2000, pp. 253–4).

Since 2000 OFWAT has commissioned a comparison of different benchmarking methods. As a methodological cross-check, DEA and SFA were compared
with OLS results by consultants. Despite some variation in the results, DEA

and SFA were seen as credible alternatives to OLS regression. OFWAT has also used international benchmarking studies such as one of supplies in Scandinavian cities (OFWAT, 2002a, 2004, 2005, p. 16). In addition, the regulator has continued to assess the efficient frontier shift using data on trends in other industries as well as in the UK water sector (Europe Economics, 2003; OFWAT, 2002b, 2003). The approach to setting the sector price caps for 2005 was therefore based on a refined version of the methods used before 2000.[32]

Discussion
The UK's experience with benchmarking or yardstick competition illustrates both its potential as a basis for price-cap setting but also its limitations. Table 6.1 summarizes the approaches adopted.

Regulators have differed in their approach to benchmarking. OFFER placed more emphasis on average performance in the industry than OFWAT, which has preferred to identify frontier performance, and OFTEL (now OFCOM) seems to have relied more heavily on international benchmarking than the other regulatory offices, reflecting the lack of domestic comparators to BT in UK telecommunications. Also, contrary perhaps to Shleifer's expectation in 1985, benchmarking in UK utility regulation has proved to be relatively difficult to implement and its results can be challenged for a number of reasons. The criticisms are as follows.

Selection and building of appropriate models
Building efficiency models that reflect true costs reasonably accurately is always likely to be a hazardous venture (Sawkins, 1995; Turvey, 2005). A recent study of different cost frontier models by Farsi and Filippini, using a sample of 59 utilities operating in Switzerland, found that, while the average inefficiency was not sensitive to the econometric specification used, the efficiency rankings varied significantly across the models (Farsi and Filippini, 2004; also see Jamasb and Pollitt, 2003; and Estache et al., 2004). They conclude that 'The estimated measures of inefficiency are, therefore, sensitive to econometric specification and should not be used as a direct instrument in benchmarking' (Farsi and Filippini, 2004, p. 3). Uncertainty about the appropriate techniques to use is reflected by the lack of consensus across the regulatory offices, and within offices over time, regarding the best approach to modelling efficiency. However, where differences in technology and data availability exist, this lack of consensus may simply indicate the necessity of employing alternative non-compatible approaches to modelling efficiency in different regulated industries.

Moreover, once a model is selected a decision has to be made regarding whether to use cross-sectional or time series data including panel data. In UK regulation, the modelling choice seems to have been dictated by data availability rather than by theoretical arguments regarding the underlying validity of the

Table 6.1   Summary of benchmarking methods used by UK regulatory offices

Market	Overall approach and individual methods
Electricity	Separation of CAPEX and OPEX
	Reliance on average benchmarks and frontier analysis NGC transmission benchmarked against Scottish transmission and frontier public electricity suppliers
	Use of operational ratio comparisons, expert judgement of future cost savings, OLS, regressions and TFP calculations
Gas	Separation of CAPEX and OPEX Reliance on average benchmarks
	Until 1998: determination of savings based on estimated cost trends of BG's own costs and cost forecasts From 1998: inter-LDZ benchmarks. From time to time comparisons of BGT with NGC's grid CAPEX : comparison with US data from FERC
	Use of operational ratio comparisons, expert judgement of future cost savings, OLS, regression and labour productivity and TFP calculations
Telecoms	Limited separation of CAPEX and OPEX Mostly reliance on average benchmarks
	Early international benchmarking from 1987, but greater reliance on BT's own costs and cost forecasts. Some domestic benchmarking as competitors developed Increased use of domestic and international benchmarking over time
	Early comparison of international service baskets, price indices and performance ratios Later: use of OLS, DEA, SFA methods and use of panel data
Water & Sewerage	Water and sewerage considered separately and separation of CAPEX and OPEX Extensive reliance on frontier benchmarks
	Some international benchmarking but reliance on domestic frontier benchmarks
	Early use of DEA; later mainly OLS regressions
	Labour productivity and TFP calculations, operational ratio comparisons and expert judgement

estimated statistical relationships. For example, OFWAT's models have been criticized by water companies for ignoring complex production relationships in the water sector, but the number of independent variables has had to be kept small because of the small number of observations available each year.[33] Moreover, despite the impact of water industry mergers in reducing even further the number of annual observations since privatization, the regulator continued to reject the use of panel data modelling on the grounds that the production function is not stable over time. OFWAT continues to rely on cross-sectional analysis (Competition Commission, 2000, pp. 263–5).[34]

Also when building their models, OFGEM and OFWAT have modelled CAPEX and OPEX separately, although the telecommunications regulator has not. It is not clear why modelling total expenditures should be correct for BT but not for electricity distribution and water and sewerage companies. Modelling OPEX separately may be sensible where there are investment outlays that would distort cost comparisons (Rossi and Ruzzier, 2000, p. 84), but this would presumably also apply to telecommunications. Moreover, separating CAPEX and OPEX may cause unintended effects. Due to a lack of suitable comparators weaker efficiency incentives may be set for CAPEX than OPEX and this could lead to a substitution of CAPEX for OPEX by the industry. However, a recent UK National Audit Office report (NAO, 2002, paras 3.6 to 3.11) noted that both regulators and companies felt that the UK price-cap system had led to a bias *against* CAPEX because of weak rewards from capital investment and a failure to include some investments in the regulatory asset base.

The accuracy of the resulting rankings

While applying the various methods, regulators in the UK have favoured an approach to setting performance targets that permits a ranking of regulated firms in terms of efficiency. Depending on the ranking, firm-specific 'catch-up' factors are used to pull inefficient firms towards the frontier. Leaving aside telecommunications and electricity and gas transmission, where such a factor is not used because there are no obvious comparators, the catch-up factor is set according to the performance of the most efficient firm or group of firms and the frontier shift is based broadly on a forecast of TFP growth and input prices in the industry compared to the economy as a whole. However, the different estimation methods used by UK utility regulators can produce different frontiers and catch-up factors (Jamasb and Pollitt, 2003); while the regulated firms, and their advisers, have consistently challenged both the regulator's computation of the catch-up and the frontier shift.[36] The firms point to efficiency rankings being biased by the use of inappropriate cost function models and criticize the regulators for overly optimistic assessments of possible frontier movements. While it is to be expected that the regulated firms will seek to find something to criticize in any process by which prices are set, the change over time in the models used by the regulators has not helped to build confidence in the resulting estimates.[37]

The limited use of international comparisons

Although the UK regulators have been keen to increase the data used in modelling both catch-up factors and frontier shifts, they have so far placed limited emphasis on international comparisons, with the exception of OFTEL. BT is dominant in the UK telecommunications market and OFTEL (now OFCOM) has commissioned international studies of performance in the absence of a domestic comparator. OFGEM has also used international comparisons alongside performance comparisons with other privatized utilities in the UK, and in 2001 OFWAT published international comparisons of performance (OFWAT, 2001). But it seems that only limited attention has been paid to the results of such studies by these regulators when determining price caps. It is the case that the results of international benchmarking are subject to error because of, for example, data heterogeneity, currency exchange rates and omitted variable problems. It is critical in performance benchmarking to have good data.[38] But at the same time, the regulators have few domestic comparators. Even in the water sector, where initially 39 water suppliers could be compared, because of mergers in the industry over the last ten years the number is now only 22 when companies under common ownership are aggregated. There is therefore a case for a renewed attempt to try to develop useful international data bases within the UK regulatory offices, despite potential difficulties. Perhaps this could occur in co-operation with regulators overseas.

Treatment of the quality of service

There have been difficulties in building service quality targets into the performance benchmarking exercise. Efficiencies in OPEX and CAPEX should not be achieved at the expense of reducing customer service or the reliability of supplies. Mikkers and Shestalova (2003) show that a yardstick competition regime that does not penalize network failures will lead to under investment and be socially sub-optimal. The socially optimal outcome is obtained by the regulator introducing penalties for under-supply equivalent to the value customers place on service failures. The result is incentives for regulated firms to achieve the socially desired level of capital enhancement and capital maintenance. But achieving this outcome in practice is not straightforward given uncertainty about the value consumers actually place on service reliability. UK regulators have used varying approaches to tackling this problem. For example, OFGEM has undertaken an 'Information and Incentives' project to address concerns about the potential trade-off between economic performance and service quality (OFGEM, 2000a, 2001a), while OFWAT (2000) imposes direct financial incentives for service quality when determining the price cap, through an X factor adjustment. However, the most appropriate method for the integration of quality of service into overall performance benchmarking remains unresolved.

An increased regulatory burden

Companies frequently complain about the regulatory burden placed on them in terms of having to submit data to the regulator to facilitate the benchmarking exercise and arrive at the price caps. The regulators have produced a growing volume of documentation at each price review. For example, the setting of the price caps for water after 2000 involved OFWAT publishing in excess of eight major documents. The regulators see this as a necessary response to demands for more consultation, accountability and transparency in price cap setting. But the companies complain about the volume of data they need to submit as part of the process: as the government's National Audit Office recently concluded:

> Benchmarking should be seen a way of simplifying the price control process. … Some of the benchmarking exercises of recent years achieve precisely the opposite – requiring the firm to account to the regulator for the way it carries out its detailed business activities. (NAO, 2002, Appx. 5, para. 39)

Uncertainty

Finally, despite the growing documentation from the regulatory offices, companies have raised concerns about what they perceive as undue uncertainty surrounding the process by which the data they submit to the regulator are used in arriving at a set of performance metrics (Competition Commission, 2000, pp. 149–51). In response to such criticism, OFWAT and OFGEM now provide companies with an audit trail to show how they have arrived at the figures in their final price control documents. But water and electricity distribution companies still complain about the uncertainty surrounding the process by which the efficiency rankings are created. Meanwhile the cost of operating benchmarking, including the compliance costs placed on regulated firms, remains unquantified. Also unknown is the extent to which changes in personnel over time within the regulatory offices have impacted on both the emphasis placed on benchmarking and the precise methods used.

Conclusions

In 1985 Shleifer proposed the use of benchmarking or yardstick competition in economic regulation so that a regulated firm's prices were not based on its own costs. In the UK benchmarking is now part of the process of setting price caps. OFTEL, OFGEM and OFWAT have experimented with both national and international benchmarking, although it appears that less importance has been placed on international data because of the difficulty of finding acceptable comparators. The main exception is in telecommunications where BT's continued dominance in the market restricts the use of domestic comparator firms.

The use of imperfect benchmarking may be better than relying only on cost information supplied by the regulated firm. At the same time, however, the operation of benchmarking has proved to be far from problem free in the UK. It has been subject to criticism relating to (1) the selection of the appropriate performance model; (2) the accuracy of the resulting efficiency scores; (3) the extent with which international benchmarking is used; (4) building in correct allowances for service quality; (5) the costs imposed on the industry; and (6) the uncertainty that is said still to surround the price-capping exercise. As Burns et al. (2005) comment, to be successful benchmarking needs to be seen as having high value and credibility, and in the UK both appear to be lacking, with the partial exception of in water industry regulation.

Notes

1. We would like to thank Phil Burns, Ian Byatt, Michael Crew, Mark Hann, Stephen Littlechild, Eileen Marshall, Colin Robinson, Ralph Turvey, Peter Vass and Tom Weyman-Jones for helpful comments on earlier drafts of this chapter. The content also benefited from comments made during a presentation of the chapter's content at Frontier Economics in London in February 2005. The usual disclaimer applies.

2. Price caps are also used in airport regulation and the regulation of the railways in the UK. Each regulatory system has some special characteristics and for reasons of space we exclude these industries from the discussion below. During the preparation of this chapter it was suggested to us that under incentive regulation it does not necessarily matter how the efficiency target is set by the regulator, except for the effect on the distribution of rewards between producers and consumers. The objective is to set a target to provide the prospect of economic profits by being efficient. While understanding the point, we do not accept that regulators can take such an approach to setting price caps in practice. Regulators need to justify their efficiency targets to the industry, consumers and government. .

3. In some studies yardstick competition is a more restricted form of benchmarking referring to the use of econometric analysis. However, as econometric techniques are rarely if ever solely used when setting the price cap, we prefer to treat the terms yardstick competition and benchmarking as equivalents.

4. Stephen Littlechild has made the point to us that the reasons for this were (a) it was not part of his terms of reference since the concept did not then exist; (b) there was not the time to do it; (c) whether the concept would have been accepted was unclear; and (d) whatever he said would have been largely irrelevant given the way the price cap would necessarily have been set at that time. Nevertheless, the fact remains that no guidance existed as to how the 'X' factor should be determined.

5. The resulting tariff will generate a net present value of zero provided that the revenue forecasts are correct and OPEX and CAPEX are in line with forecasts. This is equivalent to the firm's IRR (internal rate of return) being equal to its projected cost of capital (Estache et al., 2003). The purpose of the price cap is to provide incentives to 'outperform' and earn higher profits.

6. Bös (1991) criticises yardstick competition precisely because the threat of bankruptcy may not be credible in the case of firms producing essential services.

7. This issue has arisen in the UK given the common ownership of several electricity distributors as well as several water companies by common parent firms.

8. The Törnqvist index, as originally developed in Törnqvist (1936), is a discrete approximation to a continuous Divisia index. It can yield the same productivity measure as a flexible form production function, although it does assume constant returns to scale. Further assumptions are that all firms are cost minimisers and revenue maximisers. This is often inappropriate for regulated firms. In addition, price subsidization and cross-subsidisation can distort the resulting productivity measure because prices are used as weights.

9. Production function analysis can only measure technical efficiency, while cost functions reflect both technical and allocative efficiency through the choice of the optimal input mix given factor prices. For this reason, cost functions are usually favoured over production functions in performance benchmarking. A firm is technically efficient when it is not possible to use less inputs to produce the given output. This is a necessary but not sufficient condition for cost efficiency; for a good introduction to efficiency measurement see Coelli et al. (1998).

10. A distance function may be either input or output oriented. An input orientation considers how far the input vector may be proportionately contracted with the output vector held fixed. By contrast, the output orientation expands the output vector while holding the input vector fixed.

11. In SFA cost function analysis the error term ε is composed of two independent components and is defined as $\varepsilon = v+u$, where v is a two-sided error term which captures random shocks and is assumed to be symmetrically and independently distributed $N(0, \sigma^2)$. By contrast, u is a non-negative, one-sided error term to capture inefficiency and is usually assumed to have a half normal (or sometimes a truncated normal or gamma) distribution. A potential criticism of SFA is that there is no clear justification for the chosen distribution for u. However, arguably the assumptions of SFA are more valid than simply assuming that all measurement error is inefficiency, which is the implicit assumption in a COLS model.

12. For a more detailed appraisal of the use of each of these methods within a regulatory environment, see Coelli et al. (2003).

13. An input oriented model is usually adopted for utility analysis because a utility's output may be largely outside the discretion of management due, for example, to universal service obligations.

14. The DEA frontier is deterministic and all distances from the frontier are therefore attributed to inefficiencies rather than to modelling error. There have been some developments in the estimation of non-parametric stochastic frontiers, involving stochastic DEA models (Khumbhakar and Lovell, 2000), but non-stochastic mathematical modelling still dominates.

15. As Newbery (2004, p. 14) explains, this form of benchmarking in Chile was established well before privatisation and overcame many of the problems of securing the potential benefits of privatization.

16. In the UK regulators tend to reject the term negotiation as an accurate description of the process of price setting. They form a view and make a proposal, which the firms can then accept or reject. The regulators may then vary their proposal to reflect the companies' objections. This is not exactly a process of negotiation, but it does involve the 'give and take' which lies at the heart of negotiating.

17. In practice the cost frontier could also be estimated directly using SFA or DEA techniques.

18. The following discussion is based on the publications of the UK regulatory offices, especially the *Price Control Reviews* and related documents, which in part are available from the regulators' websites and in part from the regulators' libraries, and government publications, especially the National Audit Office's report on *Pipes and Wires* (NAO, 2002). We would like to thank OFGEM, OFWAT and OFCOM for assistance in tracking down relevant material.

19. In the UK the MMC (now CC) reviews licence modification disputes between the regulator and companies, including disputes over price caps.

20. However, in contrast to the other utility regulatory offices in the UK, OFTEL has not favoured separate benchmarking of OPEX and CAPEX.

21. In early 2005 OFGEM sanctioned the sale of four gas distribution networks by National Grid Transco, noting that: 'Separate ownership and management of the gas distribution networks will enable Ofgem to compare and contrast the performance of gas distribution companies. This will allow gas consumers, for the first time, to benefit from efficiency gains of the kind that successive price controls have secured for electricity distribution customers' (OFGEM, 2005a). This statement seems to confirm the limitations of earlier benchmarking experiments in gas regulation.

22. As discussed in Saal (2003) substantial regulatory pressure was subsequently exerted in order to promote competition in generation. This was because the initial industry structure established at privatization was excessively concentrated. Similarly, initially distribution and supply of electricity were operated as separate businesses with separate accounts though within the

same companies. The Utilities Act 2000 required legal separation of the activities to facilitate effective competition .

23. The electricity industry in Northern Ireland is separately organised and regulated
24. DEA was also employed but the results were considered unreliable and were not used.
25. From 2000 price controls were applied to NGC separately for its transmission asset ownership and system operation. For the systems operation side of the NGC, trading function staff costs have been benchmarked against similar costs in companies with trading functions in other sectors of the economy.
26. In 1999 and 2004 OFGEM used the top quartile of companies to establish the efficient frontier for OPEX. In contrast, OFWAT uses the performance of a single company when determining the efficient frontier for the water industry.
27. For example, Burns et al. (2005) note that in the 2004 review the relative efficiency rankings of the companies derived from benchmarking and the initial price controls set were very different, underlining the fact that benchmarking did not play a critical role in price setting.
28. The water industries of Scotland and Northern Ireland are separately organised and are still publicly owned.
29. Saal and Parker (2000) subsequently suggested that there may be some economies of scope between water and sewerage services and also provide evidence suggesting that water and sewerage costs may be non-separable.
30. A best performing firm may be disqualified as the frontier company if OFWAT judges it to be atypical in some respect, for example size. Information on performance supplied by the regulated companies is subject to scrutiny by official appointed 'reporters' in an attempt to ensure that information is consistent and reliable.
31. OPEX targets were set initially using 1997/98 data from the companies and then adjusted on receipt of 1998/99 data.
32. In the 2004/5 price review once again a number of consultancies were involved in assisting OFWAT, including Babtie Engineering on the cost base, Mott MacDonald on company capital maintenance submissions, CEPA/Europe Economics on the cost of capital, and Deloitte & Touche for company tax projections; for a more complete listing see OFWAT, 2005, p. 48.
33. We accept Ofwat's argument that its approach of separately estimating efficiency for each of approximately 18 different disaggregated water and sewerage activities allows it to account for some of the complexity of water industry operations. This is the case, because it potentially allows for the inclusion of the most appropriate explanatory factors for each disaggregated model, while in contrast, data limitations would severely restrict the number of explanatory factors that could be employed in a cross-sectional model of aggregate water company efficiency. Nonetheless, this modelling approach cannot account for cost interactions and scope economies, such as those identified by Saal and Parker (2000), and Stone and Webster Consultants (2004a).
34. Although the resulting models have not been used directly in its efficiency assessments, recent work commissioned by OFWAT has explored panel based approaches to modelling total and OPEX costs in the water industry (Stone and Webster Consultants, 2004a, 2004b).
35. It must be noted that the water industry does not operate the standard RPI – X price cap regime, but instead operates a RPI + K regime where K is Q – X, where X is the standard X factor. The addition of the Q factor is to allow for the anticipated capital requirements associated with mandated environmental and drinking water quality investment programmes. This alternative price cap regime may influence the incentives for capital investment in the water sector, but further discussion of this issue is beyond the scope of this chapter.
36. A potential alternative approach would be greater employment of panel-based productivity decomposition methods, such as those that were recently identified by Pacific Economics Group (2004) as being applicable for electricity regulation. This work, which was commissioned by the Essential Services Commission in Victoria, Australia, highlights the potential advantage of such methods because they allow the simultaneous estimation of both a firm's catch-up factor and its potential frontier shift, using data drawn solely from the set of firms subject to price-cap regulation. Also, Stephen Littlechild has drawn our attention to the growing volume of comparative industry data provided by the private sector, which is largely used by the companies to benchmark and assess their performance against other firms. City analysts

also produce performance comparisons for investors. Perhaps more use could be made of these data by regulators.

37. Of course, it would have been wrong if the methods had not adapted over time as lessons were learned. The point here is not that changes should not have occurred, but that they have not necessarily occurred in a way that has helped to build confidence in the process of benchmarking.

38. Ian Byatt, the former water industry economic regulator for England and Wales, emphasized this point to us after reading an earlier version of the chapter. He also emphasized the importance of adopting reasonable but not necessarily correct price limits in a world in which there are time pressures for regulators to improve efficiency in their industry and the correct price limits are unknown. Stephen Littlechild, the former UK electricity industry regulator, has similarly emphasized to us the distinction between the economist's 'ideal world' and the reality facing regulators. We accept the legitimacy of both of these arguments.

References

Bauer, P., Berger, A., Ferrier, G. and Humphrey, D. (1998) 'Consistency Conditions for Regulatory Analysis of Financial Institutions: A Comparison of Frontier Efficiency Methods', *Journal of Economics and Business*, **50**, 85–114.

Bernstein, J. and Sappington, D.E. (1999) 'Setting the X Factor in Price Cap Regulation Plans', *Journal of Regulatory Economics*, **16**, 5–25.

Bogetoft, P. (1994) 'Incentive-efficient Productive Frontiers: An Agency Perspective on DEA', *Management Science*, **40**, 959–68.

Bogetoft, P. (1997) 'DEA-based Yardstick Competition: The Optimality of Best Practice Regulation', *Annals of Operations Research*, **73**, 277–98.

Bös, D. (1991) *Privatization: A Theoretical Treatment*, Oxford: Clarendon Press.

Burns, P., Jenkins, C. and Riechmann, C. (2005) 'The Use of Benchmarking in Regulation', mimeo, London: Frontier Economics.

Competition Commission (2000) *Sutton and East Surrey Water plc: A Report on the References under Sections 12 and 14 of the Water Industry Act 1991*, London: Stationery Office.

CEPA (2003) *Productivity Improvements in Distribution Network Operators*, Office of Gas and Electricity Markets, September.

Coelli, T. and Perelman, S. (1999) 'A Comparison of Parametric and Non-parametric Distance Functions: With Application to European Railways', *European Journal of Operational Research*, **117**, 326–39.

Coelli, T., Estache, A., Perelman, S. and Trujillo, L. (2003) *A Primer on Efficiency Measurement for Utilities and Transport Regulators*, Washington, DC: World Bank.

Coelli, T., Rao, D.S.P. and Battese, G. (1998) *An Introduction to Efficiency and Productivity Analysis*, Dordrecht: Kluwer.

DTe (1999) *Price Cap Regulation in the Electricity Sector: Information and Consultation Document*, The Hague: Netherlands Electricity Regulatory Service.

DTe (2000) *Guidance for Price Cap Regulation in the Dutch Electricity Sector in the Period from 2000 to 2003*, The Hague: Netherlands Electricity Regulatory Service.

DTI (1998) *A Fair Deal for Consumers: Modernising the Framework for Utility Regulation. The Response to Consultation*, London: Department of Trade and Industry.

Europe Economics (2003) *Financial Performance and Expenditure of the Water Companies in England and Wales*, Europe Economics, March.

Estache, A., Pardina, M.R., Rodríguez, J.M. and Sember, G. (2003) 'An Introduction to Financial Economic Modelling for Utility Regulators', *World Bank Policy Research Working Paper 3001*, Washington, DC: World Bank.

Estache, A., Rossi, M.A. and Ruzzier, C.A. (2004) 'The Case for International Coordination of Electricity Regulation: Evidence from the Measurement of Efficiency in South America', *Journal of Regulatory Economics*, **25** (3), 271–95.

Farrell (1957) 'The Measurement of Production Efficiency', *Journal of the Royal Statistical Society, Series A*, **120** (3), 253–81.

Farsi, M. and Filippini, M. (2004) 'Regulation and Measuring Cost Efficiency with Panel Data Models: Application to Electricity Distribution Utilities', *Review of Industrial Organization*, **25** (1), 1–19.

Fischer, R. and Serra, P. (2000) 'Regulating the Electricity Sector in Latin America', *Economia*, **1** (1), 155–98.

Jamasb, T. and Pollitt, M.G. (2001) 'Benchmarking and Regulation: International Electricity Experience', *Utilities Policy*, **9**, 107–30.

Jamasb, T. and Pollitt, M.G. (2003) 'International Benchmarking and Regulation: An Application to European Electricity Distribution Utilities', *Energy Policy*, **31**, 1609–22.

Khumbhakar, S. and Lovell, C.A.K. (2000) *Stochastic Frontier Analysis*, Cambridge: Cambridge University Press.

Littlechild, S.C. (1983) *Regulation of British Telecommunications' Profitability*, London: HMSO.

Mikkers, M. and Shestalova, V. (2003) *Yardstick Competition and Reliability of Supply in Public Utilities*, Bath: Centre for the Study of Regulated Industries, University of Bath.

MMC (1995) *Scottish Hydro-Electric plc: A Report on a Reference under Section 12 of the Electricity Act 1989*, London: HMSO/Monopolies and Mergers Commission.

MNR (2001) *Transco Price Control Review 2002–2007*, London: Mazars Neville Russell, 7 September.

NAO (2002) *Pipes and Wires*, London: National Audit Office, Stationery Office.

NERA (2000) *The Comparative Efficiency of BT. A Report for Oftel by NERA*, London: Office of Telecommunications.

Newbery, D.M. (2004) *Privatising Network Industries*, Munich: CSEifo.

OFFER (1994) *The Distribution Price Control. Proposals*, London: Office of Electricity Regulation, August.

OFFER (1995) *The Distribution Price Control. Revised Proposals*, London: Office of Electricity Regulation, July.

OFFER (1996) *The Transmission Price Control Review of the National Grid Company. Proposals*, London: Office of Electricity Regulation, October.

OFFER (1999a) *Reviews of Public Electricity Suppliers 1998–2000: Distribution Price Control Review. Final Proposals*, London: Office of Gas and Electricity Markets, December.

OFFER (1999b) *Reviews of Public Electricity Suppliers 1998–2000: Supply Price Control Review. Initial Proposals*, London: Office of Gas and Electricity Markets, August.

OFGAS (1994a) *Price Controls on Gas Transportation and Storage. The Director General's Decision*. London: Office of Gas Supply, August.

OFGAS (1994b) *Proposed Price Controls on Gas Transportation and Storage. A Consultation Document*, London: Office of Gas Supply, June.

OFGAS (1996a) *1997 Price Control Review: British Gas Transportation and Storage. The Director General's Final Proposals*, London: Office of Gas Supply, August.

OFGAS (1996b) *1997 Price Control Review: Supply at or Below 2,500 Therms a Year: British Gas Trading. The Director General's Initial Proposals*, London: Office of Gas Supply, November.

OFGAS (1998) *Review of British Gas Trading's Domestic Supply Tariffs. A Decision Document*, London: Office of Gas Supply, July.

OFGAS (1999) *Review of British Gas Trading's Price Regulation. Initial Proposals*, London: Office of Gas and Electricity Markets, November.

OFGEM (1999) *Reviews of Public Electricity Suppliers 1998 to 2000: Supply Price Control Review. Final Proposals*, London: Office of Gas and Electricity Markets, December.

OFGEM (2000a) *Review of Transco's Price Control from 2002. Initial Consultation Document*, London: Office of Gas and Electricity Markets, May.

OFGEM (2000b) *The Transmission Price Control Review on National Grid Company from 2001: Transmission Network Owner. Initial Proposals*, London: Office of Gas and Electricity Markets, September.

OFGEM (2000c) *NGC System Operator Price Control and Incentive Schemes under NETA. Initial Proposals*, London: Office of Gas and Electricity Markets, December.

OFGEM (2000d) *Review of Public Electricity Suppliers 1998 to 2000: Supply Price Control Review*, London: Office of Gas and Electricity Markets, June.

OFGEM (2001a) *Review of British Gas Trading's Price Regulation. Final Proposals*, London: Office of Gas and Electricity Markets, February.

OFGEM (2001b) *Review of Transco's Price Control from 2002. Final Proposals*, London: Office of Gas and Electricity Markets, September.

OFGEM (2003a) *Separation of Tranco's Distribution Price Control. Final Proposals*, London: Office of Gas and Electricity Markets, June.

OFGEM (2003b) *Electricity Distribution Price Control Review. Second Consultation*, London: Office of Gas and Electricity Markets, December.

OFGEM (2003c) *NGC System Operator Incentive Scheme from April 2004. Initial Consultation Document*, London: Office of Gas and Electricity Markets, December.

OFGEM (2004a) *Electricity Distribution Price Control Review. Policy Document*, London: Office of Gas and Electricity Markets, March.

OFGEM (2004b) *Extending the National Grid Company's Transmission Asset Price Control for 2006/07. Initial Consultation*, London: Office of Gas and Electricity Markets, May.

OFGEM (2004c) *NGC System Operator Incentive Scheme from April 2004. Proposals and Statutory Licence Consultation*, London: Office of Gas and Electricity Markets, February.

OFGEM (2005a) 'OFGEM Approves Gas Networks Sale', Press Release R/5, London: Office of Gas and Electricity Market, January.

OFGEM (2005b) *Assessment of the Electricity Distribution Price Control Review Process*, London: Office of Gas and Electricity Markets, March.

OFTEL (1987) *International Comparison of Telephone Charges*, London: Office of Telecommunications, August.

OFTEL (1988) *The Regulation of British Telecom: A Consultative Document by the Director General of Telecommunications*, London: Office of Telecommunications, January.

OFTEL (1989) *International Comparisons of Telephone Charges Prepared by the Economics, Statistics and Accounting Branch of the Office of Telecommunications. Statistical Note*, London: Office of Telecommunications, January.

OFTEL (1991) *International Comparisons of Telephone Charges Prepared by the Economics, Statistics and Accounting Branch of the Office of Telecommunications. Statistical Note*, London: Office of Telecommunications, March.

OFTEL (1992a) *International Comparisons of Telephone Charges Prepared by the*

Economics, Statistics and Accounting Branch of the Office of Telecommunications. Statistical Note, London: Office of Telecommunications, February.

OFTEL (1992b) *The Regulation of BT's Prices: A Consultative Document Issued by the Director General of Telecommunications*, London: Office of Telecommunications, January.

OFTEL (1992c) *Future Controls on British Telecom's Prices: A Statement by the Director General of Telecommunications*, London: Office of Telecommunications, June.

OFTEL (1996a) *Network Charges from 1997. A Consultative Document*, London: Office of Telecommunications, December.

OFTEL (1996b) *Pricing of Telecommunications Services from 1997. Oftel's Proposals for Price Control and Fair Trading*, London: Office of Telecommunications, June.

OFTEL (1997a) *Comparison of Telecoms Prices for Business. A Benchmarking Report for Oftel*, London: Office of Telecommunications, November.

OFTEL (1997b) *Interim Charges for BT's Standard Services for Year Ending 31 March 1998. Determination and Explanatory Document*, London: Office of Telecommunications, July.

OFTEL (2000a) *Price Control Review: A Consultative Document Issued by the Director General of Telecommunications on Possible Approaches for Future Retail Price and Network Charge Controls*, London: Office of Telecommunications, March.

OFTEL (2000b) *Price Control Review: A Consultative Document Issued by the Director General of Telecommunications Setting out Proposals for Future Retail Price and Network Charge Controls*, London: Office of Telecommunications, October.

OFTEL (2001) *Proposals for Network Charge and Retail Price Controls from 2001*, London: Office of Telecommunications, February.

OFTEL (2002a) *International Benchmarking Study of Fixed Line Services*, London: Office of Telecommunications, June.

OFTEL (2002b) *International Benchmarking Study of Internet Access (Dial-up and Broadband)*, London: Office of Telecommunications, June.

OFTEL (2002c) *International Benchmarking Study of Mobile Services*, London: Office of Telecommunications, June.

OFWAT (1994a) *1993–94 Report on the Cost of Water Delivered and Sewerage Collected*, Birmingham: Office of Water Services.

OFWAT (1994b) *Setting Price Limits for Water and Sewerage Services: The Framework and Approach to the 1994 Periodic Review*, Birmingham: Office of Water Services.

OFWAT (1998a) *Assessing the Scope for Future Improvements in Water Company Efficiency*, Birmingham: Office of Water Services, April.

OFWAT (1998b) *1997/98 Report on Water and Sewerage Operating Costs Efficiency*, Birmingham: Office of Water Services.

OFWAT (1998c) *Capital Works Unit Costs in the Water Industry: An Analysis of the June 1998 Water Company Cost Base Assumptions*, Birmingham: Office of Water Services, December.

OFWAT (1998d) *Prospects for Prices: A Consultation Paper on Strategic Issues Affecting Future Water Bills*, Birmingham: Office of Water Supplies, October.

OFWAT (1998e) *Setting Price Limits for Water and Sewerage Services: The Framework and Business Planning Process for the 1999 Periodic Review*, Birmingham: Office of Water Services, February.

OFWAT (1999a) *Efficiency Assessments: Econometric Models*, RD 2/99, Birmingham: Office of Water Services, July.

OFWAT (1999b) *Final Determinations: Future Water Sewerage Charges for 2000–05*, Birmingham: Office of Water Services, November.

OFWAT (2000) *Maintaining Serviceability to Customers*, Birmingham: Office of Water Services, April.

OFWAT (2001) *Worldwide Water Comparison 1999–2000*, Birmingham: Office of Water Services, December.

OFWAT (2002a) *International Comparison of Water and Sewerage Service: 2000–01 Report*, Birmingham: Office of Water Services, December.

OFWAT (2002b) *Water and Sewerage Service Unit Costs and Relative Efficiency: 2001–02 Report*, Birmingham: Office of Water Services, December.

OFWAT (2003) *Updating the Overall Performance Assessment (OPA). A Consultation*, Birmingham: Office of Water Services, December.

OFWAT (2004) *International Comparison of Water and Sewerage Service: 2001–02*, Birmingham: Office of Water Services, March.

OFWAT (2005) *Annual Report of the Director General of Water Services, 2004–2005*, Birmingham: Office of Water Services, March.

Pacific Economics Group (2004) *TFP Research for Victoria's Power Distribution Industry*, Report commissioned and published by the Essential Services Commission, Melbourne: Victoria State Government.

Rossi, M.A. and Ruzzier, C.A. (2000) 'On the Regulatory Application of Efficiency Measures', *Utilities Policy*, **9** (2), 81–92.

Saal, D.S. (2003) 'Restructuring, Regulation, and the Liberalization of Privatized Utilities in the UK', in D. Parker and D.S. Saal (eds), *International Handbook on Privatzation*, Cheltenham, UK and Northampton, MA, USA: Edward Elgar.

Saal, D.S. and Parker, D. (2000) 'The Impact of Privatisation and Regulation an theWater and Sewerage Industry in England and Wales: A Translog Cost Function Model', *Managerial and Decision Economics*, **21** (6), 253–68.

Sawkins, J.W. (1995) 'Yardstick Competition in the English and Welsh Water Industry: Fiction or Reality?', *Utilities Policy*, **5** (1), 27–36.

Shephard, R. (1970) *Theory of Cost and Production Functions*, Princeton, NJ: Princeton University Press.

Shleifer, A. (1985) 'A Theory of Yardstick Competition', *Rand Journal of Economics*, **16** (3), 319–27.

Stewart, M. (1993) *Modelling Water Costs 1992–93: Further Research into the Impact of Operating Conditions on Company Costs*, Birmingham: Office of Water Services.

Stone and Webster Consultants (2004a) *Investigation into Evidence for Economies of Scale in the Water and Sewerage Industry in England and Wales*, Report commissioned and published by the Office of Water Services, Birmingham, UK.

Stone and Webster Consultants (2004b) *Investigation into OPEX Productivity Trends and Causes in the Water Industry in England and Wales: 1992–93 to 2002–03*, Report commissioned and published by the Office of Water Services, Birmingham, UK

Törnqvist, L. (1936) *The Bank of Finland's Consumption Price Index*, Bank of Finland.

Turvey, R. (2005) 'On Benchmarking and TFP Comparisons', mimeo.

Vass, P. (1999) 'Accounting for Regulation', in P. Vass (ed.), *Regulatory Review 1998/99*, London: Centre for the Study of Regulated Industries.

Weyman-Jones, T.G. (2003) 'Regulating Prices and Profits', in D. Parker and D.S. Saal (eds), *International Handbook on Privatzation*, Cheltenham, UK and Northampton, MA, USA: Edward Elgar.

7   Regulation and the cost of capital

Tim Jenkinson

Introduction

The cost of capital is one of the most important factors that regulators, and companies, have to estimate. The appropriate cost of capital for regulated industries has been debated extensively in many countries, in particular the US with its general (although not exclusive) reliance on rate of return regulation. However, in recent years, the cost of capital debate has been particularly active in the UK, where regulation tends to be on the basis of price caps (or, in some cases, revenue caps). This chapter reviews the way that regulators in the UK (including the Competition Commission[1]) have estimated the cost of capital, and discusses some important issues that remain unresolved.

With the regulatory asset values (RAVs) of the UK water, energy and rail networks alone approaching £100 billion,[2] even small changes in the allowed return on such asset bases can have significant implications for customer bills. In addition, these are by no means the only assets where the rate of return is regulated: certain airports, parts of mobile phone networks, the air traffic control system, the Royal Mail, and even Yellow Pages are also subject to explicit regulation. Furthermore, in many competition cases, the relationship of the observed rate of return to the estimated cost of capital is a key concern.

The main issues discussed in this chapter are closely related. First, we discuss the difficulties observed in practice in estimating risk, and the appropriate equity cost of capital. Second, for regulated utility companies, the trend towards high levels of debt in their capital structures has become a source of concern for regulators. We discuss the question of whether, in addition to setting the cost of capital, the capital structure of companies should be regulated. Third, as debt has increased, the issue of 'financeability' – whether the projected revenues, profits and cash flows are such as to enable the company to maintain a strong credit rating – has increasingly become a focus of attention. We consider whether adjustments to the required returns should be made to address concerns regarding financeability in the latter part of the chapter.

To provide a background to these current issues, the chapter begins by defining terms and considering the recent history of regulatory judgements on the cost of capital, and draws comparisons with some of the key market evidence.

146

How have regulators' estimates of the cost of capital evolved?

The cost of capital represents the minimum expected return required by investors in order to commit funds to a particular company or project. Much of the complexity associated with estimating the cost of capital derives from the difficulty of observing the expectations of investors. This is not too much of a problem in the case of debt investors, as interest rates provide forward-looking measures of market expectations for various credit qualities. The main problems are associated with estimating expected equity returns. In the absence of an observable market measure, it is necessary to use an appropriate asset pricing model to derive an estimate of risk and thereby the cost of equity. In the UK, regulatory bodies have almost exclusively relied on the Capital Asset Pricing Model (CAPM),[3] although lip-service is typically paid to alternatives such as the Dividend Growth Model.

In the early years in the UK following the privatization of most regulated industries, the allowed returns of companies were on a 'glide path' towards the estimated cost of capital: companies were allowed to keep part of the benefit from reducing costs more quickly than assumed by the regulators at previous periodic reviews, and consequently earned returns considerably in excess of the cost of capital. However, now that the UK regulated utility businesses have been subject to multiple reviews, the glide path has ended and the estimated cost of capital is now much more closely related to actual (and expected) returns.

Estimating the overall cost of capital using the CAPM involves the following steps. First, the risk-free interest rate is estimated. This is, generally, the most straightforward part of the exercise, as forward-looking estimates are readily available from government bond markets. The main issues relate to (a) whether to use the latest 'spot' estimates, or whether to apply some longer-term averaging (which might be important if there are concerns that current rates are unusual, and that companies may need to raise finance during the subsequent control period at very different rates), and (b) what maturity of debt to assume (this decision is usually bounded by the length of the control period – typically five years – and the economic life of the assets).

The second step involves estimating the company-specific debt premium. Again, this is normally not too difficult, especially for those companies with existing quoted debt. Even in the absence of such quoted debt, comparative information can be used from companies with similar operating and financial profiles. Issues of maturity and whether to use spot or longer-term averages apply equally to the debt premium. Combining the risk-free rate and debt premium estimates produces the overall cost of debt.

The third step then involves estimating the market's valuation of equity risk – the equity risk premium (ERP). This is probably the least straightforward issue faced by regulators, not least because views on the appropriate value for the ERP differ significantly among academics and practitioners. Unlike in the case of interest rates, market evidence of forward-looking expectations are not available, and so there tends to be a strong reliance on historical evidence as a guide to future expected returns (see the discussion in Jenkinson, 1999). However, in recent years there has been an important reassessment of what the longer-term historical evidence actually shows for the ERP – in particular the important work of Dimson et al. (2002) – which has generally resulted in downward revisions to estimates of the ERP.

The fourth step is to estimate the (undiversifiable) risk associated with the specific regulated activity. Within the context of the CAPM, this means estimating the beta coefficient, and again this necessarily relies on historical data. We will focus on the difficulties encountered in estimating beta coefficients in the next section of the chapter, but this has certainly been one of the areas where regulators have become increasingly loath to rely on the market evidence. Combining the beta and ERP estimates provides the cost of equity.

The fifth step involves weighting together the cost of debt and cost of equity to produce an overall weighted average cost of capital (WACC). Until recently, regulators tended to use actual debt/equity ratios in such calculations, but, as regulated companies have increasingly become highly geared, there has been a tendency to use 'assumed' capital structures in setting the WACC.

Finally, it is necessary to decide whether to set the cost of capital on a pre-tax or post-tax basis. Clearly, investors care about the returns they receive from the company after it has paid any corporate taxes, and they have paid any income or capital gains taxes. Regulators have the choice, however, of allowing for such tax payments in the allowed cost of capital – thereby setting a pre-tax cost of capital – or including projected (corporate) tax payments in the allowed costs of the company, and setting a post-tax cost of capital on the RAV. In practice, adopting the former approach will usually involve using an assumed tax-wedge reflecting statutory tax rates, which is applied to the cost of equity (given that interest payments on debt are tax deductible at the corporate level). The use of statutory rates is fine when viewed over the long term, or in equilibrium, but in the short term the actual tax positions of companies can deviate widely from the statutory position. Setting a post-tax cost of capital will tend to reduce incentives to increase gearing for purely tax-driven reasons, especially if any benefits from increasing gearing above assumed levels are clawed back at subsequent reviews. General concerns to reduce the incentives for companies to adopt highly geared capital structures provide one explanation for the increased tendency in recent years to set the cost of capital on a post-tax basis.[4]

In Table 7.1 we present a summary of a sample of the regulatory decisions regarding the cost of capital that have been made in recent years in the UK. For consistency, these have been put on a similar tax basis: given the trend towards using post-tax values, we have normalized on this measure.[5] Looking over the recent history of regulatory decisions, there was a general downward trend in the estimates. In part this was driven by falling real interest rates, especially as regulators started, from 1999 onwards, to put more weight on the current spot rates rather than the longer-term averages (which was the justification for the range employed, for example, by the Monopolies and Mergers Commission in the 1996 BAA case). Also, as the stock market boomed until 2001, so estimates of the equity risk premium tended to be reduced. So, for example, in the case of OFWAT the estimated cost of equity and the overall WACC fell noticeably between the periodic reviews of 1994 and 1999. Similarly, in the case of BAA the overall WACC fell by a full percentage point from 6 per cent in 1996 to 5 per cent in 2002.

However, the other noticeable trend in the UK during the last few years has been the increasing use of debt in the capital structure of, in particular, water and electricity distribution companies. In principle, under the Modigliani and Miller (1958) assumptions, changes in the capital structure should have no impact on the overall WACC, in particular when measured on a post-tax basis, as in Table 7.1. As gearing increases, the equity beta should increase linearly (provided the underlying asset beta is constant) thereby offsetting any benefit from the greater use of cheaper debt. But there has clearly been a perception among regulated companies that the increasing use of debt finance can lower the cost of capital, and as a result there has been a significant increase in gearing across the utility sector.

This has had various implications. First, regulators are increasingly concerned that their methodology for estimating the cost of capital should not encourage excessive use of debt. This in part explains the trend towards setting the cost of capital on a post-tax basis, where any tax-driven benefits from increasing gearing above assumed levels are clawed back at the next review. However, the main way that regulators have responded in recent years has been by increasing their estimates of the cost of equity finance – both in absolute terms and relative to the cost of debt. For instance, as Table 7.1 shows, in the most recent 2004 review of electricity distribution, the cost of equity has been estimated at 7.5 per cent real post-tax, whereas at the previous review in 1999 the range was estimated at 5.5–6.5 per cent. We discuss the problems regulators have encountered in estimating the appropriate cost of equity in the next section.

The second response to the increasing gearing has been for regulators to pay much more attention to financeability, and to consult those involved in the debt markets – in particular credit rating agencies – to a much greater extent. We discuss the merits of this response later in this chapter.

Measuring risk
One of the key requirements in establishing an appropriate cost of capital is clearly to estimate the risks associated with the activity. Standard finance theory informs us that investors should only require additional returns for bearing non-

Table 7.1 Selected regulatory determinations for the cost of capital

Regulator	Industry and year of the regulatory review	Risk-free rate (%)	Debt premium (%)	Post-tax cost of debt (%)	Equity risk premium (%)	Equity beta	Post-tax cost of equity	Gearing $\frac{debt}{debt + equity}$	Post-tax WACC
OFWAT	Water (2004)	2.5–3.0	0.8–1.4	2.3–3.1	4–5	1.0	6.5–8.0	55%	4.2–5.3 **5.1%**
OFGEM	Electricity Distribution (2004)			2.9		1.0	7.5	57.5%	**4.8%**
Competition Commission	London Airports – BAA (2002)	2.5–2.75	0.9–1.2	2.4–2.8	2.5–4.5	0.8–1.0	4.5–7.3	25%	4.0–6.1 **5.0%**
OFGEM	Gas Transmission and Distribution – TransCo (2001)	2.75	1.5–1.9	3.0–3.3	3.5	1.0	6.25	62.5%	4.2–4.4 **4.4%**
ORR	Railtrack (2000)	3	1.5–1.75	3.15–3.3	4	1.1–1.3	7.4–8.2	50%	5.3–5.8 **5.6%**
OFGEM	Electricity Distribution (1999)	2.25–2.75	1.4	2.6–2.9	3.25–3.75	1.0	5.5–6.5	50%	4.0–4.7 **4.6%**
OFWAT	Water (1999)	2.5–3.0	1.5–2.0	2.8–3.5	3–4	0.7–0.8	4.6–6.2	50%	3.7–4.9 **4.1%**

Monopolies and Mergers Commission	London Airports – BAA (1996)	3.5–3.8	0.3–0.8	2.7–3.2	4–5	0.7–0.9	6.3–8.3	30%	5.2–6.8 **6.0%**
OFWAT	Water (1994)	3–4	1.0	2.8–3.5	3–4	0.67–0.75	5.0–7.0	12%	4.7–6.6 **5.7%**

Note: This table summarizes the cost of capital determinations for various UK regulated companies on a consistent real post-tax basis. It should be noted that in many cases the figures quoted by the regulators were on a different tax basis; in these cases the implied post-tax figures have been computed using an assumed corporate tax rate of 30 per cent in order to compute the post-tax cost of debt. In the final column the resultant range for the WACC is presented, based solely on adding up the component parts in the previous columns. This sometimes differs from the ranges quoted by regulators, which on occasions have been narrower than the range implied by the individual estimates. The final column also includes, in bold, any quoted 'headline' cost of capital figure used by the regulator on a post-tax basis (for those regulators who use different tax bases, the headline figure has been calculated on a post-tax basis). When headline figures are not quoted, then the mid-point of the range is shown in bold. In the case of the most recent OFGEM review, little detail on the component parts of the cost of capital was published. In the interests of consistency over time and between regulators, the figures do not include small company premia that have been applied to the small water-only companies, nor any allowances for embedded debt (which were made by some regulators during 1999–2001).

Sources: OFGEM (2004b, p. 109), OFWAT (2004, p. 222), Competition Commission (2002, p. 171), OFGEM (2001, p. 73), Office of the Rail Regulator (2000, pp. 46–47), OFWAT (1999, p. 130), Monopolies and Mergers Commission (1996, p. 81), OFWAT (1994, pp. 49–50). OFWAT is the Office of Water Services, OFGEM is the Office of Gas and Electricity Markets, ORR is the Office of Rail Regulation.

diversifiable risks – which within the single-factor CAPM are captured by the beta of the company. However, one of the most difficult areas for regulators in recent years has been the estimation of such beta coefficients. Recall, also, that small changes in such estimates have significant implications: with an equity risk premium of, say, 4 per cent a movement of 0.25 in beta will change the cost of equity by 1 per cent.

As can be seen from Table 7.1, and from reading the determinations from which the figures are drawn, regulators have tended to use equity beta estimates that are surprisingly close to unity. To some extent, of course, the upward trend that can be seen in the equity betas should simply reflect the increased use of debt in the capital structure. However, it is nonetheless surprising that, for instance, water companies and electricity distribution companies – with revenues that vary hardly at all with the general state of the economy – should be assumed to have a risk profile similar to that of the average UK company.

There are various possible explanations for the high betas used by regulators. First, for some industries market evidence relevant to the regulated business has become increasingly scarce or difficult to interpret. There have always been concerns about the need to isolate regulated from unregulated activities of companies, but in some industries it has become more or less impossible to obtain a direct measure of risk. This is particularly the case in electricity distribution – where no pure electricity distribution companies with a separate stock exchange listing exist in the UK anymore – and in the case of the rail network – since the demise of Railtrack and its reincarnation as Network Rail (which is essentially funded by government-guaranteed debt). In such cases, it is possible to look at comparator companies in similar industries, or at international evidence for the same industry, but this is usually a very imperfect substitute, since details of the regulatory contract – for instance in the extent of cost pass-through, or the sharing of quantity risks through revenue caps – will have a significant impact on risk. The second, and related, explanation for the tendency to use beta estimates close to unity is that uncertainty about the 'true' value – either due to the lack of reliable evidence, or to instability in the estimates over time – should result in more weight being given to the unconditional expectation (in the absence of any specific information) that the companies are of average risk (and hence have a beta of unity). This point is specifically made by OFGEM in their most recent determination for electricity distribution (see OFGEM, 2004b, pp. 105–6). OFWAT, although acknowledging the market evidence that betas are much lower than unity, has also clearly been influenced by such views (see OFWAT, 2004, pp. 269–70). Consequently, for both the energy and water sectors, the current position is that equity beta is estimated at unity.

While acknowledging the problems faced in measuring risk, it is nonetheless extremely surprising that the cost of equity is set on this basis. Consider the evidence for the water sector – which probably provides the least bad set of data

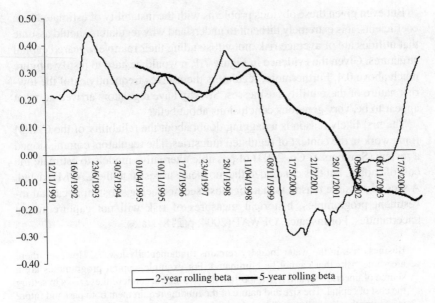

Note: This figure shows 2-year and 5-year rolling betas since privatization for the UK water sector (as represented by the *Datastream* UK Water index), relative to the FTSE-All Share index. The data frequency is daily.

Source: *Datastream*.

Figure 7.1   Beta estimates for the UK water sector

for estimating betas. In Figure 7.1 the equity betas for the water sector are computed on a two-year and five-year rolling basis since privatization. These estimates are derived using daily total returns for an index of UK listed water companies. Figure 7.1 demonstrates clearly the problems faced by regulators. For much of the 1990s the data were all pointing towards beta estimates in the range of 0.2 to 0.4. Although levels of net debt were increasing during this period there was no clear upward trend in the equity beta, as would, in principle, be expected if the underlying asset beta was unchanged.

However, the real problems with the estimates started during the stock market bubble years of 1999–2001, when estimated betas tumbled sharply and even turned negative (obviously with a lag of a few years in the case of the five-year estimate). Indeed, although the two-year beta increased significantly in 2004 and at the end of 2004 was back at around 0.3, the estimated five-year rolling beta for the water sector at the time of writing remains negative. This is clearly implausible, and suggests that the period generating such odd results should carry less (or no) weight in cost of capital calculations.

But even given these obvious problems with the instability of estimated beta coefficients, it is extremely difficult to understand why regulators should assume that utilities are of average risk, notwithstanding their relatively geared capital structures. Given the evidence in Figure 7.1, it would be hard to justify a figure much above 0.4. Furthermore, regulators themselves frequently extol the low-risk nature of these utility businesses. So why have regulators arrived at, what appear to be, very generous conclusions about beta?

The first likely reason is a nagging doubt about the reliability of the CAPM framework in the context of regulated industries. The regulators commissioned a review (Smithers & Co, 2003) of possible alternative models to estimate the cost of capital, but this concluded that no clear successor to the CAPM existed. A second possible reason is that for those sectors facing substantial capital investment programmes, historical measures of risk will not capture future uncertainties. For instance, OFWAT (2004, p. 218) states:

> Business risk in the water industry remains fundamentally low. ... However, there are some risks that cannot be eliminated. For example, capital programmes are a source of uncertainty, and it is important that we take account of these risks in setting the cost of capital. The size and nature of the funding requirement both past and future is a factor that has influenced our view on an appropriate cost of capital for the water sector.

However, it is questionable how much influence such fears regarding capital investment should have in practice. After all, the cost of capital is being applied to the *entire* regulatory asset base, which, as mentioned in Note 2, currently amounts to £35 billion in the case of water. Over the next five years, due to the large capital programme, it is anticipated that this asset base will grow to £40 billion. Do the risks associated with the existing asset base really justify a beta of unity? It is extremely difficult to see why and, indeed, the low-risk nature of the existing regulated asset base has been recognized by the relatively cheap debt financing that has been secured against it. Furthermore, it is not axiomatic that the uncertainties associated with a large capital programme will necessarily increase investors' required returns. Many of these risks are diversifiable in nature, and as long as the regulatory contract allows for a reasonable degree of symmetry in terms of enjoying the benefits of unanticipated efficiencies, as well as bearing any cost over-runs, then the impact on the cost of capital may be negligible.

Therefore, the current situation regarding assessing risk in the regulated utility sector is quite opaque and, on the face of it, seems to be rather generous. This is particularly true if the existing asset base can be thought of as having an established regulatory status, and therefore suffers little in the way of expropriation risk. Of course this says nothing about the generosity or severity of the overall regulatory settlements: a generous cost of capital may to some extent be balanced by a regulator's very challenging assumptions on future operating or capital efficiencies when setting price caps. But these are separate matters, and the objective of regulators should always be to establish an appropriate cost of capital in order to encourage appropriate investment decisions.

In this section we have considered risk in isolation from general considerations of capital structure. However, arguably the main explanation for the apparent generosity of recent estimates of the cost of equity relates to a concern that the 'flight of equity' should be halted. It is to these issues that we now turn.

Capital structure

The increasing use of debt in the capital structure has been observed across all UK utilities in the last decade. At privatization, most utilities had very little debt, and some had positive net cash balances.[6] A combination of net investment, dividend policies/share repurchases, and acquisitions has steadily increased gearing. However, it is worth remarking that it is by no means the case that companies have all adopted highly geared structures: the financial structures of utility companies, both within a particular sector and between sectors, varies considerably. Nonetheless, as can be seen from Table 7.1, the assumed level of gearing in the case of most of the regulated industries is now over 50 per cent, and this is reasonably close to the average actual gearing observed in those industries.

One obvious question is: should regulators care about capital structure? In this section we consider this question from two related perspectives. We start by considering the effect of capital structure on the cost of capital per se, and then look at the broader questions relating to whether regulators should attempt to influence, or limit, the capital structure of regulated companies.

Capital structure and the cost of capital

In the context of the cost of capital, finance theory suggests that the overall cost of capital is determined by the underlying business risks, not by how the business is financed. The main objection to this theoretical position is that it ignores the effects of taxation. However, if the cost of capital is set on a post-tax basis, then this objection may not apply. But this assumes that the CAPM is applied consistently – with reliable estimates of equity betas and debt betas – which would thereby maintain the invariance of the cost of capital to gearing. As noted in the previous section, in practice regulators have increasingly assumed an equity beta of unity, and have separately assumed a gearing level. Despite the close connection in theory between these assumptions, the relationship is much less apparent in recent regulatory decisions. So, for instance, a beta of unity was applied by OFGEM to the electricity distribution companies in both 1999 and 2004, despite the fact that the assumed gearing increased from 50 per cent to 57.5 per cent.

In this situation the gearing assumption clearly has a major influence on the out-turn WACC. If increased use of debt has no impact on the assumed equity beta, then higher gearing will always reduce the allowed cost of capital, since, implicitly, the underlying asset beta is lower.

On the other hand, if the cost of capital is being set on a post-tax basis, and tax payments are being allowed for separately as a cost, regulators would still have to determine their policy on the extent of pass-through of tax, since higher use of debt finance would tend to reduce tax bills, and hence required revenues.

It is worth noting, however, that the necessity to set an *assumed* (or *target* or *maximium*) level of gearing is not required when the cost of capital is set on a pre-tax basis. As explained earlier, the pre-tax approach tends to use statutory tax rates in computing the tax wedge to be applied to the cost of capital. In the short term, the effective tax rates of companies can deviate very substantially from these statutory rates, but over the long term the average effective rate should be similar to the statutory rate. Using this approach, the impact of capital structure is only important in the sense noted above: namely, that the estimated betas should reflect the observed gearing over the period that the betas are measured, in order that the CAPM is consistently applied.

Regulators may have some residual interest in the actual level of gearing employed by companies even when the cost of capital is being set on a pre-tax basis, depending on the relative tax disadvantage of equity (which should be reflected in the allowed tax wedge). In practice, this depends on the extent of dividend tax imputation or, as in the UK in recent years, the extent of 'shareholder relief' regarding the taxation of dividends.[7] However, companies themselves have incentives to reduce their cost of capital, and so will tend to reduce their reliance on equity when it is tax-disadvantaged. If they do increase gearing, then regulators would simply incorporate the higher observed gearing into their cost of capital calculations at the next price control and customers would, at that stage, benefit from any tax efficiencies.

Looking over the recent history of regulatory decisions on the cost of capital, the vast majority of regulators have employed this pre-tax approach to setting the cost of capital. This has been the case with the Monopolies and Mergers Commission (though not its successor the Competition Commission in its review of water charges in 2000), OFTEL (the telecommunications regulator, recently absorbed into the Office of Communications, OFCOM), the Civil Aviation Authority (CAA) (which regulates the main London airports), and Postcomm (which regulates the Royal Mail). In addition, until recently, OFGEM and the Office of Rail Regulation (ORR) also set the cost of capital on a pre-tax basis. In their most recent determinations, both have switched to a post-tax approach. The only regulator to consistently set the cost of capital on a post-tax basis has been OFWAT, who has, not surprisingly, been particularly proactive in the capital structure debate.

Should capital structure be regulated?

However, in many respects, the real debate about capital structure goes beyond issues relating to the cost of capital. In particular, in the 2004 reviews of water and electricity distribution, given the loose application of the CAPM, arguably the gearing assumption had little direct impact on the *outcome* for the overall WACC. In recent years, the main issue has been the concern that companies might adopt financial structures that over-relied on debt and were not able to absorb cost, or other, shocks, or leave capacity to fund new investment. The emergence of 'thin equity' models for utility companies has raised a number of issues relating to capital structure that, while related to the cost of capital – in particular because the way the cost of capital is determined may provide incentives for adopting a particular capital structure – raise more general issues about the regulatory contract and the operation of financial markets.

First, perhaps the most fundamental question is whether regulators should attempt to influence capital structure at all. After all, if the cost of capital is set at an appropriate level, then investors should be prepared to commit capital, and the choice of capital structure could be left to the management of the company. As noted above, incentives to optimize the capital structure (in respect of taxation, addressing principal–agent concerns, or other factors) would exist as long as the cost of capital was based at periodic reviews on the out-turn capital structure. This *laissez-faire* attitude towards capital structure broadly conforms to the approach taken by the Competition Commission over the years. I would argue that there is much to commend this general stance, and that regulators should avoid being too prescriptive about appropriate capital structures.

However, this stance raises a second important issue: what happens if a regulated company becomes financially distressed? Should regulators limit gearing, or set incentives that effectively discourage the use of debt beyond a certain point? This is one of the main concerns regarding the adoption of almost entirely debt-financed structures for some utility companies.

Again, there are different approaches that can be taken. The *laissez-faire* approach would acknowledge the potential disruption that could be caused by the insolvency of a regulated company and would make sure that robust arrangements for the transfer of the licence of the regulated activity existed. Such arrangements were in place for some, but not all, regulated companies at privatization, and subsequent legislation has generally incorporated such 'special administration' clauses into the remaining licences. However, beyond establishing such back-stop arrangements, the choice of capital structure would remain one for the management. If debt levels, for whatever reason, became unsustainable, then this should be reflected in the market values of the debt and equity, and/or result in the violation of debt covenants. It is likely that in such a situation the management would have to organize a financial restructuring, which would typically involve raising more equity financing (either directly, or by converting some debt into equity). This would doubtless be painful for the management, but there is no reason why the lights should go out or the water should stop running. In extremis, the company may be unable to raise additional financing, in which case the existing investors would have an interest in negotiating a sale of the company. There seems to be a healthy appetite for regulated companies from a variety of parties, including private equity firms, and there is no reason to believe that an orderly sale of the company could not be achieved.

The objections to this approach fall into three broad categories. First, it is possible that the insolvency of a utility company may have systemic effects that go beyond the individual entity. For instance, debt premia might rise for all companies in that sector, or in other regulated sectors. Regulation of capital structure might, therefore, be justified in order to avoid such negative externalities. This is clearly a possibility, but it is uncertain whether investors would reassess risk in this way, in particular if the problems facing the particular company were idiosyncratic.

Second, there is a concern that companies operating with high gearing – or those bought mainly with debt at valuations at, or above, the RAV – might be more likely to cut back on areas of expenditure that are important in the longer term, but may be discretionary in the short term. This relates particularly to those expenditures – such as maintenance or renewals – where the effects on outputs are not necessarily direct in the short term. This might be a particular issue if interest rates rose, and the burden of interest payments reduced free cash flow significantly. Again, this is potentially a concern, but the direct way of addressing this is to develop better systems for regulators to monitor outputs and the condition of assets. Furthermore, annual reporting of operating and capital expenditures provides regulators with early warning of abnormal trends. From the viewpoint of the company, a highly geared financial structure is likely to be heavily hedged against interest rate volatility and, in any case, the equity holders in the business ultimately care about the value of the company, and have no incentives to damage this. Again, it is not clear how valid this concern is, and regulation of capital structure is a rather indirect way of addressing it.

Third, there is a view that, at certain times, equity markets are 'closed' and therefore in the event that companies faced financial distress, or needed to finance a major investment programme, they would be unable to raise new equity. Therefore, regulated companies should keep a reasonable buffer of equity financing to see them through such eventualities.

This argument, although often heard, does not, in my opinion, withstand close scrutiny. In what sense are equity markets 'closed'? Most utility companies have high dividend yields, and if necessary dividends could be cut and the retained earnings re-invested in the regulated business. In this way debt/RAV ratios would be reduced. Furthermore, if an additional equity issue is required, then why would investors *not* subscribe? Increasingly, firms conducting secondary offerings use

deep-discounted rights issues, which do not even require underwriting. If investors do not want to commit additional funds, they can sell their rights and accept
the resultant share dilution. Although new equity issues by utility companies are
not commonplace in the UK, they have been observed – for instance United
Utilities' recent rights offer, and the sale of Northumbrian Water by Suez in 2003.
Furthermore, it seems odd to believe that equity investors would be unwilling to
commit further funds whereas debt investors are willing.

An alternative interpretation of the view that equity financing is difficult, is
that such capital raising, or dividend cutting, events give financial markets the
opportunity to express their views about the management of the company, and
that senior executives often face intense scrutiny. Therefore, it is not so much
that financing cannot be raised, but that executives may not want to go to the
equity markets. However, in the absence of any evidence of mismanagement,
it is difficult to understand why equity investors would exact management
changes if additional funding was required for, say, a major investment programme that was going to result in an increased RAV, or why they would be
unprepared to fund it (whether by debt or equity).

Therefore, although there are arguments for capital structure to be regulated,
there are also good reasons for taking a *laissez-faire* approach to capital structure
decisions. If the cost of capital is set at a reasonable level, financing should be
forthcoming, and there is no need to decide on a target, optimal or maximum
level of gearing. In the next section we consider an additional issue that has in
recent years become a significant consideration in determining required rates
of return: financeability.

Financeability

All the regulatory bodies have, as one of their duties, a requirement that the
companies they regulate are able to finance their licensed functions. One interpretation of this duty, in line with the *laissez-faire* approach explained in the
previous section, is simply that it relates to the requirement that the regulators
set an appropriate cost of capital for the regulated business. However, there has
been an increasing weight given to a second requirement – to check on the prospective financeability of the company given its future capital and operating
requirements.

For instance, OFWAT is particularly clear in its interpretation of its duties:

> We have a duty to secure that companies are able to finance the proper carrying out
> of their functions as licensed undertakers ('finance functions'). We look at this as
> having two strands. One is to secure that, if a company is efficiently managed and
> financed, it is able to earn a return at least equal to the cost of capital. The second is
> that its revenues, profits and cash flows must allow it to raise finance on reasonable
> terms in the capital markets. We refer to this second strand as financeability. (OFWAT,
> 2004, p. 217)

Financeability is particularly an issue when companies are required to undertake large capital programmes, and are therefore facing periods when depreciation allowances are insufficient to prevent negative cash flow. OFWAT go on to elaborate that in such circumstances there can be 'a deterioration in credit quality which could restrict the access of companies, despite earning their cost of capital, to capital markets or could significantly increase the cost of finance' (2004, p. 217).

The practical consequence of conducting such financeability tests is that increasing emphasis is placed on prospective financial ratios – such as various versions of interest coverage, cash flow to debt ratios, and gearing ratios – and whether companies are expected to retain a strong credit rating throughout the price control period. Regulators increasingly turn to credit rating agencies for their views on such matters, and licences have been amended in some cases to require companies to maintain an investment grade credit rating.

Such macro-level tests of the impact of the various parts of the regulatory determination on the finances of the company are clearly sensible, and have frequently been conducted by sectoral regulators and the Competition Commission. However, with the increased gearing of regulated companies, and the end of the glide path whereby past efficiency saving resulted in allowed returns well in excess of the cost of capital, financeability tests are increasingly starting to bind. This is particularly true of the water industry in England and Wales, where the recent final determinations for the 2005–10 price control period include financeability payments amounting to more than £400m in NPV terms.[8]

The effect of such financeability payments is to set allowed returns at a level above the cost of capital. However, there are arguments against this two-strand approach to judging an appropriate allowed return. First, as noted in the previous section, capital structure is largely a matter for management rather than the regulator. Financeability issues tend to follow directly from decisions over capital structure. Ideally, management should be taking a long-term view of the likely capital programmes they will be required to deliver, and set their capital structure appropriately. If they want to keep a stable dividend policy, and not tap the equity market for additional funds, then if they anticipate substantial future net investment they should retain the financial capacity by keeping current levels of gearing down at appropriate levels. If management misjudges such matters, and faces a credit downgrade, then they have to repair their credit rating by raising additional equity financing. According to this narrow interpretation of the 'financing functions' duty of regulators, there is no need for regulators to involve rating agencies in their deliberations (notwithstanding the high levels of debt employed by some companies), or for them to make additional payments over and above the cost of capital.

In practice, however, it can be difficult for management to anticipate the investment demands they are likely to face in the future. Such matters often involve all manner of government agencies and are subject to considerable political input. So in some cases it may be unreasonable to expect companies to be able to predict the future capital expenditure requirements and set an appropriate long-term strategy to finance these. In such cases, however, there are alternatives to allowing companies higher rates of return. First, it is always open to the regulator to adjust the profile of prices within a control period to match the cash-flow profile. For instance, if a company faced particularly high first-year investment, allowed revenues could be increased in this year to keep financial ratios at appropriate levels. However, this approach tends to trade off stable price paths for consumers against stable financial ratios for companies. Furthermore, it is unclear why financial markets should be unduly influenced by financial ratios in any particular year, rather than those applying over the entire control period.

Second, if the cash-flow 'problem' is such that it cannot be fixed by moving revenue around within a control period, then the regulator could alter the depreciation profile of the company and spread the effect over many years. This approach was considered, but ultimately rejected, by OFGEM for one company in their 2004 review of electricity distribution. However, advantages of such an approach are: (a) it is NPV neutral, since the extra depreciation reduces the RAV more rapidly and (b) in many cases it will lead to an equitable inter-temporal smoothing of prices over a number of control periods.

Therefore, although some regulators in the UK have added financeability allowances on top of the estimated cost of capital, I would argue that there are good arguments against this, and in favour of a narrower interpretation of their duties.

Conclusions

This chapter has reviewed some of the important issues encountered by regulators when estimating the cost of capital. Although asset pricing models such as the CAPM are easy to implement in principle, we discussed some of the issues faced by regulators in practice. One of the main concerns has been how to estimate the risk for regulated companies, especially when the relevant beta coefficients are either unstable or unavailable. The approach currently adopted by some regulators – to assume that utilities, with their current financial structure, are of average risk relative to the market as a whole – seems questionable and, perhaps, more driven by a desire to increase allowed equity returns to prevent a further substitution of equity by debt.

The chapter has also considered the related issues of the regulatory approaches to capital structure and financeability, and their relationship to the cost of capital. In general, I have argued that it was not necessary, or probably desirable, to attempt to regulate the capital structure and the various measures of financeability *in addition to* the cost of capital. If the latter is set an appropriate level, the former are, on the whole, matters for management not regulators.

Notes

1. The predecessor to the Competition Commission (CC) was the Monopolies and Mergers Commission (MMC). However, in this chapter occasionally, as a shorthand, we refer to decisions by either body as being those of the CC.

2. The regulatory asset values have recently been estimated at £35 billion for the England and Wales water sector (OFWAT, 2004), at £12.5 billion for electricity distribution (OFGEM, 2004a), at £10.7 billion for gas distribution (from NGT estimates associated with the sale of some of the local networks), at £20.2 billion for the rail infrastructure (ORR, 2003, p. 269), at around £5 billion for electricity transmission (OFGEM, 2000) and at £13 billion for gas transmission. All these figures relate to the estimated RAV at April 2005. The price bases differ somewhat (between 2000 and 2003 prices) although converting into current prices would have a minor upward effect on the estimates.

3. The overall cost of capital (WACC) is calculated as a weighted average cost of debt and equity finance: WACC $= g \times r_d + (1 - g) \times r_e$ where g is the gearing level (net debt/total value); r_d is the return required on debt; and r_e is the return required on equity. The CAPM states that a company's cost of equity is determined by the risk-free rate (r_f), the equity risk premium (ERP) for the market as a whole, and the company-specific risk parameter, *beta* (measured by the ratio of the covariance of the returns on the company's shares with the those of the market in general, divided by the variance of the market returns): $r_e = r_f + beta \times$ ERP. The cost of debt is usually estimated as the sum of the risk-free rate (r_f) and debt premium (d_p) that investors require from investments in a company: $r_d = r_f + d_p$. As an alternative to the CAPM, the cost of equity is sometimes estimated using the Dividend Growth Model, which in its simplest form assumes that dividends grow at a constant perpetual rate. In this case the cost of equity is the sum of the current dividend yield and the assumed growth rate.

4. For instance, OFGEM (the Office of Gas and Electricity Markets) consistently set the cost of capital on a pre-tax basis until the 2004 electricity distribution price control review, at which point it switched to a post-tax approach which 'allows the incentives to increase gearing to be mitigated' (OFGEM, 2004b, p. 111).

5. To further confuse matters, the terminology 'post-tax' has not been consistently applied in the past. The distinction between pre- and post-tax has tended to relate only to the cost of equity, with the cost of debt being assessed on a pre-tax basis. The figures in Table 7.1 measure both the cost of equity and the cost of debt on a post-tax basis.

6. A notable exception is the case of the National Air Traffic Services, which was sold to a consortium that financed the acquisition with 94 per cent debt. Furthermore, the ratio of debt to the regulatory asset value was 118 per cent.

7. The system whereby dividends avoided being taxed twice – once at the corporate level (via corporate tax) and once at the shareholder level (via income tax) – used to be ameliorated by the use of the imputation system involving the company issuing tax credits to individual shareholders. In the UK, such credits did not entirely remove the double taxation, but the effect was much reduced. In 1997, the tax system was significantly changed, and reclaimable tax credits were replaced by lower rates of income tax on dividend income. This is what we refer to as a shareholder relief system. For more information on these tax changes, see Bell and Jenkinson (2002).

8. A financeability payment has also been allowed by OFGEM in its recent price control review for the electricity distribution sector. For one company, an extra payment of £1.6m p.a. has been allowed to ensure that it is possible to 'maintain a credit rating comfortably within investment grade' (OFGEM, 2004b, p. 115).

References

Bell, L. and Jenkinson, T.J. (2002) 'New Evidence on the Impact of Dividend Taxation and on the Identity of the Marginal Investor', *Journal of Finance*, **57**(3), 1321–46.

Competition Commission (2002), *BAA plc: A Report on the Economic Regulation of the London Airports Companies (Heathrow Airport Ltd, Gatwick Airport Ltd and Stansted Airport Ltd)*, London: The Stationery Office, November.

Dimson, E., Marsh, P. and Staunton, M. (2002) *Triumph of the Optimists*, Princeton, NJ: Princeton University Press.

Jenkinson, T.J. (1999) 'Real Interest Rates and the Cost of Capital', *Oxford Review of Economic Policy*, **15**(2), 114–27.

Modigliani, F. and M. Miller (1958) 'The Cost of Capital, Corporation Finance and the Theory of Investment', *American Economic Review*, **48**, 261–97.

Monopolies and Mergers Commission (1996) *BAA Plc: A Report on the Economic Regulation of the London Airports Companies (Heathrow Airport Ltd, Gatwick Airport Ltd and Stansted Airport Ltd)*, London: MMC, October.

Office of the Rail Regulator (2000) *Periodic Review of Railtrack's Access Charges: Final Conclusions*, London: ORR, October

OFGEM (2000) *The Transmission Price Control Review of National Grid Company from 2001: Transmission Asset Owner – Final Proposals*, London: OFGEM, September

OFGEM (2001) *Review of Transco's Price Control from 2002*, London: OFGEM, September.

OFGEM (2004a) *Electricity Distribution Price Control Review: Update Paper*, London: Office of Gas and Electricity Markets, September.

OFGEM (2004b) *Electricity Distribution Price Control Review: Final Proposals*, London: Office of Gas and Electricity Markets, December.

OFWAT (1994) *Future Charges for Water and Sewerage Services: The Outcome of the Periodic Review*, Birmingham: Office of Water Services, July.

OFWAT (1999) *Future Water and Sewerage Charges, 2000–05: Final Determinations*, Birmingham: Office of Water Services, November.

OFWAT (2004) *Future Water and Sewerage Charges: Final Determinations*, Birmingham: Office of Water Services, December.

ORR (2003) *Access Charges Review Final Conclusions*, London: Office of the Rail Regulator, December.

Smithers & Co (2003) 'Study into Certain Aspects of the Cost of Capital for Regulated Utilities in the UK', February, Available from the OFWAT website: www.ofwat.gov. uk/aptrix/ofwat/publish.nsf/AttachmentsByTitle/cost_of_capital130203.pdf/$FILE/ cost_of_capital130203.pdf.

8 Information revelation and incentives

Phil Burns, Cloda Jenkins and Thomas Weyman-Jones

Introduction

Regulation is present in a number of utility industries, all of which have different characteristics, but competition is not expected to emerge in these sectors and, hence, regulation is expected to remain in place for some time (indeed indefinitely). The first-best world provides the benchmark case. In this situation the regulator would know, with certainty, the required efficient level of costs and demand for quality of service at all periods in time.

The challenge for the regulator is to get as close as possible to first best given the information problems that he or she faces. The range of feasible options available to the regulator, both for getting better information about efficient costs and service levels and for designing incentive mechanisms, will depend on the specific characteristics of the industry and company being regulated. For example, the number of companies in the industry will determine the feasibility of using mechanisms that are based on comparative analysis. Similarly, the extent to which managers are expected to be risk averse will influence the options available to the regulator for trading off incentives and insurance. The legal and institutional framework of the regulatory regime will also influence the choices that the regulator will make. Most notably, the regulator's ability to commit to particular mechanisms may be determined by the law, and the extent to which the regulator is independent from policymakers may influence the way in which the potentially conflicting objectives of technical efficiency, allocative efficiency and distribution objectives are balanced. Furthermore, the length of time that regulation has been in place and the data-gathering processes that have been used will influence the nature of the information problem. The environment within which the regulator makes decisions must therefore be considered, both to determine the range of options available and to assess which option is optimal given this environment. The challenge for the regulator is to understand how these factors influence the choices considered under the first question, and to ensure that they are taken into account when making decisions about the choice and design of information revelation and incentive mechanisms.

Two types of information asymmetry are modelled in the theoretical literature: *hidden information*, or adverse selection, and *hidden action*, or moral hazard. In the first case the regulator does not know the firm's type: it could be a highly productive efficient firm, or an unproductive inefficient firm. In this case the type of firm is a random variable chosen by nature before the regulatory game begins. This is the chief matter of interest here, and the regulator is compelled to consider the spectrum of high-powered, intermediate and low-powered contracts. The second case arises when the regulator's only problem is that the firm's effort in taking cost reducing action is unobservable. This is treated in other chapters, and the regulator is primarily interested in high-powered contracts. However, we do consider cases where hidden action and hidden information interact so that the power of the regulatory contract is critical. To express the power of the regulatory contract we state that the outcome will be a payment to the firm (perhaps as regulated revenue or allowed cost) which can be expressed in terms of a fixed sum and a proportion that varies with the firm's observed or reported cost. The parameter linking these is the power of the regulatory contract, with the most high-powered contract having a payment that is entirely decoupled from the firm's observed performance.

A basic model of hidden information

We begin with the simplest model[1] of regulator–firm interaction with asymmetric information, in which regulator and firm share equal certain knowledge of the firm's fixed cost, F, and the market demand curve, $Q(p)$, but the regulator is unsure of whether the firm has low or high marginal cost, and is unable to observe this. In the time line of this simplest principal–agent game with hidden information, the first move is by the exogenous force of nature, which draws a realization of the random marginal cost from the population of two values, one low and one high, (c_L, c_H), where $\Delta^c = c_H - c_L > 0$ is the excess of the high marginal cost over the low marginal cost.

This random drawing of marginal cost is observed by the agent, the role played by the firm, but not the principal, the role played by the regulator. The principal–regulator offers a menu of contracts based on a subjective probability distribution of the unobserved costs and preferences about the relative welfare weight of the agent–firm and consumers. The firm chooses to accept or reject and opts for one of the choices on the menu. If the contract menu has been efficiently designed, so that the agent both participates and responds to the incentives in the menu, the agent–firm's choice reveals the marginal cost that was unknown by the regulator.

The regulator's preferences are to deliver surplus to consumers and profit (arising from the firm's monopoly of information) to the agent–firm. If the regulator is indifferent between these, then a completely decentralized mechanism can be used whereby the agent–firm is free to choose its pricing policy and is given a profit equal to the observed consumer surplus which will be maximized by setting price at marginal cost.[2] If the regulator is reluctant to transfer resources from consumers to the agent–firm, then the efficient mechanism design is more complex. The regulator's reluctance may stem from preferences that favour the consumer, or from the fact that the transfer itself uses up resources, perhaps in the form of a tax distortion, so that delivering \$1 to the producer reduces consumer surplus by more than \$1. The regulator's problem contains three elements: induce the firm to participate by ensuring that its costs are covered whatever happens, reward it with additional profit for revealing that it has drawn a low marginal cost realization, and minimize the size of this reward because it has to be extracted from consumers.

There are two contracts on the menu, each containing two elements, a regulated price, p, and a transfer payment, T, from consumers to the firm as a contribution to its fixed cost.[3] The firm chooses between (p_L, T_L) and (p_H, T_H). The key parameter for the regulator is the relative weights attached to consumer surplus and firm's profit, which is reflected in the regulator's welfare function:

$$welfare = consumer\ surplus + (\alpha)\ firm's\ profit$$

and we assume $\alpha < 1$ for the reasons stated above. The regulator knows that the two possible realizations of marginal cost are (c_L, c_H) and the regulator has prior subjective probabilities associated with these possible marginal cost outcomes: probability of c_L is π and probability of c_H is $1 - \pi$. The efficient mechanism is

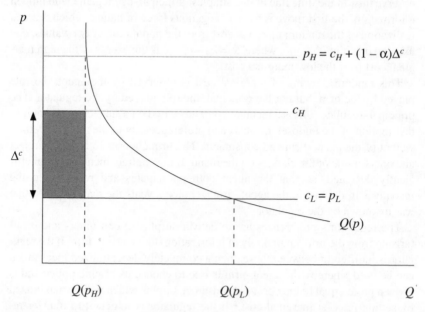

Figure 8.1 The outcome in the simplest hidden information game

illustrated in Figure 8.1. For ease of exposition we assume in Figure 8.1 that the regulator attaches equal probability to the two possible marginal costs: $\pi = 1 - \pi = 0.5$

The form of the regulation is such that after choosing one of the contracts on the menu, the firm earns $T + (p - c)Q(p) - F$. Choosing $p_L = c_L$ generates an associated transfer equal to:

$$T_L = F + Q(p_H)\Delta^c = F + Q(p_H)(c_H - c_L).$$

Consequently the firm makes positive informational profits equivalent to $Q(p_H)\Delta^c = Q(p_H)(c_H - c_L)$, and this is illustrated by the shaded area in Figure 8.1.

Choosing $p_H = c_H + (1 - \alpha)(c_H - c_L)$ generates a transfer equal to:

$$T_H = F - Q(p_H)(1 - \alpha)\Delta^c = F - Q(p_H)(1 - \alpha)(c_H - c_L).$$

Consequently the firm would make zero informational profit since

$$(c_H + (1 - \alpha)(c_H - c_L) - c_H)Q(p_H) - F + (F - Q(p_H)(1 - \alpha)(c_H - c_L)) = 0.$$

Its fixed cost is covered only incompletely by T_H and the remainder is due to a price mark-up over marginal cost. If nature has endowed the firm with c_H unknown to the regulator, the best the firm can do is to participate and just cover its costs. If nature has endowed the firm with c_L it can do better than this by choosing the contract (p_L, T_L), revealing that it has low marginal cost in return for positive informational profit. This is a separating equilibrium because it separates out the different types of agents.

How does the menu alter if the regulator's subjective probabilities of low and high cost are not equal? The contract offered for a low cost realization does not change, nor does the transfer payment available for the high cost realization. All that happens is that the regulated price cap for a high cost realization changes to $p_H = c_H + (\pi/1 - \pi)\alpha(c_H - c_L)$.

As the regulator's subjective probability of a low cost realization increases, the attraction of pretending to have a high cost realization is decreased by reducing the calculated output volume $Q(p_H)$ that will be used to generate the informational profit to the firm.

Hidden information and hidden action
We now consider a model from Laffont and Tirole (L & T) (1993) that combines the problems of hidden information and hidden action. It is known that cost depends on two factors: a firm's inherent productivity parameter, β, randomly chosen by nature, and the effort, e, devoted to lowering cost, but only the indi-

vidual firm knows the value of its productivity parameter and how much effort it will devote to lowering cost.

$$C = \beta - e$$

The regulator is aware that firms do not like expending effort, and it does know about the firm's specific *disutility of effort function*: $\psi(e)$. If a particular cost is observed, C_0, the regulator does not know whether this results from low effort by an efficient firm (productivity parameter has the value β'), or high effort by an inefficient firm (productivity parameter has the value β''). But if the regulator can discover the level of the firm's disutility (ψ) then it can infer the level of effort, e.

If the principal–regulator was fully informed about cost and effort it could insist on the *optimal level of effort* to minimize the sum of cost and disutility. This occurs when

Marginal utility of less effort = marginal cost saving ($1)
from extra effort: $- \psi'(e*) = 1$

Now consider the agent's problem. The agent is interested in the profit, U, to be made from taking on the contract. This is the transfer payment, now symbolized by the continuous variable t, less the disutility of effort:

$$U = t - \psi(e)$$

When a firm is engaged to carry out the contract, the regulator does not know which of the two productivity parameters, β' or β'', describes the firm, but let us assume initially that there is an equal probability of each. In the next illustration imagine that the regulator has constructed the profit indifference curves of the firm based on the common knowledge of the disutility of effort. The indifference curve that just ensures participation, $U = 0$, is drawn for the inefficient type of firm, and two indifference curves representing positive payoffs, $U > 0$, are drawn for the efficient type.

How can the regulator restrict the level of profit it must pay to induce the efficient firm to tell the truth? Note that there is an implicit assumption here that the regulator must prefer lower transfer payments to higher transfer payments. This could simply be a matter of preference, but Laffont and Tirole have a more relevant reason for wanting to minimize transfer payments from the regulator. They observe that every $1 paid in transfers will have cost more than $1 to raise in taxation because taxes usually distort the Pareto efficient allocation of resources.[4] The contract is:

1. Engage a firm to deliver a service, and observe the cost that is reported.
2. Pay the cost and a transfer payment that is smaller the higher the reported cost.

The regulator's dilemma is that while an inefficient firm will not pretend to be efficient, an efficient firm could easily pretend to be inefficient. The analysis is shown in Figure 8.2.

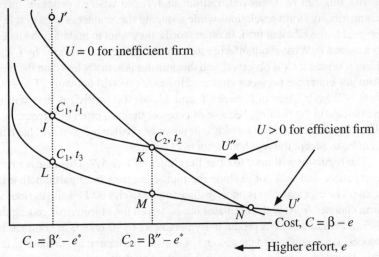

Transfer payment, t

$U = 0$ for inefficient firm

J

C_1, t_1

C_1, t_3

L

K

C_2, t_2

U''

$U > 0$ for efficient firm

M

N

U'

Cost, $C = \beta - e$

$C_1 = \beta' - e^*$ $C_2 = \beta'' - e^*$

Higher effort, e

Figure 8.2   Profit indifference curves for efficient and inefficient agents in the Laffont and Tirole principal–agent game

The axes represent C and t, total cost and the transfer payment. Moving rightwards along the horizontal axis represents reduced effort, while moving up the vertical axis represents increased transfer payment (both are 'goods'). Indifference curves further up to the right represent higher levels of profit for the agent–firm. However, an efficient firm has profit indifference curves that are much less steep than those of an inefficient firm. The argument is quite subtle here; it occurs in two stages. First, note that the slope of a profit indifference curve is the marginal utility of less effort, $-\psi'(e)$. This is so because every extra $1 of transfer payment, t, can be traded off against extra effort and still leave U unchanged. Second, for a given level of cost, C_0, the marginal disutility of effort required to lower cost at the margin $\psi'(e)$ is lower when coming from the efficient firm's cost curve than from the inefficient firm's cost curve.

Now take a specific level of effort, for example the first best optimal level, e^*. Suppose the regulator's first thought is to offer two contracts, J and K. Transfer payment t_1 if cost C_1 is observed, but transfer payment t_2 if C_2 is observed. The efficient firm is indifferent between these contracts, so we will assume it chooses J, which suggests it has the productivity parameter, β'. The inefficient firm can only choose K, since J will be on a much lower indifference curve with negative profit. So far the mechanism of offering two contracts to choose from has led to the truth being revealed. Such a contract is *incentive compatible*.

But this can be improved. Laffont and Tirole wish to maintain incentive compatibility (truth revelation) while reducing the amount of money that must be paid to the efficient firm. In other words, they want to maintain the incentive but reduce t_1. What about offering the pair of contracts represented by L and M? Here t_3 is paid if C_1 is observed, and this transfer is actually less than the efficient firm got under the previous choices. However this will not work. The efficient firm will be indifferent between L and M, but the inefficient firm will never participate in the bidding, because M is below the zero profit indifference curve. The efficient firm knows its bids will never be challenged so it will have no incentive to accept the regulator's contract choices.

The regulator will have to offer the choice of L and N. This pair is incentive compatible and will not exclude the inefficient firm from participating in the game. The efficient firm is once again assumed to choose L, while the inefficient firm chooses N. Now the regulator has achieved the objective of getting the efficient firm to reveal its productivity parameter by its choice of contract. In the process it has minimized the amount of transfer payment it has to make to induce this. However, the cost of doing so is implied by the fact that the inefficient firm is offered a contract that allows it to get away with less than the optimal effort level, say $\bar{e} < e^*$. This result arises because at N, the regulator has traded off some inefficiency in order to reduce the size of the expensive transfer payment needed to induce the efficient firm to reveal the truth about its productivity parameter. Figure 8.2 reveals this outcome because at both of the points L and M, effort is at the first best level, $e = e^*$ and cost differs only by the productivity parameter. Consequently, $-\psi'(e^*) = 1$; that is, marginal disutility of effort equals the marginal cost saving from more effort. At N, however, we see that the efficient firm's indifference curve with slope $-\psi'(e)$ is less steep than at M, requiring that $-\psi'(e) < 1$; since the marginal disutility of effort is lower, effort itself must be less. This result is also sensitive to the regulator's subjective probabilities of high and low productivity, with larger values of the probability of high productivity reducing the extent to which an inefficient firm needs to be rewarded for participation.

We summarize the following properties from the BM and L&T models:

- Offer a menu of contracts to induce firms to reveal their (productivity) type.
- Trade off inefficiency for residual profit – *intermediate power incentive regulation.*
- L, M, N lie on the tangents to the efficient firm's indifference curve.

The explanation for the last statement is that the set of optimal contracts traces out the efficient firm's profit indifference curve.[5] Label this as $t(C)$, so that the transfer payment is a function of the reported cost. We can reconstruct the curve as a series of tangents to the efficient firm's profit indifference curve, each with intercept A, and slope coefficient B: $t = A_i - B_iC$. This is the optimal mechanism drawn up by the regulator: a menu of contracts from high to low power from which the firm chooses in a way that reveals its type. The slope of each contract is the marginal disutility of effort for a firm with a given realization of cost or efficiency, and the most productive firm chooses the contract with largest intercept and steepest slope; that is, the most high-powered contract. This outcome (offer a menu and let the firm choose) is one from which neither regulator nor firm will wish to deviate, hence it is a Bayesian Nash equilibrium.

Alternatively, we could have a model that contains no transfer payment to the firm and allows the regulator to stipulate a relation between the firm's permitted price and the marginal cost that is observed. An inefficient firm may report a high marginal cost. It is allowed a high price, but if it reduces cost then price falls very rapidly. In other words, the inefficient firm can keep hardly any (perhaps none) of the cost savings it achieves. An efficient firm reporting a low marginal cost is only allowed a low price, but this does not fall when the firm reduces cost. This firm can keep all the cost savings it achieves. This is an example of Sliding Scale Regulation, see for example Burns et al. (1998).

Developments of the basic models

The discussion so far has only indicated the barest details of recent ideas on regulation under asymmetric information.[6] We briefly summarize how the field can be developed before turning to applications and practice. In particular we examine four issues that have arisen in practice:

- risk aversion;
- yardstick competition ;
- quality of service;
- and dynamics and commitment.

We assumed that the firm was risk-neutral, but if it is risk-averse it will require additional compensation in the form of insurance to participate in the game. The risk-averse firm enjoys expected profit but dislikes the variance of profit that arises from the randomness of the efficiency chosen by nature. The power of the regulatory contract must be reduced to accommodate a higher coefficient of risk aversion.

Under yardstick competition, the regulator engages with a number of firms, each of which may differ in productivity type. Laffont and Tirole suggest that the unknown productivity type may be due to two different causes: aggregative error and idiosyncratic error. In aggregative error, the random productivity of two firms is the same, and the regulatory solution is strikingly simple. By relating a firm's payment to the performance of the other firm (and in the absence of collusion), the regulator completely eliminates the firm's information monopoly. The first best outcome is achieved. This remains true even if the firms are risk-averse. Each firm has the highest incentive power and it keeps all the cost savings it makes from reducing its own costs. This is the maximum incentive power even if the firm is risk-averse and faces highly variable costs whatever its effort level. It is, however, fully insured because it can pass on the full level of costs observed from its competitors in the yardstick mechanism, and it receives the same revenue whatever the state of the world, and the level of its own marginal cost. If the productivity differences are solely idiosyncratic, then the situation is one of independent regulation of unconnected firms and replicates the basic model, where once again risk aversion will reduce the power of the regulatory contract. More generally, yardstick competition can eliminate information asymmetry arising from aggregative error, leaving only idiosyncratic error to be treated by a menu of contracts. In practice, the firms must share the same operating environment, so a benchmarking exercise is necessary to determine the efficient and consistent estimate of aggregative error. Benchmarking is examined in detail in Chapter 6 in this volume by David Parker, Thoralf Dassler and David Saal.

Quality of service regulation raises a number of issues. Armstrong and Sappington (2004) note that price-cap regulation is not well designed for this purpose since it prevents the firm from capturing the full value that some consumers may place on high quality supply. It will usually have to be supplemented by additional regulatory incentives, possibly involving intermediate power contracts such as sliding scale mechanisms. Laffont and Tirole (1993) draw a distinction between search goods, where quality can be determined before consumption or at least legally verified after consumption, and experience goods where quality is not observable until after consumption, and may not then be legally verifiable. Quality aspects of search goods can be regulated as if dealing with a multi-product monopoly, so that new problems do not arise. Where quality is verifiable additional regulatory instruments such as user panels or consumer watchdogs can be used to allow more reliance on high-powered contracts. On the other hand, with experience goods or where quality is not verifiable, a 'crowding-out' effect may occur. Firms may substitute between care for quality and cost reduction, so that the firm must be given a lower pow-ered contract, or additional intermediate power contracts related to quality issues must be available when a high-powered contract applies to the regulated price. Laffont and Tirole argue that where the regulated firm is forward looking and sensitive to its reputation in repeated supply of service then more high-powered schemes may be used. This raises the key issue of dynamic regulation, which complicates matters significantly.

We know that regulators and firms in practice are engaged in repeated interac-tions, with possibly fixed periods, for example of five years, between regulatory reviews. The key is the extent to which the regulator can perfectly commit to the regulatory contracts offered in the first period. If this is assumed to be so, then the regulator and firm can sign a long-term contract which simply replicates the static incentive compatible mechanisms in each period. However, such com-mitment is unlikely for two reasons according to Laffont and Tirole: most jurisdictions have legal restrictions on the ability of regulators to sign such long-term contracts – the political and consumer pressures are likely to be too strong, and the problem of incomplete contingent contracts arises whereby un-foreseen events lead to re-contracting. Crew and Kleinfdorfer (2002) have argued strongly that lack of credible commitment undermines the incentive compatible mechanism approach to regulation. In this case the firm may fear, and the regulator favour, a ratchet effect whereby the regulator tightens the constraint on the firm as it builds up experience of the firm's capability.

Imagine a two-period repeated game in which the regulator and the firm share a common discount factor,[7] δ. This can be analysed[8] with Figure 8.2. With complete commitment, the menu pair L and N remain optimal in each period, and the regulator signs a contract to ignore the information gained in the previ-ous period. As before, the efficient type earns positive profit in each period, with a present value depending on δ. However, the question is whether L and N are still an optimal, incentive compatible pair of menu contracts in the first period of a two-period game when there is imperfect commitment by the regulator. The answer is not if the discount factor is positive. This is because if the combination (L, N) were optimal, the regulator should offer it because it maximizes first-period welfare, and completely reveals the efficient firm's productivity for the second period. With imperfect commitment, the regulator will wish to use the information gained in the first period to reduce the efficient type's second-period profit to zero. This is the *ratchet effect* that worries many regulated firms. In this event the efficient type's present value stream is only positive in the first period and zero in the second. The inefficient type receives present value stream of zero for the two periods. In the event that the regulator cannot commit to a long-term contract that ignores information learned in the first period, a sub-optimal solution will emerge. For example, the efficient type may choose the contract represented by N by pretending to be an inefficient type, but actually earning positive discounted profit in both periods. The regulator can only counteract this by offering a higher reward to the efficient firm, for example the contract pair represented by (J, N) which was sub-optimal in the static analysis, since they do not lie on the same indifference curve of the efficient type.

The situation could be worse, leading to a strategy called by Laffont and Tirole 'take the money and run'. The higher the discount factor the greater must be the payment to the efficient firm to prevent it pretending to be inefficient when the regulator cannot commit to the two-period contract. The required contract pair might be (J', N). In this event, the inefficient firm can do better by pretending to be efficient for the first period and then refusing to supply in the second period. Of course, the efficient firm then strictly prefers J' to N. The consequence is that the regulatory mechanism tends towards a pooling outcome where the two firms are treated equally in the first period so that no information is extracted, rather than the separating equilibrium which distinguishes the two types in the basic model.

A general way round this problem of the breakdown of incentive compatible regulation, arising from the imperfect ability of the regulator to commit to a long-term contract, is to be unable to use the information from the first period. Regulators find it beneficial to delay making use of the information learned in the repetitions of the game, perhaps by preserving the firm's initial incentives over several periods, or increasing the length of time between reviews.

Lessons from regulation in practice
Theoretical models provide us with insights into the types of mechanisms that can be used to overcome the regulator's information problem. Practical regulatory mechanisms have been developed which often build on the principles that are embedded in the theoretical models, but which reflect the practical constraints and information limitations that regulators face. We discuss some of the mechanisms that have been considered in the UK and elsewhere in Europe designed to address the issue of hidden information in practice.

Role of benchmarking for information extraction: electricity distribution in the Netherlands[9]
The energy law in the Netherlands requires that the regulator (DTe) sets a CPI – X formula, and that the X factors should be the same for all companies. DTe considered the information available and recognized that it was scant. Consequently, DTe began to use the benchmarking process to elicit information from the operators, by credibly threatening to use the information it did have to arrive at a view on network efficiency. Despite the relatively large number of output and environmental factors, the spread of efficiency was large, and these scores were reflected in a wide range of individual X factors for each operator that were set by DTe in September 2000. Nearly all the firms appealed against the

first decision. The appeal court did not evaluate the appeals on content, but ruled that DTe had to determine new X factors, since according to the judge the Electricity Law required that DTe had to establish a uniform X factor for all companies. The fact that the law was so rapidly amended, indicated that the government and the parliament supported DTe's approach. This crucially buttressed the position of the regulator, and finally all operators accepted the use of benchmarking in the regulatory model. The ruling also increased the legal credibility of benchmarking in the Netherlands.

However, as the companies began to understand both the law and the methodology, it became clear that they also understood that an obvious route to avoiding a regulatory downside was to present better information to the regulator. In this sense, the incentive to provide information was clearly linked to the credibility and value of the benchmarking regime. Therefore, as a consequence, a clearly beneficial outcome of the process was better information provision in the following senses:

1. A common interpretation of the law as requiring yardstick competition as the long-run model of regulation.
2. A legally determined (and very fast) timetable for the price control.
3. A consistent methodological approach adopted by DTe at every stage of the process.
4. A clear appeals process; and
5. A legal decision that required the government to change the law and in doing so reaffirmed its commitment to DTe's approach.
6. A stipulation about a predetermined approach to regulation in law that minimized doubt about commitment and permitted the static yardstick mechanism to be repeated in future periods.

Capital expenditure forecasting: electricity distribution in the UK
In its 2004 price control determination, the UK electricity regulator, Ofgem introduced a sliding scale approach to the remuneration of capital investment. This represented a departure from previous practice, which was to establish a point estimate of the investment plans for the forthcoming price control period, based on the advice of consultants and discussions with the companies. For this price control determination, however, it was clear that Ofgem and several of the network operators would not be able to reach agreement on future capital expenditure plans, so Ofgem (2004) established a sliding scale to help reduce the scope for disagreement, and with the aim of incentivizing the companies, Distribution Network Owners or DNOs, to reveal their true investment plans. We use this case study to highlight the issues of incentive power and risk aversion.

Ofgem (2004) proposed a mechanism where each operator's business plan is compared to a report prepared for Ofgem by its own engineering consultants.

On the basis of these comparisons, each operator is then given an allowed capital expenditure, a marginal incentive rate to try and outperform this budget and some additional revenue. The mechanism is 'incentive compatible'; however, because the mechanism was introduced after the companies submitted their plans, the effect of this property will not be felt until the next price control review.

We can construct a model of the mechanism as follows. The parameters are:

- $f = DNO/C$: the ratio of the DNO's forecast requirement to the consultant's forecast requirement; this will be ≥ 100 per cent and covers a range of discrete values:
- $f \in [100\%, 140\%]$. Its value is used to determine the values of the income incentive parameters α, β that apply to a given DNO;
- an incentive multiplicative income parameter α_f which falls linearly as the ratio $f = DNO/C$ rises;
- an additional income parameter β_f which falls more than proportionately as the ratio $f = DNO/C$ rises.[10]

The values of α_f and β_f are in the ranges of discrete values: $\alpha_f \in [0.4, 0.2]$, $\beta_f \in [2.5, -2.4]$, as shown in Table 8.1.

Table 8.1　*UK electricity distribution, capital investment: incentive parameters*

DNO/C % ratio of CAPEX forecasts, f	100	105	110	115	120	125	130	135	140
Multiplicative income incentive parameter, α_f	0.4	0.38	0.35	0.33	0.3	0.28	0.25	0.23	0.2
Additive income incentive parameter, β_f	2.5	2.1	1.6	1.1	0.6	–0.1	–0.8	–1.6	–2.4

Source:　Ofgem (2004), Table 7.6.

Ofgem determines an Allowed Capital Expenditure (CAPEX) value that compromises between the DNO forecast and the independent consultant's forecast. The values of α_f and β_f that will apply to a given company are determined by $f = DNO/C$: the ratio of the DNO's forecast requirement to the consultant's forecast requirement. For each company $j = 1 \dots n$, the incentive mechanism determines the following income reward or penalty[11] depending on the difference between the allowed CAPEX, C_J, and the realized or actual CAPEX, R_j:

$$U_{jf} = (C_j - R_j)\alpha_f + \beta_f$$

The reward parameters are chosen to ensure that before CAPEX is realized the reward is maximized when $f = DNO/C$ is closest to 100 per cent; and given the values of $f = DNO/C$ and C_j, which determine the parameters α_f and β_f for the jth company, U_{jf} increases as $R_j < C_j$; that is, the company's realized CAPEX is less than its allowed CAPEX.

Therefore, each company is in principle incentivized to be conservative in its forecasts of capital expenditure, and to keep realized expenditure below allowed expenditure. However, Ofgem is only right to draw these conclusions from its stylized example if there is no uncertainty about future capital expenditure plans and the operators are risk-neutral. In practice, there is both uncertainty and risk aversion, and these may lead companies to over-state the true expected value of the investment plan.

Armstrong et al. (1994, pp. 40–42) have demonstrated this clearly in a theoretical model of the regulation of a risk-averse utility. Adapting their conclusions to this case study, we can argue as follows. The additive parameter of the mechanism depends on factors such as the reservation utility that must be covered to induce participation in the game, the expected value of the random variable representing production conditions, and the multiplicative incentive power part of the mechanism. The multiplicative incentive power parameter, in turn, depends on the coefficient of risk aversion and the amount of risk represented by the variance of the random variable; that is, uncertainty about production conditions. This emphasizes that the optimal regulatory contract has to trade off high powered incentives against insurance for uncertainty for the risk-averse firm.

It is clear that the set of payoffs adopted by Ofgem (2004) is incentive compatible assuming risk neutrality. However, it is possible that an operator may not choose to report its expected level of investment if there is uncertainty and if the operator is risk-averse. Generally, an examination of the mechanism suggests that there is little to choose in terms of expected profit between forecasting the expectation of capital expenditure or forecasting a level that would push the operator into the next bracket. Given this fact, any uncertainty relating to the future investment plans, coupled with a slight degree of managerial risk aversion, is likely to result in forecasts being submitted that exceed the expected value.

Moreover, as a consequence of forecasting a higher level of investment than is expected, operators are then pushed into a band where they face a lower incentive rate for out-performance. The consequence of this is that if there is insufficient incentive to reward choosing a forecast close to the expected value (by compensating for risk), then Ofgem risks diminishing cost efficiency. Clearly, in order to avoid this problem, there should be greater differentiation between the payoffs associated with choosing different forecasts, so that at the margin operators choose a forecast that is closer to their expected value. This demonstrates that the choice of incentive parameters has to take into account strong behavioural assumptions about the agents' preferences if inefficient outcomes are to be avoided.

In practice, a regulated company's incentive to minimize the use of inputs to produce the required level of outputs can be distorted by the way in which the incentive mechanisms themselves have been designed. The four key distortions that have arisen in practice mirror the difficulties in the theoretical models relating to timing and dynamics, ratchet effects and quality of supply.

Timing distortions The UK regional electricity distribution network operators (DNOs) are regulated under an RPI – X mechanism whereby companies were, up until 2004, allowed to retain the profits from operating cost savings made during the regulatory period (beyond those assumed by the regulator when setting the X factor) until the next periodic review.

With the five-year regulatory period, operating cost savings made in year 1 of a period were worth more than those made in year 5. This is because all savings, independent of when they were made, were shared with customers through an initial price cut (the P0 cut) at the start of the next period. Under this regime a company's decision about the optimal time to make cost reductions was distorted by the process by which savings were shared. In particular, a company had a strong incentive to make savings early in a period.

Figure 8.3 shows the change in real unit operating expenditure (OPEX) for the DNOs since privatization. At the start of each period after a price review – 1995/96 and 2000/01 – the level of cost reduction is significantly greater than in other years. This suggests that companies may have been reacting to the perverse timing distortions within the RPI – X mechanism and adjusting the decision about when to make operating cost distortions accordingly. The greater fall in OPEX immediately after price reviews could also be explained by the tightening of the price cap that occurred at each review, but it is clear that companies can then capitalize on up to five years of higher profits.

This problem was also evident in the water sector in England and Wales in the 1990s. However, in 1999 Ofwat, the water regulator, introduced a rolling incentive mechanism which allowed companies to retain the benefit of operating cost savings for five years, independent of when in the regulatory cycle the savings were made (see Ofwat, 2004 for the most recent version). This meant that the marginal benefit of a cost reduction was not affected by the timing of the periodic review and, hence, the timing distortion was removed. Ofgem is considering introducing a similar mechanism in the future but the rolling operating

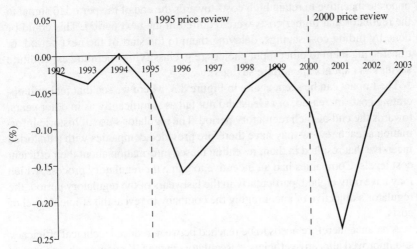

Growth in real unit operating expenditure
(Weighted industry average)

Note: Real unit operating expenditure is calculated as turnover minus operating profits minus depreciation, exceptionals, MWCA and loss on disposals.

Source: Companies' annual regulatory accounts and authors' calculations.

Figure 8.3 *Annual growth in real unit operating expenditure of electricity distribution network operators in England and Wales*

expenditure scheme was not allowed for in the most recent price determination (for the period 2005 to 2010) because of concerns about the consistency of cost reporting, Ofgem (2004, p. 76). However, a rolling incentive scheme for capital expenditure was introduced by Ofgem in the 2004 determination.

The ratchet effect At each periodic review (1994, 1999 and 2004), the electricity regulator (Ofgem), used data for the penultimate year of the regulatory period as the starting point for determining required operating expenditure in the next period. Adjustments were made to a company's own actual cost data, to ensure consistency with other companies in the sector and to ensure that efficiency was improved over the period. But the opening level of allowed operating expenditure at the start of the next regulatory period was closely correlated with the level at the end of the previous period (i.e. the year for which data were available – 1992/93, 1998/99 and 2003/04 respectively).

Companies knew that the regulator would base future price caps on historical expenditure levels and a classic ratchet effect problem may have arisen. While, as discussed above, companies had an incentive to make savings during the regulatory period – particularly the early years – they were also faced with an opposite incentive to retain high costs towards the end of the period to signal to the regulator that higher costs were required in the next period. This could be done by hiding cost savings, delaying them to the start of the next period, or transferring them to other input choices (e.g. classifying operating expenditure savings as capital expenditure savings).

The impact can be seen, again, in Figure 8.3, where we see that real unit operating costs increased, or at least did not fall as significantly as in other years, towards the end of each regulatory period. The regulator's use of historic information at each review may have therefore provided companies with a distorted incentive that resulted in them revealing biased information about their efficient cost levels. Companies had an incentive to game the regulatory process, which may have outweighed, particularly in the last years of the regulatory period, the regulator's objective of encouraging the company to reveal the efficient level of costs.

A balance therefore needs to be reached between reduced technical efficiency and improved allocative efficiency. Regulators in the UK appear to have focused on the benefit of using company-specific information in setting prices, although some adjustments are made for comparative efficiency differences, especially outside the water sector (also see Chapter 6). The regulators are therefore implicitly accepting a potential reduction in the power of the incentive regime and the costs associated with regulatory gaming. In contrast, in the Netherlands yardstick mechanisms are used. The primary focus is therefore on providing high-powered technical efficiency incentives, with companies allowed to earn a return above the average industry cost of capital if they are efficient.

A successful cost reduction incentive scheme – the UK National Grid Company

At the privatization of the electricity industry in the UK in 1990, the National Grid Company (NGC) was created to own and operate the high-voltage transmission system. Network charges that consumers paid for electricity transmission were regulated under an RPI – X mechanism. The transmission company incurred other costs that were not covered by the RPI – X regime. In particular, certain costs that depend on how well the transmission system is constructed and operated – such as the additional cost of 'constrained-on' generation (plant required to operate because of transmission constraints) and 'ancillary services' (a range of services with no common international definition, but essentially relating to paying generators to operate in a manner that assists the operation and security of the system) – were not allowed. These costs were recovered as the 'transport' component of 'uplift' payments, which were levied on all generators and electricity suppliers (retailers) in the electricity pool (the upstream wholesale market).

In response to rapid increases in costs, particularly of constrained-on generation, and recognizing that NGC had significant influence over some uplift costs, Offer (the then electricity regulator) introduced an incentive scheme, the Transmission Services Scheme (TSS) in 1994/95.[12] The scheme was based on sliding-scale incentive regulation. First, Offer set a target for transmission service costs. Then, if NGC's costs were below this target in any one year, uplift payments were reduced less than proportionately, allowing NGC to retain a proportion of the saving as additional profits. Similarly, if costs exceeded the target, uplift payments increased less then proportionately, exposing NGC to a reduction in profits. A cap on total incentive payments or penalties was established: cost variations beyond the limits implied by this cap were simply passed through one-for-one. Initially, the scheme specified that NGC retained 30 per cent of any cost savings (to a maximum of £25m, about 5 per cent of the target cost) and paid 20 per cent of any cost over-run (to a maximum of £15m). Targets were revised annually.[13] Indeed, by exposing its ability to manage these cost categories, NGC provided Offer with information it could use to set tougher targets in the future. Target costs in 1998/99, for example, were only £215m – less than half the 1994/95 target (see Offer, 1998).

The effects on transport uplift costs were impressive, as Figure 8.4 illustrates. The rapid increases in cost over the first four years of the pool's existence were reversed. In particular, the 'operational out-turn' cost category (principally constrained-on generation) fell by more than half comparing the full years before (1993/94) and after (1995/96) the introduction of the scheme.

Clearly, NGC gained substantially from the scheme. The incentive payment in 1994/95 was £22.5m and in 1995/96 it was £25m (in nominal prices, i.e. the maximum allowed payment).[14] However, the reduction in the two cost categories from 1993/94 to 1995/96 was almost £260m, about 4 per cent of the total cost of wholesale electricity in England and Wales. Ofgem (1999) also noted that NGC reduced the costs of balancing the system (excluding the cost of unscheduled availability and transmission losses) from £60m in 1993/94 to £208m in 1999/2000 (in real terms). Thus, although NGC might appear to have been the principal beneficiary, the benefits to customers were substantially greater.

Information and quality of service regulation
One consequence of providing a company with high-powered cost reduction incentives is that it may have an incentive to reduce quality of service (outputs) in order to earn a higher return. In response to this distortion regulators have tended to develop quality of service regulatory mechanisms alongside, or within, price control mechanisms.

The design of an ideal quality of service mechanism requires the regulator to have information about the efficient level of service given the marginal cost of providing the service and the marginal benefit, or willingness to pay, of custom-

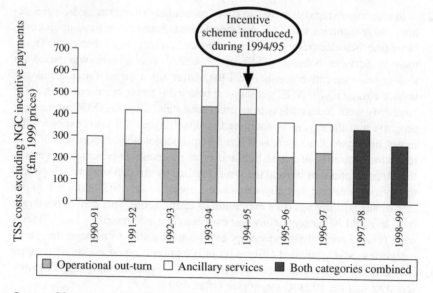

Source: Ofgem documents such as NGC System Operator Incentives, Transmission Access and Losses Under NETA, consultation document (1999), available at http://www.ofgem.gov.uk/temp/ofgem/cache/cmsattach/1447_nsodec.pdf

Figure 8.4   Uplift costs

ers obtaining the service. Furthermore, regulators need to be able to observe and measure the level of quality of service delivered to ensure that penalties for under-delivery are credible. Information is therefore also key to the regulation of quality of service.

Electricity distribution in Norway
Revenue caps are used to regulate electricity distribution companies in Norway, with a minimum and maximum return on capital applied. In 2002 a further element was added to the assessment of allowed revenue, an adjustment for quality of service performance.[15] The quality measure used is the value of energy not supplied to consumers. Before introducing the revenue adjustment the Norwegian energy regulator, NVE, introduced mandatory reporting of interruptions longer than three minutes for end-users at all voltage levels in 2000 (data were collected from 1995).

Furthermore, survey evidence was available on the value that customers place on an interruption. The surveys were undertaken by The Centre for Research in Economics and Business Administration, on behalf of NVE, between 1989 and 1991. Those surveyed provided information on the direct costs associated with

interruptions of different lengths and at different points in time. The survey results were updated to reflect information on average interruption duration
throughout the year (not at peak load times only) and general price increases.[16]
This provided NVE with information on willingness to pay for a reduction in
service interruptions, allowing for an estimate of the optimal service–revenue
trade-off to be made. The NVE, therefore, appears to have recognized how to
limit the information requirement for quality regulation and ensured that the
required information was collected in a consistent manner for all companies.

The survey evidence was used to calculate average cost of energy not supplied
(actual CENS), which was used as an input in the benchmarking analysis for
the 2002 revenue caps.[17] The expected cost of energy not supplied (expected
CENS) was used as an output in the benchmarking analysis. The expected level
of energy not supplied was estimated for each company using a regression
model. The regression analysis was based on data for the period 1996 to 1999
for all companies. Variables included actual levels of interruptions (forced out-
ages and planned disconnections) that lasted more than three minutes and a
range of structural control variables including energy supplied, network extension, number of distribution transformers, wind and geographical dummies.

The average interruption costs were calculated, at company level, using survey evidence on the expected cost of the interruption to different customer
categories. The quality adjustment to the revenue cap linked actual quality of
supply to the expected level of quality of supply. Specifically, companies with
a quality of supply below the expected level had a reduction in the level of allowed revenue and those with a quality of supply above expectations had an
increase in the level of allowed revenue. The revenue adjustment reflects the
difference between expected and actual interruption costs.

Under this regime companies have an incentive to move towards the actual
optimal level in the revenue adjustment regime. The company has no incentive
to reduce quality because of the offsetting reduction in revenues, or to increase
it beyond the level suggested by the survey evidence because of the absence of
any reward for such overinvestment in quality. Specifically, the company makes
decisions that ensure that its marginal costs of providing quality are equal to the
marginal customer-specific interruption costs. The incentive regime is therefore
based on internalized information about the costs and benefits of providing
quality of supply rather than on the expected level of quality used in the
assessment.

The Norwegian regulator has introduced an incentive scheme for quality of
service that links quality performance to allowed revenue, placing a clear and
transparent financial incentive on the companies. Furthermore, the assessment
of the required level of quality, and performance relative to that, is based on information about customer willingness to pay. This scheme, therefore, appears
to closely match incentive mechanisms suggested by economic theory.

Limitations with the scheme remain, however. The value of an interruption is assumed to be fixed, in real terms, over time, which may not be the case. Furthermore, the determination of average quality of supply is not updated, suggesting that the benefits of yardstick performance are not used to assess company behaviour over time.

The adjustment mechanism, and the process involved in preparing for the introduction of this quality of supply regulatory regime, does, however, show how the availability of information can improve the quality of the regulatory regime that is in place.

Conclusions

The clearest message from this survey of the information revelation issue is the unresolved complexity of the topic. We began by examining the theoretical contributions with key points:

1. The static basic model has a separating equilibrium in which it is the choices made by agents from a menu of rewards which reveal information.
2. The menu covers a spectrum of high-powered to low-powered contracts with some inefficiency from the low-powered contract needed to minimize the high-powered reward to the most efficient type of firm. A useful way of implementing a menu of contracts is by sliding scale regulation, in which the regulated companies choose their pay-off control parameters from a range offered by the regulator.
3. The basic results are compromised by practical difficulties. Compensation is necessary for risk aversion. Lack of regulatory commitment seriously undermines the outcome of repeated interaction. Quality requires specific intermediate-power incentives such as sliding scale if it is not to be crowded out by cost reduction effort. Yardstick competition, which requires bench-marking, can be a powerful regulatory tool to deliver first best outcomes when firms are correlated in the random variable of efficiency type.

In examining regulation in practice, we discovered that regulatory pressures can elicit information when there is strong and credible government support, but that incentive schemes with limited differentiation of rewards and penalties may be ineffective. Electricity distribution in the Netherlands and in the UK were shown to be examples of these phenomena. In the UK case study of capital expenditure forecasts and outcomes, we examined a two-part information incentive mechanism designed by the electricity regulator. This provided incentives for conservative forecasts and realizations below allowed expenditure. However, the incentives depend critically on the parameter values, and the theoretical models demonstrate the need to take account of managerial risk aversion in setting these parameters. It will be very interesting to monitor the development and adoption of such models by regulators. The prognosis for the UK model is uncertain because of the complexity of the game. On the one hand, the regulator has to set incentives to take account of risk aversion, and this may require very expensive rewards. In fact, as Farrell (2000) demonstrates, the cost of compensating a single agent for risk aversion may be so high that the regulator prefers an X-inefficient outcome. On the other hand, the presence of other regulated companies in a yardstick competition game can greatly reduce the cost of compensating for risk. Both of these ingredients, uncertainty and benchmarking, are present in the UK case study.

The next difficulty identified in the theoretical models concerns dynamics, timing and commitment. Two practical examples were examined. The timing of the redistribution of regulatory cost savings to consumers was shown to have a strong effect on the power of incentives. Under repeated regulatory review, there is a danger of losing incentive power towards the end of the current regulatory period if the cost savings will be immediately redistributed at the next review. We discussed approaches to this in both UK electricity and water regulation. The theoretical models indicated the need to delay using information about efficient performance in order to maintain incentive power, and evidence for this is clear from the evolution of operating expenditures over time in the UK utilities. A closely related issue is the ratchet effect and this arises because of the inability of the regulator in practice to commit to a long-term contract with the companies that will allow the regulator to ignore information gained in earlier stages of the game. The loss of incentive power because of the failure to commit appears to have had significant costs when we examined the UK electricity industry. The implication, as Crew and Kleindorfer (2000) demonstrate, is that incentive regulation is undermined.

These conclusions point to the difficulty of implementing information incentives in practice, but there have been successes. We examined a successful sliding scale mechanism in the case study of UK electricity transmission, where the compensation to the company, although substantial, has delivered significant benefits to the consumer. One caveat, however, is that successful incentive regulation appears to be easier where the regulatory problem is more concentrated on hidden action rather than on pure hidden information. Our final case study did address a specific hidden information issue. The theoretical models demonstrate that, in addition to a price control, specific incentives for quality of supply may be needed, and these may need to be more low-powered than hidden action based price control regulations. We examined a procedure for quality of supply rewards in Norway. Instead of concentrating on capital expenditure allocation, this specifically addressed the issue of willingness to pay for continuous supply. The initial results of the mechanism seem to suggest that it has useful lessons for other regulatory jurisdictions.

It is clear that regulators across the world have adopted a wide variety of different incentive mechanisms, which reflect both the corporate and legal environment, and political and social preferences of the jurisdiction concerned. Nevertheless there is a substantial consensus on the importance of incentive regulation despite the theoretical and practical difficulties. We repeatedly discovered that dynamic issues of commitment (or lack of it) and the timing of regulatory review are absolutely critical in the effectiveness of regulation for information revelation. This situation is a repeated game and this means that, in order to achieve high-powered efficiency incentives, regulators have to delay the use of information learned in the regulatory process to avoid the ratchet effect. We found that carefully designed intermediate-power incentive mechanisms could deliver cost reductions almost as well as high-powered schemes. We discovered that regulation of quality of service raises serious difficulties. The crowding-out effect necessitates intermediate-power incentive mechanisms for quality to run alongside high-powered mechanisms for cost reduction. Such complexity of design is only just being addressed and much work remains to be done, especially on consumer valuation of quality of supply. Although we have covered a large range of material and learned much, our lack of experience and knowledge of optimal information revelation remain a challenge.

Notes

1. Our analysis is drawn largely from Armstrong et al. (1994), Armstrong and Sappington (2004), and Laffont and Tirole (1993). The basic analysis, known as the BM model, is from Baron and Myerson (1982).
2. This is the Loeb-Magat mechanism, see Armstrong and Sappington (2004).
3. The analysis and notation are taken from Armstrong and Sappington (2004).
4. Laffont and Tirole quote US empirical studies that suggest the distortion effect costs about 30 per cent of the size of the transfer.
5. The fact that the optimal contracts lie on the efficient firm's indifference curve results from its incentive compatibility constraint being binding at the optimum; the participation constraint binds for the inefficient firm.
6. Further detail is in Armstrong and Sappington (2004) and Laffont and Tirole (1993).
7. The discount factor in period t is $\delta = (1 + i)^{-t}$ where i is the common discount rate; larger values of δ are associated with lower values of i.
8. This analysis is taken from Laffont and Tirole (1993), pp. 377–9.
9. See Burns et al. (2006) for a fuller description of the information revelation process.
10. Ofgem (2004) states that both parameters are linearly related to DNO/C but a simple plot of the values shows this not to be true of the additive income parameter.
11. Ofgem (2004) does not implement a precise formula, instead it reports a table of rewards with the possible R_j, C_j values in the rows and columns of the incentive matrix.
12. In addition, incentives were introduced into the payments made *by* NGC to the providers of ancillary services, abandoning the previous approach of simple remuneration of cost.
13. Note that sharing ratios and caps changed as the scheme developed. Later schemes also provided for different sharing rules and profit/loss caps for different components of TSS costs.
14. It is worth noting that the first payment was below the maximum available while the second was at the maximum. Even in this second year, NGC's performance did not result in costs substantially below the levels at which the maximum payment was triggered. If this had happened, it would be reasonable to conclude that incentives were not the principal driver of the cost reduction. The receipt of two payments close to the maximum suggests (but does not prove) efficient response to incentives on NGC's part.
15. Details of the revenue adjustment can be found in Langset (2001).

16. The updating of the cost information assumes that, apart from inflationary effects, customers' preferences for quality of service do not change over time. This may not be the case, however, and there may be a need to update the surveys themselves at regular intervals to check for any change in preferences.
17. Energy not supplied is estimated as the amount of energy that would have been supplied to the customers if interruption did not occur, reflecting the duration of the interruption. A standardized methodology is in place under the Electricity Network Regulations for estimating this variable.

References

Armstrong, M. and Sappington, D. (2004) 'Recent Developments in the Theory of Regulation', in R. Bresnahan, J. Vickers, M. Armstrong and R.H. Porter (eds), *Handbook of Industrial Organization (Vol III)*, New York: Elsevier North-Holland.

Armstrong, M., Cowan, S. and Vickers, J. (1994) *Regulatory Reform: Economic Analysis and British Experience*, Cambridge, MA: MIT Press.

Baron, D. and Myerson, R. (1982) 'Regulating a Monopolist with Unknown Costs', *Econometrica*, **50** (4), 911–30.

Burns, P., Jenkins, C., Mikkers, M. and Riechmann, C. (2006), 'The Role of the Policy Framework for the Effectiveness of Benchmarking in Regulatory Proceedings', in Tim Coelli and Denis Lawrence (eds), *Performance Measurement and Regulation of Network Utilities*, Cheltenham, UK and Northampton, MA, USA: Edward Elgar (forthcoming).

Burns, P., Turvey, R. and Weyman-Jones, T. (1998) 'The Behaviour of the Firm under Alternative Regulations', *Scottish Journal of Political Economy*, **45** (2), May, 133–57.

Crew, M. and Kleindorfer, P.R. (2002) 'Regulatory Economics: Twenty Years of Progress', *Journal of Regulatory Economics*, **21** (1), 5–22

Farrell, J. (2000), 'Monopoly Slack and Competitive Rigor', in Eric Rasmusen (ed.), *Readings in Games and Information*, Oxford: Blackwell Publishers.

Laffont, J.-J. and Tirole, J. (1993) *A Theory of Incentives in Procurement and Regulation*, Cambridge, MA: MIT Press.

Langset T (2001) *Quality Dependent Revenues – Incentive Regulation of Quality of Supply*, Oslo: The Norwegian Water Resources and Energy Directorate (NVE).

Offer (1998) *Transmission Services Incentives Scheme: Proposals*, Office of Electricity Regulation archived at Ofgem, London: Office of Gas and Electricity Markets.

Ofgem (1999) *NGC System Operator Incentives, Transmission Access and Losses and NETA: A Consultation Document*, London: Office of Gas and Electricity Markets.

Ofgem (2004) *Electricity Distribution Price Control Review Final Proposals*, London: Office of Gas and Electricity Markets.

Ofwat (2004) *Future Water and Sewerage Charges 2005–10 Final Determinations – Periodic Review 2004*, Birmingham: Office of Water Services.

9 Regulatory governance and the lessons from UK practice

Peter Vass

Introduction[1]

This chapter focuses on regulatory governance; that is, the framework of regulatory structures and processes that should be designed to achieve, and sustain, good regulatory outcomes. Much effort has, and is, put into analysing regulatory objectives (the market and conduct failures to be addressed) and the means (instruments) by which regulators might meet those objectives, but it is equally important to recognize that regulators themselves need to be 'controlled' if good regulation is to be achieved and sustained in practice. The regulatory 'framework' is therefore an important policy question for all governments, and certain generic aspects can be seen to apply. Important features include the legal framework, the separation of roles and responsibilities, identification and codification of the principles of good regulation, institutionalizing a 'whole of government view', and designing effective processes for regulatory accountability. The provision and use of information play a vital role in these control mechanisms.

Regulatory governance is therefore about achieving regulation that can be shown to be in the public interest, and which maintains public confidence and support. Such regulation should be demonstrably cost-effective. Yet this is not about a single, rigid solution. Regulatory governance is also about flexibility and adaptation to meet changing circumstances or heeding the lessons of past failures.

To illustrate the principles and practice of regulatory governance in this context, the chapter first sets out some general characteristics of the regulatory state, and suggests that recent developments may be resulting in a new regulatory paradigm which integrates an earlier tradition of self-regulation with the modern imperatives of an all-pervading regulatory state. The chapter then focuses on the principles and practice of regulatory governance in the UK. In this way the chapter illustrates, through a specific country example, the path of policy exploration and decision that all countries might take with respect to regulatory governance if they are to create an effective regulatory state designed to meet their particular circumstances.

The elements of regulatory governance

The aims and practice of regulatory governance have much in common with corporate governance. Corporate governance has been simply defined as 'how companies manage themselves'. It is about how the board manages all the material risks the company faces. The commercial objective may be simply stated – maximize sustained economic profits – but to achieve that requires effective corporate governance. Similarly, regulatory governance is about how regulators and, in a broader context, 'the regulatory state', manages itself. In this respect, therefore, we can talk quite properly of the governance of the regulatory state. Equally, just as we expect directors of companies to treat corporate governance seriously, we should expect politicians to take regulatory governance seriously – and ensure that it is managed properly (Foster, 2005).

However, there are differences. For company directors there are clear disciplines on them to have regard to good corporate governance. Typically, companies operate in a competitive environment – and might go bankrupt – and face the prospect of take-over if shareholders are persuaded that another company can do a better job with the resources than the incumbent management. In this sense, directors are held accountable by the customers and shareholders. And where company directors (the 'agents') can abuse their position in relation to shareholders (the 'principals') governments typically attack this power, among other things, by competition policy (which promotes more effective competition and erodes monopoly power) and regulatory reporting requirements (helping to redress problems of asymmetry of information). But what disciplines are there on politicians and regulators to manage the regulatory state effectively? While voters could be said to be the equivalent of customers and shareholders for the services of the regulatory state, the immediate relationship is, for the most part, less forceful and transparent. For this reason, the state can abuse its regulatory power and regulators may succumb to their own 'conduct' failures, leading to bureaucratic regulators, misaligned incentives, and perverse regulatory outcomes. The answer is to build up internal control systems in the regulatory state which focus on achieving effective accountability, and thereby create the discipline on regulators, and the regulatory state, to improve governance and performance.

These straightforward aims immediately beg two questions. First, to what purpose is the governance directed, and, second, how do we judge whether the governance is good or bad? The first question concerns objectives, or desired outcomes – which provide the benchmark for answering the second question – performance evaluation based on comparing the actual outcome with the planned outcome. Yet there is another aspect of the second question that goes beyond straightforward comparison of plans with actual outcomes, but concerns internal control by mechanisms and processes that are put in place to help sustain or achieve good performance over time. Conformance (or compliance) with

Table 9.1　The elements of regulatory governance

Elements	Characteristics	Guiding principles
Regulatory purpose	Objectives (outputs); 'The problem to be addressed'	Objectivity, coherence, rationality
Regulatory means	Instruments (inputs); 'The options available to solve the problem'	Proportionality, targeting, consistency
Regulatory framework	Structure and process (governance); 'The control mechanisms aimed at optimizing regulatory outcomes'	Transparency, accountability

Table 9.2　The regulatory framework

Structure and process considerations	Three stages of accountability
• the legal framework • separation of roles and responsibilities • principles of good regulation • forming a 'whole of government view' • provision of relevant information	• giving reasons for decisions • exposure to scrutiny • the possibility of independent review

well-designed internal control processes facilitates good performance in terms of achieving desired outcomes (Banaga et al., 1995). For this reason it is necessary at the start of this chapter to separate out the elements of regulatory governance so that each can be separately addressed. Table 9.1 sets out the three elements – regulatory purpose, regulatory means and the regulatory framework – and identifies each of their key characteristics and guiding principles that should inform the design of both the regulatory state and the actions of its constituent regulators.

Important aspects of the regulatory framework are set out in Table 9.2. Under the three stages of accountability, 'giving reasons for decisions' should be seen to be encompassed more generally in the preparation of regulatory impact assessments (RIAs) by regulators; 'exposure to scrutiny' would include effective consultation processes as well as the independent audit of regulatory activities by Parliamentary committees and other authoritative bodies, such as national audit offices. 'The possibility of independent review' refers to courts and other tribunals which have the power to overturn regulatory decisions that are either *ultra vires*, inequitable or unreasonable. The structure and process considerations are concerned with entrenching the regulatory framework through codification and institutionalization, which is an important aspect of the design of the regulatory state. In effect, regulating the regulators requires the same control sequence of setting standards, monitoring and enforcement that the regulators apply to regulated companies – but applied to themselves. The historical development of codification and institutionalization in the UK has been covered by Moran (2003). A key transition in this regard is from the tacit to the explicit.

Separation of roles and responsibilities is an important feature for achieving effective accountability and effective regulation. One aspect of this, the development of the so-called 'independent' regulator, may be misunderstood, however, and cause concern that a wedge has been driven between the requirements for democratic accountability of the regulatory state and the decision-making of independent, technocratic regulators. This need not be the case, and the answer is to see independence as 'within', rather than 'of', the state.

An analogy is usefully found in company corporate governance, whereby a board divides itself up and expects directors to play different parts: some are executive directors, some are non-executive directors. All are directors, and have a collective responsibility for achieving sustained, good performance from the company; yet they play different roles in achieving this, for reasons of internal control, and as a check on each other. Having chosen the 'board' design, it is important that the company respects the particular roles being played by directors. In the same way, when the government has decided that a regulator should be empowered to act independently of government ministers with the purpose of promoting consistency and investor confidence (thereby avoiding short-term political interference which would otherwise increase political risk and hence the cost of capital), then this independent role needs to be respected.

Characteristics of the regulatory state

The characteristics of the regulatory state have been well analysed by Hood et al. (2001). They sought to answer the question why regulatory regimes varied, and why some seemed poorly aligned with the arrangements which might have been expected based on an objective (or normative) 'public interest' theory of the regulatory state. This model is typically founded in arguments about market failures, and the methods by which the state can correct for these (hence it is often judged to be econocentric in outlook), but can be generalized to include both market and non-market failures (Baldwin and Cave, 1999). 'Conduct failures' might therefore be a better description. Inequitable distributional outcomes resulting from the market place can be incorporated as a form of 'market failure' because the market has not delivered an outcome acceptable to the community, and thereby the regulatory state seeks to correct for it (for example, by requiring equal opportunities for the disabled or by lump sum transfers of income through social security and welfare systems).

Hood et al.'s answer was found by asking the question: how does context shape content in risk regulation regimes? They identified three 'shapers':

1. 'market failure' pressures (e.g. monopoly power, externalities, missing markets and public goods);
2. 'opinion-response' pressures (e.g. public opinion);
3. 'interest-driven' pressures (e.g. from organized self-interested groups).

All were found to have significant explanatory power for various extant regulatory regimes, thereby harnessing both normative and positive models in describing the distribution of regulatory regimes.

The key question for this chapter is whether the distribution of regulatory regimes remains essentially static, and subject to all three drivers depending on the circumstances, or whether the regulatory state has mechanisms that promote the 'public interest' drivers and militate against the special interest and 'capture' drivers. The UK perspective is that promoting good regulatory governance through effective accountability processes provides those mechanisms, supported by an 'institutionalized' framework of principles of good regulation and internal checks and controls. Codification of the principles of good regulatory governance is therefore essential to create a climate of expectations about regulatory conduct that provides a discipline on regulators to operate in the 'public interest', and to develop and reform the regulatory framework as necessary to that end.

An emerging regulatory paradigm

This assertion is perhaps supported by the broad development of UK government through the three 'ideal types' over the last two hundred years. These could be termed: the 'framework' state of the early nineteenth century; the 'providing' state of the mid-twentieth century, with its commitment to publicly owned industries and services; and the 'regulatory' state of the late twentieth century, still in force to date.

In the post-privatization or 'liberalized' world of the regulatory state, the emphasis is on regulating behaviour (via policy not service provision, i.e. 'steering' not 'rowing'). The consequence of this is two complementary trends – an extension of the regulatory state, whereby it 'envelops' previously self-regulatory activities within its sphere of interest, but operating at the strategic level such that it delegates or devolves responsibility for securing public interest outcomes to (apparently) self-regulating industry arrangements. In this way, markets are harnessed to achieve effective, but 'light touch' regulation. These arrangements could be termed 'co-regulation' between the regulatory state and empowered 'industry' bodies (Bartle and Vass, 2005). The self-regulatory arrangements, as part of co-regulation with the regulatory state, could range from the formal to the informal (perhaps on a scale demarcated as co-operative, delegated, devolved, facilitated or tacitly supported).

Figure 9.1 illustrates the idea of the new regulatory paradigm involving what might be seen to be a form of regulatory 'subsidiarity', whereby the detailed implementation and achievement of regulatory outcomes can be delegated ('downwards') to industry bodies and private sector agreements. This debate has been well analysed by Michael Moran when considering the transformation of self-regulation. As Moran notes 'The dominant analytical paradigm for the modern regulatory state pictures it as an institution concerned with steering self-regulating networks' (2003, p. 69).

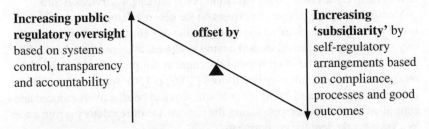

Increasing public regulatory oversight based on systems control, transparency and accountability

offset by

Increasing 'subsidiarity' by self-regulatory arrangements based on compliance, processes and good outcomes

Figure 9.1   The new regulatory paradigm

However, representation of the regulatory state as 'the governor of the machine' (Moran, 2003, p. 13) has to be accompanied by a 'better regulation' agenda. This is both to control the activities of the regulatory state, which has become 'all-embracing', and to provide the necessary legitimacy to a representative democracy, which operates through technocracy rather than decision-making by direct participative methods of democracy. The new wave of self-regulation should not therefore be seen so much as a 'deregulatory' agenda, but as a more efficient and effective mode of operation for the regulatory state – a 'better' regulatory agenda. Accountability of both the regulators and the regulated, through transparency of process and reporting, is the essential mechanism required to maintain the new regulatory paradigm or settlement. From the regulated companies' point of view, it requires effective compliance regimes by industry to ensure that public interest outcomes are achieved and performance builds public confidence and consent.

In the UK, the Communications Act 2003 incorporates a duty on the Office of Communications (Ofcom) to promote self-regulation. Yet if the government seeks to emphasize the deregulatory elements of a better regulation agenda, then the potential for misunderstanding caused by the terminology of self-regulation needs to be addressed if there is to be public confidence in the process (National Consumer Council, 2000). Self-regulation by an 'industry' or an incumbent in relation to activities for which it has monopoly power will always be viewed sceptically, given concerns over potential abuse resulting from concerted actions or predatory behaviour. The regulatory state can only 'tolerate' self-regulation in these respects where it demonstrably meets public purposes (i.e. it substitutes for action that would otherwise be taken directly by the regulatory state). The development of 'co-regulation' is therefore not so much an agreement between equal parties, as a delegated relationship with the principal party being the public oversight body. In this respect, for example, the UK's Advertising Standards Authority – an industry player – is carrying out functions delegated by, and on behalf of, Ofcom. Similar developments can be seen in the UK legal profession, where traditional 'self-regulation' (termed 'professionally led' regulation) is now to be overseen by a public oversight body, the Legal Services Board.

Moran also notes a danger consequent on the new regulatory paradigm, which is that governments embark on hyper-innovation as a consequence of the regulatory state being entrenched in, and having enclosed, all aspects of the modern polity. Expectations build up without the capacity for politicians to deliver the outcomes, and the result is policy fiascos (2003, p. 156). Again, improved accountability is the means by which policy fiascos can be effectively reduced and controlled – once again emphasizing the importance of regulatory governance as a key agenda item for governments.

Applying regulatory governance in the UK – a case study

The purpose and context of regulatory governance have been stated, but how is it applied in practice, and what policies do governments need to consider? This section examines issues of regulatory governance in the light of a recent inquiry by the UK Parliament into the accountability of regulators. It provides a relevant framework because the accountability of regulators in the UK has improved, is improving and, it is hoped, will continue to improve. There are many reasons for this, and its effects, particularly over the last ten years, have been beneficial in both redressing the perceived imbalance between the regulators and the regulated with respect to the disciplines imposed on them to achieve good governance, and in improving regulatory outcomes. A key conclusion is that effective accountability is necessary for effective regulation. It exposes regulators, and thereby undermines arbitrary and irrational regulation by providing a discipline on regulators to seek out, and apply, cost-effective regulation. It also helps to avoid regulatory capture. The governance perspective of this discussion is developed, therefore, from UK experience but the principles are generally applicable and, it is hoped, persuasive. Nevertheless, their application internationally has to be mindful of the context of each country in question (Kirkpatrick et al., 2005; Minogue, 2005).

Context

The privatization of the United Kingdom's utilities and network industries (water, energy, transport and communications) from 1984 onwards was accompanied by the establishment of independent regulators – a new form of regulator to be at 'arm's-length' from ministers (in practice, the powers were vested in individuals as director generals rather than a regulatory authority, although this has now been changed in the UK in favour of regulatory boards). Concern over the democratic mandate for the actions of these technocratic regulators, particularly where they were seen to be trespassing on policy issues, was the first reason for the development of a renewed debate on the accountability of the regulatory state and its constituent organizations. Not surprisingly, the regulated were at the forefront of promoting that debate (Vass, 2003). This debate was given a renewed impetus following the privatization of the regional water authorities in England and Wales in 1989 and the UK electricity industry from 1990. The profits being made and directors' rewards (including salary, bonuses and share options) grew so dramatically that by 1995 customers and the public generally (or at least their vocal representatives – politicians, the press and the National Consumer Council) had become outraged. The profits and salaries were seen as a failure of the regulatory system, and the political consequence was that New Labour's electoral prospectus included a review of utility regulation, with major reforms in prospect, should they win power from the Conservatives in the 1997 election. If regulatory mistakes had been made, then clearly increased accountability was required.

When Labour was elected to power in 1997 the review of regulation took place almost immediately (DTI, 1998). The resulting recommendations turned out to be less radical than perhaps many had hoped – some with their desire to reassert direct state and ministerial control over matters that perhaps had seemed to slip from their grasp with the introduction of the concept of 'public services – privately provided'. This was because, as with any government coming to power, the review gave the opportunity for deeper analysis of the issues than is perhaps available when developing the political rhetoric of an election manifesto. New Labour found that the key objectives and mechanisms of incentive regulation (the RPI – X price rather than profit control system), which was policed by independent regulators, were well designed to meet many of the public interest objectives that they espoused. If there had been a failure, then it was a failure of the previous government, when privatizing, to set sufficiently challenging price controls for the water and electricity industries at the outset, rather than a set of post-privatization regulatory failures. From this realization came the one-off 'retribution' of the windfall tax on the privatized utilities. This was designed to claw back some of the perceived excess returns to shareholders since privatization and designed to be one-off, to avoid erosion of the very incentives to efficiency that the government had found from its inquiry to be such an important characteristic of the regulatory system bequeathed by the Conservatives.

Given the inherited regulatory foundations were found to be 'fit for purpose', the Labour government, having put the past behind it with the imposition of the windfall tax, proceeded to reform the system, in effect, by building on the extant foundations. The results were sometimes surprising – more plans for privatization and more introduction of competition wherever possible (in part to 'bypass' regulation) – and sometimes window-dressing – putting in place reforms that were more political form than regulatory substance (although they were sacred cows for some of the critics of regulation) – the three most notable being:

1. regulatory boards to replace individual director generals;
2. independent consumer bodies to replace the consumer committees of the regulatory bodies;
3. promoting customer protection to the formal statutory status of a 'primary' duty on regulators.

Unfortunately, of these three, the first two, as noted below, may prove to have a 'downside' of undermining effective regulatory accountability, and hence effective regulation. With regard to the third, the regulators had already pursued this objective, with consumer protection being a primary rationale for their establishment in the first place.

A clearer recognition that ministers have to take responsibility for setting social and environmental standards was, however, engendered, particularly as a result of the 'cost of quality' debate taken forward by Ian Byatt, the water regulator, in response to rising water bills driven by a succession of environmental directives from the European Commission in the early 1990s. The outcome was to ensure that ministers considered both costs and benefits when setting quality standards. A new documented process was born – formal 'ministerial guidance' – which reinforces ministers' accountability for defining the 'outputs' to be met by the licensed or contracted private providers.

Real progress: better regulation not deregulation

In one respect, however, the results of the review have been a radical development for the UK regulatory state. These are in the 'process reforms' to improve accountability and hence regulatory governance. Corporate scandals and collapses have contributed over the years to a progressive demand for improved accountability and internal control by company boards, culminating in 2003 with the Combined Code (of Practice) on Corporate Governance, which was first developed by the Cadbury Committee in 1992 (Financial Reporting Council, 2003). Internationally, similar developments have taken place, as with the Sarbanes-Oxley Act in the United States, which followed the Enron scandal and company collapse; an event which also brought down the company's external auditor, Arthur Andersen. In a similar way, the lack of a demonstrably effective regulatory (and 'providing') state led to calls for improved regulatory governance, resulting in a wide range of codes of practice (The Independent Commission on Good Governance in Public Services, 2004).

Under the Conservatives regulatory governance was presented as a 'deregulatory agenda', but this was inevitably found wanting because some market and conduct failures inevitably call for the attention of the regulatory state. The review of utility regulation was one mechanism for shifting the balance towards a 'better regulation' agenda – regulating where necessary and cost-effectively. It was complemented by a new institutional focus, most notably through the government's Better Regulation Task Force (BRTF), which published its five 'principles of good regulation', and by a recognition that good regulation requires formal processes, most notably articulation of the objectives and reasoning behind specific regulations (Better Regulation Task Force, 2003a). Regulatory Impact Assessments (RIAs) became the new process tool, and are set to become the foundation stones for regulatory governance and the effective accountability of regulators in the UK (see Chapter 12 for a full discussion of RIA). To promote and coordinate this, the government established the Regulatory Impact Unit in the Cabinet Office.

The BRTF principles of good regulation are transparency, consistency, proportionality, targeting and accountability. These principles reflect an emphasis on implementation and practice, and can be criticized for an absence of unifying regulatory objectives (such as coherence, objectivity and rationality) or for being opaque. Transparency is perhaps not overly clear (does it refer primarily to clarity of regulatory objectives for example?), and is consistency about consistency with past decisions, equality of treatment (one person with another) or alignment of regulation with the fundamental objectives of the regulatory system? Hood et al. have also criticized them because 'better regulation principles often turn out to be a set of "contradictory proverbs" … without any practical guidance on what to do when one proverb clashes with another' (2001, p. 180). Nevertheless, the principles have arguably 'delivered' in the sense of providing an inescapable cultural context and norms for regulatory governance and practice. 'Guidance and interpretation' is delivered through the central departments of state formally charged with promoting better regulation, including the Cabinet Office, HM Treasury and the Department of Trade and Industry.

The Parliamentary review
In the light of these developments in the regulatory state, a Parliamentary inquiry was held in 2003–2004. The Constitution Committee's report was published in

May 2004, entitled *The Regulatory State: Ensuring its Accountability* (House of Lords, 2004a). It identified many of the important generic characteristics required for effective regulatory governance, and thereby provides a relevant case study.

The Committee's line of reasoning is succinct: 'Our starting point is that regulation is a means to an end, not an end in itself', and that 'Regulation can only be in the public interest where it serves a clear purpose' (p. 5). The problem is crisply set out too: 'We have to resist the danger of regulatory creep. … This regulatory tendency has to be checked, and the best means is effective accountability. Necessary, and cost-effective, regulation can be properly identified; unnecessary regulation can, and should be removed' (p. 5).

The Committee notes in particular the changed context of recent years, identifying, first, the establishment of arm's-length independent regulators and, second, 'the progressive changes to the rights of the regulated in recent years, perhaps most clearly exemplified by the incorporation of the European Convention of Human Rights into UK Law' (p. 6). This underpins the idea that appeals against regulatory decisions should go beyond the traditional grounds for judicial review, and be allowed on 'the merits of the case' (which looks to the principle of 'reasonable' decisions by regulators, rather than the traditional view in UK judicial review that a regulator's decision cannot be overturned unless it was so unreasonable that no reasonable person could have made it – in effect, irrational). Given the higher expectations of those exposed to regulatory decisions about their rights, the Committee observed that 'we can only expect the progressive consolidation of those rights and expectations into law and judicial review procedures to continue' (p. 6).

The Committee asked 'who does what and why, and how?' The why and how questions were brought together in the conclusion that 'regulators should be accountable for effective regulation which meets rational, well-defined objectives' (p. 6). This defines the purpose of their regulatory governance processes. Regulators must choose appropriate instruments to tackle regulatory problems; not 'sledgehammers to crack nuts'. The who does what questions, however, meant that the issue of effective coordination among regulators had to be addressed, since separate agencies might be established to tackle particular issues of concern to the regulatory state (Robens, 1972). A broad distinction between economic, environmental and social regulation could be clearly discerned, and the former is reflected in the fact that the UK has economic regulators, both national such as the Office for Fair Trading and the Competition Commission, and sectoral such as the Office of the Director General of Water Services (Ofwat), the Office of Rail Regulation (ORR) and the Gas and Electricity Markets Authority (GEMA), the latter supported by its office, Ofgem. While environmental effects (externalities on third parties) and social concerns (distributional issues such as inclusion, access and affordability) typically require the close involvement of ministers in approving standards and taking responsibility for the 'democratically mandated' judgements involved, there are normally specialist regulatory agencies created, such as the Environment Agency, and social security departments, such as the Department of Work and Pensions.

One of the key principles of the regulatory arrangements that accompanied privatization was the 'unbundling' of the regulatory state, such that independent regulators were put in place at 'arm's length' from ministers (albeit independent within, rather than of, the regulatory state). The advantage was public accountability of the regulators, secured on the basis of their own statutory powers and duties. This gives confidence to investors that they will be protected from arbitrary interventions by politicians ('political risk'), although it has to be recognized that with independence came discretion ('regulatory risk'). In the UK, the pressure for replacing 'individual' regulators (director generals) with 'Authorities' (regulatory boards) has come primarily from regulated companies, arguing in favour of more 'balanced' decision-making. However, given effective accountability mechanisms, it is difficult to see why the decisions of boards should in principle be any better than those of an individual regulator (who normally involved advisory boards in any event). The suspicion is that both governments and regulated companies might feel it is easier to work with authorities than with the high profile, and personally highly accountable, individual director generals.

The regulatory framework: accountability to all parties
The regulatory state is therefore a complex system that has separate regulators addressing different problems, and set within a process that needs communication between the regulatory bodies over time, if balanced and cost-effective outcomes are to be achieved. There are two consequences: first, that regulators must satisfy a '360° view' of accountability to all interested parties, including those regulated (not just formal accountability 'upwards'), and second, the need for a 'whole of government view' of regulation, whereby the government takes responsibility for ensuring an integrated and coordinated design for the regulatory state (perhaps best seen as the regulatory framework or 'blueprint'). The OECD has suggested that a particular department should be charged with this responsibility in order to promote consistency of practice (OECD, 1997, 2002a, 2002b). The Committee's diagram of its 360° view of accountability is shown in Figure 9.2.

The consequences are clear. Regulated companies are accountable to regulators for the proper performance of their tasks, but equally regulators are accountable to the companies for the proper performance of their tasks. Nevertheless, the Committee (as the shading in Figure 9.2 shows) 'drew a distinction between regulators exercising a duty to explain – [extending to all the bodies identified in Figure 9.2] – and being required to respond to demands made by

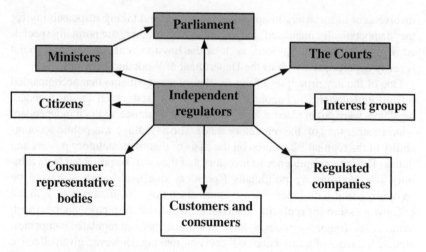

Source: House of Lords (2004a), p. 20.

Figure 9.2   The 360° view of regulatory accountability

those who gave them their powers or control of the legal application of their powers' (House of Lords, 2004a, p. 21). Ministers too are directly accountable in this hierarchy, either as direct regulators or as those responsible for operating the regulatory system, including appointing suitable independent regulators.

Parliament does not escape responsibility either. As the Committee observes 'Improving parliamentary scrutiny is essential' but

> it is not just a question of the answerability of regulators to parliament, but also one of the duty of parliament to ensure that its scrutiny is effective'. Scrutiny at the moment is dependent on individual (select) committees deciding that inquiry is necessary into a particular regulator or regulatory decision. It is both fragmented and inconsistent. There is no means of establishing a coherent overview of the regulatory regime operating within the United Kingdom. We believe there should be. (House of Lords, 2004a, p. 7)

The elements of accountability

The elements, or steps, by which accountability is given effect therefore required analysis, and the Committee noted the insight provided by Sir Derek Morris's evidence (then chairman of the UK's Competition Commission).[2] From this it identified the three key elements, all of which are required for effective regulatory governance and accountability, namely the duty to explain; exposure to scrutiny; and the possibility of independent review. From these it can be seen why the Committee concluded that 'we have not found a conflict between independence and accountability' (p. 6). Accountability is not an end in itself, but is there for the purpose of achieving sustainable, effective regulation. In effect, it is a control system – the control system of regulatory governance. The duty to explain incorporates the preparation of regulatory impact assessments (RIAs) (Cabinet Office, 2003). As the Committee observes 'Properly done it reveals whether regulators have subjected their decisions to cost–benefit analysis (where this should be taken to mean costs and benefits in their broadest sense). ... These RIAs need to be conducted retrospectively as well as prospectively, to ensure that that cost-effectiveness is constantly under review' (House of Lords, 2004a, p. 7). The cost–benefit test is not only concerned with average benefits exceeding average costs, but in ensuring that, at the margin, the incremental benefit of having a standard at the chosen level is approximately equal to the incremental cost of having the standard at that level. The methodology of RIAs has therefore to be carefully examined and periodically reviewed (National Audit Office, 2005; Ofgem, 2005a, 2005b).

The Committee drew together the main principles and practices in a diagram of regulatory governance, and this is reproduced as Figure 9.3. It is succinct and self-explanatory. Figure 9.3 shows clearly how the process of maintaining an effective regulatory state starts and ends with Parliament. The time dimension, shown by moving anti-clockwise around Figure 9.3, not only demonstrates the different but inter-related roles the constituent parts of the regulatory state play

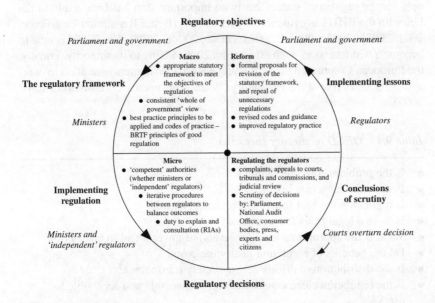

Source: House of Lords (2004a), p. 23.

Figure 9.3   The circle of accountability through the regulatory cycle

at various stages during the regulatory cycle, but also draws attention to the importance of 'iterative' arrangements between regulators if balanced outcomes are to be achieved. Hence, for example, ministers propose initial environmental standards, and the implications of these for costs and customers' bills can then be assessed by the economic regulator, and the implications for affordability taken on board by ministers in making their final judgements.

Entrenching the regulatory framework

Effective regulatory governance depends therefore on two key developments. First, that parliaments and legislatures take the opportunity to focus their attention on improved scrutiny of the regulatory framework and the regulatory state as a whole. Second, those scrutinizing the executive (including judges as part of an improved judicial review process) focus their attention on Regulatory Impact Assessments as the primary documentation for framing their inquiries. In this way RIAs will be forced to be 'fit for purpose' by preparers, and the proper balance between the accountability of the regulators and the regulated thereby achieved. This should also focus increased attention on regulatory accounts, too often an underutilized source of information and accountability.

The need to 'entrench' such institutional and process requirements should therefore not be underestimated if countries are to achieve an overall effectiveness for the regulatory state. Clearly an important start has been made in the UK with the BRTF, as evidenced by its outputs (Better Regulation Task Force, 2001, 2003b, 2003c, 2003d, 2004a, 2004b, 2004c, 2005). The BRTF is now to become a 'Commission' with effect from 2006, adding to its authority. Equally, the European Commission is addressing governance matters in relation to managing its own role as a regulatory 'state' (European Commission, 2001, 2002).

Table 9.3   OECD regulatory check list

- Is the problem correctly defined?
- Is government action justified?
- Is regulation the best form of government action?
- Is there a legal basis for regulation?
- What is the appropriate level (or levels) of government to take action?
- Do the benefits of regulation justify the costs?
- Is the distribution of effects across society transparent?
- Is the regulation clear, consistent, comprehensible and accessible to users?
- Have all the interested parties had the opportunity to present their views?
- How will compliance be achieved?

The OECD's recommendations also emphasize the importance of entrenching regulatory governance, identifying the goals of transparency, accountability, legitimacy, efficiency and policy coherence, and noting that transparency is an essential part of all phases of the regulatory process, as well as the management of the regulatory system.

The work of the OECD can also be commended for producing a checklist for regulatory legislation and decision-making, shown in Table 9.3. The checklist came out of a recommendation of the OECD on Improving the Quality of Government Regulation in 1995, which adopted for the first time an internationally accepted set of principles on ensuring regulatory quality (OECD, 2002a).

Regulatory governance in practice

The consequences of accountability for regulatory governance are dramatic, and emphasize the key importance of the provision of information in securing effective accountability and regulatory governance. They include (the associated references illustrate mainly with respect to the recent regulatory review of water prices in the UK – similar types and volumes of documentation are published by all of the UK's regulators):

- setting out clearly the objectives and proposed methodology at the start (Ofwat, 2003a);
- consulting at each stage and publishing the results of that consultation, including giving reasons why consultees' comments have or have not been accepted (Ofwat, 2003b);
- being transparent in relation to each stage and the final outcomes (Ofwat, 2003c, 2004a);
- setting out forward plans and reviewing outcomes in each annual report (Ofwat, 2005a, 2005b);
- establishing codes of conduct as to the procedures that will be followed;
- being subjected to scrutiny from a wide range of interested parties, including Parliamentary select committees (National Audit Office, 2002; Public Accounts Committee, 2002; Environment, Food and Rural Affairs Committee, 2004; Environmental Audit Committee, 2004);
- comparative analysis to benchmark performance (Ofwat, 2004b, 2005c);
- and post-completion review of the degree to which the periodic review has been properly conducted and in accordance with the principles of good regulation (Ofwat, 2005d).

The UK government formally responded to the Committee's report and participated in the subsequent Parliamentary debate (House of Lords, 2004b). The debate on the Committee's report took place on 2 December 2004 and gave the opportunity for the government, while accepting the broad thrust of the report, to argue why it did not accept some significant recommendations (Hansard col. 609). The chairman of the Constitution Committee, Lord Norton of Louth, opened the debate, and had prepared the ground for some of his more trenchant remarks (Norton, 2004a, 2004b). The government's response was arguably weakest in the area of 'coherence' of regulatory policy and process as a whole. Rather than focusing on the need for improved coordination and a lead government department to sustain a consistent regulatory model, the government chose to question the breadth of definition of regulation adopted by the Better Regulation Task Force: 'so wide as to encompass almost everything' (Hansard col. 612).[3] Yet this is an important definition given the context of the modern regulatory state, and the need for it to be accountable for the whole range of its activities.

Good examples of the weakness with which the government approaches the 'institutional' task of projecting a 'whole of government view' of regulation, are:

1.   that no one body is given overall responsibility for coordinating principles and practice, and being the advocate of efficiency and effectiveness in the regulatory state, unaffected by specific departmental interests;
2.   existing coordinating arrangements are not evidently transparent;
3.   and the principles of good regulation are not seen as important, generic statutory duties to be applied to regulators.

Without attention to these weaknesses, there is a danger that regulatory independence, in particular, might be undermined in the future (Glaister, 2004).

Conclusions

The relevance of the UK's experience to the international development of regulatory governance depends most fundamentally on whether generically relevant principles and practices have been identified. If so, then there is a template of fundamentals which can be mapped onto different cultural and institutional settings, adapted to their particular requirements, and then tested to see if the fundamental principles have been maintained. It is consensus on the fundamental principles that has to come first, before the development of law, processes and institutions in local settings, through which the fundamental principles of regulatory governance can be given effect. Simply transferring institutional blueprints and processes, without the prior consensus on objectives and outcomes is highly exposed to the risk of failure.

By focusing on the development of regulatory governance in the UK the chapter has aimed to demonstrate four fundamental lessons. First, that effective regulation is dependent on effective accountability of regulators. Second, that codification of the principles of good regulation is necessary to create the right climate of expectations. Third, that institutionalization of the processes of accountability has to be secured in order to ensure that the control system works in practice. Finally, that achieving sound regulation and an effective regulatory state is an evolving process, where mistakes are made and lessons learned. For this reason the regulatory state must be flexible enough to adapt and develop in the light of the fundamental principles of good regulation.

The UK Parliament has revisited the longstanding debates on accountability, and 'codified' the principles and practices into a set of conducts which can be seen to underpin a modern and effective regulatory state. There is strong evidence to suggest that the UK government is inexorably moving along the path to full implementation of the vision which the recent House of Lords report has articulated, albeit that 'inertial' forces may slow down the arrival point. The most recent example is the Hampton Report, launched by the Chancellor of the Exchequer as part of the 2005 Budget in the context of the government's deregulatory programme (HM Treasury, 2005). It takes forward the regulatory governance agenda, and reflects international best practice, citing the OECD's work: 'The OECD, in its most recent thinking on regulatory matters, recommends that governments develop a strategic centre for thinking and performance management of regulation' (OECD, 2002c).

Notes

1. This chapter develops work initially published by the author in the *CRI Regulatory Review, 2004/2005*, edited by the author, entitled 'Accountability in the Regulatory State Revisited', Chapter 11, University of Bath, 2005.
2. 'I do think that there are three different and equally important levels of accountability. The first, to give it an epithet, would be transparency. People have to know what you are doing and how you have done it, and in trying to explain that and in being forced to explain there is an element of accountability. ... The second is more penetrating. It is not just transparency. It is actually being questioned, if you like grilled, on what you have done and how effective have you been in doing it. The decisions cannot be changed but you can be cross-questioned. There, fairly obviously, the role of the select committees is paramount. The third level is where, of course, the decisions can be changed, and that is in our case through judicial review and to the High Court. (House of Lords, 2004a, p. 27)
3. 'Regulation may widely be defined as any measure or intervention that seeks to change the behaviour of individuals or groups' (BRTF, 2003a, *Principles of Good Regulation*, p. 1, para. 1).

References

Baldwin, R. and Cave, M. (1999) *Understanding Regulation – Theory, Strategy and Practice*, Oxford: Oxford University Press.

Banaga, A., Ray, G. and Tomkins, C. (1995) 'A Conceptual Framework for Corporate Governance and Effective Management', *Corporate Governance – An International Review*, **3** (3), July, 128–37.

Bartle, I. and Vass, P. (2005) 'Self-regulation and the Regulatory State – A Survey of Policy and Practice', *CRI Research Report 17*, University of Bath, UK.

Better Regulation Task Force (2001) *Economic Regulators*, London: Cabinet Office.

Better Regulation Task Force (2003a) *Principles of Good Regulation*, London; Cabinet Office.

Better Regulation Task Force (2003b) *Environmental Regulation: Getting the Message Across*, London: Cabinet Office.

Better Regulation Task Force (2003c) *Imaginative Thinking for Better Regulation*, London: Cabinet Office.

Better Regulation Task Force (2003d) *Independent Regulators*, London: Cabinet Office.

Better Regulation Task Force (2004a) *The Challenge of Culture Change: Raising the Stakes, Annual Report 2003–2004*, London: Cabinet Office.

Better Regulation Task Force (2004b) *Avoiding Regulatory Creep*, London: Cabinet Office.

Better Regulation Task Force (2004c), *Make It Simple – Make It Better*, London: Cabinet Office.

Better Regulation Task Force (2005) *Regulation – Less is More: Reducing Burdens, Improving Outcomes, A BRTF Report to the Prime Minister*, London: Cabinet Office.

Cabinet Office (2003) *A Quick Guide to Regulatory Impact Assessment, and Better Policy-making: A Guide to Regulatory Impact Assessment*, London: Cabinet Office.

Department of Trade and Industry (DTI) (1998) *A Fair Deal for Consumers – Modernising the Framework of Utility Regulation*, London: DTI.

Environment, Food and Rural Affairs Committee (2004) *Water Pricing: Follow-up, 19th Report of Session 2003–04*, HC 1186, London: House of Commons.

Environmental Audit Committee (2004) *Water: The Periodic Review 2004 and the Environmental Programme, 4th Report of Session 2003–04*, HC 416, London: House of Commons.

European Commission (2001) *European Governance – A White Paper, 428, Final*, Brussels: EC.

European Commission (2002) *Communication from the Commission on Impact Assessment, Com276, Final*, Brussels: EC.

Financial Reporting Council (2003) *The Combined Code on Corporate Governance*, London: FRC.

Foster, Sir C. (2005), *British Government in Crisis*, London: Hart Publishing.

Glaister, S. (2004) *British Rail Privatisation – Competition Destroyed by Politics*, CRI Occasional Paper 23, Bath: University of Bath.

HM Treasury (2005), *Reducing Administrative Burdens: Effective Inspection and Enforcement*, Philip Hampton, London: HM Treasury.

Hood, C., Rothstein, R. and Baldwin, R. (2001) *The Government of Risk – Understanding Risk Regulation Regimes*, Oxford: Oxford University Press.

House of Lords Select Committee on the Constitution (2004a) *The Regulatory State: Ensuring Its Accountability, 6th Report of Session 2003–04, Vols I–III*, HL Paper 68 I-III, London.

House of Lords Select Committee on the Constitution (2004b) *The Regulatory State: Ensuring Its Accountability – The Government's Response, 12th Report of Session 2003–04*, HL Paper 150, London.

The Independent Commission on Good Governance in Public Services (2004) *The Good Governance Standard for Public Services*, London: Office of Public Management and CIPFA.

Kirkpatrick, C., Parker, D. and Zhang, Y.F. (2005) 'Price and Profit Regulation in Developing and Transition Economies: A Survey of Regulators', *Public Money and Management*, **25** (2), April, 99–105.

Minogue, M. (2005) *Apples and Oranges: Comparing International Experiences in Regulatory Reform*, CRI Occasional Lecture 13, Bath: University of Bath.

Moran, M. (2003) *The British Regulatory State – High Modernism and Hyper-Innovation*, Oxford: Oxford University Press.

National Audit Office (2002) *Pipes and Wires*, London: NAO, HC723, Session 2001–02.

National Audit Office (2005) *Evaluation of Regulatory Impact Assessments Compendium Report 2004–05*, London: NAO, HC 341.

National Consumer Council (2000) *Models of Self-regulation: An Overview of Models in Business and the Professions*, London: NCC.

Norton, P., Professor the Lord Norton of Louth (2004a) 'Regulating the Regulatory State', *Parliamentary Affairs*, **57** (4), 785–99.

Norton, P., Professor the Lord Norton of Louth (2004b) *Who Regulates the Regulators*, CRI Occasional Lecture, 8 September, Bath: University of Bath.

OECD (1997) *Report on Regulatory Reform*, Paris: Organisation for Economic Co-operation and Development.

OECD (2002a) *Regulatory Policies in OECD Countries – From Interventionism to Regulatory Governance, Reviews of Regulatory Reform*, Paris: Organisation for Economic Co-operation and Development.

OECD (2002b) *United Kingdom – Challenges at the Cutting Edge*, Paris: Organisation for Economic Co-operation and Development.

OECD (2002c) *Government Capacity to Assure High Quality Regulation*, Paris: Organisation for Economic Co-operation and Development.

Office of Gas and Electricity Markets (Ofgem) (2005a) *A Review of Ofgem's Regulatory Impact Assessments*, Oxford: Regulatory Policy Institute.

Ofgem (2005b) *Guidance on Impact Assessments – Revised Guidance*, London: Office of Gas and Electricity Markets.

Ofwat (2003a) *Setting Water and Sewerage Price Limits for 2005–10: Framework and Approach (Periodic Review 2004)*, Birmingham: Ofwat.

Ofwat (2003b) *Summary of Consultation Responses and Conclusions (to Setting Water and Sewerage Price Limits for 2005–10: Framework and Approach)*, Birmingham: Ofwat.

Ofwat (2003c) *Overview of Companies' Draft Business Plans (for Setting Water and Sewerage Price Limits for 2005–10: Framework and Approach)*, Birmingham: Ofwat.

Ofwat (2004a) *Future Water and Sewerage Charges 2005–10: Final Determinations*, Birmingham: Ofwat.

Ofwat (2004b) *Financial Performance and Expenditure of the Water Companies in England and Wales, 2003–2004 Report*, Birmingham: Ofwat.

Ofwat (2005a) *Ofwat Forward Programme 2005–06 to 2007–08*, Birmingham: Ofwat.

Ofwat (2005b) *Annual Report of the Director General of Water Services 2004–2005*, Birmingham: Ofwat.

Ofwat (2005c) *International Comparison of Water and Sewerage Service – 2005 Report Covering the Period 2002–03*, Birmingham: Ofwat.

Ofwat (2005d) *Report into the Conduct of the 2004 Ofwat Periodic Review – A Report Commissioned by Ofwat from the Independent Steering Group*, Birmingham: Ofwat.

Public Accounts Committee (2002) *Pipes and Wires, 50th Report of Session 2001–2002*, HC 416, London: House of Commons.

Robens, The Lord (1972) *Safety and Health At Work, Report of the Committee 1970–72*, Cmnd 5034, London: HMSO.

Vass, P. (2003) *Accountability of Regulators, in Regulatory Practice and Design – A Collection of Reviews Relating to Utilities and Network Industries*, CRI Collections Series 2, Chapter 1, pp. 1–16, first printed in *CRI Regulatory Review* (1994), Chapter 12, Bath: University of Bath.

10 Regulation and consumer representation

Michael Harker, Laurence Mathieu and Catherine Waddams Price

Introduction

A separate chapter on consumer representation might seem redundant in a handbook on regulation – surely consumer interest is precisely the purpose of regulation? We explore the specific roles of consumer organizations in a regulatory framework. Regulation itself is often characterized as protecting consumers by imposing ex ante constraints on firms' actions. In contrast, competition policy ensures that markets are structured so that consumers can exercise their own power through informed choice, and threatens ex post punishment for firms who restrict such choice through exploitation of their market power. Consumer representative bodies play a part in both situations. In the United Kingdom there is an apparent irony that independent consumer bodies were established by the same legislation which enhanced the importance of consumer protection in the regulators' duties. One reason may be that sources of consumer information become particularly important when competition is introduced into a previously monopolized market.

A large range of organizations purport to represent consumers: some speak for consumer interests as a whole, while others focus on particular groups (low income, the elderly or other groups perceived as vulnerable); some are general and others focus on a particular sector (e.g. energy); some are statutory and others voluntary. In regulated sectors they may arise because, although the regulator's duties include consumer protection, there are particular challenges in catering to consumers who of necessity share a regulated network and its characteristics, including reliability.

Within regulated industries, consumer representation covers a number of dimensions. The industries concerned are usually utilities which are regarded as 'essential'.[1] Expenditure on their products increases with income, but at a decreasing rate, so that the proportion of income spent on these services is higher for lower income households. In developed countries, most consumers are attached to a network to supply the relevant services; in countries and industries where this is not the case, extension of the network, or other means of making the product universally available, is generally a major objective of the government. Because of its politically sensitive nature, supply has in the past often been provided below cost, sometimes below marginal cost, by publicly owned monopolies. The privatization process, itself often politically divisive, usually engenders the need for explicit regulation, at least of the monopoly network element; new arrangements for consumer representation are sometimes made at the same time.

Consumer representation in privatized utilities has three distinct explicit roles. The first two relate to the consumer body as a whole, namely to ensure that the consumer *voice* is heard where there is monopoly; and to ensure that consumers are able to exercise their right of *exit* where retail choice is introduced. Consumers may need assistance or information in these markets because exit is a new and unfamiliar freedom. Those who are not used to making choices about telephone and energy suppliers may not fully understand the distinction between monopoly wires and choice of retail providers, and may need help in finding the information needed for such a choice. This important role of consumer bodies in 'jump starting' a market and helping consumers to ensure that it becomes competitive should generally mean they become victims of their own success in these markets. Once a market is judged sufficiently competitive to move from ex ante regulation to reliance on general competition law and ex post scrutiny, consumer representation might be judged to have been successful in this transitional role, and a separate sector specific body may no longer be required.

The third consumer body function is for individual consumers, to advise them in any disputes with the companies – we can call this role *resolution*.

For the monopoly network activities, where consumers have no choice, the exit function of consumer bodies is irrelevant. The functioning of these networks affects most directly the quality of service which consumers experience, for example continuity of supply. Moreover, since consumers sharing a single network must also share its reliability, regulators need to determine an appropriate balance between quality and price. Is it appropriate to have a consumer body separate from the regulator in such circumstances? This would be most appropriate where there is danger of regulatory capture either by the regulated company or by the government. We label this as our fourth potential role for consumer bodies – that of *supervision* of the regulator. If this is not a concern, then it would probably be more efficient for the regulatory body to incorporate the consumer representation function itself, so that it has more immediate access to the information generated.

If the consumer body is not a direct guardian for the regulatory watchdog, there might still be advantages in having a separate 'regulatory' voice to be heard by the media, government and public, but separation could be costly, both in terms of administration and potential distortion of decisions. Baron (1985) showed that separating environmental from economic regulation would result in lower pollution, higher costs, and higher profits for the regulated firm, higher consumer prices and lower welfare because the firm can use its superior information to extract rents. Similar effects could result from any 'single issue' body which focuses on a particular aspect of consumer welfare, or the welfare of particular consumers, without having to take account of potentially negative impacts (for example, lower prices or better conditions for one group of consumers may result in higher prices for another group).

In this chapter we first use a detailed case study of one example of consumer representation to illustrate and develop these four facets of voice, exit, resolution and supervision. We examine the development of consumer representative bodies for regulated utilities and suggestions for further reform in the UK, one of the leaders in privatization and deregulation, focusing particularly on the energy sector as our example. We then survey consumer representation in the EU, Australia, New Zealand, the United States and some Latin American countries. From this broad overview we identify examples of each type of consumer representation function from other country contexts. The final section of the chapter uses evidence from these studies to draw some general conclusions about the role and effectiveness of consumer representation in regulated sectors.

UK institutions

The economic concept of market failure in natural monopolies usually leads to the establishment of explicit regulatory institutions when utilities are privatized, as recommended by the World Bank (Guislain, 1997). Such regulatory institutions are often complemented by bodies charged with the function of representing the consumer interest. The UK's experience over the last two decades can be characteristic of an evolution of institutional design, for example: regulatory bodies have been merged and their make-up reformed, notably from single regulators to regulatory boards; where competition has been introduced, the tools of regulation have shifted from prescriptive ex ante controls through licensing to the use of the general competition law, also recently reformed. Together with these changes, there has been a general shift towards stronger consumer representation, with the establishment of independent bodies having significant powers of supervision over both the regulated firms and the regulators. Established in November 2000, *energywatch* – the consumer council for the energy sector in Britain – was one of the first of these new breed of councils. However, as is discussed in this chapter, although a relatively new innovation, there have been a number of calls for the reform of these institutions. In particular, questions have arisen over the way in which they interpret the consumer interest and the degree of inconsistency between sectors. These calls for reform provide a focus for issues we explore further in this chapter.

Background

Reform of the consumer bodies accompanied more general changes in utility regulation. Shortly after coming to power in May 1997 the UK Labour government announced a comprehensive review of the regulation of the utilities (privatized by predecessor Conservative governments between 1984 and 1995). Reform followed, with the enactment of the Utilities Act 2000 in respect of gas and electricity markets, the Communications Act 2003 in respect of telecommunications, and the Water Act 2003 in respect of water and sewerage services.

Following the review, the government consulted on legislative change publishing a Green Paper entitled *A Fair Deal for Consumers: Modernising the Framework for Utility Regulation* (DTI, 1998a). The central thrust of the Green Paper was that the interests of shareholders had been given priority over those of consumers and, more specifically, that the benefits of competition were not being shared fairly by all consumers, in particular the vulnerable and disadvantaged. To address these concerns a new hierarchy of duties was proposed for the regulators with a primary objective to promote the interests of consumers *wherever appropriate* through the promotion of effective competition (emphasis added). The legislation provided specific guidance that this primary objective should be achieved by securing that reasonable demands are met and licence holders are able to finance relevant activities, suggesting that the Authority would need to balance different considerations and stakeholder interests within its overall consumer objective. This new primary duty to consumers in general was to be complemented by a requirement on the regulators to have regard to the interests of vulnerable and disadvantaged consumers (including a new responsibility for those on low incomes) in respect of all aspects of supply, including price. With the enactment of the Utilities Act 2000, these duties were incorporated into the Gas Act 1986 and the Electricity Act 1989.[2] An additional duty to carry out its functions in the manner best calculated to contribute to sustainable development was imposed on the Authority under the Energy Act 2004, mirroring similar duties imposed on the Water Regulator under the Water Act 2003.

The nature of consumer representation
In the Green Paper the government stated its belief 'that consumers should have an effective and powerful voice within the regulatory system' (DTI, 1998a, para. 1.20). In respect of the new overriding duty, it was thought that the consumer interest could only be realistically protected 'if the real interests of consumers are properly understood' (DTI, 1998a, para. 3.10). While all of the different models of consumer representation had their strengths, it was thought that the model best placed 'to argue the consumers' case' with the regulators would be that of independent consumer councils. Separating consumer representation from the regulators' offices (where they had mostly been based hitherto[3]) could encourage more open debate on regulatory decisions and raise the profile of consumers within the regulatory process (para. 3.11).

In addition to the provision of greater independence for the new consumer bodies, the government proposed a substantial augmentation of their powers, principally in respect of their ability to require information from both the regulated companies and their cognate regulators (DTI, 1998a, para. 3.12). Where retail competition was present, they were also to have responsibility for providing consumers with comparative price information (DTI, 1998a, paras 3.42–3.44).

The composition and powers of the new consumer body for the energy sector, *energywatch*, are discussed in detail below. Reform for the other sectors took more time than originally anticipated. The Water Act 2003 provides for a body broadly similar to that of energywatch, while the Communications Act 2003 introduced a significantly different model for telecommunications, as is also discussed below.[4]

Other (non-statutory) consumer bodies have been created to reflect the interests of particular consumer groups. Large and commercial users have formed a number of groups to lobby and make representations of their common interests to the regulator. The principal organizations here are the Major Energy Users Council, the Utilities Buyers Forum and the Intensive Energy Users Group. In respect of domestic consumers, various voluntary organizations represent the interests of specific groups of individuals who have particular needs in respect of energy services, examples being the Royal National Institute for the Blind and Age Concern. Others, such as the Public Utilities Access Forum (PUAF) (a group set up by organizations representing individuals on low incomes), have exercised considerable influence over the regulators especially in relation to the Social Action Plan, an ongoing initiative set up to address problems of disadvantaged consumers having access to competitive energy markets.[5]

The regulator is able to hear cases for particular consumer interests from these non-statutory groups. In contrast, a consumer council seeking to represent the general interests of consumers will normally present a compromise between competing interests in the advice and representations it makes to the regulator. Perhaps somewhat ironically, this argument suggests that the regulator, in considering the needs of a variety of stakeholders, will be able to make the decision better if he or she hears the individual voices of different consumer interests. This does not mean that the 'aggregate' consumer voice is not important too, but that the regulator may need to know how its constituent parts contribute.

Following consultations on the Green Paper, a White Paper heralded the endorsement of consumer councils with responsibility 'for pro-actively promoting and advocating the interests of consumers' (DTI, 1998b, para. 17). The new consumer bodies would be the 'primary point of contact' with all consumers, with responsibility 'in the first instance for handling consumer complaints', although the enforcement of regulatory obligations would remain with the regulator (DTI, 1998b, para. 17). While the government was of the view that the councils should represent the interests of all consumers, it confirmed its intention that it should also have an explicit role in promoting the interests of the disadvantaged (DTI, 1998b, para. 18). The gas regulator, in particular, who had had experience of an independent consumer body before reform, recognized the inherent tensions, discussed above, which exist in representing the interests of all consumers:

> In making representations to the regulator, the consumer council may find consider-able difficulty in practice in balancing the potentially conflicting needs of the wide spectrum of domestic customers. [I]t will be even more difficult for the council to balance the needs and views of industrial and commercial customers with those of domestic customers, particularly if it is charged with the particular role of represent-ing disadvantaged customers. (Ofgas, 1997, p. 3)

Consumer voice and exit: consumer representation in a competitive environment
A further initiative was mooted in the Green Paper. In markets where effective competition is achieved, the government suggested that it might be appropriate to replace the consumer councils with an ombudsman, acting as 'an independent intermediary between customers and companies' (DTI, 1998a, para. 3.18); any residual policy advice could be provided by Advisory Committees. The gas regulator offered her support to the idea, arguing that the relevant legislation ought to include a 'sunset' provision for the replacement of the council (Ofgas, 1998, p. 10).[6] However, in the face of objections from consumer groups, the government judged that any discussion of the replacement of the consumer councils with ombudsman schemes was premature, although it did not rule this out in the longer term (DTI, 1998b, para. 21). As is discussed later, the ombuds-man model was resurrected by the Government for the telecommunications sector.

In practice, some consumers have experienced difficulties in exercising their power of exit in the energy market, especially those in debt. This suggests either that competition is not yet mature in the industry, in which case the original ar-guments for consumer representation may still be valid; or that this is a more general issue, not specific to energy, which should be addressed through com-petition law or trading standards offices. Even where ex ante price controls are removed and competition is well established, some argue that the nature of the commodity implies a need to ensure that the benefits of competition are shared fairly by all consumers These discussions are reflected and summarized by the Department of Trade and Industry, see Table 10.1.

However, sunset clauses for explicit consumer representation in retail markets that have become competitive ignore the need for continuing regulation of the natural monopoly elements of the gas, electricity and water industries,[7] and the need for consumer voice to inform an appropriate level of quality and price. These factors are also included in Table 10.1.

Table 10.1   Market characteristics that justify sector-specific consumer representation (UK)

	Water	Energy	Post	Comms	Financial services	Air
Degree of monopoly power	●	◐	●	◐	○	○
Degree to which it is an essential service	●	●	◐	◐	○	○
Degree of information problems in the market	○	◐	○	◐	●	○
Market size (annual household spend £m)	£5,493	£15,038	£884	£14,629	n/a	£10,590

● High
◐ Medium
○ Low

Source: DTI and HM Treasury (2004).

The 'energywatch' model of consumer representation

Under the Utilities Act 2000, the original regulators for the gas and electricity sectors (Ofgas and Offer) were merged into a single entity known as Ofgem.[8] For this reason a single consumer council for the energy sectors was created, namely energywatch.[9] The Water Act 2003 provided for a new statutory consumer council[10] with a structure and powers similar to that of energywatch. The picture is somewhat different in telecommunications, reflecting the rapidly changing technology and greater competitive development in some areas.[11] Under the Communications Act 2003 (section 16) the telecommunications regulator, Ofcom, is required to establish a consumer panel to provide policy advice on the needs of consumers, including the disadvantaged and those living in rural areas. However, beyond the provision of advice, the panel does not have any of the information gathering powers of its counterpart in energy, nor does it enjoy institutional independence from the regulator. Consumer complaints – a principal function of energywatch – are dealt with by (self-regulatory) ombudsman schemes.[12]

For the rest of this section we focus on energywatch, outlining its principal powers and duties, its formal relationship with the economic regulator, and reviewing the nature of some of its work in the first four years of its existence.

The organization, duties and powers of energywatch

The Secretary of State, rather than the regulator, appoints members of energywatch.[13] To guarantee the independence of the council from the regulator, the council's budgets are set and agreed with the sponsoring department (i.e. the Department of Trade and Industry) rather than with the regulator. Since the necessary resources are raised via licence fees, it was accepted that the sponsoring department would need the power to issue an instruction to the regulator to raise such monies (DTI, 1999, para. 14), and this was established by the Utilities Act 2000 (section 8). Without such a power of direction, energywatch would be reliant on the regulator raising a satisfactory level of payments to meet its expenses, thereby undermining its independence from Ofgem.

Energywatch's principal role is to act as advocate for the interests of consumers, including vulnerable and disadvantaged consumers. It has the broad function of obtaining and keeping under review information about consumer matters and the views of consumers in the different areas of Great Britain (Utilities Act 2000, section 18(1)). The meaning of consumers is aligned to the definition contained in Ofgem's duties, and includes both existing and future consumers; energywatch is required to have regard to the interests of the disabled, the chronically sick, those of pensionable age, those on low incomes, and those residing in rural areas (section 17).[14] While both energywatch and Ofgem have identical duties as far as consumers are concerned, the regulator alone is given additional specific guidance on securing that reasonable demands are met and licence holders are able to finance relevant activities, as was discussed above. The additional duty with respect to sustainable development is also restricted to the regulator. This distinction suggests that energywatch can pursue the consumer objective, where it can be identified, more single mindedly, unencumbered by the Authority's need to balance different considerations, within the overall consumer objective.

Energywatch has the function of making proposals, providing advice and information on consumer matters to public authorities, licensees and 'other persons whose activities may affect the interests of consumers', subject to some restrictions, concerned mostly with commercial confidentiality (section 19). Energywatch also has a general power to publish any advice or information about consumer matters where this would 'promote the interests of consumers', subject to similar restrictions (sections 20–21). More specifically, it publishes statistical information on the levels of performance achieved by firms in respect of energy efficiency targets, on complaints, and on standards of performance set by Ofgem.

The government intended that all consumer matters should, in the first instance, be channelled through energywatch, providing a 'one-stop shop' for consumer complaints and removing any confusion on the part of consumers about the division of responsibilities between the consumer body and the regulator. Energywatch is required to *investigate* complaints made to it by any customer in respect of any activity connected with the supply of gas or electricity (Utilities Act 2000, section 22). However, if it cannot reach a settlement, the only course of action open to it is to refer the matter to Ofgem who retains the sole power to take enforcement action.

Energywatch has new powers to obtain information from licensees and the regulator. The Utilities Act 2000 provides energywatch with the power to direct either Ofgem or the licensees to furnish it with such information 'as it may require for the purpose of exercising its functions' (section 24).[15] In exercising a supervisory role over the regulator, it has ex post rights of access to information on the deliberations of Ofgem, an important power which may reduce potential risks that the regulator's relationship with the industry would undermine its independence.[16] In this way it can provide an important check against regulatory capture.

Emphasis was placed on the need to put in place a legislative framework that promoted cooperation and coordination between the regulator and the council. While there would be a clear delineation of functions, there would need to be 'close interdependencies, and a need for an effective framework for collaboration' (DTI, 1998c, para. 11). To achieve this it was envisaged that the statutory framework would require the regulator to consult on specified regulatory decisions. As a consequence, there are formal requirements on both the regulator and energywatch to consult one another, for example on their 'forward work programmes' (Utilities Act 2000, section 4). Much of the framework for coordination between the council and the regulator would be too detailed to be set in statute and such detail might inhibit the flexibility necessary 'in order to respond to developments and experiences in running the two bodies in parallel' (DTI, 1998c, para. 12). Instead, Ofgem and energywatch have a statutory obligation to agree on a 'memorandum of understanding' to govern their mutual coordination and cooperation in the exercise of their functions (DTI, 1999, para. 10; Utilities Act 2000, section 7).

Consumer advocacy in practice Energywatch was established as a strong, independent consumer council, as 'the public advocate for utility consumers', presenting an informed consumer view not only to the regulators, but to the government, Parliament and the media (DTI, 1998c, para. 9).

Since its inception, energywatch has focused considerable resources on this 'lobbying' role. It has contributed evidence to the UK Parliament's Select Committee on Trade and Industry on several occasions, particularly on the issue of fuel poverty (energywatch, 2002, p. 9; 2003, p. 15; 2004, p. 12). It has campaigned to end disconnections for vulnerable consumers, exerting pressure through Parliament and the media (energywatch, 2004, p. 12). With its role in handling complaints, it has been able to highlight some of the principal consumer concerns with regard to the operation of the competitive market. There have been three particular areas of concern. First, energywatch has been highly critical of the marketing practices of some firms, resulting in Ofgem levying a £2 million fine against one of the worst offending companies and, after the investigation, the public intervention of the Energy Minister (energywatch, 2003, pp. 12–13). A new standard condition has been incorporated into the supply licences to increase the regulator's powers to intervene in such circumstances (energywatch, 2004, p. 6). Second, its concern about late billing (which constituted 59 per cent of complaints received in 2003/4) led to an investigation by Ofgem (energywatch, 2004, p. 8). Third, in the face of increasing energy wholesale prices, energywatch has been highly vocal in national and regional media in encouraging consumers to switch suppliers, particularly away from the incumbents whose prices tend to be significantly higher than those of entrants. While in many areas there has clearly been cooperation between energywatch and Ofgem, the former has occasionally criticized the regulator, for example for removing price restraints on prepayment tariffs, which affect some of the poorest of consumers (energywatch, 2003, p. 13).

An effective voice for consumers?　　The powers given to energywatch enable it to scrutinize effectively both the regulator and the regulated firms. The regulator is required to consult energywatch on all its key decisions and its forward work programme. The latter requirement is significant since that programme contains the regulator's operational and policy priorities. Together with the institutional safeguards which guarantee its independence, energywatch has the potential to campaign for and advocate powerfully the interests of consumers, though both bodies are bound by formal requirements to engage positively with each other.

　　While the government hinted that energywatch would have specific responsibility to represent the interests of disadvantaged consumers, there is no such formal provision in the legislation, in which energywatch's duties mirror those of the regulator with respect to such consumers. The diverse nature of the consumer interest and the breadth of the definition of consumer (including commercial, industrial and residential consumers) present energywatch with a challenge in representing a single consumer interest. As the government noted: 'Industry lobbies the regulator hard in pursuit of its interests. That is to be expected, but it should be balanced by proper and full representation of consumers' concerns'[17] (DTI, 2000, para. 7.5.3).

　　Governments and regulators will find it easier to notice and respond to the interests of highly organized interest groups rather than those which are diverse and disparate, such as residential consumers, and this may well be the justification for governmental intervention in the form of statutory bodies charged with representing such consumers' interests (Howells, 2000, p. 298). Despite the ambiguity of energywatch's duties, it has in practice focused its attentions on poorer consumers. In the longer term, however, it claims to have an 'overall objective of systemic change to company practices and consumer behaviour' (energywatch, 2004, p. 5).

In a competitive environment, one effective way for consumers to express their preferences is through the market mechanism. However, market mechanisms are not a panacea. Particular consumers may not be in possession of all the relevant information or have the incentives to collect this information, necessary to make decisions effectively. Such limitations may apply particularly to some consumer groups. It should not be forgotten that while the government lauded many of the benefits of competition, a major concern in its review of utilities was that the benefits of competition should be enjoyed 'fairly' by all consumers, especially the vulnerable and disadvantaged. This was a particular concern because price changes in utilities have a disproportionate impact on poorer consumers' budgets, a fact which energywatch has emphasized in the context of rises in wholesale energy prices (2004, p. 23). In the early days after privatization, market liberalization resulted in some rebalancing of tariffs between different consumer groups. The introduction of competition in the bulk energy supply market resulted in a rebalancing of tariffs in favour of large industrial consumers at the expense of domestic users. Even within the latter consumer group, since the introduction of competition in domestic supply there has been concern about potential tariff rebalancing to reflect cost conditions in two respects: tariffs for credit and prepayment meters (used disproportionately by lower incomes groups) might increase relative to automated bank debit tariffs; and fixed charges might increase relative to rates per unit (increasing prices for those who use less energy, who generally also have a lower income; ONS, 2004). Placed in the context of the government's ongoing policy objective to reduce fuel poverty, it is unsurprising that consumer groups charged with the promotion of the consumer interest should focus on the needs of lower income consumers. While the regulator is ultimately responsible for balancing these competing interests, their identification can be assisted considerably by consumer bodies representing particular perspectives (for an example of this view see Ofgas, 1998, pp. 3–4).

Although there was some rebalancing in anticipation of competition (Waddams Price and Hancock, 1998), more recent figures suggest that these early concerns have not so far been reflected in practice (Waddams Price, 2005). It is not yet clear whether the expected rebalancing has not materialized because firms have revised their understanding of underlying costs, which was reflected in their early pricing behaviour (Otero and Waddams Price, 2001); or whether their view of costs remain unchanged and companies have not rebalanced because of external pressure, including representations made by consumer bodies. Such pressure can be exerted through the regulator, either where ex ante price caps remain or through an implicit threat to seek their reinstatement; or directly on the companies, who wish to maintain a good image, not only with the regulator but also with the media and wider public. This leaves the question of exerting pressure informally through media and public opinion. If it is indeed such informal pressure that has prevented rebalancing of prices in order for them to become more cost reflective, this raises other concerns. Efficiency gains from better cost signalling to consumers are sacrificed, and the trade-off between such efficiency gains and distributional issues is obscured rather than elucidated. This is far from the more open debate intended in establishing statutory consumer bodies. Finding the most appropriate trade-off through such informal and tacit means would seem to be more a matter of luck than judgement; in particular, such a process deprives the government of the central role which it should properly assume in such a fundamental discussion.

Moreover, particular concerns for low income groups remain for a number of reasons. If that remains unchanged, further rebalancing may be expected at some time in the future. In any case the *level* of energy prices is expected to rise in the future to reflect environmental concerns and raw material costs. Such price rises may be exacerbated by residual market power (either unilateral or multilateral) in the deregulated energy market, and, as already noted, would have a disproportionate effect on low income consumers.

Consumers who switch supplier in the competitive markets have made savings compared with those who stay with incumbents, and energywatch has been active in encouraging switching. Benefits of competition may not be restricted only to those who switch supplier, if incumbents lower their prices in response to entrants' pressure. But evidence for this is mixed six years after the markets opened, with concerns about coordinated effects between suppliers, as well as remaining dominance by incumbents (Ofgem, 2004; Waddams Price, 2005).

International experience

Just as in the UK case, consumer protection for regulated sectors is usually provided in addition to general provisions for promoting consumer interests. One major factor in the structure, powers and duties of such consumer bodies in network industries such as transport, post, telecommunications and energy, is the ownership of the industries themselves. Where they are publicly owned, as in most EU countries, both regulatory and consumer bodies play a rather different role from that when they are in the private sector, as in the UK. Publicly owned industries are often regulated internally, with the interests of consumers as one of their own objectives, explicit or implicit. In particular, conditions for prices and charges may be incorporated into their own statutes or regulations. For example, we see few organizations representing water consumers because water in most countries is still publicly supplied. In the UK guidance on the public interest was restricted to general phrases in the nationalization Acts, which required corporations to cover costs, taking one year with another, and not to discriminate unduly against any consumer or group of consumers.

The ownership, objectives and constraints of the industries, in turn, affect the perceived need for and establishment of sector specific consumer bodies. Private sector monopolies are generally expected to pursue profit maximizing objectives, and be subject to maximum regulatory constraints on their profit or price levels; while public sector industries are more likely to pursue policies of maximizing revenue, and be subject to constraints that minimize their burden on the exchequer.[18] The short-term consumer interest may be highly vocal where it becomes a political issue, particularly when the industries concerned are owned by local governments.

All governments have some bodies that focus on consumer protection, using a variety of institutions from government departments and agencies to collective actions through the legal system and Ombudsmen to adjudicate, sometimes with powers of redress (DTI, 2003). Within the European Union 15,[19] each member state has special ministerial departments with responsibility for protecting the economic interests of consumers, though not always with specific sector responsibilities. In some member states (Belgium, Denmark and Austria), consumer organizations are also involved in market surveillance. For the regulated sectors, consumer bodies are often incorporated within the overall regulatory body. The telecommunications sector typically has greater consumer representation, reflecting its role as one of the first of the traditionally publicly owned monopolies to be privatized.

Beyond the EU a variety of models are apparent. In New Zealand, where sectoral regulation was initially rejected in favour of using general competition law, an Electricity Commission was established in 2003 to oversee the industry, in response to concerns about security of supply and the dramatic Auckland power failure in 1998. The Commission includes provision for consumer information and there is an independent Energy Complaints Commissioner for dispute resolution. Regulation of other utility sectors is undertaken within the Commerce Commission, and consumer representation is similarly shared with general competition oversight, though consumers of State Owned Enterprises can make a complaint to the office of the Ombudsmen. In Australia, too, power failures have led to the establishment of a new national energy regulator. Individual states and territories have jurisdiction-specific ombudsman schemes to deal with consumer complaints and we discuss below recent initiatives on consumer representation. The Australian Communications Authority was established in 1997 and deals with questions of consumer representation and complaints.

In the United States, most consumer representation and support is based at state level. Regulation of interstate trading is provided through sectoral regulators: the Federal Energy Regulatory Commission and the Federal Communications Commission. A federal code lays down consumer rights for representation and for reimbursement of costs for electric utilities, but individual states make their own arrangements for consumer representation. The Senate Energy Bill in May 2005 sought to create a Consumer Advocate as an independent watchdog to represent consumers at the Federal Energy Regulatory Commission, at judicial hearings, and at other federal agencies. In Canada the National Energy Task Force has been established by the Consumers' Association, itself an independent, not-for-profit, volunteer-based, charitable organization. The task force coordinates interventions on behalf of consumers before various energy boards across the country, and 'will pursue involvement in all aspects of energy pricing and inform consumers on policies put forward by various governments and how these policies will affect consumers' (Consumer's Association of Canada, 2004). This is one of several voluntary consumer associations and lobby groups in North America. In Latin America, which has a long experience of introducing private ownership and competition to utility industries, including telecoms and energy, there are few separate statutory bodies for consumer representation. Consumer complaints are generally handled by the sector regulators.

Table 10.2 summarizes the variety of institutions that are available to protect and represent consumer interests in the energy and telecommunications sectors in a range of countries.[20] If consumers are represented directly in the regulatory body, this is shown with a tick in the third column. Bodies whose *main* objective is consumer representation (rather than protection) are listed in the final column. These organizations are classified as administrative (i.e. an agency of government, A), independent statutory bodies (IS), or voluntary (V). Among the countries and sectors included, only the UK uses the independent statutory body model described earlier in the chapter.

International examples of consumer body functions

It is useful to explore how far regulatory agencies in other regimes perform the various tasks we have identified for energywatch in the UK, focusing in turn on each of the four roles that body performs. The recent review of consumer representation in the Australian energy sector provides an interesting example of such issues in regulated utilities, particularly as competition is introduced. Thus for example, in its review, KPMG identified the role of a consumer body as being to 'provide advocacy on behalf of consumers, through one focused point, to the Australian Energy Market Commission (AEMC) and the Australian Energy Regulator (AER)' (National Consumers Electricity Advocacy Panel, 2005).

At the time of review in 2005 various bodies represented consumers, and the National Energy Code Administrator provided funding for this role in electricity.

Table 10.2 Sector-specific regulatory agencies and consumer representation

Country	Consumer protection	Consumer representation on regulatory body	Consumer representation
Denmark	Danish Energy Regulatory Authority (DERA) http://www.ks.dk/ National Telecom Agency (Telestyrelsen) http://www.tst.dk/	✓	
Finland	Energy Market Authority (Energiamarkkinavirasto) http://www.energiamarkkinavirasto.fi/ Telecommunication Administration Centre (Telehallintokeskus) http://www.thk.fi/		
France	Office of Energy Regulation (Commission de Régulation de l'Energie or CRE) http://www.cre.fr/ Telecommunications Regulatory Authority (Autorité de Régulation des Télécommunications or ART) http://www.art-telecom.fr/	✓	
Germany	Regulatory Authority for the Electricity and Gas Markets http://www.regtp.de/ Regulatory Authority for Telecommunications and Post (Regulierungsbehörde für Telekommunikation und Post or RegTP) http://www.regtp.de/		
Norway	The Norwegian Water Resources and Energy Directorate (Norges Vassdrags – og Energidirektorat or NVE) http://www.nve.no/ Norwegian Post and Telecommunications Authority (Post- og Teletilsynet or PT) http://www.npt.no/		

Table 10.2 continued

Country	Consumer protection	Consumer representation on regulatory body	Consumer representation
Sweden	Swedish Energy Agency (STEM) http://www.stem.se/ Swedish National Post and Telecom Agency (Post och Telestyrelsen or PTS) http://www.pts.se/		
UK	Office of Gas and Energy Markets (OFGEM) http://www.ofgem.gov.uk/ofgem/ Office of Communications (OFCOM) http://www.ofcom.org.uk/		Energywatch http://www.energywatch.org.uk/, IS
Australia	Australian Energy Regulator (AER) http://www.accc.gov.au Australian Communications Authority (ACA) http://www.aca.gov.au/	✓	Energy and Water Ombudsman (New South Wales) http://www.ewon.com.au/, A Energy Consumer protection office (Queensland) http://www.ecpo.qld.gov.au/, A Electricity Ombudsman (South Australia) http://www.eiosa.com.au/, A Electricity Ombudsman (Tasmania) http://www.energyombudsman.tas.gov.au/, A Energy and Water Ombudsman (Victoria) http://www.ewov.com.au/, A
New Zealand	Electricity Commission http://www.electricitycommission.govt.nz/		Electricity and Gas Complaints Commission http://www.egcomplaints.co.nz/, V
Canada	National Energy Board http://www.neb.gc.ca/ Canadian Radio-television and Telecommunications Commission (CRTC) http://www.crtc.gc.ca/		National Energy Task Force http://www.consumer.ca/1527, V

Country	Agency	URL
USA	Federal Energy Regulatory Commission (FERC)	http://www.ferc.fed.us/
	Federal Communications Commission (FCC)	http://www.fcc.gov/
Argentina	National Regulatory Entity of Gas (Ente National Regulator des Gas or ENARGAS)	http://www.enargas.gov.ar/
	National Regulatory Entity of Electricity (Ente National Regulator de la Electricidad or ENRE)	http://www.enre.gov.ar/
	National Commission of Communications (Comision National de Comunicaciones or CNC)	http://www.cnc.gov.ar/
Brazil	Electricity Regulatory Agency (Agência Nacional de Energia Eléctrica or ANEEL)	http://www.aneel.gov.br/
	National Telecommunications Agency (Agência Nacional de Telecommunicações or ANATEL)	http://www.anatel.gov.br/
Chile	National Commission of Energy (Comision Nacional de Energia or CNE)	http://www.cne.cl/
	Chile's Telecom Regulator (Subsecretaría de Telecommunicaciones or SUBTEL)	http://www.subtel.cl/
Peru	Energy Regulatory Agency (Organismo Supervisor de la Inversión Energía or OSINERG)	http://www.osinerg.gob.pe/
	Telecommunication Regulatory Agency (Organismo Supervisor de la Inversíon Privada en Telecomunicaciones or OSIPTEL)	http://www.osiptel.gob.pe/
	US National Low Income Energy Consortium	http://www.nliec.org, V

✓

Note: A, administrative organization; IS, independent statutory body; V, voluntary organization.

Source: The World Bank Group, International Directory of Utility Regulatory Institutions, available from: http://www.worldbank.org/html/fpd/psd/ifur/directory/ (accessed 20 June 2005).

225

The panel administering the funds includes a representative of each of business users, domestic users, electricity retailers and generators, with an independent chairman. The first principle laid down for them is 'there should be diversity in the allocation of funding with respect to the number of end users represented, the nature of the interests represented and the issues which are the subject of the application for funding' (clause 8.10 of the National Electricity Code). Under this system, balance of consumer (and other) views had been sought through funding a variety of different 'voices'. The options considered in 2005 included a variety of (statutory) organizational structures ranging from separate institutions to committee models to present a single voice to the government and regulator, a task similar to that performed by energywatch in the UK.

Many voluntary groups represent the voice of a particular group of consumers, for example the US National Low Income Energy Consortium states its objectives as

> finding common ground among diverse groups that work with, serve or represent low-income energy consumers; exploring, exchanging, and promoting innovative ideas and successful efforts that improve the ability of low income consumers to access and afford energy; and setting an agenda for low income energy policy at the federal, state, and local levels. (National Low Income Energy Corsortium, 2004)

Such groups can sometimes become captured by particular political or industry interests, which makes the 'representativeness' of a statutory body particularly important.

Similarly, there is no paucity of information providers in newly competitive markets to help consumers in exercising their right of exit. Here the effect of an organization's advice on the profitability of business organizations, as well as on consumer welfare, is immediate, and so the format and reliability of the information provided are very sensitive. In Michigan, the Public Service Commission, a part of the state government, itself provides comparisons between the costs of different suppliers. A comparison service is often operated through commercial websites which provide information free to consumers, such as *uswitch* in the UK and *energyshop* in the US. However consumers often seek reassurance that the information really is independent, a role energywatch provides in approving the search tools available from its website, and Michigan State answers by providing the comparisons directly itself.

Specific dispute resolution, the third of energywatch's roles, is traditionally provided through offices of an ombudsman. In Scandinavia, where the term and concept originated, such ombudsmen generally operate across all sectors, sometimes with a particular section of the office specializing in energy. In Sweden the Ombudsman is Director General of the statutory Consumer Agency; as part of her responsibility for consumer interests across markets, she filed a group action against an electricity company which went bankrupt at the end of 2002, leaving consumers who had signed up to fixed price contracts to find alternative suppliers at higher prices. Here, although the action was on behalf of 7000 consumers, the redress sought was specific to this particular group of consumers, rather than a change in overall policy. Of course such specific cases often lead to a change in the rules, but this is not the primary objective of the initial action. Ombudsmen typically gain their power through the courts, since this is where the evidence uncovered in their findings is presented. While energywatch has a less direct role within the legal system, we have seen that its handling of many complaints about misselling has led to regulatory enquiries and action.

The role of ombudsman offices in utilities is sometimes complicated by their initial institution to deal with public sector complaints. This is the case, for example, in Ireland.[21] So the oversight offered by the ombudsman may cease, or need to be specifically extended, when public sector providers are privatized, a time at which some might feel they are most needed.

All groups that provide voice, exit and dispute resolution exercise some constraints on the actions of providers, regulators and government, through public opinion and informal pressure. We have noted that the UK energy market shows clear signs of such informal constraint, for example through the reluctance of companies to raise tariffs where such actions might be seen as disadvantaging the poor, even after formal regulation has been removed. However, examples of direct powers with respect to the regulator, such as energywatch exercises in terms of access to information, are less common. Where there is more open general access to information about decisions made by official bodies, such powers might be exercised without having to assign them in advance to a particular body. For example, in the US the Center for Public Integrity has used the Freedom of Information Act to obtain information and launch a campaign about links between the Federal Energy Regulatory Commission and energy companies (Bogardus, 2004). Elsewhere it is assumed that the regulator's accountability to the legislature would be sufficient to monitor its actions. It is perhaps a function of the UK's tradition for rather closed government that has led to the particular information acquisition powers of energywatch, which do not seem to be mirrored elsewhere, notwithstanding the recent introduction of the Freedom of Information Act 2000.[22]

The international survey shows that the arrangements for consumer representation, like regulation itself, depend on the legislative and political environment within which regulation functions. Part of this environment is the general consumer policy in each regime, a topic beyond this chapter, but reviewed recently by the UK Department of Trade and Industry (DTI, 2003).

Conclusions

In practice the presence of regulatory institutions, typically associated with ex ante regulation in a sector, seems to increase rather than curb the presence of bodies with explicit consumer representation duties, suggesting that regulation and a separate consumer 'voice' may be complements rather than substitutes. We have argued that sector-specific consumer representation in regulated industries is appropriate either to provide consumer voice, where exit is impracticable, or to help overcome information problems to assist consumers to exercise their right of exit, where this is possible. In the first role, representing consumer interests independently of the regulator's organization can provide protection against capture of the regulator by the government or companies. But it is costly, both in terms of administration and because having a separate body, campaigning on more narrow issues, may distort decisions from those which best balance the broader interests with which the regulator is entrusted. The simultaneous institution of energywatch with the establishment of consumer protection as the primary objective of the regulator in the UK suggests that guarding against regulatory capture may have been a major concern to the government at that time.

However the model has been criticized. The government has suggested that the current nature of consumer representation – fragmented across a number of different sectors – may be an ineffective and inefficient mechanism for securing consumer voice. Sectoral bodies may become too reactive to both the regulators and the complaints they receive, instead of concentrating on the 'underlying causes of market failure' in their respective industries (DTI and HM Treasury 2004, pp. 29–32). Sectoral consumer bodies might be more prone to capture by their corresponding regulators or companies in the industry. The National Audit Office, which assists Parliament in scrutinizing public expenditure, argues that energywatch should define better the types of consumer issues where intervention is necessary or otherwise; in particular, the NAO argues that relying on consumer complaints to prioritize its work is not necessarily a means by which the overall nature of consumer problems can be identified (NAO, 2004, para. 1.23). However, the consumer council for the postal sector, Postwatch, was also criticized for being too reliant on its network of regional committees for the identification of consumers' priorities (para. 123).[23]

To address these issues, one proposal is to extend Consumer Direct, a recently established national helpline and online service for consumer advice, to cover the utility sectors, supplanting the sectoral consumer bodies in their key role of providing information for and dealing with the complaints of utility consumers (DTI, 2004, para. 5.7). This would fit a pattern that we have seen is common in other countries. Another, complementary, proposal is to merge the sectoral consumer bodies to form a 'National Utilities Consumer Council'. This body would presumably be less subject to capture by companies or the regulator, but might be more vulnerable to government capture.

Perhaps concern to guard against regulatory capture has diminished as boards have replaced individual regulators (another initiative of the Utilities

Act 2000 and corresponding legislation in communications and water). In this case, a single body, ideally the regulator, which can be trusted to weigh all the costs and benefits of regulatory decisions in an overall 'welfare' assessment, and gathers information about different consumer preferences (or voice) internally, would render better outcomes. It is only if some additional safeguard is needed that the costs and potential distortions of a consumer body are likely to be justified. Energywatch costs about £13 million a year to run and employs 300 staff, compared with a cost of £38 million for Ofgem with its 291 staff. Perhaps some of the energywatch resources could be more effectively used within the regulatory body, if its supervisory role is not paramount. Energywatch's responsibilities include assisting consumers to exercise their right of exit in the market. The discussions in the UK about merging the sector-specific bodies or integrating them within a more general consumer organization suggest that energywatch has successfully fulfilled its transitional role to assist in the newly opened market, and that these functions can be safely consigned to and may be more effectively exercised by other bodies concerned with increasing consumer 'empowerment' across a range of sectors. Proposals to reform the UK system and the variety of international arrangements surveyed in this chapter show that functions of consumer advocacy and information can be delivered in a variety of ways, and that no single model is superior in all countries at all times.

Notes

1. For examples of this view see Ernst (1994), Prosser (1997).
2. A reordering of duties in telecommunications came with the Communications Act 2003, and for water a similar change was included in the Water Act 2003. All the utility regulators enjoy concurrent powers with the OFT (Office of Fair Trading) to apply the Chapter I and II provisions under the Competition Act 1998 (modelled on Articles 81 and 82 of the EC Treaty). In so doing, however, they are not bound to have regard to their sectoral duties.
3. The exception was the gas industry, which had an independent consumer council established at privatization.
4. For a full review of the consumer bodies originally put in place at the time of privatization see Graham (2000), chapter 5.
5. National Energy Action campaigns for the eradication of Fuel Poverty, and the National Right to Fuel Campaign and the Consumer Association have also been particularly vocal in advocating the case of the fuel poor.
6. She did, however, add that consumer representation ought to continue in respect of the monopolistic parts of the industries.
7. The prospects for competition in water supply are limited; there will be some competition for bulk water supply as a result of the Water Act 2003, but residential consumers will continue to be served by their incumbent monopolist. For a fuller discussion see Chapter 17.
8. The Gas and Electricity Market Authority under the statute.
9. The Gas and Electricity Consumer Council under the statute.
10. It is expected that this new council will be brought into being in October 2005.
11. In telecommunications the local loop remains largely monopolistic, although there is inter-network competition from cable operators and some consumer groups, particularly students, do not subscribe to fixed-line telecommunications networks at all, preferring mobile phones.

12. These schemes are subject to the approval of and supervision by Ofcom (Communications Act 2003, sections 50–55). All telecommunications providers are required to belong to such a scheme for the purpose of dispute resolution between themselves and domestic and small business consumers. The main ombudsman scheme is known as the Office of Telecommunications Ombudsman, to whom 96 per cent of fixed line operators belong.

13. The only statutory criterion for appointment is the desirability of appointing one or more members who either have experience of the special needs of disabled persons or have a disability (Utilities Act 2000, Schedule 2, para. 1(4)). Members (including the chairman) are appointed for a term not exceeding five years, and can only be removed by the Secretary of State on the 'ground of incapacity or misbehaviour' (Utilities Act 2000, Schedule 2, para. 2(2)).

14. However, as with the corresponding provision for Ofgem, energywatch retains the freedom to have regard to the interests of other consumers as well.

15. In so doing it is required to 'have regard to the desirability of minimising costs, or any other detriment, to [Ofgem] or the licence holder'. This provision curbs the informational burden faced by licensees by reducing the 'double jeopardy' of an investigation by both Ofgem and energywatch. Where Ofgem fails to comply with a direction to provide information, it is placed under a duty to give reasons for such a failure. Where a licence holder fails to comply with a direction to provide information, energywatch may refer the matter to Ofgem, which then determines whether the licensee is entitled to withhold the information concerned (section 27).

16. For the detailed rules governing the provision of information see: The Utilities Act 2000 (Supply of Information) Regulations SI 2000/2956. The main flaw in the information rules is that it is Ofgem who decides whether or not it is entitled to withhold information from energywatch, although the legislation does provide for the appointment of an independent arbiter in this regard.

17. The word 'consumer' here denotes final consumers, rather than industrial or commercial customers.

18. This was the case in the UK, where financial targets were set for nationalized industries to achieve a minimum return on net assets in the 1960s.

19. The EU 15 refers to the 15 member states of the EU before the accession of the ten new member states in 2004.

20. Only sector-specific regulatory bodies are included.

21. The Ombudsman Act 1980.

22. The Act came into force in January 2005 and is less extensive than freedom of information legislation in some other countries, including the USA.

23. The House of Lords Select Committee on the Constitution recently echoed these criticisms, expressing concern that there was no commonality of approach in the way in which consumer bodies gathered information on consumers' concerns and preferences (2004, para. 64).

References

Baron, D. (1985) 'Noncooperative Regulation of a Nonlocalized Externality', *Rand Journal of Economics*, **16**, 553–68.

Bogardus, K. (December 2004) 'Federal Energy Regulators Smooth the Way for Liquefied Natural Gas Terminals', *Energy Bulletin*, Washington, DC: Center for Public Integrity, available from: http://66.102.9.104/search?q=cache:PUMJ1GFQ4EcJ:www.Energybulletin.net/3551.html++information+energy+regulators&hl=en (accessed 20 June 2005).

Consumer's Association of Canada (2004) *Energy*, available from: http://www.consumer.ca/1527 (accessed 20 June 2005).

DTI (1998a) *A Fair Deal for Consumers: Modernising the Framework for Utility Regulation, Green Paper*, London: The Stationery Office.

DTI (1998b) *A Fair Deal for Consumers: Modernising the Framework for Utility Regulation, White Paper*, London: Department of Trade and Industry.

DTI (1998c) *Public Consultation Paper on Consumer Councils*, London: Department of Trade and Industry.
DTI (1999) *Consumer Councils: The Response to the Consultation*, London: Department of Trade and Industry.
DTI (2000) *A New Future for Communications*, London: Department of Trade and Industry.
DTI (2003) *Comparative Report on Consumer Policy Regimes*, London: Department of Trade and Industry.
DTI (2004) *Extending Competitive Markets: Empowered Consumers, Successful Business*, London: Department of Trade and Industry.
DTI and HM Treasury (2004) *Consumer Representation in Regulated Industries*, London: Department of Trade and Industry.
energywatch (2002) *Annual Report November 2000 to March 2002*, London: energywatch.
energywatch (2003) *Annual Report April 2002 to March 2003*, London: energywatch.
energywatch (2004) *Annual Report April 2003 to March 2004*, London: energywatch.
Ernst, J. (1994) *Whose Utility?: The Social Impact of Utility Privatization and Regulation in Britain*, Buckingham: Open University Press.
Graham, C. (2000) *Regulating Public Utilities: A Constitutional Approach*, Oxford: Hart.
Guislain, P. (1997) *The Privatization Challenge*, Washington, DC: The World Bank.
House of Lords Select Committee on the Constitution (2004) *The Regulatory State: Ensuring its Accountability*, HL Paper 68 I, London: The Stationery Office.
Howells, G. (2000) 'Consumers and Participation', in N.D. Lewis and D. Campbell (eds), *Promoting Participation, Law or Politics?*, London: Cavendish, pp. 291–318.
NAO (2004) *Energywatch and Postwatch: Helping and Protecting Consumers*, London: TSO.
National Consumers Electricity Advocacy Panel (2005) *Consumer Advocacy in the Australian Energy Market, Consultation Paper*, Victoria: NCEAP, available from: http://www.advocacypanel.com.au/documents/PanelSubmissiontoSCOonAdvocacy.pdf (accessed 20 June 2005).
National Low Income Energy Consortium (2004) *What is NLIEC?*, available from: http://www.nliec.org/what.htm (accessed 20 June 2005).
Office of National Statistics (2004) *A Report on the 2002–03 Expenditure and Food Survey*, London: ONS.
Ofgas (1997) *Review of Utility Regulation: Submission of the Director General of Gas Supply*, London: Ofgas.
Ofgas (1998) *Response to the Government's Public Consultation Paper on Consumer Councils*, London: Ofgas.
Ofgem (2004) Domestic *Competitive Market Review 2004, A Review Document*, April, London: Ofgem.
Otero, J. and Waddams Price, C. (2001) 'Price Discrimination in a Regulated Market with Entry: The Residential UK Electricity Market', *Bulletin of Economic Research*, **53** (3), July, 161–75.
Prosser, T. (1997) *Law and the Regulators*, Oxford: Clarendon Press.
Waddams Price, C. (2005) 'Effect of Liberalising UK Retail Energy Markets on Consumers', *Oxford Review of Economic Policy* (forthcoming).
Waddams Price, C. and Hancock, R. (1998) 'Distributional Effects of Liberalising UK Residential Utility Markets', *Fiscal Studies*, **19** (3), 295–319.

11 Regulatory impact assessment

Colin Kirkpatrick

Introduction[1]

Although there is no generally agreed definition of regulation, it can be broadly understood to refer to a government measure which is intended to affect individual or group behaviour. Alongside fiscal policy (taxation and government expenditure), regulation is the main policy tool that government can use to affect the outcomes of markets, and the design of effective regulatory policy is now the focus of much interest among policymakers in all parts of the world. The member countries of the OECD are each active in pursuing regulatory reform programmes aimed at improving the operating environment for investment and, more generally, enhancing the quality of public governance processes (OECD, 2002). Regulatory reform is a key component of the process of establishing the institutional infrastructure of a market economy in the transitional economies of central and eastern Europe (OECD, 2004a; Jacobs, S., 2004). In developing countries, regulatory reform is a central component of the development policy framework (World Bank, 2004b).

With the emergence of the 'regulatory state' (Majone, 1994, 1997) as the dominant paradigm in public sector management, increasing attention has been given to the design and implementation of 'good' regulation which contributes to the goals that are set for the regulatory system. Regulatory Impact Assessment (RIA) is a method of policy analysis which is intended to assist policymakers in the design, implementation and monitoring of improvements to regulatory systems, by providing a methodology for assessing the likely consequences of proposed regulation and the actual consequences of existing regulations.

The aim of this chapter is to review existing RIA methodologies and experience in their use in a range of different countries and contexts. The next section discusses the different definitions of RIA and describes the considerable variation in the scope and coverage of RIA in different countries. The following section identifies the core principles of RIA in terms of its outcome and process dimensions, and locates the role of RIA in the wider context of evidence-based decision-making. Later the evolution of RIA as a tool for better policy design is described and the experience with RIA in a range of developed, transitional and developing countries outlined. Also 'good practice' guidelines for RIA are discussed and a number of general lessons from the experience of applying RIA in practice are drawn. Towards the end of the chapter the ex post evaluation stage of RIA is examined, focusing on the alternative methods that have been used to assess the performance and quality of RIA. The results of these quality evaluation studies are summarized. The final section of the chapter provides a brief summary and conclusion.

Definition of regulatory impact assessment (RIA)

'Good' regulation will be both *effective* and *efficient*; effective in the sense of achieving its planned goals and objectives, and efficient in terms of achieving these goals at least cost, in terms of government administrative costs and the costs imposed on the economy in terms complying with regulations. There is, therefore, a compelling case for the systematic appraisal of the positive and negative impacts of any proposed or actual regulatory change. *Regulatory impact assessment* (alternatively referred to as *regulatory impact analysis*) provides a methodological framework for undertaking this systematic assessment of benefits and costs of regulation, and for informing decision-makers of the consequences of a regulatory measure.

There is no single or generally agreed definition of regulatory impact assessment or of the 'regulations' that are covered by RIA (Lee, 2002). The UK defines RIA as 'a tool which informs policy decisions. It is an assessment of the impact of policy options in terms of the costs, benefits and risks of a proposal' (Cabinet Office, 2003, p. 5). The OECD, which has been active in developing 'best practice' guidance on RIA as part of its programme on regulatory reform practice, defines regulation broadly in the following terms: 'regulation refers to the diverse set of instruments by which governments set requirements on enterprises and citizens' (OECD, 1997). A more comprehensive definition of RIA is:

> An information-based analytical approach to assess probable costs, consequences, and side effects of planned policy instruments (laws, regulations etc.). It can also be used to evaluate the real costs and consequences of policy instruments after they have been implemented. In either case, the results are used to improve the quality of policy decisions and policy instruments, such as laws, regulations, investment programmes and public investments. Basically, it is a means to inform government choices: choices about policy instruments, about the design of a specific instrument, or about the need to change or discontinue an existing instrument. (SIGMA, 2001, p. 10)

In practice, the scope of RIA is often narrower than is implied by the definitions above. Lee (2002, p. 10) notes that RIA may be limited in its application according to the levels of administration; the levels of the regulatory measures; the type of measure; and the sectors to which the measures apply or which they affect. The focus of RIA may also be narrowed by concentrating on a specific target, rather than the higher level strategic goals of regulatory policy as a whole. For example, the RIA may aim to reduce the number of existing regulations and the quantity of administrative red-tape, or reduce the financial costs of regulation

Table 11.1   RIA adoption in selected OECD countries

Country	Year that RIA was adopted	Scope of coverage
Australia	1985, strengthened 1997	• Primary laws, subordinate regulations, international treaties and quasi-regulations that have business or competition impacts (150 regulations per year out of approximately 2000 regulations) • Business impacts arise in case of significant market impact • Reviews of existing regulations should adopt the RIS (Regulatory Impact Statement) framework
Canada	1978, strengthened 1986	• RIA is required only for subordinate regulations • Memorandum to Cabinet (MC) similar to RIA is required for primary laws and policies
Czech Republic	Developed since 2000	• All primary laws including their 'substantial intents' and government decrees. Partial impact analysis is done in case of some major subordinate regulations in particular areas, however, this is not systematic
Germany	1984, strengthened 2000	• Primary laws and subordinate regulations • The RIA process can be applied to the review of existing regulations
Greece	Developed since 2001	• Primary laws and subordinate regulations
Hungary	1987, strengthened 1996	• Primary laws and subordinate regulations (all acts and decrees) • The analysis process is applied to the existing regulations
Italy	1999	• Primary laws and subordinate regulations
Mexico	1996, expanded 2000	• Primary laws and subordinate regulations • RIA does not apply to the review of existing regulations
The Netherlands	1985, strengthened 1994–1995	• Primary laws in major regulations. Subordinate regulations in major regulations. Also applied to the review of existing regulations

Table 11.1   continued

Country	Year that RIA was adopted	Scope of coverage
Poland	2002	• All legislative proposals (primary laws and subordinate regulations); but the Budget Act is excluded from that procedure • RIA is not required to review existing regulations
United Kingdom	1985, strengthened 1996 and 1998	• Any proposal for which regulation is an option – including both primary and secondary legislation – that would have a non-negligible impact on business, charities or the voluntary sector should have an RIA • RIA is also applied to reviews of existing regulations • Regulations affecting only the public sector are currently subject to a Policy Effects Framework (PEF) assessment, which was brought within RIA in 2004
United States	1974, strengthened 1981	• Primary laws in selected cases and all subordinate regulations
European Commission	2002	• Major regulatory and/or non-regulatory proposals with significant economic, social and/or environmental impacts • Proposals with a significant impact on major interested parties • Proposals that constitute a new policy, policy reform and/or significant change to existing policy • Proposals that involve major regulatory issues (subsidiarity/proportionality/choice of regulatory instrument) • The new procedure does not apply to Community decisions that derive from the executive powers of the European Commission, for example adoption of EU-funded projects, decisions on the application of EC competition law, etc.

Source: OECD (2004b) in Jacobs (2004).

to businesses, rather than assessing the impact of regulatory measures on the broader goals of economic and social development.

Comparative information on the variation in coverage of RIA systems in a sample of different countries is provided in Table 11.1. The table shows, for example, the variety of approaches to ex ante and ex post assessment, the use of preliminary screening of proposals and the range of goals that are used in assessing impacts.

The principles of regulatory impact assessment
There are two dimensions to a 'good' regulatory system (Ogus, 2001). The first relates to the instruments or legal forms selected to achieve the desired outcomes, which will be defined by the regulatory objectives. RIA helps in identifying the root cause of the problem that regulation is designed to address. The second relates to the procedures or processes by which the instruments are formulated and applied. RIA can contribute, therefore, to both the *outcome* and the *process* dimensions of policy processes. The outcome contribution of RIA can be assessed against the goals that are set for regulatory systems. These goals are discussed in detail later in the chapter. The process contribution of RIA can be assessed in terms of the principles of 'good governance'. There is a broad consensus that these principles encompass *proportionality*, the regulation should be appropriate to the size of the problem it is intended to address; *targeting*, the regulation focuses on the problem and does not cause unintended consequences in other area of the economy or society; *consistency* in decision-making, to avoid uncertainty; *accountability* for regulatory actions and outcomes; and *transparency* in decision-making (Parker, 2002).

The contribution of RIA to better regulatory decision making rests on the systematic assessment of the impacts of a regulatory measure, and the adherence to the principles of proportionality, targeting, consistency, accountability and transparency. The purpose of an RIA is

> to explain the objectives of the [regulatory] proposal, the risks to be addressed and the options for delivering the objectives. In doing so it should make transparent the expected costs and benefits of the options for the different bodies involved, such as other parts of Government and small businesses, and how compliance with regulatory options would be secured and enforced. (NAO, 2002, p. 51)

A properly conducted RIA, therefore, systematically examines the impact arising or likely to arise from government regulation and communicates this information to decision-makers. It should also set out *the consequences of not regulating* (NAO, 2002. p. 1). It also encourages public consultation to identify and measure benefits and costs and thereby has the potential to improve the transparency of governmental decision-making. It can promote government accountability by reporting on the information used in decision-making and by demonstrating how the regulation will impact on society. The result should be an improved and more consistent regulatory environment for both producers and consumers.

It is important to recognize that RIA, even when operated well, is not a tool that substitutes for decision-making. Rather, it should be seen as an integral part of the policymaking that aims to raise the quality of debate and therefore the quality of the decision-making process. As Jacobs, S. (2004, p. 287) points out, 'the most important contributor to the quality of government decisions is not the precision of calculations, but the action of asking the right questions, understanding real-world impacts, and exploring assumptions'.

RIA is an evidence-based approach to policymaking where the decision is based on fact finding and analysis that define the parameters of action according to established criteria (OECD, 1997, pp. 14–15). It has the potential to strengthen regulation by systematically examining the possible impacts arising from government actions and communicating this information to decision-makers in a way that allows them to consider (ideally) the full range of positive and negative effects (benefits and costs) that are associated with a proposed regulatory change. Equally, RIA has the potential to improve the monitoring of existing regulatory policies (SIGMA, 2001). This might lead to revisions to an existing regulation to improve its performance. RIA may also help to constrain economically damaging regulatory discretion and expose cases of regulatory conflicts (e.g. between agencies).

RIA practice and experience
Guidelines on undertaking RIAs and on the issues to cover have been published by the OECD, and the majority of OECD countries have adopted formalized RIA arrangements. In March 1995, the Council of the OECD adopted a *Recommendation on Improving the Quality of Government Regulation*, which made reference to the use of RIA (OECD, 1995). In 1997 ministers of the member countries endorsed the OECD *Report on Regulatory Reform*, which recommended that governments 'integrate regulatory impact assessment into the development, review, and reform of regulations' (OECD, 1997). Jacobs (2002) reports that 20 out of the then 28 OECD countries were using RIA in some form by 2001, although Radaelli (2002) found that national guidelines for undertaking RIAs existed in only nine OECD countries. While the detail of the way in which RIA is being applied varies between countries, there is a degree of commonality in terms of the main characteristics of the procedures that have been adopted, as summarized in Table 11.2.

The origins of RIA can be traced to the United States There the formal adoption of RIA in the 1970s was in response to a perceived increase in the regulatory burden associated with a surge in regulatory activity since the mid-1960s, together with concerns that this might be adding to inflationary pressures in the

Table 11.2   Common characteristics of RIA

---

1. *Statement of problem.* Is government intervention both necessary and desirable?
2. *Definition of alternative remedies.* These include different approaches, such as the use of economic incentives or voluntary approaches.
3. *Determination of physical effects of each alternative, including potential unintended consequences.* The net should be cast wide. Generally speaking, regulations or investments in many areas of public policy can have environmental implications that must be kept in mind.
4. *Estimation of benefits and costs of each alternative.* Benefits should be quantified and where possible monetized. Costs should be true opportunity costs, not simply expenditures.
5. *Assessment of other economic impacts,* including effects on competition, effects on small firms, international trade implications.
6. *Identification of winners and losers.* Those in the community who stand to gain and lose from each alternative and if possible, the extent of their gains and losses.
7. *Communication with the interested public*, including the following activities: notification of intent to regulate; request for compliance costs and other data; public disclosure of regulatory proposals and supporting analysis; and consideration of and response to public comments.
8. *A clear choice of the preferred alternative*, plus a statement defending that choice.
9. *Provision of a plan for ex post analysis of regulatory outcomes.* It is important, for example, to establish current conditions to have a benchmark to measure performance against. Planning is needed to ensure that procedures are in place for the collection of data to permit such benchmarking.

Source: OECD (2004b), p. 27.

US economy (Anderson, 1998). Over time, there has been a broadening of the scope of assessments to consider all types of significant regulatory costs and benefits (i.e. not only costs falling on the business sector), accompanied by an emphasis on the role of economic analysis in the assessment of these costs and benefits (Lee, 2002, p. 5). Since 1995 the Office of Management and Budget (OMB) has been required to report on the costs and benefits of government regulations and in 2000 the OMB published guidance on how to conduct RIAs. This widened the scope of RIA to include non-quantifiable costs and benefits and put more emphasis on risk assessment and the quality of information collection (OMB, 2001).

In the United Kingdom the systematic assessment of the impact of regulation by government began in the 1980s as part of the Conservative government's deregulation initiative. Concern that excessive government intervention in industry might inhibit economic growth, especially small business activity, led to the establishment of a Deregulation Unit in the Department of Trade and Industry, together with eight Business Task Forces, with responsibility for reducing the existing burden on business, charities and voluntary organizations. For new regulations, the emphasis was placed on calculating business compliance costs and consulting business about these costs before legislating (NAO, 2001, appendix 1). In the mid-1990s the Deregulation Unit was transferred to the Cabinet Office and the Business Task Forces were replaced by a single Deregulation Unit. At the same time, risk assessment was added to the assessment process, and Ministers were required to sign risk assessments and cost compliance assessments to certify that the regulatory benefits and costs were appropriately balanced.

The Better Regulation Task Force was established as an independent advisory body in 1997 to advise government on regulatory issues, and is supported by the Regulatory Impact Unit located in the Cabinet Office. The Task Force's terms of reference are: 'to advise the government on action which improves the effectiveness and credibility of government regulation by ensuring that it is necessary, fair, and affordable, and simple to understand and administer, taking particular account of the needs of small businesses and ordinary people'. In 1998, the Prime Minister announced that no proposal for regulation should be considered by Ministers without a regulatory impact assessment being carried out. Guidelines for carrying out RIAs were published, and encompass risks, and costs and benefits not only to business but more widely. The RIA reports are published for public scrutiny. In 2000, revised RIA Guidelines were introduced. The main changes were: submission of an initial assessment to Ministers, before they choose the regulatory option; consultation with small business; emphasis on early informal consultation with those likely to be affected; greater emphasis on identifying non-regulatory options and making clear the benefits of proposals; more thorough assessment of costs and benefits; and a statement from the Minister responsible for the proposal that 'the benefits justify the costs' (Cabinet Office, 2000, 2003; Owen and Courtney, 2002).

Canada's RIA programme has evolved since the late 1970s, and in 1986 a formal government-wide regulatory policy was introduced with the requirement for an RIA for all regulation proposals. The Treasury Board Secretariat has developed a standard format for all RIAs and the Regulatory Affairs Directorate acts as the central agency responsible for reviewing proposals in draft form. It focuses on demonstrating through training and communication the benefits of conforming to the regulatory policy. This approach is judged to have been more effective in changing attitudes and enlisting cooperation than the 'gatekeeper' approach operated from 1986 to 1991, when the Directorate had to formally approve all RIAs. The approach 'focuses more on influencing regulatory culture within sponsoring departments than battling each regulatory proposal that falls short of the full requirements of the regulatory policy' (Treasury Board of Canada, 2001). Regulatory departments have the flexibility to adopt different approaches to meeting RIA requirements. At the same time, 'proposals which clearly violate the regulatory policy are systematically challenged at the Cabinet table' and 'in the highly collegial and consensus-oriented world of Ottawa decision-makers, that represents a significant deterrent to regulators' (Treasury Board of Canada, 2001).

In common with the UK and Canada, New Zealand made it compulsory from April 2001 for all proposals submitted to Cabinet to have a Regulatory Impact Statement (RIS). This, where appropriate, should also include a Business Compliance Cost Statement (BCSS) explicitly recording the likely cost implications for business. Both the RIS and the BCSS are published on the responsible department's website after agreement from the responsible Minister and/or Cabinet. The RIA Unit, in common with those in other OECD countries, is responsible for advice, guidance and training.

In recent years there has been a drive to reduce costs of excessive bureaucracy, under the leadership of the Ministerial Panel on Business Compliance Costs, aimed at obtaining a balance between achieving the government's policy objectives and reducing unnecessary costs to business. The New Zealand government has also recognized the importance of seeking impartial assessment and has commissioned both university research centres and institutes of economic research to report to its Treasury and relevant departments, such as the Ministry of Consumer Affairs.

In the European Union, regulatory impact assessment is an important part of the 'better governance' agenda, which aims to improve the quality of legislation and make governance more transparent, responsive and accountable (Radaelli, 2003). The Goteborg European Council meeting in June 2001 agreed that 'sustainable development should become the central objective of all sectors and policies ... careful assessment of the full effects of a policy proposal must include estimates of its economic, environmental and social impacts inside and outside the EU' (EC, 2001, p. 1), and established procedures to ensure that each major legislative proposal is informed by an assessment of the potential impacts of the measure, both inside and outside the Union. The 2002 Communication of the European Commission on Impact Assessment commits the Commission to undertake an impact assessment of all major policy proposals in order 'to improve the quality and coherence of the policy development process, [and to] contribute to an effective and efficient regulatory environment and further, to a more coherent implementation of the European strategy for Sustainable Development' (EC, 2002a, p. 2). In 2003, the Commission began implementing the new integrated system for the systematic use of impact assessment, which consists of the 'preliminary' assessment of all proposals in the Commission's work programme (Lee and Kirkpatrick, 2006).

Although the transitional economies of central and eastern Europe share a common history of Soviet or communist rule, there are considerable variances in the use of RIA, which suggests that history alone is not a sufficient explanation of the way reforms develop within government. Issues of administrative capacity, institutional infrastructure and incentives to carry out an RIA, all affect the reform process in transitional economies (Jacobs, 2005). The adoption of RIA is also seen as advantageous in terms of promoting the democratic principles of 'good government'. RIAs support legal government, which observes the rule of law with proportionate and equitable law. An accountable government is promoted through assessing direct costs and benefits that citizens will incur and selecting policies on the basis of best value for money, taking into account redistribution effects – that is, who gains and who loses. Consultation with consumers, business and civil society also helps build legitimacy and promotes issues of equity and fairness among citizens. This is particularly important in transition economies where NGOs and voluntary non-state institutions have been sluggish to develop and the role of civil society in shaping government is incipient and weak (Jacobs, C., 2004).

In developing countries there is a growing recognition among policymakers that RIA can be used in the design and implementation of regulatory reform programmes to bring about improvements in the quality of regulatory governance and policymaking (World Bank, 2004b, pp. 73–4). However, evidence on the use of RIA in developing countries is limited. For a small number of middle-income developing countries that are members of the OECD, notably South Korea and Mexico, there is information on the use of RIA in the country reviews of regulatory reform. The approaches adopted in these two countries are similar to those found in developed economies and are consistent with OECD principles. Nevertheless, their experiences appear to illustrate some of the challenges that may arise in adopting the OECD model in countries where institutional capacity is less well developed. More comprehensive information on RIA in developing countries is reported in Kirkpatrick et al. (2004), based on responses to a questionnaire that was sent to 311 departments with regulatory responsibilities in 99 countries. Overall, the findings from the questionnaire survey suggest that the level of awareness and application of RIA in developing countries is perhaps higher than might have been expected based on the limited information previously available. The survey findings indicate that RIA is already being applied in a number of lower-income economies, though it is still at an early stage of development. Forty per cent of the countries sampled returned completed questionnaires and the respondents suggested that RIA (or similar) is being used in the majority (75 per cent) of these countries. The coverage of RIA,

Table 11.3   OECD RIA checklist

---

1. Is the problem correctly defined?
2. Is government action justified?
3. Is regulation the best form of government action?
4. Is there a legal basis for regulation?
5. What is the appropriate level (or levels) of government for this action?
6. Do the benefits of regulation justify the costs?
7. Is the distribution of effects across society transparent?
8. Is the regulation clear, consistent, comprehensible, and accessible to users?
9. Have all interested parties had the opportunity to present their views?
10. How will compliance be achieved?

Source: OECD (1995).

both in terms of types of regulation and number of regulation proposals appears, however, to vary widely between countries, and few countries appear to be applying RIA consistently to regulatory proposals affecting economic, social and environmental policies. While there is a general recognition of the desirability of including benefits as well as costs in an RIA, methods of quantification are generally underdeveloped. These findings lead to the conclusion that there is a need to improve understanding and practice of RIA in developing countries. In this context, while the OECD 'best practice' guidelines (Table 11.3) provide some pointers to how an RIA framework might be developed, they are unlikely to be a complete template or model for transfer and adoption in countries with very different institutions and objectives. The OECD guidelines need to be translated to reflect the particular issues that arise when regulating in developing countries, including issues to do with regulatory capacity, poverty reduction and development goals.

'Good practice' guidelines and the lessons of RIA experience
As already discussed, guidelines on undertaking RIAs have been published by a number of international organizations, including the OECD and the European Commission (OECD, 1995; EC, 2002b). There are variations in these 'good practice' guidelines, reflecting differences in legal, legislative and administrative traditions or systems (Mandelkern Group, 2001), but they follow a broadly similar approach. As an example, Table 11.3 sets out the OECD checklist, issued in 1995, of questions that should be addressed in an RIA.

The publication of international guidelines should not be interpreted as advocating a 'one-size-fits-all' best practice approach to regulatory assessment. Rather, the principles and criteria for RIA practice that are described should be viewed strictly as a guide to developing an RIA system that meets the particular needs and resource constraints of an individual country, rather than as best practice standards. These general guidelines can be supplemented by a number of practical lessons drawn from the experience of countries that have implemented some form of RIA.

First, RIA needs the development of RIA skills within the government machinery, including skills in enumeration and valuation of costs and benefits. Generally, qualitative effects will involve more judgmental or subjective evaluation, and physical units introduce serious problems of aggregation. There may be a temptation, therefore, to diminish the RIA to include only an evaluation of measurable financial costs and benefits. Or, the assessment could be reduced to looking solely at the cheapest way of achieving the regulatory outcome (in effect providing a cost-effectiveness study only) in which the benefits are taken as given. This lesser form of RIA risks ignoring important differential benefits from different forms of regulation.

Second, RIA requires the extension of consultation procedures to ensure that appropriate information is collected and analysed in reaching a view on the regulatory impact. There may be little tradition of consulting widely before undertaking regulation, or those chosen for consultation in the past may have been selected on political grounds. The need to consult and evaluate can be time consuming and resource heavy within hard-stretched governments. RIAs may involve multiple stages with each new regulation facing an initial RIA, another RIA after consultation and redrafting, and a final RIA on the legislation as passed by the legislature. A sensible approach to minimize these costs is to prioritize where detailed RIA should be undertaken, by using a screening procedure to identify when a regulation is likely to have major effects on the economy, society or the environment. It is important, however, that the decision on when to use a RIA is not made simply on political grounds.

Third, RIA needs to be championed across government if it is to be used consistently and become a normal feature of regulatory policymaking. It therefore needs clear and powerful political support within government if it is to overcome bureaucratic and political inertia. In the UK the Regulatory Impact Unit in the Cabinet Office monitors progress and encourages the implementation of RIA across government. Similar bodies exist in a number of other OECD countries (Radaelli, 2002, p. 9).

Fourth, to achieve these improvements in regulatory governance may require a cultural change within government, involving more open policymaking as part of a broader process of governance reform.

Finally, RIA must also confront the possibility of 'regulatory capture'. In practice, the nature and content of regulation are likely to be 'captured' by special interest groups who have the time, resources and incentives to invest in influencing the regulatory process. In market economies, resources flow to where the perceived returns are highest and this is no less true in the shaping of regulation policy. There will be constant pressure from external groups and their spokespersons within the legislature and government to advance regulations that promote their members' economic rents. For this reason, regulatory policymaking may not be the objective and rational process that RIA presumes, with its emphasis on fact finding and disinterested decision-making. At the same time, however, RIA can help to control rent seeking activity within government by promoting wider consultation and by requiring the explicit identification and evaluation of costs and benefits. RIA, by making the regulatory process more transparent and accountable, provides a means of weakening regulatory capture.

RIA has the potential to form an integrating framework within government to improve regulatory design and implementation. A properly carried out RIA will usefully address both regulatory goals and the regulatory process and by so doing should lead to improved regulatory capability, effectiveness, efficiency, and accountability.

Evaluating the quality of RIA

As the scope and scale of RIA practice have grown, there has been increasing recognition of the need for ex post evaluation of regulatory quality. Ex post evaluation can improve the quality of RIA, first, by contributing to the body of empirical evidence on which the design and implementation of future regulatory proposals can be assessed, and second, by placing evaluation results in the public domain, thereby making policymakers more accountable for their regulatory decisions. The OECD defines regulatory quality as follows:

> *Regulatory quality* refers to the extent to which a regulatory system pursues its underlying objectives. These objectives involve the specific policy objectives which the regulatory tool is being employed to pursue and the efficiency with which these objectives are achieved, as well as governance based objectives including transparency and accountability. (OECD, 2004b, p. 8)

The purpose of the evaluation of RIA, therefore, is to improve the effectiveness and efficiency of the RIA system, in terms of the goals that are set for it. These goals can be set in narrow or broad terms. In a restricted sense, the goals can be expressed in terms of improving the performance of the RIA procedures in contributing to 'better' regulation and regulatory governance. In a broader sense, the evaluation can be in terms of the goals of the regulatory reform process as a whole.

Almost all of the RIA evaluation work undertaken so far has focused on the narrower level. There are three basic approaches to 'narrow' evaluation, each of which contributes to the understanding of regulatory performance (OECD, 2004b):

- *Compliance tests* are input based, and evaluate formal compliance with the individual elements of the RIA procedures and process.
- *Performance tests* go beyond the question of formal compliance with procedural requirements, and measure the quality of the analysis undertaken. They link the inputs and the outcomes of the RIA process by assessing whether RIA is functioning adequately.
- *Function tests* are outcome focused, and evaluate the actual effect of RIA on the quality of the regulatory outcomes.

Compliance tests

Compliance testing typically involves a 'scorecard' assessment against the benchmark of the guidelines for good practice, such as the OECD checklist for regulatory decision-making shown in Table 11.3. In the United States, RIA evaluation studies have benchmarked actual RIA against published guidelines issued by the OMB. In a review of 48 RIA completed between 1996 and 1999, Hahn et al. (2000) found that many of the assessments failed to conform to the relevant guidelines. In a recent evaluation of UK RIAs, Ambler et al. (2003) compare compliance across different periods and find limited improvement over time. Overall, the authors conclude that 'The impression remains that in many cases compliance of RIAs remains a bureaucratic task to be despatched with as little effort as possible' (p. 23).

Vibert (2004) undertakes a compliance evaluation of the reports prepared by the European Commission during the first year (2003) of implementing Extended Impact Assessments. The scorecard benchmarks three main aspects of RIAs, namely their approach to the quantification of costs and benefits, procedural aspects such as whether alternative approaches to a policy question have been considered, and whether the lessons emerging from the RIA exercise are being taken into account in the outcome. The results of the evaluation show that, while little progress has been made towards being able to quantify and monetize the costs and benefits of proposed regulatory measures, the assessment process has contributed to greater transparency in the Commission's law making processes.

Performance tests

Performance evaluation tests focus on the quality of the various components of the process, rather than simply asking whether the required procedures were in place. A recent example of the performance testing approach to evaluation is provided by the UK National Audit Office reports on RIAs prepared by UK government departments and agencies (NAO, 2001, 2004). Using a sample of 10 RIAs, the evaluation methodology involved asking six high-level questions, each of which was broken down into more detailed sub-questions (Table 11.4).

246 International handbook on economic regulation

Table 11.4   National Audit Office, UK: framework of questions

---

1. Was the RIA process started early enough?
   Did the department have clear objectives for the regulation?
   Did the department allow a realistic timetable for the RIA process?
   Did the department consider the risks?
   Did the RIA consider a range of options?
   Were alternatives to regulation considered?
   Were alternative regulatory tools considered?

2. Was consultation effective?
   Was effective consultation started early in the process?
   Did the department use appropriate consultation techniques?
   Did the department explain clearly the impact of the regulation?
   Did the department consult all interested groups of stakeholders?
   Did the department consider the impact on small businesses?
   Were the results of the consultation used well in formulating the
   regulation?

3. Did the RIA assess the costs thoroughly?
   Were the implementation and policy costs on all affected taken into
   account?
   Did the department identify all parties on whom costs would fall?
   Did the department consider the costs to small businesses?
   Did the department identify all likely costs?
   Did the department assess the costs of all options?

4. Did the RIA assess benefits realistically?
   Did the department identify all parties who would benefit?
   Were the benefits realistic and relevant to the regulation?
   Was the methodology for quantifying/scoring the benefits robust?

5. Did the RIA realistically assess compliance?
   Was possible non-compliance factored into the analysis?
   Did the department assess the existing level of compliance?
   Were ways of increasing compliance considered?

6. Will the regulation be effectively monitored and evaluated?
   Did the RIA contain procedures for monitoring and evaluating the extent
   to which the regulation meets its objectives?

Source: Humpherson (2004).

Perhaps not surprisingly, the study identified the use of a number of practices and approaches across UK government departments, evidence of good practice and areas in need of improvement. There were a number of main findings (Humpherson, 2004). First, RIA was well embedded within government as part of the policymaking process and all new regulations are subject to RIAs. Second, within the sample, there was an insufficient degree of attention paid to the generation of alternative options, including 'do nothing', and to the analysis of options. Third, there had been improvement in the form, content and timing of consultations, although there was scope for improvement in the integration of consultations into the final RIA report. Fourth, quantifying costs and benefits was weak. Quantification of risks and hazards that the regulation was intended to reduce was attempted in some cases, but benefits were rarely quantified. Data uncertainties were often ignored and excessive accuracy attached to the quoted figures. Finally, there was insufficient consideration given to the enforcement, sanctions and evaluation of the RIAs.

Lee and Kirkpatrick (2006) carried out a performance evaluation of a sample of EC Extended Impact Assessments undertaken by the European Commission. The reports were evaluated in five main areas, each of which was disaggregated into more detailed sub-categories. Each area and sub-category is assessed and given a score which recorded the quality in terms of a scale which ranged from 'A – generally well performed, no important tasks left incomplete' to ' F – very unsatisfactory, important tasks poorly done or not attempted'. The study identified a number of areas of weakness, including poor identification of the problem, unbalanced coverage of different types of impacts and lack of clarity in the explanation of the analysis, and weaknesses in the presentation of the RIA findings.

Function tests
Function tests are focused on the outcomes of the RIA, and attempt to demonstrate the difference that the RIA has made to the quality of the regulatory system. Methodologically, a function test is intended to measure impact against the counterfactual 'do nothing' situation. A number of different types of RIA function tests have been applied in practice (OECD, 2004b, p. 35). The most frequently used method of evaluating RIA outcomes is to assemble data on the frequency with which regulatory proposals are revised or abandoned as a result of the RIA. This type of functional test faces the standard methodological difficulty of determining whether the observed change is the direct result of the RIA, or whether other factors have influenced the outcome. Also, a part of the impact will be unobservable if regulatory proposals are withdrawn in anticipation of an unfavourable RIA. Ambler et al. (2004) examined a sample of 200 RIAs conducted by UK government departments between mid-1998 and mid-2002. They found little evidence that RIAs had caused legislation to be aborted, with

only 11 cases of final RIAs being identified where this was a possibility. However, this may understate the impact of the RIA process, since the authors were unable to track initial and partial RIAs that were subsequently withdrawn. Vibert (2004) evaluated the first year of extended impact assessments undertaken by the European Commission, and found that 'there is not a single case where EU action has been assessed to have negative net benefits or where the inability to quantify the net benefits has led to the conclusion that the measure should be withdrawn or that no policy would be the best policy' (p. 9).

A second method of evaluating outcomes is to conduct an audit trail in relation to the RIA process and focus on how suggested changes to the initial regulatory proposal have been dealt with. This approach has the advantage of reviewing the process of managing the consultation suggestions and the internal decision-making involved in the preparation of the RIA. It is likely, however, to be relatively resource intensive (Yarrow, 2004). It also requires access to the key actors within government, which external evaluators may have difficulty in obtaining, since this increases the pressure on the regulators to be transparent and to justify their decisions.

A third evaluation approach extends the audit trail method, and tests the effect of the RIA on the organizational and regulatory culture; that is, 'how and whether RIAs are instrumental in instilling a greater appreciation and understanding of the benefits of the RIA process, and thereby encouraging a proactive rather than reactive use of the RIA as a policy development tool' (OECD, 2004b, p. 38). This type of evaluation is largely qualitative in nature, which can pose problems in the interpretation of the results. It does have the merit, however, of providing a more direct measure of the extent to which the goal of RIA has been achieved. Interestingly, the National Audit Office, which has legal authority to investigate internal procedures within UK government, found that its RIA evaluations had a significant impact on accountability – 'in essence, therefore, the fact of the NAO evaluation can help concentrate the minds of departments: a point borne out by the feedback discussions held with departments whose RIAs were in the pilot sample, following the completion of the first year's work by the NAO' (Humpherson, 2004, p. 281). A further example of this approach being applied is the independent study of the Canadian RIA system, which found that the implementation of RIA in Canada had induced a cultural change among regulators: 'More attention is paid to alternatives and costs and benefits ... Officials were sensitive to RIA requirements and departments had systems in place to consider regulatory options and costs and benefits ... and a core of expertise was available in several departments' (Delphi Group, 2000, pp. 5–6).

Evaluation at the 'broader' level involves assessing the impact of RIA on the regulatory environment and on the benefits that this provides, in terms of the goals of the regulatory reform process. This approach to evaluation is considerably more complex and methodologically challenging than the 'narrow' approach that has been discussed above. The causal chain from inputs to outcomes is extended by two additional stages: from the outcomes as measured in terms of the RIA process to changes in the overall regulatory framework, and from changes in the overall regulatory environment to the goals to which regulatory reform is expected to contribute. The methodological problems of establishing a counterfactual baseline from which to assess changes, and the difficulties of attributing changes to the initial RIA process, have limited the application of this evaluation approach to RIA.

The contribution of RIA to the quality of the overall regulatory reform effort might be evaluated by assessing the scope and coverage of the RIA process in relation to the regulatory environment. This would involve aggregating the evaluation results from the compliance and performance evaluation tests, to obtain a measure (or order of magnitude) of the significance of the total impact of RIA on the quality of the regulatory framework. So far there has been no systematic evaluation of the impact of RIA as a whole on the quality of the regulatory environment in any country.

There have been efforts, however, to evaluate the impact of changes in the regulatory environment on the broader societal goals. The OECD country reviews of regulatory reform have provided empirical evidence of a relationship between regulatory reform and better economic performance. Gains in terms of higher productivity and economic growth are found in countries such as Canada, the US and the UK, which have had a lengthy period of RIA. The general conclusion is that 'countries with explicit regulatory policies consistently make more rapid and sustained progress than countries without clear policies. The more complex the principles, and the more concrete and accountable the action program, the wider and more effective was reform' (OECD, 2002, p. 40). Evidence of the relationship between regulatory reform, particularly as it affects the business sector, and economic performance in a large number of developing and transitional countries, has been assembled by the World Bank (2004a). However, the supporting data are largely associative in nature, and provide little convincing evidence of causality. The World Bank has also gathered measures of the quality of regulatory governance in different countries (World Bank, 2004b), which has been used to test for a causal relationship between regulatory quality and economic performance. Jalilian et al. (2004) use multiple regression analysis to test for the impact of regulatory quality on economic growth in a sample of developed and developing countries. Their results are consistent with the argument that improving the efficiency, effectiveness and transparency of regulatory policymaking can have a significant positive effect on economic growth.

To conclude this section, a common limitation of most RIA systems is the limited attention given to the monitoring and evaluation of results. This is a significant weakness, given that the systematic and transparent evaluation of ex post impacts can contribute to a better understanding of successes and failures, and thereby to improved performance of RIA and regulatory systems. However, establishing the links between RIA and improvements in the quality of the overall regulatory environment, and between the regulatory environment and society's economic, social and environmental goals for national development, is a highly challenging exercise. But the discipline of so doing, if only in terms of the order of magnitude, is almost certainly justified in terms of the indirect impact that learning from experience will have on the RIA process and the quality of the regulatory framework.

Conclusions

Globally, the past decade has seen a major shift in the role that the state plays in the process of economic growth and development. This has led to interest in new approaches to policymaking with the aims of improving the quality of legislation and making governance more transparent and accountable. Regulation policy has been at the centre of this move towards 'better' policy and governance.

Regulatory impact assessment provides an analytical framework for assessing the effects that the introduction of a new regulation is likely to have, and also for assessing the actual impact of existing regulatory measures. By providing decision-makers with evidence on the effects of their regulatory choices, RIA can contribute to more informed policy choices, thereby improving the efficiency and effectiveness of regulation policy.

RIA was initially adopted in the OECD countries but is now being used in a growing number of transitional and developing economies. The way in which RIA has been implemented has varied between countries, reflecting differences in the objectives selected, institutional capacity and resource constraints. For many of these countries, RIA has been adopted within government only recently, and there is limited evidence available so far on the impact that it has had in terms of improving the quality of regulation decision-making. But for those countries where there is sufficient experience on which to make an evaluation of RIA performance, the results suggest that the impact has been positive in terms of more efficient regulation and also in the contribution to the broader goal of better governance.

RIA is a tool for decision-making, not a decision-making tool. It should be seen, therefore, as an integral part of the policymaking process. The aim of its application is to raise the quality of the regulatory decision-making process and in this way contribute to society's goal of economic, social and environmental advancement.

Note
1. This chapter draws heavily on work on regulatory policy undertaken with David Parker. See Kirkpatrick and Parker (2003), Parker and Kirkpatrick (2003), Kirkpatrick et al. (2004).

Bibliography
Ambler, T., Chittenden, F. and Shamutkova, M. (2003) *Do Regulators Play by the Rules? An Audit of Regulatory Impact Assessments*, London: British Chambers of Commerce.
Ambler T., Chitterden F. and Obodoviski M. (2004) *Are Regulators Raising their Game?*, London: British Chambers of Commerce.
Anderson, J.E. (1998) 'The Struggle to Reform Regulatory Procedures, 1978–1998', *Political Studies Journal*, **26** (3), 482–98.
Better Regulation Task Force (2003) 'Imaginative Thinking for Better Regulation', BRTF website.
Blake, S. (2002) 'Setting up a Regulatory Impact Unit – the UK Experience', Second Workshop of the APEC–OECD Co-operative Initiative on Regulatory Reform, Merida, Mexico, April.
Cabinet Office (2000) *Good Policy Making: A Guide to Regulatory Impact Assessment*, London: Cabinet Office.
Cabinet Office (2003) *Better Policy Making: Regulatory Impact Assessment*, London: Cabinet Office.
Delphi Group (2000) *Assessing the Contribution of Regulatory Impact Analysis on Decision Making and the Development of Regulations*, Ottawa, ON: Delphi Group.
DFID (2000) 'Making Markets Work Better for the Poor: A Framework Paper', mimeo, London: Department for International Development.
European Commission (2001) *Communication: A Sustainable Europe for a Better World: A European Union Strategy for Sustainable Development*, COM(2001)264 Final. Brussels: EC.
European Commission (2002a) *Communication from the Commission on Impact Assessment*, 5 June 2002, Brussels: EC.
European Commission (2002b) *Better Regulation for the Commission's White Paper on European Governance*, www.europe.eu.int/comm/governance
European Parliament, DG for Research (2002) *Working Paper on Development and Current Practices in the EU Member States, on the EU Level and in Selected Third Countries*, Legal Affairs Series, Luxembourg: European Parliament.
Hahn R.W., Burnett J.K., Chan Y.I., Mader E.A. and Moyle P.R. (2000) 'Assessing Regulatory Impact Analyses: The Failure of Agencies to Comply with Executive Order 12866', *Harvard Journal of Law and Public Policy*, **23** (3), 859–84.
Humpherson, E. (2004) 'The National Audit Office's Evalution of RIAs: Reflections on the Pilot Year', *Public Money & Management*, **24** (5), 277–82.
Jacobs, C. (2004) 'The Challenge of Accession in Central and Eastern Europe: Reflections on the Baltics', *Public Administration and Development*, **24**, 321–31.
Jacobs, C. (2005) 'Improving the Quality of RIA in the UK', draft paper for Centre for Regulation and Competition, Manchester University, January 2005.
Jacobs, S. (1997) 'An Overview of Regulatory Impact Analysis in OECD Countries', in OECD, *Regulatory Impact Analysis: Best Practices in OECD Countries*, Paris: OECD.
Jacobs, S. (2002) 'Convergence in Impact Analysis: Toward an Integrated Framework

for RIA and SIA in European Institutions', paper presented at the *Sustainability Impact Appraisal Seminar*, British Embassy, Brussels, April 2002.

Jacobs, S. (2004) 'Regulatory Impact Assessment and the Economic Transition to Markets', *Public Money & Management*, **24** (5) 283–90.

Jalilian, H., Kirkpatrick, C. and Parker, D. (2004) 'The Impact of Regulation on Economic Growth in Developing Countries: A Cross-section Analysis', Centre on Regulation and Competition Working Paper 54, University of Manchester.

Kirkpatrick, C. and Parker, D. (2003) 'Regulatory Impact Assessment: Its Potential for Use in Developing Countries', *Public Administration and Development*, **24**, pp. 1–12.

Kirkpatrick, C., Parker, D. and Zhang, Y.-F. (2004) 'Regulatory Impact Assessment in Developing and Transition Economies: A Survey of Current Practice', *Public Money & Management*, **24** (5), 291–6.

Lee, N. (2002) 'Developing and Applying Regulatory Impact Assessment Methodologies in Low and Middle Income Countries', Centre on Regulation and Competition Working Paper no. 30, University of Manchester.

Lee, N. and Kirkpatrick, C. (2006) 'Evidence-based policy making in Europe: an evaluation of European Commission integrated impact assessments', *Impact Assessment and Project Appraisal* **24** (1), 3–21.

Majone, G. (1994) 'The Rise of the Regulatory State in Europe', *West European Politics*, **17**, 71–101.

Majone, G. (1997) 'From the Positive to the Regulatory State', *Journal of Public Policy*, **17**, 71–111.

Mandelkern Group (2001) *Final Report on Better Regulation*, Brussels: European Council.

Morrall, J.F. III (2001) 'Regulatory Impact Analysis: Efficiency, Accountability and Transparency', Paper presented at the launching conference of the APEC–OECD Cooperative Initiative on Regulatory Reform, Singapore, February.

National Audit Office (NAO) (2001) *Better Regulation: Making Good Use of Regulatory Impact Assessments*, Report by the Comptroller and Auditor General HC 329 Session 2001–02, November, London: NAO.

NAO (2004) *Evaluation of Regulatory Impact Assessments Compendium Report 2003–04: Report by the Comptroller and Auditor General*, HC 358 Session 2003–04, 4 March 2004, London: NAO.

OECD (1995) *Recommendation on Improving the Quality of Government Regulation*, Paris: OECD, 9 March.

OECD (1996) *Regulatory Reform: Overview*, Paris: OECD.

OECD (1997) *The OECD Report on Regulatory Reform: Synthesis*, Paris: OECD.

OECD (1999) *Regulatory Reform in Mexico*, Paris: OECD.

OECD (2000) *Regulatory Reform in Korea*, Paris: OECD.

OECD (2002) *Regulatory Policies in the OECD Countries: From Intervention to Regulatory Governance*, Paris: OECD.

OECD (2004a) *Ministerial Report on Regulatory Governance in SEE Countries, OECD and the Stability Pact, and South East Europe Compact for Reform, Investment Integrity and Growth*, Paris: OECD.

OECD (2004b) 'Regulatory Performance: *Ex Post* Evaluation of Regulatory Tools and Institutions', *Working Party on Regulatory Management and Reform*, Draft Report by the Secretariat, OECD: Paris.

Ogus A. (2001) 'Regulatory Institutions and Structures', Working Paper no. 3, Centre on Regulation and Competition, University of Manchester, UK.

OMB (Office of Management and Budget) (2001) *Making Sense of Regulation: 2001 Report to Congress on the Costs and Benefits of Regulations and Unfunded Mandates on State, Local and Tribe Entities*, Office of Information and Regulatory Affairs, Washington, DC: OMB.

Owen, P.W. and Courtney, M. (2002) 'The Policy Framework for "Better Regulation"', in P. Vass (ed.), *Accountability and Regulation – Reporting Performance*, University of Bath: Centre for the Study of Regulated Industries.

Parker, D. (2002) 'Economic Regulation: A Review of Issues', *Annals of Public and Cooperative Economics*, **73** (4), 493–519.

Parker, D. and Kirkpatrick, C. (2003) 'Researching Economic Regulation in Developing Countries: A Methodology for Critical Analysis', in P. Cook, C. Kirkpatrick, M. Minogue and D. Parker (eds), *Leading Issues in Regulation, Competition and Development*, Cheltenham, UK and Northampton, MA, USA: Edward Elgar.

Parker, D. and Kirkpatrick, C. (2005) 'Privatisation in Developing Countries: A Review of the Evidence and the Policy Lessons', *Journal of Development Studies*, **41** (4), 513–41.

Parker, D., Kirkpatrick, C. and Zhang, Y.-F. (2005) 'Price and Profit Regulation in Developing and Transition Economies: A Survey of the Regulators', *Public Money and Management*, **25** (2), 99–106.

Radaelli, C. (2002) 'The Politics of Regulatory Impact Analysis in the OECD Countries', mimeo, University of Bradford, UK.

Radaelli, C. (2003) 'Impact Assessment in the European Union: Innovations, Quality and Good Regulatory Governance', Paper prepared for DG Enterprise, European Commission, December.

Radaelli, C.M. (2004a) 'The Politics of Regulatory Impact Analysis in the OECD Countries: Best Practice and Lesson-drawing', *European Journal of Political Research*, **43**, 735–43.

Radaelli, C.M. (2004b) 'Getting to Grips with Quality in the Diffusion of Regulatory Impact Assessment in Europe', *Public Money & Management*, **24** (5), 271–6.

SIGMA (2001) *Improving Policy Instruments through Impact Assessment*, SIGMA Paper No. 31, Paris: OECD.

Stern, J. and Holder, S. (1999) 'Regulatory Governance: Criteria for Assessing the Performance of Regulatory Systems. An Application to Infrastructure Industries in the Developing Countries of Asia', *Utilities Policy*, **8**, 33–50.

Treasury Board of Canada Secretariat (2001), Paper No. 14 on *Regulatory Reform through RIA: The Canadian Experience*, at www.tbs-sct-gc.ca/pubb

Vibert F. (2004) *The EU's New System of Regulatory Impact Assessment – A Scorecard*, London: European Policy Forum.

World Bank (1995) *Bureaucrats in Business: The Economics and Politics of Government Ownership*, Oxford: Oxford University Press for the World Bank.

World Bank (2001) *World Development Report, 2000/2001*, Washington, DC: World Bank.

World Bank (2004a) *World Development Report 2005*, Washington DC: World Bank and Oxford University Press.

World Bank (2004b) *Doing Business in 2004: Understanding Regulation*, World Bank and IFC, Washington, DC: World Bank and Oxford University Press.

Yarrow, G. (2004) 'Evaluation of Regulatory Communication and Consultation Mechanisms: Approaches, Methodologies, and Some Guiding Principles', Paper prepared for the OECD Project on ex post Evaluation of Regulatory Tools and Institutions, OECD, Paris.

12 Economics of environmental regulation: instruments and cases[1]

Anthony Heyes and Catherine Liston

Introduction

The imperative of managing the exploitation of the natural environment is not a new one. Institutions – formal or informal – aimed at preventing inappropriate private exploitation of water, land and other resources were put in place or evolved in all ancient civilizations.

In modern market economies, as pressures on the natural environment have intensified, robust and efficient environmental regulation has become a central ambition of most governments. Despite differences in view as to how heavily to weight environmental protection, the underlying rationale for regulation is well understood and has its roots in market failure. In particular in the notion of public goods and externality.

Many components of the natural environment (clean air, biological diversity, water, quiet, aesthetically pleasing views, etc.) are public or quasi-public goods. Formal ownership rights for the environment are frequently non-existent. Even where such rights could be established and enforced there is a deep-seated attachment to the view that many of the key elements of the natural environment should remain in common 'ownership'. In the absence of policy intervention the social cost of use of a common resource will exceed private cost and the public good will be over-exploited, to the detriment of social welfare (Coase, 1960). After a famous article published in the *Science* almost forty years ago this phenomenon has come to be referred to as the 'tragedy of the commons' (Hardin, 1968).

The over-exploitation of a public good such as the environment is an example of the more general market failure due to externality. An externality arises when the actions of one agent (say A) impact the utility of some other (B) in a way that is not priced. Acting in self-interest, without altruistic motives, Agent A has no incentive to take account of any negative impact that her choice of actions has on B and others. When choosing to drive her car an extra mile, dump waste into a river, or shoot an elephant, for example, she does not take account of the costs to others that the additional environmental degradation resulting from such a choice imposes.

Whether couched in the language of public goods or externality theory the ambition of efficient policy is clearly understood, namely: to restrict access and use of the commons to 'efficient' levels, or to make agents act as if the full implications of their actions were on themselves.

Non-regulatory approaches to the management of shared resources may evolve, and have been the much studied by economists (both theoretical and experimental), anthropologists and others in recent years. Of particular interest is the evolution of social norms in common property resource (CPR) games. Social norm-driven behaviour arises when members of a population adhere to standards of behaviour higher than those coerced by formal laws or regulations because, for example, they fear ostracism, community disapproval or other informal punishment. Sethi and Somanathan (1996), among others, have shown how such social norms can evolve and be evolutionarily stable. Ostrom (1990) and Ostrom and Gardner (1993) provide excellent analyses, and compelling real-world examples of contexts in which communities in CPR environments have sustained patterns of cooperative behaviour in the absence of a coercive governmental authority.

Though the appeal of 'regulation' without regulation is obvious, these informal approaches do not interest us here. In general the settings in which they are likely to flourish are ones characterized by comparatively small populations, with low population turnover (relatively few itinerants) and frequent interaction in a context in which bad behaviour is publicly observed and has negative impacts that are largely contained within that neighbourhood. While this sort of setting can still be found – the exploitation of rivers or forests in village settings in less developed countries, anti-social parking in suburban neighbourhoods, etc. – informal control based on peer pressure and self-restraint is unlikely to go far to address most of the pressing environmental problems faced by modern market economies.

Institutions aimed at protecting the environment have, as we have already noted, existed for many centuries. The burning of coal was prohibited in London in 1263 by Royal Proclamation because it was prejudicial to health. In recent history, in most Western countries environmental policies were predominantly command-based – the regulator placing restrictions on what a polluting firm could do, for example by putting a cap on its emissions or mandating particular technologies.

The primary objective of an environmental regulatory programme is to restrict use of or damage to the environment. A secondary objective is to achieve that end without generating excessive economic burdens. Dissatisfaction with traditional regulatory instruments – sometimes referred to as command and control approaches – grew not out of their inability to deliver the former, but the latter. Particularly in settings where regulators did not 'know best' – either due to insufficient expertise or, more charitably, because of insufficient access to information – it seemed likely that the economic burden of achieving given environmental objectives might be reduced by the adoption of incentive or economic instruments of one sort or another. Economic theory backed up that claim, and incentive instruments have come into widespread use in many countries in the past decade or so.

Regulation: basics and a whistle-stop tour of instruments

Our aim here is to provide a brief overview of the characteristics of the major classes of regulatory instrument available, and to provide examples of the use of each.

The theory underlying instrument choice is often traced back to the famous paper 'Prices vs. Quantities' by noted Harvard economist Martin Weitzman (Weitzman, 1974). He stated that under certainty it made no difference whether the regulator chose a price-based instrument (such as a tax) or a quantity-based instrument (such as an emissions permit). Preference between instruments in a static setting should, then, be determined by issues of uncertainty. Understanding this paper should be the starting point for anyone interested in understanding the instrument choice debate.

Weitzman's world was a simplified one, and much of the research since can be seen as relaxing the assumptions of his model. So doing allows other things to matter in determining the performance of alternative instruments.

Two important strands of work have considered the *dynamic* performance of alternative approaches to policy, in particular their ability to induce efficient levels of green R&D (Downing and White, 1986), and to consider the general equilibrium impacts of policy (Bovenberg and Goulder, 1996, 2001; Jorgenson and Wilcoxen, 1990).

Naturally, the characterization of instruments themselves and the policy environments in which they operate, is stylized in any discussion of this sort. Mathematical analysis is provided only where it is needed to establish important efficiency results, elsewhere established results are stated and justified intuitively.

Legal liability

At the heart of the problem of externality is the absence of effective property rights. In his celebrated analysis of the problem of social cost, Coase (1960) demonstrated that, in the absence of other complications, well-defined property rights would lead a society of self-interested individuals to make socially optimal choices of behaviour regardless of how those property rights were distributed.

So one natural approach to the problem of externality is to make polluters liable to victims for damage done. The effect of doing so successfully is to establish property rights, such as to internalize the externality. While it is not uncommon to refer to the 'law versus regulation' debate, here we are using the term regulation in its broad sense, and treat 'law' as a regulatory instrument (or portfolio of instruments).

Liability for environmental and natural resource damage can be imposed either by statute or under the common law. Liability for environmental damage has been imposed under a variety of statutes in many countries; in the United States, for example, under the Comprehensive Environmental Response, Liability and Compensation Act (CERCLA) and the Clean Water Act. Under common law, both nuisance and property law have been used to prevent environmental damage (by injunction) or to secure compensation for damage done (see Dewees, 1992, for discussion).

Environmental liability can be imposed on a variety of different bases, but under the broadest characterization liability may be either *strict* or *negligence-based*. Under a regime of strict liability, the polluter is held liable for the full value of damage done, regardless of care taken. A well-functioning regime of strict liability institutionalizes the *polluter pays principle* in its simplest form – the polluter pays for damage without reference to behaviour.

Under a negligence-based liability rule, a responsible party is held liable only if it fails to exercise due care in its conduct of the externality-generating activity.

The ability of either type of liability rule to induce efficient care levels can readily be understood by means of a simple model (this version follows that presented by Segerson, 1995).

Assume unilateral care – that is the damages imposed depend only on the care level of the polluter. Care by the polluter might be expected to reduce the probability of damage being done (if damage is associated with accidental events), the amount of damage done if an event occurs, or both, depending on context. If the polluter chooses a level of care of monetary value x, let $p(x)$ be the probability that the prospective victim will suffer damages of $d(x)$. Under standard assumptions (including, in particular, risk neutrality of all agents) the socially optimal choice of x minimizes precaution costs plus expected external damages,

$$x + p(x)d(x).$$

Given convexity this implies that x^* is implicitly defined by the associated first-order condition

$$-p'(x^*)d(x^*) - p(x^*)d'(x^*) = 1.$$

Social efficiency requires that the care level is increased up to the point at which the marginal cost of care (the right-hand side) equals the marginal social benefit in terms of reductions in expected environmental damage (left). Care may reduce expected environmental damage either by reducing the probability of a pollution incident, or the impact of an incident, or both.

In the absence of regulation or other incentives the polluter, on the other hand, chooses x to minimize

$$x + p(x)l(x)$$

where $l(x)$ denotes the polluter's liability payment in the event of an incident.

Under a textbook regime of strict liability the polluter is liable for all damage done, such that $l_{strict}(x) = d(x)$, and is induced to choose an efficient level of care. The regime acts to fully internalize the externality, bringing private costs into correspondence with social costs.

Under a negligence rule the polluter is liable for the full amount of damage done if and only if he fails to take due care in the conduct of his operations. What constitutes due care may be defined by regulation, legal precedent or a court judgement as to how an agent engaged in an externality-generating activity could reasonably be expected to behave. If we denote as x^s the minimum level of care required to satisfy the negligence rule, then the polluter's liability payment in the event of an incident depends discontinuously on its precautionary effort. In particular $l_{negligence}(x) = d(x)$ if $x < x^s$, equals 0 otherwise.

Provided x^s is set equal to x^* – the negligence rule is specified efficiently – the profit maximizing firm will choose that socially efficient level of care.

In the context of unilateral care, then, either strict liability, or negligence-based liability with an appropriately set due care standard, can be used to induce efficient pollution control. The outcomes differ in terms of distribution. In equilibrium the expected damage flow from the activity under optimal pre-cautionary effort, $p(x^*)d(x^*)$, is incident on the polluter, who has to compensate victims, under the strict regime, but on the victim(s) under the negligence-based alternative.

Given the stochastic nature of outcomes in this stylization, the two regimes also imply a different allocation of risk between agents. In most settings it might be reasonable to suppose that polluters (firms) will be less risk-averse than prospective victims (individuals), perhaps because they are better placed to insure any risks that they face. This would imply that, other things being equal, a preference for the allocation of risk generated by the regime based on strict liability.

The strict regime, as described here, also generates efficient incentives for the choice of scale of the activity. Because under a negligence-based regime the external damage associated with pollution remains, in equilibrium, external to the polluter, the regime effectively subsidizes that polluting activity. To achieve efficient choice of scale the negligence-based regime needs to be supplemented by some additional regulatory management of entry to the activity.

Despite environmental liability regimes being in place in all countries, and under various international laws and conventions, they do not form the backbone of environmental policy except in very select settings. Notwithstanding the optimistic predictions of the textbook analysis just presented, there are a plethora of real-world 'frictions' that do not feature in the stylized world in which we have just characterized the operation of the alternative regimes. The performance of liability as an instrument of regulation turns out to be highly sensitive to these frictions. Even where its use is important (for example in the context of contaminated land in the US) its use will typically be overlaid with a complementary regulatory apparatus, designed to correct for those sensitivities.

Among the more important frictions are: (a) the difficulty and expense that a victim faces in demonstrating causation and – where applicable – negligence; (b) the risk that a polluter would not have the wherewithal ex post to pay required damages – what Shavell (1986) referred to as the problem of 'judgement proofness'; this is more likely to be a problem in low probability/high consequence contexts and competitive industries populated by a large number of firms with low capitalization; (c) the dispersed nature of the victim population and the transactions costs of that population organizing itself to coordinate litigation. In the case of many of the commonest and most important environmental problems – urban air quality, global warming, beach pollution – the damage is characterized by a large population, with each member suffering a small loss. The problem can be partly mitigated by construction of party suits, but there are additional transactions and coordination difficulties associated with such solutions. An additional approach is to allow designated NGOs – such as the Sierra Club in the US – to bring public interest suits, but again there are incentive and funding issues that arise; and (d) bilateral care issues. In many – probably most – pollution contexts, prospective victims can engage in 'defensive' expenditures or adaptations in behaviour to reduce the impact on them of a given pattern of pollution. Individuals living near noisy industrial sites can install double-glazing; people can reduce their exposure to poor quality urban air by staying inside more, or to dirty beaches by spending less time at the beach, and so on. In these settings efficiency requires optimal abatement activity by producers and optimal defensive effort by potential victims. Conventional liability regimes, as described, find it difficult to generate such two-sided incentives (under a well-functioning strict regime, for example, individuals have no incentive whatever to act defensively).

Contributory negligence or comparable provisions may be addended to liability-based systems to mitigate these problems, but the practical difficulties of application become significantly more complex.

Example 1: Strict versus negligence-based liability in the European Union
Environmental liability provisions in the nation states that make up the European Union vary, reflecting the variety of legal traditions. The United Kingdom, for example, typically operates on a negligence basis, while countries such as Germany and the Netherlands have a tradition of strict liability.

A concerted attempt to harmonize approaches was made by the EU in the early and mid-1990s with the publication of the 1993 EC Green Paper *Remedying Environmental Damage* (Cm. (3)47).

The impetus for this was not simply a desire to identify and implement the best available approach per se, but also a desire to homogenize legal and regulatory approaches between nation states as part of the development of the level playing field requisite for economic integration and operation of the Single European Market. As we have seen, even where the two approaches induce the same level of precaution strict liability for damage imposes a greater liability burden on producers. This has the potential to confer a competitive disadvantage on producers subject to such a regime.

After prolonged consultation, national governments – each representing countries with long legal traditions of one type or the other – were unable to agree on a common approach, and diversity remains.

Example 2: Contaminated land in the United States
Perhaps the most studied, and among the most contentious uses of liability as an instrument in an environmental setting has been in the context of contaminated land in the United States.

The Comprehensive Environmental Response, Liability and Compensation Act (CERCLA) was enacted in 1980, both as an instrument to provide incentives for safe future land use, but also as an endeavour to fund the clean-up of the large stock of contaminated sites already in existence at that time.

The Act imposes strict, retroactive, joint and several liability on a variety of 'responsible parties'. In essence joint and several liability means that where several entities have contributed to contamination at a site – because a particular piece of land has been shared among a group of businesses, for example, or a given plant has had several operators over the years – any one of those contributors can be held liable for the whole damage, however small the fraction of the total contamination that can be directly subscribed to them.

The EPA in the US has been proactive in identifying sites in need of remediation, particularly during periods of activism in the late 1980s and early 1990s. At the end of 1996 approximately 40,500 contaminated sites had been identified and some 1475 placed on the National Priorities List (NPL) for expeditious pursuit. About 400 of these were 'construction complete' and around 950 were at least at the stage of a remediation programme having been designed.

The stipulation that liability be strict and joint and several has greatly facilitated the EPA in recovering the costs of clean-up from responsible parties (by 1999 it had reached settlements with polluters totalling more than US$16 bn). To provide up-front funding for the clean-up process, and to cover the costs in those cases where clean-up expenses cannot be fully recovered from responsible parties, CERCLA also authorized a tax on the petroleum and chemical industries. In the first five years of operation of the tax it raised something over US$5 bn, that money constituting the Superfund. The Superfund is used to fund clean-up at sites where insufficient costs can be extracted from responsible parties.

Particularly contentious in the United States has been the width with which CERCLA and the associated 1986 Superfund Amendment and Reauthorization Act (SARA) envisaged throwing the net of 'potentially responsible parties' (PRPs), to include not just owners of land in contaminated sites but other related parties such as transportation companies and banks who had lent to the offending owner. After much early dispute, the burden faced by lenders was reduced by a series of EPA clarifications in the early 1990s.

Command-and-control
The term command-and-control has come to mean different things to different people. Here we will use it to refer to approaches in which the regulator makes prescriptions regarding the technology to be used in abatement and/or engagement in the externality-generating activity. For example, the regulator may mandate the attachment of catalytic converters to new cars, or the retrofitting of sulphur scrubbers to all coal-burning power plants.

The likely efficiency of a regime of command-and-control based regulation will depend largely on the ability of the regulatory agency to determine the optimal choice of technology in any given case. In settings where the technology and economics are fairly standard, as for example with the fitting of catalytic converters to cars, it can be one of the most straightforward and efficient ways to implement policy.

In most environmental regulatory settings, however, heterogeneity between polluters will make the task of determining best technology at any given location very difficult. There may be a wide set of revisions to product or process (or both) that would allow a welfare-motivated firm to implement a cost-efficient environmental policy. But (a) what works best may vary substantially between firms and (b) the firm has private information about what works for it. In that case the application of a 'one size fits all' technology-based policy is likely to generate a considerable excess burden. The flexibility offered by market-based or incentive mechanisms is likely to work significantly more efficiently.

Where command-and-control has been stipulated in legislation, it has often been tempered to recognize this need for flexibility – the need for setting-specific trade-offs between costs and benefits. The 1956 Clean Air Act in the United Kingdom, for example, required that polluters employ *best practicable technology* (BPT) with practicable defined as 'reasonably practicable having regard to local conditions and circumstances, to financial implications and the current state of technology'. In other pieces of legislation from a variety of countries similarly unhelpful definitions are provided for concepts such as *best available technology* (BAT), and *best available technology not entailing excessive cost* (BATNEEC).

Green taxation

In designing policy to ration use of the environment economists have for many years – and perhaps not surprisingly – been attracted by the mechanism of price (tax).

Pigou (1938) famously characterized the optimal tax on pollution (or other environmental degradation) as being equal to marginal damage. Consider an industry populated by N firms indexed i. Each firm derives a benefit(profit) from production of some good. Production of that good by firm i is both privately costly, c_i, and also generates emissions, e_i, which impose a disamenity on some third party or parties. We can write the firm's benefit function as

$$B_i = pq_i - c_i(q_i, e_i)$$

where q_i is the level of output. For simplicity the price of the output is taken to be fixed at p, an assumption normally justified by assuming that the output market is perfectly competitive, and the firm's costs are decreasing and convex in emission.

In the absence of intervention the firm will set a level of emissions above the socially desirable level because the damages associated with the emissions are external to the firm.

The optimal tax is straightforward to derive. Assuming that the value of external damage depends on aggregate emissions according to a strictly increasing and convex $D(\cdot)$ the social planner chooses a unit tax τ to maximize

$$\sum_i B_i(e_i) - D\left(\sum_i e_i\right)$$

subject to the set of incentive compatibility constraints

$$e_i = \arg\max_{e_i}\{B_i(e_i) - \tau e_i\}.$$

In other words, the planner sets the tax to maximize net benefits, subject to the constraint that each firm determines its own emission level to maximize its own (net) benefit. Since the representative firm's problem is concave, each constraint can be replaced with the associated first-order condition:

$$B_i'(e_i) - \tau = 0.$$

The planner's problem can then be expressed as a Lagrangian

$$L = \sum_i B_i(e_i) - D\left(\sum_i e_i\right) - \sum_i \lambda_i (B_i'(e_i) - \tau)$$

where $D(\cdot)$, the value of environmental damage, depends only on aggregate emissions.

For most classes of pollutant the underlying science of the pollution process leads us to expect an increasing marginal rate of damage, that is to say $D' > 0$, $D'' > 0$. Without presenting the optimality conditions, it is straightforward to derive the optimal tax

$$\tau^* = B_i'(e_i) = D'\left(\sum_i e_i^*\right)$$

The tax is set to equate with marginal damage, which is precisely Pigou's (1938) result.

In more complex settings the tax would need to be tailored to take account of the impact of pollution according to factors such as location, time of day, concentration, where these factors influence the impact of the discharge of a given total volume (Sterner, 2003).

It is worth noting the properties of the outcome that implementation of such a tax implies. By setting unit tax equal to marginal social damage, the firm is bearing the full marginal cost of its activity and so its privately optimal choice of action will coincide with the socially optimal one. Individual and aggregate emissions will be set at their first-best level. The burden of abatement will be distributed cost-effectively across firms – that is to say in the way that minimizes system costs.

The oft-cited efficiency benefits of a price-based system, (a) flexibility and (b) devolution of decision-making to those with private information, are apparent here. Each firm is confronted with the full marginal cost of its actions, but left to make its own abatement decisions. The system is flexible because different firms can choose a different emissions level, depending on their own particular abatement cost conditions, and will do so in a socially efficient way.

Implementing such a tax regime is informationally undemanding in the sense that the planner needs only information about the *impact* of pollution, not on the firm-specific cost of its reduction. It is the latter over which firms are commonly (and plausibly) supposed to have private information.

The assumption that marginal damages are increasing in total emissions implies that a Pigovian tax will lead to the socially optimal population of firms only when firms are small. If firms are not small (in the formal sense) then a tax set at the Pigovian level can lead to too little of the taxed activity. This is because a large firm, in making an entry decision, will take account of the fact that its entry will impact industry emissions and therefore the tax rate. A small firm takes the tax rate as given.

If a tax is to be set in a context where pollutants are prone to accumulate in the environment (where the pollutants are not of the pure 'flow' type) things become more complicated. Greenhouse gases accumulate in the atmosphere, for example, and heavy metals and other pollutants may accumulate in soils and bodies of water. In that case, damage at any time *t* will depend not just on emissions at *t*, but on the profile of past emissions. The precise temporal relationship between the emissions profile and damaging impacts is often complex and uncertain and policy analysis requires that explicit attention be paid to 'stock dynamics', the way in which the stock of the pollutant evolves through time.

Example 1: Pollution taxes in Central and Eastern European (CEE) transition economies

Many CEE transition economies have experienced rapid economic reform and growth since the 1980s, and in many cases this has been associated with a deterioration in the condition of the natural environment.

Bluffstone and Larson (1997) and Sterner (2003) illustrate that environmental taxes and fees have been a key instrument of environmental policy in these economies during transition.

The application of taxation has, in some cases, been comparatively sophisticated. In Estonia, for example, individual taxes on emissions are differentiated according to the size and sensitivity of the polluted area such that the tax burden on firm *j* is:

$$T^j = \sum_i e_i^j g_i^j t_i$$

where e_i^j is firm *i*'s vector of emissions, t_i the pollutant-specific tax rates, and g_i^j are multipliers set to reflect the sensitivity of the location in which the pollution takes place (whether it is an area of recreational use, population density and demographics, and so on).

While in general taxes have been set below their Pigovian level, they are still at a level high enough to make a significant impact. The political acceptability of the new taxes has in many cases been enhanced by the earmarking of funds. Taxes had been in use prior to 'marketization' in these economies. Though they had been useful in revenue generation they had comparatively modest incentive effects in the planning period in which plant managers faced soft budget constraints. Bluffstone (1999) provides evidence of the enhanced incentive effect following the post-transition hardening of budget constraints.

Example 2: Fuel taxation and road pricing in Singapore and elsewhere
Road use is an area of policy in which charges/taxes/pricing have been embraced in many different places around the world. This is true both in the context of urban road use and long distance out-of-town settings.

The externalities generated by car use include those that might be regarded as conventionally environmental – the contribution of vehicle emissions including CO_2 to global warming, or of particulates to urban air quality. In addition car use by any individual imposes a congestion externality on other road users, lengthening travel times and increasing accident risks.

Policies can have a number of impacts. They might reduce the number of cars on the road, and/or the pattern of usage of any given stock of cars, and/or the level of emissions per unit of use. The first two of these channels can address both the environmental and the congestion elements of the road use 'problem'.

In most jurisdictions regulation involves a mixture of technological fixes and use of price (tax) instruments.

Domestic fuel prices vary considerably between countries, largely due to differences in taxation. Standard gasoline prices in the UK in 2004 were approximately US$1.30 per litre, higher than in most of the rest of the EU, while prices in Argentina, Canada and Australia were around half that level.

In addition to taxing car ownership and use (through fuel taxation) increasingly popular are efforts to tax road use directly.[2] A well-known example of a particularly sophisticated car ownership and road pricing scheme is that in place in Singapore. Very high duties are placed on imported (i.e. almost all) cars, and a very high vehicle registration fee is added (195 per cent of the vehicle's value). An electronic tolling system came into operation in 1998, with an electronic dashboard-mounted gadget being detected by a roadside device, allowing drivers to be charged according to distance driven, time of day, and so on.

Emissions standards (tradable and non-tradable)
Quantity-based regulation has been favoured by policy-makers in many contexts. The imposition of an emissions limit or quota on polluters has been applied in a variety of national and international settings.

If the regulator has good information about each firm's marginal cost and damage functions then the operation of such a system is, in principle at least, straightforward. Firm i's emissions limit is set to equate the marginal cost of abatement with the marginal damage associated with the emissions. The resulting pattern of abatement will then be both cost-effective and cost-efficient. However, such an approach is not workable when firms face significantly different abatement costs, and that heterogeneity is hidden from the regulator.

A major innovation of the past two decades has been the development of approaches that make standards or allowances tradable. *Tradable emissions permits* (TEPs) allow firms to buy and sell the right to pollute with one another and are designed to mitigate this difficulty. The formal analyses of the operation and properties of such a regime date back to at least Crocker (1966) and Dales (1968). A well-known and rigorous demonstration of a number of basic properties of permits is provided by Montgomery (1972).

Permits can be applied to many points in the production to pollution chain, but here we restrict our attention to tradable emissions permits (TEPs) – permits denominated in terms of *quantity of emissions*. There are at least two different styles of emission-based TEP programme. The most common – and the one we will focus on here – is referred to as 'cap and trade'. Assuming a homogeneous pollutant the regulator (a) sets an upper bound on aggregate allowable emissions, (b) issues the corresponding number of permits in sufficiently small denomination units, (c) allows firms to trade those permits at market-determined prices, and (d) sets up institutions for monitoring and enforcement to ensure that firms only emit units of pollution for which they hold permits. Under a credit-based programme, emissions reductions credits (ERCs) are generated when a firm cuts its emissions below some previously determined baseline. These credits can be used by that same firm in a subsequent period, or by another source to satisfy its own baseline. Other hybrid approaches (such as those based on emissions averaging) have also been discussed.

Tradability, if trade is competitive, generates some attractive efficiency properties. Tradability commoditizes the right to pollute so the act of polluting generates an opportunity cost. That cost is the opportunity forgone to sell the corresponding permit, the value of which equals the prevailing market price.

Consider the following formalization of how a market for TEPs works. There are a large number of small firms, such that each acts as a price taker in the market for permits, and let e_i' be the initial endowment of permits given to firm i. Then each firm i will choose a level of emission to maximize

$$B_i(e_i) - P^{TEP}\{e_i - e_i'\},$$

where P^{TEP} is the prevailing price of a permit, $B_i(e_i)$ is the benefit that the firm derives (in terms of forgone compliance expenditures) from being allowed to pollute, while $P^{TEP}\{e_i - e_i'\}$ is the amount that it has to spend on acquiring permits. Naturally this can be negative, and will be if $e_i < e_i'$; that is, the firm is a net seller of permits. We can denote the solution to this maximization problem as $e_i^*(P^{TEP})$, implicitly defined as a function of the price of permits by firm i's first-order condition:

$$B_i'(e_i) = P^{TEP}.$$

A well-functioning competitive market for permits will then ensure that P^{TEP} emerges to clear the market – to ensure that the sum of excess demands is zero. That is:

$$P^{TEP} : \sum_i (e_i^* (P^{TEP}) - e_i') = 0.$$

Ignoring possible issues arising out of non-convexity, multiple equilibria and so on, it is immediately apparent that the process of trading ensures two things. First, the environmental objective is satisfied. That is to say, the total pollution done will equal $\Sigma_i e_i'$, the sum of the endowments that the regulator issued at the start of the programme. Here quantity is fixed and price adjusts. This is in contrast to the outcome under taxation where price (the rate of tax) was fixed and quantity is free to adjust. Second, the outcome is cost-effective – the reduction in aggregate emissions is achieved in a least cost way. This can be inferred from the fact that $B_i'(e_i)$ are equalized across all firms. Any divergence between B_i' and B_j' creates opportunity for trade and the differential will be arbitraged away. Cost-effectiveness is a characteristic of the outcome shared with taxation.

The model can be complicated to include the firms' choices of output levels. In that case under standard restrictions an increase in P^{TEP} will tend to reduce both the level of output of the representative firm and the emissions-intensity of its choice of technique.

If firms are identical (including receiving identical endowments) then no trade occurs and the tradability of the permits is trivial. But in that case achieving cost-effectiveness is also trivial. The benefits of TEPs – as with other incentive instruments – emerge when firms differ in their compliance costs in ways that the regulator does not observe, or is able to observe but only imperfectly.

Cost-effectiveness can be achieved even with no information regarding compliance costs. It should be noted, though, that we have not up to this point addressed the question of how the regulator should decide how many permits to distribute in the first place. On the cost of compliance side, the information burden is relieved in the sense that the regulator needs only to know the distribution of cost types in the population of firms – for any *given* disbursement of permits it can rely on trade to get those permits into the 'right' hands. At the industry level, though, cost efficiency requires the regulator to set the aggregate number of permits issued such that the resulting equilibrium price equals the corresponding level of marginal damage:

$$P^{TEP} = D'\left(\sum_i e_i^* (P^{TEP}) \right).$$

The equivalence with the Pigovian tax is apparent from this solution. Firm *i*'s emissions in the tax problem are a function of the tax rate in the same way as the demand for permits is a function of the permit price, both reflecting the marginal benefit to the firm of the emission (or the marginal abatement cost saved). Provided the total disbursement can be chosen to make P^{TEP} coincide with the Pigovian tax then the incentives generated by the two regimes will be the same.

The policy problem in setting up a *TEP*-based regime is (a) to determine the optimal aggregate level of permits, and (b) to create a legal environment within which a market for their exchange can operate smoothly and competitively.

None of this analysis presupposes any particular initial *allocation* of permits, and an attraction of this approach is that the efficiency properties of the equilibrium just sketched are (in principle) invariant to how those permits are initially assigned. This is an application of the classic insight of Coase (1960) that in the absence of transactions costs a system of well-specified property rights over any good will ensure an efficient use of that good, regardless of the initial assignment of those rights.

The initial assignment of the permits will have major income distribution effects that may be controversial. In most cases policy-makers have opted for some sort of grandfathering of allocations, issuing to firms according to some formula based on past output. In principle concerns over distributional issues (such as the desire to compensate) can be addressed separately – by appropriate initial endowments or lump-sum compensations – without the need to generate inefficiency in the resource use.

In repeated settings issues also arise as to the intertemporal efficiency of abatement. A number of current TEP regimes (such as the sulphur dioxide permits created under the 1990 Clean Air Act Amendments in the US) allow for banking or borrowing of allowances over time. A source that emits within its allowed limits in period *t* can carry its shortfall – subject to certain rules – into period *t* + 1. A growing academic literature has sought to explore the positive and normative implications of banking and borrowing and to characterize efficient intertemporal trading rules. In general, allowing intertemporal transfer can be expected to enhance the performance of a TEP regime, though often the specification of models is such that optimality could be achieved without intertemporal trading by a sequence of single-period permit markets in which the total number of permits issued each period is optimally chosen (Cronshaw and Kruse, 1996; Rubin, 1996).

The achievement of cost-effectiveness – and, for the correct aggregate assignment of TEPs, cost-efficiency – is predicated on the assumption that we have a 'perfect' market in which those TEPs are exchanged. In real settings such a market may be hard to achieve, or even approximate, and considerable attention has been paid to thinking about the role of imperfections in TEP markets.

The standard textbook analysis of TEPs assumes zero transactions cost – there are no administrative or other frictional costs associated with trading (buying or selling) the permits. This is unrealistic. Atkinson and Tietenberg (1991) outline six empirical analyses that found trading levels in permit markets were lower than theory suggested they should have been. This is strong *prima facie* evidence that there may be costs to trading.

Hahn and Hester (1989) provide an in-depth case study of a water pollutant TEP programme introduced on the Fox River in the United States, that points to substantial transactions costs to trade. Those transactions cost can offset, partially or even completely, the benefits from trade. Stavins (1995) notes that under the programme of criteria for air pollutants operated by the EPA in the US, perhaps the best known trading programme, the market may be thin such that there is no straightforward means for buyers and sellers to identify one another. Buyers often therefore pay significant fees to agents and consultants to search out sellers.

The conclusion that equilibrium permit allocations – and therefore aggregate compliance costs – are independent of initial TEP allocations is not sustained when costs of transactions are taken into account. Stavins (1995) formalizes the impact in a simple model. In essence, such costs mean that less trade happens than otherwise would occur, such that marginal compliance costs are not equalized (except in trivial cases where no trade is required to ensure equalization). The exact mapping depends on the particular relationship between transactions costs and the size of trade.

Understanding that transactions costs matter has implications for the design of TEP-based regimes. A lot of designs are similar in spirit to more generic attempts to make asset markets less frictional. Simple systems that concentrate on things that can be measured reasonably cheaply (such as marketed inputs into production) can be expected to generate lower transactions costs. In implementing TEPs government should encourage thick markets and encourage competitive supply of commercial brokerage services to facilitate trade at minimum costs.

The other main area of concern here is the scope for buyers and/or sellers in the permit market to exercise market power. Once one or more actors in the TEP market ceases to act as a price-taker it is apparent that the welfare properties of the equilibrium are likely to be compromised (Hahn, 1984).

Example 1: Individual transferable quotas (ITQs) in Iceland, New Zealand and Chile
One of the areas in which tradable permits have been widely and productively used is in the context of fisheries regulation.

While not a 'pollution' problem in the conventional sense, fishing is an exploitation of a natural resource. In the absence of well-specified and enforceable ownership rights we would expect over-harvesting of a fish population, so regulation or stock management is targeted at restricting the harvest rate. While local, community-based management has proved effective in many small-scale fisheries, for larger operations it is less likely to work effectively. Early regulatory approaches, based on catch or technology, for example, are being replaced or supplemented by tradable permits to fish, individual transferable quotas (ITQs), in many settings.

Though the principle of ITQs is straightforward, practical application is more complex. Sterner (2003) provides an excellent summary of many applications with an emphasis on the variations in approaches (see for example his Table 28.1).

Iceland has a long history as a fishing nation and implemented the first major ITQ regime in the world in 1979. Its initial locus was herring, but by 1990 it had expanded to cover all commercially fished species. The Ministry of Fisheries sets system-wide total allowable catches (TACs) based on scientific assessment of sustainability, and issues quotas based on that aggregate. The initial distribution of permits has been based on grandfathering (rather than auction), and monitoring is funded by fees based on a percentage of the value of the catch.

The market for tradable permits has been thick. Since 1986, 20–30 per cent of permits have been traded each year, with this figure much higher for some species (96 per cent, for example, in the case of Atlantic pollack). This high rate of trading is consistent with a high variance in the marginal cost of fishing for these species and provides *prima facie* evidence of substantial welfare gains due to the implementation of the ITQ regime.

ITQs have similarly been introduced to cover 32 species of fish and shellfish in the coastal waters of New Zealand, with permits there being granted in perpetuity (in contrast to the annual rights on offer in Iceland). In Chile ten-year ITQs have been issued to cover cod and shrimp, with the Chilean approach distinguished by its use of initial allocation based on an auction rather than historic or other claims.

Example 2: The US lead trading programme (1982–1987) and Title IV of the Clean Air Act Amendments (1990)

The elimination of lead from gasoline in the United States in the 1980s was done very effectively, with dramatic improvements in ambient lead concentrations throughout the country.[3]

To reduce the cost burden of the lead reduction, a lead trading programme was introduced in 1982. This provided flexibility to refiners to produce gasoline with a higher or lower lead content than that prescribed by the national standard, but allowed those producing with lower-than-standard content to claim credits. These could be sold to other producers refining at higher-than-standard, or banked for later use. The national standard provided a *de facto* allowance around which tradable credits or debits were accumulated.

About 15 per cent of the tradable permits earned were traded, and the US Environmental Protection Agency estimated that the mechanism of trading reduced the overall cost of the lead reduction achieved by 20 per cent.

Title IV of the Clean Air Act Amendments (1990) established the US Acid Rain Program, calling for a substantial reduction of SO_2 emissions between 1990 and 2000. The design of the trading system has been widely analysed and written about (see, for example, Stavins, 2000). In broad terms firms are able to achieve reductions in emissions above those legally required, and sell the resultant credits to other firms. 'A robust market of bilateral SO_2 trading has emerged, resulting in cost savings ... on the order of $1 bn annually compared with the costs under command-and-control regulatory alternatives' (Stavins, 2000, pp. 39–40).

'New' approaches: voluntary agreements, corporate social responsibility and information as an instrument

Necessarily in a brief overview of the sort that a chapter such as this can provide, we arrive at a point where we have covered – albeit at some speed – the most important parts of regulation in the past.

Over the past decade or so a number of new instruments or quasi-instruments have emerged as potentially influential contributors to environmental management control going forward. These can be classified around the theme of social responsibility or self-regulation.

Since about 1990 the term 'voluntary agreement' or VA has come in to the common parlance of regulatory economists. By 2000 in the US, for example, the Environmental Protection Agency estimated that upward of 13,000 firms were party to one of the Agency's voluntary initiatives.

There is no well-cast definition of a VA. To regard a VA as an *instrument* implies a level of abatement beyond what would be achieved purely voluntarily, and agreement implies something other than a unilateral decision by the polluter (Sterner, 2003). The term is generally used to refer to a sort of negotiated contract between regulators and polluting firms. A firm agrees to go beyond legal requirements in exchange for an enhanced relationship with the regulator, positive publicity, or some other favour or regulatory forbearance. In effect, the problem of regulation becomes one of procurement – disbursement of favours of one sort or another in order to buy enhanced performance.

In Segerson and Miceli (1996) firms agree to 'voluntary' emissions cuts under the threat of (more costly) regulatory intervention in the event that such voluntary cuts are not forthcoming. In Heyes and Rickman (1999) a firm overcomplies in one area in which it deals with the regulatory agency, in exchange for the agency turning a 'blind eye' to its non-compliance elsewhere. In Boyd et al. (1999) a company is willing to make significant investments in abatement in exchange for fast-track treatment of its application for regulatory approval.

For many years scholars and policy-makers have been interested in the extent to which 'corporate social responsibility' (CSR) can drive pro-social behaviour. A review of stakeholder theory and its implications for environmental policy is well beyond the scope of this chapter.

Broadly speaking, economists have tended to accept and embrace only instrumental motives for CSR – that is CSR behaviour driven by corporate self-interest. There is extensive and compelling evidence that the environmental and financial performance of firms is positively correlated. Consumers may be willing to pay a premium to buy a 'green' product, employees may have higher moral codes and be more productive when working for a green organization (Brekke et al., 2004), a subset of firms may favour tougher environmental regulations that confer a comparative advantage on themselves over rivals (Salop and Scheffman, 1983), or voluntary achievement of improved standards may pre-empt stricter mandatory standards (Maxwell et al., 2000).

The CSR trend has coexisted with an increasing recognition that firms can be punished by the 'communities' in which they exist. Community here can mean those who are geographically close, industry peers, the community of investors, or others. Pargal and Wheeler (1996) provide empirical evidence that local communities in a developing country setting are able to encourage local polluters into improved treatment of the environment. There is also a substantial body of event study evidence that points to the fact that infringement of environmental regulations or poor environmental performance can hurt firms (for examples Khanna et al., 1998; Badrinath and Bolster, 1996).[4]

In the past two decades we have witnessed an explosion in green marketing – whereby firms disburse information about their own performance. Large corporations now routinely publish annual reports on their social and environmental performance – akin to their financial reports – in a way that would have been unheard of 20 years ago.

All of this points to an important function that a regulatory agency might play as a collator and disseminator of information regarding the environmental performance of firms. It also points to the potential role labels – whether governmentally or privately run – might play in providing the information that consumers and others will need to exercise their own preferences for responsible treatment of environmental resources.

Example 1: VAs in the US – '33/50' and 'Responsible Care' Programs
The 33/50 Program established by the USEPA in 1991 captures the flavour of many VA initiatives. The EPA wrote to about 5000 companies asking them to consider voluntary reductions in their emissions and transfers of a list of 17 toxic

substances, in particular to achieve a reduction of 33 per cent by the end of 1992 and 50 per cent by the end of 1995. Around 750 companies subscribed.

Arora and Cason (1995) provided a careful empirical exploration of the impact of the 33/50 scheme. There were indeed marked reductions in releases of the listed substances that were subject of the scheme. Other changes in policy and business environment were changing around the same time. *Toxic Release Inventory* (TRI) data were published from 1988, for example, and there is evidence that some firms were shamed by the figures into improved performance. The authors could find only weak evidence of any independent impact of 33/50.

The *Responsible Care Program* initiated by the Chemical Manufacturers Association in 1988 is probably the highest-profile industry-initiated programme. Firms that participate adopt six codes of conduct intended to promote environmental performance.

Example 2: Eco-labelling – the Nordic Swan, German Blue Angel and Dolphin Protection in the USA

The German Blue Angel (1977) was the first national eco-labelling scheme. The *Blue Angel* is a governmental programme, though NGOs assist in its operation. It applies life cycle analysis to some 4500 products in 77 different product categories.

The *Nordic Swan*, established by the Nordic Council of Ministers in 1989, is a widely accepted and understood product label in Scandinavia, appearing on a high proportion of products of certain types sold there (about 65 per cent of laundry detergents, 50 to 70 per cent of other cleaning products).

In contrast the *Green Seal* scheme in the United States is entirely privately operated, as is *Environmental Choice* in Canada.

Since these pioneer labelling initiatives, a host of others have appeared, some government operated but many run or endorsed by environmental NGOs. Karl and Orwat (2000) is an excellent source of institutional detail, while Heyes and Maxwell (2004) provide some theoretical analysis of the comparative incentives effects of government versus private run programmes.

Although implementation of eco-labels is widespread, there has been comparatively little systematic research on their impacts and effectiveness. One of the best available case studies is that by Teisl et al. (2002) on the labelling of dolphin-friendly tuna. Canned tuna is the most important seafood product in the United States in terms of quantity consumed. Much of the tuna comes from the Eastern Tropical Pacific where, traditionally, fishing methods have inflicted a high number of incidental deaths on dolphins. Prior to 1972, the number of dolphins being killed in this way was estimated to be around 100,000 per year by the US fleet, and in the 1970s dolphin populations were endangered. Media attention on the issue was particularly intensive in the 1980s and there were calls for consumer boycotts of the yellowfin tuna. The three largest tuna canners in the US announced a dolphin-safe labelling policy in 1990. The government in the US followed this up with the 1990 *Dolphin Protection Consumer Information Act* (DPCIA), which defined 'dolphin-friendly' and how it should be verified. Teisl et al. provide detailed empirical evidence that US consumers responded substantially to the labels, and that the market share of canned tuna increased because of the labelling initiative.

Conclusions

The regulation of the environmental behaviours of individuals and organizations is an evolving craft.

While approaches to policy vary across countries, across environmental issues, and through time, it is possible to detect broad phases. The early years of policy activism in this field were dominated by prescriptive command-and-control methods, combined with legal approaches. Since the early 1980s, as policy imperatives have tightened and the burden on industry of compliance costs has risen, there has been a steady rise in interest in and implementation of the variously called economic, market-based or incentive instruments – primarily green taxes and tradable permits. Current thinking is now pushing towards what have been referred to as 'third wave' instruments such as labelling schemes, mandating green corporate accounts, and community right-to-know legislation. These involve giving information to private agents and empowering them to discipline producers – through their interactions in product markets, investment markets, and so on – to induce responsible behaviour.

Through time experience is accumulated and policy agencies are able to design and operate instruments in more refined ways. There is also increasing recognition that there is no single 'best way' to do things, and that 'smart' regulation will likely involve the application of several instruments at once. The way in which sticks and carrots can best be combined and managed to deliver the desired environmental outcomes at minimal economic cost remains a potent academic and policy challenge.

Notes

1. We are grateful to Peth Tuppe and the editors for helpful comments on this chapter.
2. While enjoying a renaissance, charging for use of roads is not, of course, a new idea – road tolls were a common feature of life in most European countries in the sixteenth and seventeenth centuries, with most of the money raised being used to fund the construction or maintenance of the road.
3. Average ambient lead concentrations in the US fell by 87 per cent between 1980 and 1989 (Gilpin, 2000).
4. An event study uses stock market data to investigate the impact of some event on the capitalized value of the firm.

References

Arora, S. and Cason, T. (1995) 'An Experiment in Voluntary Environmental Regulation: Participation in EPA's 33/50 Program', *Journal of Environmental Economics and Management*, **28** (3), 271–86.

Atkinson, S. and Tietenberg, T. (1991) 'Market Failure in Incentive-based Regulation: The Case of Emissions Trading', *Journal of Environmental Economics and Management*, **9** (1), 101–21.

Badrinath, S.G. and Bolster, P. (1996) 'The Role of Market Forces in EPA Enforcement', *Journal of Regulatory Economics*, **10** (2), 165–81.

Bluffstone, R. (1999) 'Do Pollution Charges Reduce Pollution in Lithuania?', in T. Sterner (ed.), *The Market and the Environment*, Cheltenham, UK and Northampton, MA, USA: Edward Elgar.

Bluffstone, R. and Larson, B.A. (1997) *Controlling Pollution in Transition Economies*, Cheltenham, UK and Lyme, USA: Edward Elgar.

Bovenberg, A.L. and Goulder, L.H. (1996), 'Optimal Environmental Taxation in the Presence of Other Taxes: General Equilibrium Analysis', *American Economic Review*, **86** (4), 985–1000.

Bovenberg, A.L. and Goulder, L.H. (2001) 'Environmental Regulation and Taxation in a Second-best Setting', in A. Auerbach and M. Feldstein (eds), *Handbook of Public Economics*, 2nd edn, Amsterdam: North-Holland.

Boyd, Mazurek J., Krupnick, Alan and Blackman, Allen (1999) 'The Competitive Implications of Facility-Specific Environmental Agreements: The Intel Corporation and Project XL', in E. Petrakis, E. Sartzetakis and A. Xepapadeas (eds), *Environmental Regulation and Market Power*, Chelternham, UK and Northampton, MA, USA: Edward Elgar, pp. 96–115.

Brekke, B., Arne, K. and Nyborg, K. (2004) 'Moral Hazard and Moral Motivation: Corporate Social Responsibility as Labor Market Screening', Memorandum 25/2004, Frisch Centre, University of Oslo.

Coase, R.H. (1960) 'The Problem of Social Cost', *Journal of Law and Economics*, **3**, 1–44.

Crocker, T.D. (1966) 'The Structuring of Atmospheric Pollution Control Systems', in H. Wolozin (ed.), *The Economics of Air Pollution*, New York: W.W. Norton.

Cronshaw, M. and Kruse, J. (1996) 'Regulated Firms in Pollution Permit Markets with Banking', *Journal of Regulatory Economics*, **9** (2), 179–89.

Dales, J.H. (1968) 'Land, Water and Ownership', *Canadian Journal of Economics*, **1** (4), 791–804.

Dewees, D. (1992) 'The Role of Tort Law in Controlling Environmental Pollution', *Canadian Public Policy*, **18** (4), 57–138.

Downing, P.B. and White, L.J. (1986) 'Innovation in Pollution Control', *Journal of Environmental Economics and Management*, **13**, 18–27.

Gilpin, A. (2000) *Environmental Economics: A Critical Overview*, Chichester: John Wiley & Son.

Hahn, R.W. (1984) 'Market Power and Transferable Property Rights', *Quarterly Journal of Economics*, **99** (4), 753–65.

Hahn, R.W. and Hester, G.L. (1989) 'Marketable Permits: Lessons for Theory and Practice', *Ecology Law Quarterly*, **16**, 361–406.

Hardin, G. (1968), 'The Tragedy of the Commons', *Science*, **162**, 1243–8.

Heyes, A.G. and Rickman, N. (1999) 'A Theory of Regulatory Dealing', *Journal of Public Economics*, **72** (3), 362–78.

Heyes, A.G. and Maxwell, J.W. (2004) 'Public versus Private Regulation', *Journal of Environmental Economics & Management*, **48** (2), 978–96.

Jorgenson, D.W. and Wilcoxen, P.J. (1990) 'Intertemporal General Equilibrium Modeling of US Environmental Regulation', *Journal of Policy Modeling*, **12**, 715–44.

Karl H. and Orwat, C. (2000) 'Economic Aspects of Environmental Labelling', in H. Folmer and T.H. Tietenberg (eds), *The International Yearbook of Environmental and Resource Economics 1999/2000*, Cheltenham, UK and Northampton, MA, USA: Edward Elgar.

Khanna, M., Rose, W.R., Quimio, H. and Bojilova, D. (1998) 'Toxic Release Information: A Policy Tool for Environmental Protection', *Journal of Environmental Economics & Management*, **36** (2), 243–66.

Maxwell J., Lyon, T.P. and Hackett, S. (2000) 'Self-regulation and Social Welfare: The Political Economy of Corporate Environmentalism', *Journal of Law and Economics*, **43** (2), 583–617.

Montgomery, W.D. (1972) 'Markets in Licenses and Efficient Pollution Control', *Journal of Economic Theory*, **5**, 395–418.

Ostrom, E. (1990) *Governing the Commons: The Evolution of Institutions for Collective Action*, Cambridge: Cambridge University Press.

Ostrom, E. and Gardner, R. (1993) 'Coping with Asymmetries in the Commons: Self-governing Irrigation Systems Can Work', *Journal of Economic Perspectives*, **7** (4), 93–112.

Pargal, S. and Wheeler, D. (1996) 'Informal Regulation of Industrial Pollution in Developing Countries: Evidence from Indonesia', *Journal of Political Economy*, **104** (6), 1314–27.

Pigou, A.C. (1938) *The Economics of Welfare*, 4th edn, London: Macmillan.

Rubin, J. (1996) 'A Model of Intertemporal Emissions Trading, Banking and Borrowing', *Journal of Environmental Economics and Management*, **31**, 269–86.

Salop, S. and Scheffman, D. (1983) 'Rising Rivals' Costs', *American Economic Review*, **73** (2), 267–71.

Segerson, K. (1995) 'Liabilities and Penalties in Policy Design', in D.W. Bromley (ed.), *The Handbook of Environmental Economics*, Oxford: Blackwell.

Segerson, K. and Miceli, T.J. (1996) 'Voluntary Environmental Agreements: Good or Bad News for Environmental Policy', *Journal of Environmental Economics & Management*, **36** (2), 109–30.

Sethi, R. and Somanathan, E. (1996) 'The Evolution of Social Norms in Common Property Resource Use', *American Economic Review*, **86** (4), 766–88.

Shavell, S. (1986) 'The Judgement Proofness Problem', *International Review of Law and Economics*, **6** (1), 45–58.

Stavins, R.N. (1995) 'Transactions Costs and Tradeable Permits', *Journal of Environmental Economics and Management*, **29**, 133–48.

Stavins, R.N. (2000) 'Market-based Environmental Policies', in P. Portney and R.N. Stavins (eds), *Public Policies for Environmental Protection*, 2nd edn, Washington, DC: Resources for the Future Press.

Sterner, T. (2003) *Policy Instruments for Environmental and Natural Resource Management*, Washington, DC: RFF Press.

Teisl, M.F., Roe, A. and Hicks, R.L. (2002) 'Can Eco-labels Tune a Market? Evidence from Dolphin-safe Labeling', *Journal of Environmental Economics & Management*, **43** (3), 339–59.

Weitzman, M. (1974) 'Prices *vs.* Quantities', *Review of Economic Studies*, **41**, 683–91.

13 The economics of access and interconnection charges in telecommunications

Timothy J. Tardiff

Introduction

In telecommunications and other industries, certain providers must rely on other firms when delivering products and services to their customers. While this situation is not new, the nature of such dependencies (or interdependencies), as well as the economic analysis that suggests how such arrangements should be priced, are becoming increasingly complex as technologies advance and formerly separate markets converge. The following examples of interconnection and access arrangements from the telecommunications industry – the empirical focus of this chapter – illustrate the myriad ways in which firms and regulators have addressed the need for firms to exchange certain critical inputs and set prices for such facilities, services and transactions: (1) two adjacent, non-competing, telephone networks establish facilities so that subscribers on one network can call the subscribers on the other; (2) long-distance carriers obtain access to the facilities of a local service provider and compete against that provider in providing long-distance services to a common customer base; (3) traditional wireline telephone and new wireless (mobile) carriers establish interconnection arrangements so that subscribers of a traditional phone service can call wireless subscribers, and vice versa; (4) new competitive local telephone carriers obtain certain network elements from the incumbent carrier and at the same time establish interconnection arrangements, so that they can both capture subscribers in the common service territory and allow their subscribers to call subscribers that remain on the incumbent's network; (5) customers of the incumbent telephone carrier make telephone calls to their dial-up Internet Service Provider, which in turn is a customer of a competing local carrier; and (6) firms offering a service in which part of the call is routed by Voice over Internet Protocol (VoIP) interconnect with traditional local service providers to complete the call.

The numerous and complex situations where interconnection and access arrangements occur are accompanied by (1) comparably complex real-world terms and prices, often established by regulation, (2) a large number of stated or proposed objectives for pricing access and interconnection, and (3) a growing economic literature with the common purpose of how to establish efficient

278

access and interconnection prices, albeit with differing conclusions that depend on the specific aspects of the overall problem that are addressed as well as the particular assumptions employed to describe how consumers and firms respond to such prices. In addition, real-world pricing takes place in a rapidly changing technological and competitive environment. As a consequence, as Armstrong (2002, p. 381) observed in concluding his comprehensive treatment of the economics of access pricing, it is difficult for economic theory to keep up with the problems it is designed to solve:

> An important next step in the theoretical research in this area is, I believe, to provide a proper analysis of the *dynamics* of access pricing, focusing on the need to provide long-run, stable incentives for the incumbent (and other firms) to invest efficiently in infrastructure and innovation.

Similarly, once access and interconnection prices have been established, outcomes may well differ considerably from what was expected, because existing and new competitors may respond in ways that were unanticipated by either contemporary theory or practice.

For example, in the early days of local telephone competition in the United States, a common belief was that new entrants would tend to serve customers such as large businesses that originated more calls than they received, suggesting, in turn, that incumbent carriers would terminate a disproportionate number of calls from competitors' networks. Accordingly, incumbents tended to favour relatively high interconnection charges, while entrants typically advocated low (or even zero – 'bill and keep') charges.[1] In fact, certain entrants attracted customers that received many more calls than they made (i.e. Internet Services Providers) and the resulting payments of interconnection charges to these competitors came to be viewed as a serious problem, particularly by the incumbents. Of course, industry participants and regulators do respond to such problems, but there is a real question of whether they can react early or rapidly enough in light of the pace of change in the industry.

The remainder of this chapter is organized as follows. The second section defines the two major categories of interconnection arrangements – one-way and two-way – and the economic and public policy objectives access and interconnection prices are intended to satisfy. The following two sections describe the findings from the economic literature and outline practical policy issues for one-way and two-way interconnection prices, respectively. The final two sections of the chapter describe the historical trends and future directions in US access and interconnection pricing and summarize the conclusions and implications for other industries.

Access and interconnection: definitions and objectives

Types of interconnection and access

Previous analyses of access and interconnection pricing have distinguished between cases in which providers must obtain inputs from another provider in order to offer service to their customers (*one-way interconnection*) and situations in which two or more carriers must connect their facilities (or networks) so that customers of one carrier can call customers served by other carriers and vice versa (*two-way interconnection*).[2] One-way interconnection situations include those in which the firm supplying the inputs does not compete with the purchasers of the inputs; for example, in the first several years after the divestiture of AT&T in the United States, long-distance carriers such as AT&T, MCI and Sprint obtained access from local exchange carriers that were legally prohibited from offering ubiquitous long-distance services. However, in most of the rest of the world, as well as in the United States in recent years, the providers of access also offer long-distance services in direct competition with the carriers that purchase access services. These arrangements are examples of vertical integration[3] and, as we discuss in detail below, the focus is often on whether the combination of access prices (the upstream input used by competitors) and the access provider's long-distance prices (the downstream service that is subject to competition) permits the most efficient downstream provider to compete successfully.

Similarly, two-way interconnection can involve situations in which there is (1) no competition between the carriers exchanging traffic (e.g. international long-distance, or calling between customers of two adjacent local exchange networks); (2) competition between carriers offering services that are close substitutes (e.g. competition among carriers serving the same territory); as well as (3) arrangements between carriers offering services that may not be close substitutes, such as the exchange of calls between traditional wireline and wireless networks.[4] The relationship between interconnecting firms is sometimes described as a vertical one in that a call between customers served by different carriers requires 'inputs' from both carriers. However, unlike the one-way interconnection case, the carriers do not fit neatly into an upstream input provider and a downstream competitor. Further, the fact that interconnection arrangements can involve payments between carriers in both directions creates interesting theoretical and practical problems not encountered in one-way interconnection.[5]

Finally, one-way and two-way arrangements can co-exist – in particular, when new entrants obtain parts of their networks from incumbent providers and then exchange traffic with the incumbent. In this case, the elements obtained from the incumbent, such as the telephone wires between customers and switching facilities, are upstream inputs in the standard vertical integration sense, while there is no obvious upstream–downstream designation for the two-way intercarrier payments.

Access and interconnection pricing objectives[6]

Economic theory and regulatory practice have ascribed several, not necessarily compatible, objectives for access and interconnection prices. Such prices should promote *economic efficiency*. Efficiency consideration include: (1) *allocative efficiency*; consumers of final products should pay prices that reflect the economic cost of the resources consumed in providing the products or services (e.g. the calls to other customers) and at the same time, they should not be discouraged from consumption when the value exceeds the production cost; (2) *productive efficiency*; in competitive situations the most efficient provider should not be precluded from serving customers; and (3) *dynamic efficiency*; all firms, both entrants and incumbents, should have proper incentives to invest in technologies that lower cost and/or expand product offerings.

In addition to the economic efficiency objectives, public policy in certain countries has enunciated objectives of promoting competition and universal service.[7] While from an economic perspective there is no conflict between promoting competition and proper consideration of the various manifestations of economic efficiency, public policy at times has attempted to 'jump start' such competition and shape its form, through policies that resemble 'infant industry' protection in other contexts.[8] Similarly, there is a long regulatory history in which charges for basic services (e.g. the monthly charge for a basic residential telephone service) have been maintained at below-cost levels in some situations in order to encourage widespread subscribership. Also, recently, interconnection charges in the form of payments to wireless carriers for call terminations have been set at high levels in some countries, so that charges to wireless subscribers could be kept low in order to facilitate rapid expansion of wireless demand. In both the traditional wireline universal service policy and the newer wireless termination charge policies, expansion of subscribership is considered to capture an externality benefit that makes the service increasingly more valuable to all subscribers as the total number of subscribers increases.[9]

One-way access and interconnection

Much of the initial theoretical and practical work on access and interconnection has focused on the one-way situation (Laffont and Tirole, 2000, p. 179); that is, where an incumbent firm offers 'upstream' inputs to other firms that offer services in 'downstream' markets.[10] This literature has primarily addressed the issue of how access prices should be set and secondarily, what are the competitive consequences resulting from access charges that depart from the marginal cost of providing the service in question. For both issues, the efficient component pricing rule (ECPR),[11] explained below, has served as a prominent reference point.

Public policy objectives in establishing access prices

The analysis of the proper level for access prices has produced numerous objectives that these prices are intended to satisfy.[12] First, whether or not the incumbent provider of the upstream input participates in downstream markets, the access price should provide downstream firms the proper incentive to acquire that input from the incumbent when it is least costly to do so. For example, in the early period of long-distance competition in the United States, the per-minute usage charges for accessing local exchange carriers' customers were more than ten times higher (in nominal terms) than current charges. Consequently, there was considerable concern that long-distance carriers would find other ways to 'bypass' the local exchange carriers in reaching customers and, as a result, local exchange carriers would suffer substantial revenue losses. The systematic and steady reduction of access charges from the initial levels was explicitly designed to mitigate the bypass threat.

Second, when the incumbent access provider also competes against entrants in downstream markets, the access price should be set so that (1) the most efficient downstream provider has a legitimate opportunity to win the business and (2) downstream customers are provided the proper price signals to consume the services efficiently.

Finally, the theoretical literature routinely produces the result that access prices can be set to offset imperfections in retail price levels. For example, if public policy requires the price of a basic local service to be uniform, regardless of any cost differences in providing that service (and there is no other way to rectify distortions caused by the departure from cost-based prices), then the efficient access price would be correspondingly higher when retail prices are above cost and correspondingly lower for below-cost retail prices. Similarly, when competition is less than perfect in downstream markets, that is, when downstream prices would exceed marginal cost[13] if access were priced at its marginal cost, then 'second best' access prices would be set below cost in order to offset market-power in the downstream market.

Summary of previous findings

In this subsection, we review the findings on (1) the efficient level for access prices[14] and (2) the competitive consequences of setting access prices at particular levels. To set the stage, it is useful to describe the ECPR, which facilitates the discussion of both issues.

The ECPR establishes a relationship among (1) the price the incumbent charges for the downstream service, (2) the efficient price for access, and (3) the marginal costs the incumbent incurs to produce the access and downstream services. In particular,

$$p_a = mc_a + (p_r - mc_r).$$

In words, the ECPR establishes the access price (p_a) as the sum of the marginal cost (mc_a) and the profit (or contribution to the firm's shared and common costs) – price less marginal cost – contained in the incumbent's downstream service ($p_r - mc_r$).[15] For example, if the incumbent's price for its retail service were 5 cents and the marginal cost for supplying that service were 2 cents, then the retail margin between price and cost would be 3 cents (5 – 2). The ECPR specifies that this margin be added to the marginal cost of supplying access to competitors. Therefore, if the marginal cost of access were 1 cent, the ECPR would produce an access price of 4 cents (1 + 3).

The rationale for ECPR being an efficient price is that if the downstream market is competitive *and* only the incumbent produces the upstream input, that is, it is an essential facility, then (1) the incumbent firm should be indifferent between producing the downstream service and providing access to a competitor, which in turn supplies that service instead of the incumbent; and (2) the firm with the lowest combination of access and downstream costs will serve the market, thus achieving productive efficiency in that market.

As Laffont and Tirole (2000, p. 122) and Armstrong (2002, p. 336) explain, ECPR provides efficient (welfare maximizing) prices in special circumstances, in particular when (1) entrants have no market power in providing the downstream service, (2) the cost of providing access to the incumbent and its competitors is the same, (3) the incumbent and entrants have the same costs in the downstream market, and (4) the incumbent and competitors face symmetrical demand conditions in the downstream market. When these four conditions are not met, the determination of the efficient access price becomes more complex. In particular, the deviation of the access price from its marginal cost is determined by a Ramsey-like inverse elasticity rule, where the elasticities in question include the own and cross-price elasticities of the incumbent and entrants in the downstream market (Laffont and Tirole, 2000, pp. 102–4). It is also the case that certain specific demand curves bring cost differences into play. For example, when the incumbent and an entrant face symmetric linear demand curves, the efficient access price would exceed ECPR when the entrant has lower costs, and be lower than ECPR when the incumbent is more efficient.[16] For purposes of practical implementation of access prices, the importance of these generalizations of the ECPR is the amount of information necessary to determine such prices, which we will discuss in the next subsection.

Finally, the effects of access prices on downstream competition are noteworthy. Weisman (2003) summarizes the literature in this area and presents the major findings from that literature and his own research. Interestingly, the competitive consequences depend on whether firms compete on the basis of price (Bertrand competition) or quantity (Cournot competition). With regard to Bertrand competition, Weisman reports that when a regulator sets the access price according to the ECPR, the incumbent has no incentive either to discriminate against its rivals (in particular anti-competitively increase their costs) or to engage in a price squeeze – that is, set a downstream price that includes a smaller mark-up than that which is contained in the access charge established by the regulator. However, when the access price is set higher than the ECPR, the unequal margin conditions reflective of a price squeeze are present. When the access price is set at a level less than the ECPR, the incentive to engage in non-price discrimination or sabotage (i.e. raising a rival's costs) is present.

The Cournot competition findings are somewhat different. In particular, when the incumbent is at least as efficient as the entrant in the downstream market, Weisman found that it has incentives to raise its rival's costs. However, if the entrant is sufficiently more efficient than the incumbent, the incentive to discriminate disappears. Evidently, in this case, the incumbent's profit-maximizing choice is to 'buy' the downstream functionality from its rival, rather than 'make' it by deploying its own network.

Weisman's Cournot competition findings are similar to those reported by Weisman and Kang (2001). Based on a model in which the incumbent's profits can be affected by discriminating against rivals (by raising their costs) and by the extent of the regulator's ability to detect such discrimination, the authors also find that incentives to discriminate are lower when the rivals are more efficient than the incumbent. Other factors that reduce incentives to discriminate include a high market elasticity for the downstream product and/or more competing firms (both of which tend to lower the downstream price and thus make discrimination less profitable), greater ability of the regulator to detect discrimination, and higher access charges (because successful discrimination results in lower profits from supplying access to rivals).

Practical implementation of one-way access prices
The discussion in the previous section illustrates that when access prices are the only policy instrument to facilitate efficient competition, meet other objectives such as universal service (Baumol, 1999), and provide for recovery of the incumbent's fixed shared and common costs,[17] not only are they carrying a heavy policy load, but the information required to determine efficient price levels can also be quite demanding. For this reason, to the extent that there are other politically acceptable means to meet some of these objectives, the determination of efficient access charges would become easier. For example, the need for above-cost access charges would decrease to the extent that universal service is ensured through a combination of rebalanced rates and targeted subsidies and/or through mechanisms such as broad-based revenue taxes (or surcharges).[18]

In the most general case, establishing efficient access rates involves the following information. First, to the extent that competition for downstream services is at issue, it is necessary to define the markets for those services and determine the prices and price structures that prevail. While the theoretical literature often posits fairly simple services, such as a single toll service with a uniform per-minute price, in the real-world downstream offerings are becoming considerably more complex, for example packages of services that combine local, long-distance, advanced features, and even wireless. In these circumstances, determining prices, costs, and forgone profit (as defined by ECPR) becomes increasingly difficult.

Second, except in the case of perfect competition (or contestability), determination of the efficient access price requires information on the demand elasticities of incumbent and competing carriers. Further, such information is likely to become increasingly difficult to obtain, as well as subject to change, as carriers enter, exit, and expand their product offerings through the introduction of increasingly complex packages of services.

Third, determining the efficient interconnection price, at a minimum, requires information about the incumbent's cost for access and possibly a downstream service. While regulators rely on estimates of these costs in many situations, such estimation nonetheless can be highly controversial. Telecommunications networks tend to deploy capital-intensive equipment, which at the same time has a long (but uncertain) economic life, is subject to relatively rapid technological progress, and where the demand for the wholesale and retail services provided by the network is highly uncertain.[19] When cost information on one or more competitors is required, the information requirements are even more demanding. These competitors may well have different network configurations, deploy different technologies, and otherwise create costing information requirements well beyond what regulators typically have access to in currently available cost analyses.

Fourth, the definition of market power in the downstream market (and the use of lower, perhaps even below-cost access prices to offset it) is quite narrow: any price that exceeds its marginal cost indicates some degree of market power.[20] However, being network-based firms in their own right, downstream competitors will very likely have their own fixed shared and common costs, which are often reflected in the prices that unregulated firms charge. In these circumstances, tasking access prices with offsetting a 'problem' that is pervasive in unregulated markets may be ill-advised.

Finally, the fundamental premise that access services (or particular unbundled elements) are essential facilities is becoming increasingly less descriptive of the industry.[21] For example, even with respect to the quintessential example of long-distance services, the advent of VoIP has allowed certain carriers to compete without using traditional carrier access services. Such developments not only provide additional impetus to access charge and intercarrier compensation reform proposals (which we discuss later in this chapter), but ultimately call into question the premise that one-way access should be set by regulators, rather than in the market.[22]

Two-way interconnection

Two-way interconnection is becoming increasingly prominent in both the economic literature and in practice. The growing number of examples where it has or may occur is accompanied by increasing complexity in models used to analyse efficient prices and supplier behaviour. Not surprisingly, conclusions drawn from these models can differ, depending on the particular aspects of the complex interconnection problem that are emphasized and the specific assumptions about the interconnecting firms that are maintained. As DeGraba (2002a, p. 62) cogently observed:

> More generally, determining appropriate interconnection rates is an empirical matter. The interconnection charge regime will affect a vast number of decisions, including usage levels by customers, subscription levels of customers, regulatory arbitrage, and decisions made by regulators. An appropriate policy must balance the costs and benefits among all of these decisions.

Two-way interconnection framework

At the most general level, two-way interconnection deals with the situation in which two customers jointly consume a service (e.g. a telephone call), which may be provided by more than one firm. In addressing questions such as (1) how to establish an optimal interconnection charge (in the economic literature, this charge is usually represented as a usage-based, e.g. per minute charge, paid by the provider whose customer originates a call to the provider of the receiving party), (2) how firms will establish retail prices for their services (and possibly compete for customers) once the interconnection charges have been set, and (3) whether acceptable interconnection charges can result from market forces and/or negotiation among interconnecting firms, numerous factors come into play. Further, these factors can vary in ways that suggest different optimal interconnection rates (e.g. equal to cost, above cost, or zero 'bill and keep'), and/or different reactions by firms (e.g. acceptable versus anticompetitive negotiated interconnection rates) in different interconnection situations. In addition, while certain optimal outcomes are sometimes easy to state, for example that the sum of the prices charged to the originator and receiver of a call should equal the total cost of producing the call, the way in which interconnection charges facilitate (or hinder) this outcome again can depend on the particulars of the relationships among firms and their customers, as well as the particular modelling assumptions used to represent them.[23]

Turning first to the customers, important considerations include (1) the quantity of calls *made* and how that calling level responds to a retail price, (2) the quantity of calls *received* and how that calling level responds to a retail price, (3) whether customers make more calls than they receive, receive more than they make, or experience an approximate balance, (4) how customers choose among competing networks in response to the retail prices offered by available providers, (5) how customer choose among different retail calling plans that may be offered by networks that attract heterogeneous customers, and (6) whether or not certain customers subscribe to any service at all, given the retail pricing options offered by competing carriers.

With regard to firms, issues that might be considered include (1) whether and to what extent the firms compete; for example, are the calls offered by the interconnecting firms close substitutes, (2) how do these firms price their services to their customers, (3) whether there are explicit interconnection payments between firms,[24] and (4) what the firm's cost structure is and whether it differs from the cost structure of other interconnecting firms.

On the customer (or demand) side, some of the differences in actual conditions, which may or may not be reflected in a particular model, include whether the party that originates a call receives the same benefit as the recipient, which in principle can differ with the nature of the call. Similarly, while in some situations the number of originating and terminating calls could be fairly balanced (e.g. between networks that attracted similar mixes of customers), in other situations it clearly will not be (e.g. calls from an incumbent's network to an entrant that has attracted Internet Service Providers (ISPs) as customers and/or from a wireline to wireless network will be disproportionately in one direction). So while subscription to a particular network (or type of network) may be nearly ubiquitous (e.g. traditional telephone service in North America) for newer technologies, such as wireless in its early years, new customers can be attracted by favourable retail prices.

Perhaps the greatest complexity in describing interconnecting firms, as well as the largest discrepancy between typical models and reality, is in the price and cost structures. While the models typically represent calls as having a simple price structure based on a usage charge, real firms are offering increasingly complex packages of services with pricing plans that may be far removed from particular calls within or across networks. For example, in recent years, US residential customers have been offered a growing variety of plans, some of which offer unlimited local and long-distance calling for a fixed monthly rate. On the cost side, not only might the cost structures of interconnecting carriers differ, but it is also far from clear that each increment of usage has an equal marginal cost. For example, certain components of the switching equipment used in providing calls within and between networks do not vary with calling volumes and the other components are usually sensitive to usage only in peak periods, yet typical models (as well as traditional usage tariffs) assume there is a cost for each minute.[25] These developments raise the question of how properly to define the units of output that are the source of the consumer benefits and the concomitant marginal costs.

Finally, while the differences in the particulars of an interconnection arrangement may imply different interconnection charges in theory, such as cost-based charges in the case of one pair of firms but above cost in another, some regulators (e.g. in the US) have stated a clear preference for uniform charges. At least with respect to incumbent networks, because interconnection arrangements typically do not differ with the nature of the other interconnecting networks (e.g. similar facilities are used to interconnect both competing local carriers and traditional long-distance carriers to an incumbent's network), any variations in interconnection charges produced by theoretical models would reflect factors such as cost differences between the incumbent and interconnecting networks, differences in the vigour with which they competed with the incumbent, and differences in the type of customers they served. Not only would detecting such differences pose challenging information requirements, maintaining interconnection charge differentials could be a significant enforcement problem.

Implications and findings from the economic literature
As was the case for one-way interconnection, the theoretical literature suggests that interconnection charges may be called on to serve multiple objectives. First, because each interconnecting network enjoys some degree of market power – it is typically the only connection, hence a bottleneck, between a firm's customers and customers of other networks – there is some concern that carriers could exploit this market power if they set their own interconnection charges.[26] Second, as in the case of one-way interconnection charges, the literature suggests that two-way charges be lowered to offset less than perfect competition in retail markets. Third, in models that explicitly consider a call as jointly consumed between sender and receiver, the interconnection charge has been viewed as a mechanism to induce retail prices that reflect the relative benefits that each party receives. Similarly, in the case in which (1) callers to one network benefit from calling subscribers of the other, and (2) attractive prices would encourage more subscribers to join the latter's network, above-cost access prices have been suggested as a means for subsidizing the subscribership growth. Finally, to the extent that interconnection charges are designed to contribute to the recovery of the fixed, shared and common cost of a network, departures from purely cost-based pricing would ensue. Clearly, when the proposition that prices tend towards costs in competitive market is used as a reference point, these various considerations would cause deviations from costs in either direction, with the precise magnitude dependent on the particular facts and/or assumptions at issue. Although there are potentially many factors that affect the efficient level of access charges, it is useful to classify the literature into two broad categories: (1) models and analyses that implicitly assume that the calling party receives all of the benefits of the exchange, and (2) models that start from the premise that both parties might benefit.

Calling party is the benefit recipient   The first broad category is in many ways an extension of the one-way interconnection literature. That is, models start with a characterization of the amount of competition that prevails in retail markets (the analogue to downstream competition with one-way interconnection), then essentially view interconnection as similar to an essential facility, and finally determine the retail prices that would result from the competitive structure in question, as well as the interconnection charges that would arise from that competition and/or would be set by a regulator to maximize welfare.

For example, Laffont and Tirole (2000, pp. 190–96) model the case of duopoly competition, employing the symmetric Hotelling model to depict the competition for the common subscriber base in the service territory. The implications of the model are (1) in the absence of the need to recover fixed shared and common cost, a regulator would set the interconnection charge at less than cost (to offset the effect of less than perfect retail competition),[27] (2) depending on the magnitude of the fixed costs, the socially efficient access charge could be above or below cost, and (3) *if* the competitors were allowed to collude to set an interconnection price that generated monopoly prices, the interconnection charge would exceed cost.

The possibility that unregulated termination charges could exceed the socially optimal levels has been one motivation for introducing complications into the representation of two-way interconnection representations. For example, Poletti and Wright (2004) consider whether the following influence the extent to which voluntary interconnection prices depart from optimal levels: (1) the existence of heterogeneous customers (high versus low volume customers, with perhaps different splits of placing and receiving calls), (2) whether low volume customers subscribe at all, given the available prices (participation constraint), and/or (3) whether carriers are able to price discriminate between high and low volume customers, based on alternative price plans (incentive-compatibility constraint). Although the authors find that firms would negotiate cost-based prices when customers are homogeneous, the negotiated interconnection prices could depart substantially from optimal levels when customers are heterogeneous and the incentive and participation constraints bind.

Calling and called parties share the benefit   Approximately coincidental with the FCC's ongoing investigation of intercarrier compensation (which encompasses both one-way and two-way interconnection charges), a number of articles based on a call as a jointly consumed product emerged. As part of that investigation, DeGraba (2000 and 2002b) listed three premises in support of his 'bill and keep' proposal – eliminating interconnection charges in certain situations:[28] (1) that both calling and called parties benefit from a call, (2) competition works more effectively when networks charge their own customers, because interconnection payments are made to other carriers that possess a bottleneck to gaining access to their customers, and (3) bill and keep would eliminate the arbitrage opportunities arising from similar access arrangements being priced differently for different types of carriers. DeGraba also noted that the per-minute charges that are pervasive in interconnection tariffs (and extremely prominent in the theoretical literature) are difficult to determine and, as noted earlier, may not align with the way costs are incurred.

In response to the FCC's request for comments on DeGraba's and other proposals, Hermalin and Katz (2001) presented a formal framework for evaluating the bill and keep concept. Focusing on the premise that both the calling and the called party may benefit from the call, they present a model in which two networks exchange traffic and charge customers for both originating and receiving calls.[29] The fundamental question is then what level of interconnection charge would induce the networks to set efficient retail prices (for making and receiving calls).

When sender and receiver have the same demand conditions; that is, enjoy the same benefit from calling, then the efficient calling and receiving prices are the same, and under perfect competition their sum would equal the sum of the marginal costs of the two networks. Consequently, the interconnection charge would be the amount necessary for the each carrier to just break even:

$$a = (c_2 - c_1)/2$$

where c_1 is the marginal cost of the first network and c_2 is the second network's cost.[30] Note that (1) if the networks have the same cost characteristics, the interconnection charge is zero (bill and keep),[31] and (2) the charge would be negative if the calling party's network had higher costs.[32]

Accounting for demand considerations would reduce the interconnection charge paid to the receiving party's network if the called party valued the call less than the calling party and vice versa if the called party received the greater benefit.[33] For example, in a commentary on DeGraba's bill and keep proposal, Wright (2002) suggested that the benefits to wireline customers might be greater if there were more wireless customers that could be called. This, in turn, suggests the wireline customers pay a higher price for calling, which in turn would be reflected in higher (i.e. most likely greater than zero) interconnection payments to wireless carriers.

Finally, although some derivations of bill and keep as potentially efficient are based on the presence of retail charges for receiving calls, there are other derivations that suggest that bill and keep is an approximately efficient outcome. For example, when analysing efficient interconnection charges for dial-up calls to ISPs, Wright (2004) first observed that the efficient charge for interconnection when the ISP is served by another network would be the difference between the price of a local call (in this case to the ISP) and the cost of an end-to-end call reduced by the cost the caller's wireline network avoids because it does not have to terminate the call to a customer on the same network.[34] He then makes the practical observation that termination charges may be so small that the cost of measurement outweighs any benefits from nonzero interconnection charges.[35] In fact, when there is no retail charge for each local call (which is typically the case for residential customers in the US), Wright's equal markup approach would imply a negative interconnection payment; that is, the carrier serving the ISP would pay the calling party's network, which would offset the losses incurred from pricing local usage below its marginal cost.

Further, even though bill and keep is possibly an efficient outcome for a two-way interconnection arrangement, proposals for unified intercarrier compensation mechanisms, such as the US FCC's ongoing investigation, may be applied in typical one-way arrangements as well, hence if there were a bill and keep arrangement for a particular form of interconnection, long-distance carriers would pay nothing for call origination or termination.[36] In this context, Gilo and Spiegel (2004) derive the interesting result that if there were competing local networks (which themselves had a two-way interconnection arrangement) to which a long-distance network could originate and terminate its calls, bill and keep for the long-distance carrier is an outcome that could result from unregulated negotiations among the local and long-distance networks.

Two-way interconnection: summary and implications for interconnection pricing policy

The alternative frameworks for analysing two-way interconnection produce somewhat different fundamental outcomes. When the calling party is viewed as the only source of demand, the interconnection charge becomes a mechanism for ensuring that the customer faces the full cost associated with a call. However, because of factors such as demand conditions for local calling, the nature of retail competition for local calling, and the possibility that the interconnection charge may need to recover fixed shared and common costs and/or subsidies such as those supporting universal service, there can be Ramsey-like departures of optimal interconnection prices from cost. Thus not only are the information requirements challenging, but also determining whether optimal charges would be above or below cost depends on the empirical data and the analytical approach used in particular instances.

When both the calling and called parties are assumed to benefit from a call, an interconnection charge would reflect the relative benefits, as well as possible cost differences, between interconnecting networks. When parties enjoy the same benefits from calling and their networks have the same costs, then the optimal interconnection charge would be zero-bill and keep. Of course, departures from this outcome would be the result of comparably complex considerations that arose in the alternative framework.

The practical implication of these results is that the complexity of the task of establishing these charges can be reduced if recovery of fixed shared and common costs and/or subsidies can be accomplished through other means, i.e. there is no need to include 'taxes' in interconnection charges. However, both demand conditions and cost differences between networks would still pose formidable information requirements and the outcomes from such analyses can be both unexpected (e.g. payments from the network of the called party to the calling party's network) and controversial (depending on which networks have substantial interconnection payments or receipts).

Accordingly, the favourable reception bill and keep proposals have received in some circles is quite understandable. Eliminating explicit payments between carriers not only considerably reduces if not eliminates much of the information that would otherwise be required (and hence the cost of regulation), but it would also have the prospect of shifting the competitive energies from figuring out ways to extract payments from competitors to investing in order to provide innovative services that attract customers.

Access and interconnection pricing in the US: historical trends and future direction

The existing system of interconnection and access prices that prevails in the US and how that system has evolved illustrate many of the theoretical and policy issues discussed in the preceding sections. Before the divestiture of AT&T in 1984, there was little competition for either local or long-distance services (legal or otherwise) and long-distance prices were well above cost, in order to provide a subsidy for the basic telephone service. The AT&T divestiture created perhaps the prototypical one-way interconnection arrangement, with the newly divested local exchange carriers providing the upstream service and AT&T and its long-distance competitors providing the downstream service. From that time until the early part of the 2000s, the former affiliates of AT&T were for the most part precluded from competing in the downstream market. This arrangement eliminated the potential for anticompetitive problems to arise when a vertically integrated provider competes with dependent firms in the downstream market.

But the fact that the initial access charges inherited the subsidy burden previously carried by long-distance prices created an ongoing concern that long-distance carriers would have incentives to inefficiently 'bypass' the local exchange access services and in the process severely undermine the generation of subsidies for universal service.

Consequently, there has been a long-running trend of per-minute access charge reductions, offset by increasing monthly charges assessed directly on customers and in surcharges (essentially taxes) applied to the revenues of certain classes of carriers. In particular, the initially high per-minute access charges were reduced by almost a half (in nominal terms) between 1984 and 1989, while a charge assessed to end-users increased from US$0.00 to US$3.50 per month. Shortly after the passage of the 1996 Telecommunications Act, the FCC (1) established rules for establishing two-way interconnection charges at rates that were well below the prevailing access charges for long-distance services,[37] and (2) shifted certain costs that were not deemed to be usage-sensitive to monthly end user charges. In 2000, the FCC (2000) approved a plan developed by a consortium of local exchange and long-distance carriers that continued the shift from per-minute usage charges to end-user charge.[38] Table 13.1 illustrates these developments.[39]

Table 13.1   History of US interstate long-distance access and residential subscriber line charges (US$)

Year	Monthly customer charge (residential primary line), US$*	Per minute access charge, US$
1984	0.00	0.1726
1989	3.50	0.0911
1997	3.50	0.0604
2000	3.50	0.0285
2004	5.96	0.0144

Note: *   Higher charges for business lines have also been assessed. Beginning in 1998, the FCC established a separate charge for non-primary residential lines which was $5.00 in 1998 and $6.00 subsequently.

The trends depicted in Table 13.1 reflect some harmony in the positions of regulators and competing carriers: to the extent possible, costs not associated with usage should be removed from per-minute charges and replaced, if necessary, with flat rate charges assessed on end users. Thus, while at any particular time incumbent carriers may oppose unilateral reductions in per-minute charges, and the carriers that purchase these services may advocate cost-based rates,[40] the disagreements arise more because of factual disputes (such as the magnitude of costs) and how the transition from current rates to more reasonable and sustainable ones can be implemented rather than because of conflict over the generally desirability (for both theoretical and practical reasons) to have regulatorily imposed per-minute access and interconnection charges as low as possible.

The per-minute charges presented in Table 13.1 are the averages paid by long-distance carriers for originating and terminating calls subject to the jurisdiction of the FCC (i.e. between states) in the territories of the large (non-rural) local exchange carriers. Numerous other rates apply for other interconnection arrangements, including access for intrastate long-distance calls for large carriers, interstate and intrastate access rates for smaller rural carriers, interconnection between wireline and wireless carriers, and interconnection of incumbent and entrant local exchange carriers. Even more significantly, these rates vary considerably. For example, ICF (2004, Appendix C) – the Intercarrier Compensation Forum – reports interstate rates for one end of a call well under US$0.01 per minute, which is consistent with the level shown in the table. These large carriers charge over four times as much for intrastate long-distance access. Small incumbent (rural) carriers charge two to three times as much as large carriers for interstate and intrastate access and the corresponding rates for local exchange entrants are somewhere in between. However, for the exchange of local traffic, which under the Telecommunications Act must equal the additional cost a carrier incurs to terminate the traffic, average costs are approximately US$0.002 for non-ISP traffic and US$0.001 for ISP traffic, or several times lower than the interstate access charges for large incumbents. Indeed, there is a 50-fold difference between the lowest average per-minute rate (US$0.001) and the highest (US$0.05) charge by small incumbent local exchange carriers for intrastate long-distance access.

In large part motivated by these big discrepancies, the FCC (2001b) initiated a review of intercarrier compensation, with the objective of unifying the disparate charges. According to the FCC, such reform was necessary to overcome the following inefficiencies and problems in current rules and prices: (1) the arbitrage incentives from widely varying rates for similar interconnection services, (2) the possible exercise of market power by terminating networks, (3) possible inefficiencies arising from cost difference between interconnecting networks, (4) the possibility that inefficient interconnection rates could be reflected in inefficient retail prices, and (5) the possibility that inefficient interconnection rates could result in inefficient customer choices among competing carriers. A major focus of the FCC's investigation has been DeGraba's bill and keep proposal, which was discussed in an earlier section.

Because, in part, of the large amount of revenue raised by current charges[41] and the otherwise sweeping nature of a unified compensation regime, the FCC has yet to order a plan, although there have been specific proposals from various parties. For example, following a process somewhat similar to that which resulted in the FCC's 2000 approval of a consortium's access charge reform proposal, the ICF[42] has offered a proposal that includes four major elements. First, for the facilities that interconnect networks, the plan designates which carrier is responsible for arranging the facilities and, in the case of interconnecting with an incumbent local exchange carrier, regulates the monthly charges for these facilities.[43] Second, the plan calls for unified default per-minute charges within three years of the plan's beginning at a rate of US$0.000175, which is only a fraction of the lowest per-minute charge that currently prevails. Subsequently, over a three-year period, that unified charge would be lowered to zero-full bill and keep for all formerly usage-based charges.[44] Third, end-user charges added to basic service prices would gradually increase from an initial level of US$6.50 per month (somewhat higher than the current average charge) to US$10. Fourth, the universal service funding source would shift from a percentage surcharge on the revenues of certain types of carriers to a per month assessment, based on working telephone numbers and other non-switched connections to end use customers. At the time this chapter was written, the FCC (2005) had just begun a proceeding that requested comments on this and other comprehensive proposals. There will undoubtedly be disagreement with the form and particulars of the competing proposals that will emerge from the proceeding.[45] Nevertheless, the general changes proposed by ICF – more uniform and lower per minute charges, higher charges for basic services, the need for clear and consistent responisbilities between carriers seeking interconnection, and the establishment of sustainable universal service funding for high-cost areas – will probably characterize the next interconnection and access charge regime, if and when it emerges.

Conclusions

Establishing efficient, yet at the same time practical, interconnection charges in telecommunications is challenging because of the breadth and complexity of interconnection arrangements. In particular, factors such as (1) the historical use of above-cost prices to subsidize universal service, (2) the growing need for interconnection arrangements among carriers offering customers different services with different technologies (e.g. wireline and wireless), and (3) the difficulty in aligning increasingly complicated prices for consumer products with the underlying cost structure of interconnection and access facilities, make the establishment of access and interconnection charges that have the welfare-enhancing properties predicted by particular theoretical models a difficult task. Also, while such charges have traditionally had a volume-sensitive component (e.g. a per-minute charge), there has been an inexorable trend towards much lower usage charges in the US – a trend that almost certainly will continue, perhaps culminating in no ('bill and keep') interconnection and access charges. That trend is the result of the combination of (1) the fact that the associated marginal (or incremental) costs for interconnection are relatively low, and (2) the theoretical and practical difficulties of establishing and maintaining above-cost charges.

The application of the findings from the telecommunications literature to other industries, such as electricity, most likely lies in one-way interconnection applications because, unlike a telephone call, most products are consumed exclusively by the buyer.

Consequently relationships among interconnecting firms are likely to be the classical vertical arrangements that underlie the analysis of one-way interconnection. Accordingly, the key issues are establishing interconnection charges that facilitate efficient, non-discriminatory competition in downstream markets. To the extent that prices and access charges are usage-sensitive, the theoretical findings from the telecommunications literature would apply. Accordingly, as in telecommunications, the challenge in designing access charges in practice is aligning downstream prices and access charges with the cost structure of access.

Notes

1. Laffont and Tirole (2000, p. 139) describe how in 1996 two incumbents in California claimed that 'bill and keep' for interconnection with competing carriers was tantamount to a taking of their property. As I discuss in more detail below, some incumbents, including the corporate parent of one of the two California incumbents, have endorsed 'bill and keep' interconnection charges. Under a 'bill and keep' interconnection arrangement, interconnecting carriers exchange traffic with a volume-sensitive charge equal to zero. There may be flat charges (e.g. fixed monthly rates) for the interconnection facilities themselves.
2. See, for example, Armstrong (2002) and Laffont and Tirole (2000, Chapters 3–5).
3. See, for example, Weisman (2003).
4. Wireless (primarily mobile) and traditional wireline services have not been very close substitutes when the former is a relatively new service, wireless prices are high and/or subscribership is low. However, when wireless and wireline prices become much closer and (as in some countries) wireless subscribership approaches or even overtakes that of the traditional telephone service, the two technologies become closer substitutes. As we discuss later, access and interconnection prices must account for this development.
5. The amount of these intercarrier payments can be significant, even when they are purportedly close to the cost of providing interconnection. And to the extent that the interconnection rates are above cost (e.g. for fixed to mobile call completion in countries such as Brazil), intercarrier payments can constitute a large proportion of the revenues of certain carriers.
6. These issues are also discussed in Noam (2002).
7. For example, the 1996 Telecommunications Act in the United States clearly stated an objective of promoting competition. At the same time it contained detailed prescriptions for funding universal access to traditional wireline telephone service; see, Kahn et al. (1999) and Tardiff (2002).
8. For example, in upholding the FCC's rules for setting the prices of unbundled network elements pursuant to the Telecommunications Act of 1996, the US Supreme Court noted: 'The Act thus appears to be an explicit disavowal of the familiar public-utility model of rate regulation ... presumably still being applied by many states for retail sales, ... in favor of novel ratesetting designed to give aspiring competitors every possible incentive to enter local retail telephone markets, short of confiscating the incumbents' property' (Supreme Court of the United States, 2002, Majority: 16–17). See also Weisman (2002b).
9. For example, the number of possible connections is given by $P(n) = n(n-1)/2$, where n is the number of subscribers.
10. As described earlier, there are different one-way access arrangements, such as per-minute call origination and termination charges assessed by local exchange carriers on long-distance carriers, and monthly rental changes for unbundled subscriber loops provided by incumbent local exchange carriers to new competitive carriers in a common service territory, etc. The discussion in this section generally applies to all such one-way arrangements.
11. See, for example, Baumol and Sidak (1994).
12. Indeed, as we discuss below, because such prices can become a multitask workhorse, the question of whether other policy instruments should be used for some of the tasks arises.

13. The downstream marginal cost would be the sum of the marginal cost of the access service obtained from the incumbent plus the additional costs incurred by the downstream firm.

14. A corollary of the efficient access price problem is establishing the minimum pro-competitive price (price floor) for the incumbent's downstream service. The findings discussed in this section apply equally to determining such minimum prices; see, for example, Hausman and Tardiff (1995) and Weisman (2002a).

15. Armstrong (2002, p. 311) provides a more general statement of the ECPR: 'access charge = cost of providing access + incumbent's lost profit in retail markets caused by providing access'. The statement generalizes the version of the ECPR stated in the text, because demand and/or cost conditions may be such that the lost retail profits differ from those contained in the incumbent's downstream price.

16. This outcome would appear to have perverse dynamic efficiency consequences: efforts by the incumbent to lower costs in the downstream market would in turn decrease the access charge its competitors would pay.

17. Laffont and Tirole (2000, p. 102) explain how universal service obligations can be treated as a component of the incumbent's fixed costs.

18. See, for example, Tardiff (2002) and Armstrong (2002, pp. 334–5).

19. See, for example, Laffont and Tirole (2000, pp. 149–57) and Hausman (2003).

20. When market power is defined as the ability to charge prices that result in supranormal profits, a price that is above marginal cost does not necessarily imply market power. Firms with fixed shared and common costs must charge above marginal cost in at least some markets to earn normal profits.

21. Indeed, in the US, at the directive of the DC Circuit Court, the FCC (2004c) recently removed end-office switching from the list of network elements incumbent local exchange carriers are required to provide to competitors at regulated prices.

22. Armstrong (2002, pp. 319–21) presents a version of the ECPR that accounts for the possibility of substitution away from the access input provided by the incumbent. The erosion of the essential nature of access also has implications for establishing minimum prices for the incumbent's downstream services. For example, Weisman (2002a) proposes that the amount of forgone contribution called for by ECPR be multiplied by the proportion of a competitor's downstream output that requires the incumbent's access input. Consequently, as the access input becomes ubiquitously competitively supplied, the incumbent's minimum pro-competitive price would be its marginal (or incremental) cost, without any mark-up for forgone contribution (Hausman and Tardiff, 1995).

23. Models that address various aspects of interconnection pricing include the following examples: Armstrong (2002, 2004), Berger (2005), Cambini and Valletti (2004), DeGraba (2000, 2002a, 2002b, 2003, 2004), Dessein (2004), Hermalin and Katz (2001), Gilo and Spiegel (2004), Jeon et al. (2004), Laffont and Tirole (2000), Poletti and Wright (2004) and Wright (2002, 2004).

24. While these payments are typically usage-based charges from the firm serving the calling party to the firm serving the called party in practice, theoretical models can produce negative charges in some cases.

25. In some recent regulatory proceedings in the US, there has been movement away from per-minute cost and price structures for switch usage. For example, the FCC's Wireline Competition Bureau (2003) and the California Public Utilities Commission (2004) establish a flat monthly rate in lieu of a per-minute rate for wholesale switching provided by incumbent firms to competing local carriers.

26. In fact, in the US because of concerns that entrant competitive local carriers were charging long-distance companies too much to terminate calls on their networks, the FCC (2001a) limited the size of such charges, based on comparisons with comparable rates of incumbent local carriers.

27. The intuition behind setting interconnection prices at cost if retail competition were perfect is that (1) the calling party should face the full marginal cost of the call and (2) the cost of terminating the call on the called party's network is part of that full cost.

28. As we describe in more detail below, the FCC's investigation and DeGraba's proposal encompass both one-way and two-way interconnection payments.

29. The authors employ a similar approach in Hermalin and Katz (2004).
30.' The calling party's network incurs a cost of c_1 and pays the other network an interconnection charge of $(c_2 - c_1)/2$, resulting in total costs of $(c_1 + c_2)/2$, or half of the total costs of the call.
31. Armstrong (2004, p. 389) also observes that if there is a retail charge for receiving calls, the optimal interconnection arrangement could be bill and keep.
32. It is interesting to contrast this property of efficient interconnection charges with how carriers that terminate calls to ISPs are typically compensated. For ISP-bound calls, (1) both the calling party (the ISP's customer) and the called party (the ISP) benefit from the transaction and (2) the costs to terminate the Internet call (at least when assessed on a per-minute basis) are likely to be lower than the costs incurred on the calling party's network. Thus, Hermalin and Katz's analysis suggests that the ISP's network should pay the calling party's network, and not vice versa as happens in the real world. However, Hermalin and Katz note that if the more expensive network received the interconnection payment (regardless of the direction of the call) there would be perverse incentive properties, i.e. investments that reduced network costs would result in higher interconnection payments. DeGraba (2003, p. 213) also observes that efficient interconnection charges can be negative when the costs of the terminating party's network are lower.
33. See, for example, Jeon et al. (2004, p. 88).
34. This observation is equivalent to Armstrong's (2004, p. 380) 'equal markup' rule.
35. Similarly, Berger (2005) concluded that when the called party benefits from a call but only the calling party pays, efficient interconnection charges are less than cost (in order to capture the network externality) and in certain circumstances, the efficient charge would be zero.
36. Future recovery of costs that were covered by such charges would be shifted to local carriers' customers under unified mechanisms.
37. For example, while the average access charge under the FCC's jurisdiction was approximately US$0.03 per minute in 1996, the FCC's local competition rules (FCC, 1996) established a default rate of US$0.0015 per minute.
38. The consortium included three of the four large incumbent local exchange carriers (Verizon, SBC, and BellSouth) and two of the three largest long-distance carriers (AT&T and Sprint).
39. FCC (2004a, pp. 1–5, 1–6). The access charges are the sum of originating and terminating charges on both ends of the call – the charge at a single end is approximately half of the list value. These charges apply to services under the FCC's jurisdiction. Each state has separate rates for calls it regulates.
40. For example Armstrong (2002, p. 336) observes that entrants generally favour cost-based pricing, while incumbents favour the ECPR.
41. For example, usage-based interstate access charges accounted for about US$4.4 billion in 2002, which because of the rebalancing that began in 2000 was over 50 per cent lower than the US$9.7 billion from 1999 (FCC, 2004b, p. 164). In the case of rural carriers, Glass (2004) reports that fully half of their revenues are payments for other carriers intended to keep customer rates lower than what cost-based rates would require in these typically high-cost areas.
42. The ICF includes the three major long-distance carriers, one of the four large incumbent local exchange carriers (SBC), a rural telephone company, and local exchange entrants. Although the other three large local exchange carriers (Verizon, BellSouth, and Qwest) have not at this time signed up to the specific provisions of the ICF proposal, all had previously endorsed some form of bill and keep arrangement for usage charges, at least in the case of two-way interconnection of local exchange networks.
43. DeGraba's proposal contained a similar provision, which would require the calling party's network to arrange facilities that connect with the switching locations (central offices) of the called party's network.
44. The ICF proposal would allow interconnecting parties to negotiate rates that differ from the default usage charges specified in the plan, e.g. when the 'bill and keep' provisions take effect, parties could agree to establish a positive charge for exchanging traffic.
45. For example, the Alliance for Rational Interconnection Compensation (2004), a group of rural, high-cost carriers, disagrees with the rationale DeGraba offered for a bill and keep regime.

References

Alliance for Rational Interconnection Compensation (2004) http://www.naruc.org/associations/1773/files/aric-ic0804.pdf

Armstrong, M. (2002) 'The Theory of Access Pricing and Interconnection', in M.E. Cave, S.K. Majumdar and I. Vogelsang (eds), *Handbook of Telecommunications Economics, Volume 1: Structure, Regulation and Competition*, Amsterdam: North Holland, Chapter 8.

Armstrong, M. (2004) 'Network Interconnection with Asymmetric Networks and Heterogeneous Calling Patterns', *Information Economics and Policy*, **16**, 375–90.

Baumol, W.J. (1999) 'Having Your Cake: How to Preserve Universal Service Cross-subsidies while Facilitating Competitive Entry', *Yale Journal on Regulation*, **16**, 1–17.

Baumol, W. and Sidak, J.G. (1994) *Toward Competition in Local Telephony*, Cambridge, MA: The MIT Press.

Berger, U. (2005) 'Bill-and-Keep vs. Cost-based Access Pricing Revisited', *Economic Letters*, **86** (1), 107–12.

California Public Utilities Commission (2004) 'Opinion Establishing Revised Unbundled Network Element Rates for Pacific Bell Telephone Company DBA SBC California', Decision 04-09-063, 1 October.

Cambini, C. and Valletti, T. (2004) 'Access Charges and Quality Choice in Competing Networks', *Information Economics and Policy*, **16**, 391–409.

DeGraba, P. (2000) 'Bill and Keep at the Central Office as the Efficient Interconnection Regime', Federal Communications Commission, OPP Working Paper, No. 33.

DeGraba, P. (2002a). 'Bill and Keep as the Efficient Interconnection Regime?: A Reply', *Review of Network Economics*, **1** (2), 61–5.

DeGraba, P. (2002b) 'Central Office Bill and Keep as a Unified Inter-carrier Compensation Regime', *Yale Journal on Regulation*, **19**, 37–84.

DeGraba, P. (2003) 'Efficient Intercarrier Compensation for Competing Networks when Customers Share the Value of a Call', *Journal of Economics and Management Strategy*, **12** (2), 207–30.

DeGraba, P. (2004) 'Reconciling the Off-Net Cost Pricing Principle with Efficient Network Utilization', *Information Economics and Policy*, **16**, 475–94.

Dessein, W. (2004) 'Network Competition with Heterogeneous Customers and Calling Patterns', *Information Economics and Policy*, **16**, 323–45.

Federal Communications Commission (1996) *Implementation of the Local Competition Provisions in the Telecommunications Act of 1996*, CC Docket No. 96-98, First Report and Order, 8 August.

Federal Communications Commission (2000) *Access Charge Reform*, CC Docket No. 96-262, *Price Cap Performance Review for Local Exchange Carriers*, CC Docket No. 94-1, *Low-volume Long Distance Users*, CC Docket No. 99-249, and *Federal–State Joint Board on Universal Service*, CC Docket No. 96-45, Sixth Report and Order in CC Dockets Nos. 96-262 and 94-1, Report and Order in CC Docket No. 99-249, and Eleventh Report and Order in CC Docket No. 96-45, 31 May.

Federal Communications Commission (2001a) *Access Charge Reform: Reform of Access Charges Imposed by Competitive Local Exchange Carriers*, CC Docket No. 96-262, Seventh Report and Order, 27 April.

Federal Communications Commission (2001b) *Developing a Unified Intercarrier Compensation Regime*, CC Docket No. 01-92, Notice of Proposed Rulemaking, 27 April.

Federal Communications Commission (2003) *Petition of WorldCom, Inc. Pursuant to*

Section 252(e)(5) of the Communications Act for Preemption of the Jurisdiction of the Virginia State Corporation Commission Regarding Interconnection Disputes with Verizon Virginia Inc., and for Expedited Arbitration and Petition of AT&T Communications of Virginia, Inc. Pursuant to Section 252(e)(5) of the Communications Act for Preemption of the Jurisdiction of the Virginia State Corporation Commission Regarding Interconnection Disputes with Verizon Virginia Inc., CC Docket Nos. 00-218 and 00-251, Memorandum Opinion and Order, 29 August.

Federal Communications Commission (2004a) *Trends in Telephone Service*, May.

Federal Communications Commission (2004b) *Statistics of Communications Common Carriers: 2003/2004 Edition*, October.

Federal Communications Commission (2004c) 'FCC Adopts New Rules for Network Unbundling Obligations of Incumbent Local Phone Carriers', Press Release, 15 December.

Federal Communications Commission (2005) *Developing a Unified Intercarrier Compensation Regime*, CC Docket No. 01-92, Further Notice of Proposed Rulemaking, 3 March.

Gilo, D. and Spiegel, Y. (2004) 'Network Interconnection with Competitive Transit', *Information Economics and Policy*, **16**, 439–58.

Glass, V. (2004) 'Universal Service Reform for a Multi-media World', Presented at the Rutgers University, Center for Research in Regulated Industries, Advanced Workshop in Regulation and Competition, 17th Annual Western Conference, San Diego, California, 24 June.

Hausman, J. A. (2003) 'Regulated Costs and Prices in Telecommunications', in Gary Madden (ed.), *International Handbook of Telecommunications Economics, Volume 2: Emerging Telecommunications Networks*, Cheltenham, UK and Northampton, MA, USA: Edward Elgar, Chapter 10.

Hausman, J.A. and Tardiff, T.J. (1995) 'Efficient Local Exchange Competition', *The Antitrust Bulletin*, **40** (3), Fall, 529–56.

Hermalin, B.E. and Katz, M.L. (2001) 'Network Interconnection with Two-sided User Benefits', University of California, Berkeley, Working Paper.

Hermalin, B.E. and Katz, M.L. (2004) 'Sender or Receiver: Who Should Pay to Exchange an Electronic Message?', *RAND Journal of Economics*, **35** (3), 423–48.

Intercarrier Compensation Forum (2004) *Developing a Unified Intercarrier Compensation Regime*, CC Docket No. 01-92, Ex Parte Brief in Support of the Intercarrier Compensation and Universal Service Reform Plan, 5 October.

Jeon, D.-S. Laffont, J.-J. and Tirole, J. (2004) 'On the "Receiver Pays" Principle', *RAND Journal of Economics*, **35** (1), 85–110.

Kahn, A.E., Tardiff, T.J. and Weisman, D.L. (1999) 'The 1996 Telecommunications Act at Three Years: An Economic Evaluation of its Implementation by the FCC', *Information Economics and Policy*, **11** (4), 319–65.

Laffont, J.-J. and Tirole, J. (2000) *Competition in Telecommunications*, Cambridge, MA: The MIT Press.

Noam, E. (2002) 'Interconnection Practices', in Martin E. Cave, Sumit K. Majumdar and Ingo Vogelsang (eds), *Handbook of Telecommunications Economics, Volume 1: Structure, Regulation and Competition*, Amsterdam: North Holland, Chapter 9.

Poletti, S. and Wright, J. (2004) 'Network Interconnection with Participation Constraints', *Information Economics and Policy*, **16**, 347–73.

Supreme Court of the United States (2002) *Verizon v. FCC*, Case No. 00511, 13 May.

Tardiff, T.J. (2002) 'Universal Service', in M.A. Crew and J.C. Schuh (eds), *Markets, Pricing, and Deregulation of Utilities*, Boston, MA: Kluwer.

Weisman, D.L. (2002a) 'The Law and Economics of Price Floors in Regulated Indus-
tries', *The Antitrust Bulletin*, **47** (1), Spring, 107–31.
Weisman, D.L. (2002b) 'Did the High Court Reach an Economic Low in Verizon v.
FCC', *Review of Network Economics*, **1** (2), 90–105.
Weisman, D.L (2003) 'Vertical Integration in Telecommunications', in G. Madden (ed.),
*International Handbook of Telecommunications Economics, Volume 1: Traditional
Telecommunications Networks*, Cheltenham, UK and Northampton, MA, USA:
Edward Elgar, Chapter 7.
Weisman, D.L. and Kang, J. (2001) 'Incentives for Discrimination when Upstream Mo-
nopolists Participate in Downstream Markets', *Journal of Regulatory Economics*, **20**
(2), 125–39.
Wright, J. (2002) 'Bill and Keep as the Efficient Interconnection Regime?', Review of
Network Economics, **1** (2), 54–60.
Wright, J. (2004) 'Pricing Access to Internet Service Providers', *Information Economics
and Policy*, **16**, 459–73.

14 Regulation and the structure of the telecommunications industry

Gregory M. Duncan and Lisa J. Cameron

Introduction[1]

What will the telecommunications industry look like in five or ten years? Certainly not the way it looks today. What role will regulators have in five or ten years? Certainly not the one they have today. Ignoring the rapidly emerging competitive trends, we currently have a traditional telephone company (called the ILEC, short for incumbent local exchange carrier) competing with a number of smaller telephone companies (called the CLECs, short for competitive local exchange carriers) for 'wireline' (a technology) customers wanting to make phone calls – this is called a 'voice' service. Then we have the cable-TV company (usually only one in an area unless it is a major metropolitan area), which sells 'video' services and high-speed access to the Internet (a 'data' service) using 'cable' (a technology). The cable company competes with satellite (a technology) companies (DISH Network and DIRECTV) for video customers and wireline companies for Internet customers. Then there are the wireless companies who compete with both the wireline and cable companies. The conventional wireless companies (like Cingular and T-Mobile) compete mostly with the wireline companies for voice services, but we have some new-to-the-market companies that offer wireless (Wi-Fi and WiMAX) data services for connecting to the Internet.

What role does regulation play in the current scenario? Currently, the regulators (both federal and state) generally apply a very light-handed approach to all these service providers except the ILECs. This approach is based on the belief that the ILECs wield market power because of their traditional position as local monopoly providers and would be able to drive their competitors out of the market in the absence of regulation. Rather than debate this issue, we look to the future role regulators will have in the new environment where there is competition between and among technologies – intermodal competition.

We develop and use a technology-based model to predict what the telecommunications industry will look like in the not-so-distant future: a few regional (perhaps national) phone companies, a few regional (perhaps national) cable companies, several wireless and satellite companies, and perhaps a few specialized broadband providers. This prediction is based on the cost structures of the underlying technologies used to provide service, which dictate the ability (or lack thereof) of carriers to expand or contract their networks in response to changes in demand. Where technologies exhibit *de minimis* short-run marginal costs and high initial capital and/or startup costs, only one firm with homogeneous products will survive. This cost structure applies to the wireline and cable companies because they are required to build networks with an eye to 'ultimate' demand since customer lines in their networks are not interchangeable.[2]

For technologies where short-run marginal costs are constant or increasing (i.e. technologies that exhibit constant or decreasing returns to scale), many firms operating in the same area can survive, although the number of survivors is a matter of conjecture. The technologies used by wireless, satellite and fixed-wireless companies exhibit these characteristics. In contrast to wireline and cable companies, firms using spectrum-based technologies do not need to build to ultimate demand because they can expand their networks at relatively low cost as demand increases.

Once we know what the competitive environment will look like in the future, we can examine the role of regulation in this environment. Regulators will still be needed where there is no effective competition, mostly to protect that segment of wireline consumers who (whether due to location, income, or other reasons) do not have a choice of service providers despite the trend towards intermodal competition. We have little doubt about the type of regulation: price caps. The central question for regulators in the new environment will be: how should price caps be implemented when a wireline company produces both non-competitive services, such as local telephony in less populated regions of the country, as well as other services, such as local telephony in urban areas that are subject to significant intermodal competition from other telecommunications providers.

The structure of this chapter follows the opening paragraphs: we discuss each of the important telecommunications technologies and develop the economic model based on their cost characteristics. We use our model to predict the future structure of the industry and to determine the remaining role, if any, for Federal Communications Commission (FCC) and state public utility commission (PUC) regulation in the USA. We also use our model to analyse the impact of various policies on industry outcomes and show that observed outcomes are consistent with the predictions of the model.

Services, players and technologies
In this section, we discuss a number of key telecommunications technologies: (1) wireline; (2) cable; (3) VoIP (Voice over Internet Protocol), which is a communications protocol that can be used to provide voice service over any broadband technology; (4) conventional wireless; and (5) other wireless technologies, including fixed wireless, Wi-Fi, WiMAX, and satellite. We discuss the economic characteristics of each technology and the implications of that technology for competition within and across technologies. Where relevant, we also

provide some background on the roles played by companies traditionally identified with specific technologies. Our continuing theme is that the cost and production characteristics of these technologies dictate the future structure of the industry.

Wireline

Traditional wireline phone companies (both ILECs and CLECs) provide voice services called Plain Old Telephone Service (POTS) over the Public Switched Telephone Network (PSTN) and a variety of ancillary services, including call waiting and voice mail.[3] Wireline companies also provide consumers with broadband access and data services via high-capacity digital subscriber lines (DSLs).[4] DSL technology expands the carrying capacity of copper-wire pairs by 20-fold or more by relying on sophisticated digital processing techniques to use the full bandwidth of a copper pair, as opposed to analogue-modem technology, which is confined to 4 kHz of audible spectrum. Eventually, wireline companies may provide video and other data-related services. However, this section focuses on voice communications, the service for which wireline companies are best known.

We begin our discussion by following the path of an individual phone call. Currently, wireline companies (both ILECs and CLECs) connect calls to their destination by maintaining a dedicated and continuous physical path through the network for the duration of the call. This mode of connecting calls is referred to as circuit-based switching.[5] When someone (in telephony referred to as a calling party) dials a number, the called number is sent from the phone across a pair of copper wires (a line) to a network interface device (NID), which is usually a small grey box attached to the outside of the customer's home or business.[6] Each line from inside the house or business connected to the NID is then connected aerially (to a terminal box on a telephone pole) or underground (to a terminal box on the ground). This part of the telephone company's network is called its distribution network.

The lines go from the terminal box to a cable, which then is connected to larger and larger cables until it finally reaches a computerized switch located in a local wire centre, also called a central office. The cables that carry the lines from the terminal box to the central office make up the telephone company's feeder network. The distribution and feeder networks are part of the telephone company's outside plant network, and are like branches on a tree. A small branch (a customer line) is connected to a larger branch, and then to another even larger branch, and then to the tree's trunk – the local wire centre or central office.

Once the call reaches the local wire centre, a switch determines if the called number can accept the call. If the switch cannot establish a connection, it provides a signal or a recorded announcement to the calling party stating why it cannot connect the call (e.g. the line is busy, no circuits, not a good number). If the switch finds an open path to the called number, it connects the call. The connection can be to another line served by the same switch, another switch in its local network, or to a network owned by another company (other local telephone companies, long-distance and international companies, or wireless, cable, and satellite companies).[7]

Having provided this brief overview of the wireline network, we can now explain how its features drive the economic model discussed in this chapter. The first salient feature is the cost associated with the wireline provider's distribution and feeder networks, which consist mainly of lines, poles, conduits and cables. These networks are extremely expensive to build, as it typically involves tearing up streets, putting up poles, or laying cables, including the attendant delay and costs of obtaining construction permits and rights-of-way across private land. Because of the cost, it is optimal to repeat this process as few times as possible. As a result, wireline companies typically build to ultimate demand; that is, they estimate what future demand will be and create a network to support this demand. Thus, as demand increases, the network is in place to handle it.

A second key economic feature of the wireline network is that it is designed so that 99 per cent of all calls made during the busy hour of the busiest season of the year can be connected unless the destination phone is busy. Ignoring instances of network trouble, almost all calls are completed when dialled (and the called number is available) except on occasions like Christmas and Mother's Day or widespread regional emergencies. This means that for most of the year, the short-run marginal cost of handling additional call volume is essentially zero.[8]

A third key feature of the wireline network is the nature of maintenance costs. The costs of sending a technician to fix a damaged cable or make repairs at the local wire centre are tied to the number of lines per square mile in the serving area. Maintenance costs include having a readily available repair labour force and such things as trucks, tools and test equipment. These maintenance costs do not vary with the number of subscribers, but instead increase with the number of lines and with the geographical dispersion of the lines. It does not matter if all the lines in an area are assigned to customers or if only half are assigned, the costs of fixing a network outage remain the same.

The final key feature of the wireline network is that only a small amount of available capacity is being used at any given time, even when the network is performing its primary function of providing voice services. The copper-wire loop that connects a customer's premises to the local wire centre can carry many frequencies at the same time without interference. Voice calls occupy only a range of the lower bandwidth frequencies, whereas data calls travel over the higher frequencies.[9] As a result, the theoretical capacity of the network is enormous, although other physical limitations may come into play.[10] With this existing excess capacity, wireline companies probably can offer additional levels of service in the short run at a marginal cost that is small or negligible relative to the initial or even the long-run marginal cost of the network.

These four features of the traditional wireline network (i.e. the cost of constructing the network, the requirement to accommodate peak capacity, the nature of maintenance, and the enormous capacity of the network) have important implications for the number of companies that can provide wireline service in a given geographic area. In the context of the model, these features render multiple competitors using current wireline technology in the same geographic area inefficient because of duplication, since any one competitor can serve all possible demand. In addition, any new entrant in this business cannot survive on its own merits because the incumbent will always be willing to reduce prices to short-run marginal cost to retain customers.[11] New firms cannot survive if they can only recover short-run marginal costs, which here are essentially zero; these entrants must also recover their capital investment and other startup costs, which are significant. Another way to look at this issue is as follows. Because incumbent short-run marginal costs are zero, unless service provision is absolutely free, the firm with the larger customer base (typically the incumbent) wins. To see this, assume that two companies try to serve the same 100 customers and the annual costs for both companies are the same, $10,000. If both firms serve half the customers, a $200 annual fee per subscriber covers costs and is an equilibrium that allows both firms to survive. However, the equilibrium is unstable. If the first firm acquires ten customers from the second firm, then the first firm can charge $167.67 and cover its costs, while the second firm must charge $250. If the first firm initially serves all 100 customers and the second firm is the new entrant, the first firm can charge as little as $100 and cover its costs. The entering firm must incur a loss since at $100 it cannot attract customers or cover its costs. If the new entrant lowers its prices to capture the incumbent's customers, it will not cover its costs. Moreover, if the incumbent matches the new entrant's prices, the new entrant will still not be able to gain customers. Rather than getting into a losing price war, the rational entrant should choose not to enter. Hence, the firm with the larger market share wins – the incumbent. This argument depends critically on the assumption that the new entrant and incumbent provide the same services and there is no product differentiation. If there is product differentiation, even a zero price might not attract all demand. For example, if POTS were free, wireline companies would probably keep most of their customers (although the reverse is probably not even close to being true). Note, too, if somehow an entrant grabbed more than half the market share, it would win. However, there would still be only one firm producing the service.

In summary, a view of the telecommunications industry with multiple wireline competitors providing the same set of services is inconsistent with the basic economics of the industry in the long run. Moreover, any artificial maintenance of such an inefficient structure will almost certainly fail. We will return to this point later when we discuss intermodal competition among wireline providers and companies using other communications technologies.

Cable

The economic features of cable and wireline networks are very similar: the network is optimally built to ultimate demand, resulting in a relatively low short-run cost to accommodate new customers within the cable company's operating area. Similarly, a market structure with multiple competitors producing identical services with cable technology at essentially zero short-run marginal costs is inconsistent with basic economics. Naturally, there may be cable companies in adjacent areas, but it is not economically viable for these companies to compete in the same area over the long term. Of course, this predicted industry structure presupposes that the cable companies cannot use product differentiation to distinguish themselves.

Cable companies specialize in providing video and high-speed data services through cable modems. A cable modem connects a customer's personal computer to a network node that is shared by about 350–700 customers (with the expectation that only some fraction of the customers will use the system at any given time). Each shared network in turn connects to the computers at a cable company's main office that are connected to the Internet backbone network. The cable company acts as its customers' Internet service provider.[12]

In providing data services, cable companies compete with the DSL offerings of wireline providers. Cable companies also are expanding into voice and other services. As noted in the previous section, wireline companies currently rely primarily on 'circuit'-switching equipment to provide voice services. Circuit-switching equipment connects a call to its destination by maintaining a dedicated and continuous physical path through the network for the duration of the call. In contrast, cable companies with broadband capabilities may be well suited to providing voice services using more economical packet-switching technologies.

VoIP

VoIP is a communications protocol that can accommodate any broadband technology, including the wireless technologies discussed below. Its importance is that it makes voice communications over cable viable. VoIP uses the Internet's packet-switching capabilities to provide voice communications services, giving VoIP several advantages over circuit switching. For example, packet switching allows multiple telephone calls to occupy the same amount of space on a circuit that is occupied by only one call in a circuit-switched network.

One of the chief issues with using VoIP or packet-switching technology for voice or two-way communications is a slight delay called *latency*. In networking, latency is the amount of time that it takes a packet to travel from source to destination plus the time the terminal equipment uses to assemble the packets in the proper order; in voice communications, this would cause a slight, but noticeable, delay in the conversation, which might be irritating to some people.[13] Consequently, at this time, the quality of voice communications over cable is inferior to that provided by circuit-based switching technology over copper or fibreoptic lines. Indeed, much of the phone service provided by cable companies in the USA actually travels over phone lines leased from the ILECs.[14] In addition, emergency or the E911 service is unsatisfactory. Because of the nature of the protocol, an E911 operator would have no way of knowing where a call originated, in contrast to the usual case where the phone number, and therefore the address, is provided by modern digital systems. This issue is under intense scrutiny but is as yet unresolved.[15]

As long as VoIP calls remain inferior to traditional wireline calls, cable and wireline companies can offer differentiated products and avoid a price war. However, as VoIP improves, it will probably become the standard – so both wireline and cable carriers will have to rely on VoIP. Such developments remove features that currently differentiate wireline from cable companies. We argue below that if VoIP improves enough to compete with voice communications provided by circuit-based switching, this lack of product differentiation would spell the end of either the wireline or cable companies in their current forms.

Wireless
A wireless network has different cost characteristics from wireline and cable networks, because its distribution network is wireless and its services are mobile. These differences have important economic implications for the construction and expansion of a wireless network. Because marginal costs are constant or increasing, multiple competing wireless companies have the potential to survive in the same operating area, as explained below.

For cellular wireless companies, the local distribution network is a group of adjacent cells, each with an antenna in the middle.[16] Calls travel from a handset to an antenna using a slice of dedicated radio spectrum, and then are routed from the antenna into the wireless carrier's backbone network and to their destination. If a mobile caller stays in the same cell, completing the call is as simple as that. If the caller moves from one cell to another, a handoff must occur from the antenna of the first cell to that of the second or the call will be 'dropped'.

Unlike their wireline and cable counterparts, wireless carriers have no need to build to ultimate demand, for two reasons. First, the radio spectrum that carries the calls can be reused by another customer as soon as one customer disconnects or moves to another cell. In contrast, on a wireline network, when a customer is not using his or her line to the local wire centre, no one else can use it; it remains idle.[17] Further, when a customer moves out of his or her house, the physical facility into the house remains idle until someone else moves into the house.

Second, the cells that comprise a wireless distribution network can be split in response to increased demand. While cell splitting requires the wireless company to provide more antennae and imposes additional construction and location costs, it also increases the number of calls that can be carried. For example, if one cell capable of handling 100 calls is split, each of the new cells created can handle 100 calls. Signal power is reduced in each of the new cells so that the calls do not interfere with one another. Because the wireless network is not built to ultimate demand, new equipment must be added to accommodate increased demand. If the new equipment always increases in direct proportion to demand, we have constant returns to scale; that is, doubling the equipment doubles the capacity. So, at best, the wireless network exhibits constant returns to scale with corresponding constant short-run marginal cost; at worst, it has decreasing returns to scale and increasing short-run marginal cost. Economic analysis tells us that both cost structures are consistent with competition.

Thus, as in wireline and cable, if multiple cellular wireless providers in the same operating area produce identical services, prices naturally will be driven to short-run marginal cost. Unlike wireline and cable, price competition may not be ruinous for wireless carriers as they have non-zero marginal costs. Moreover, if the wireless carriers' marginal costs are increasing, then there will be an amount in excess of short-run average cost that will be available for the recovery of startup and capital costs. Consequently, it should not be surprising to find multiple cellular wireless carriers competing in a given area. How many competitors can coexist depends on the optimal cell size and demand. The total demand in the cell divided by the size of the optimal cell is the maximum number of firms the cell can economically support.

Our opinion is that five or six competitors can survive in the larger markets; some financial analysts and other telecommunications experts put this number at three or four, and some as low as two. Time will tell. Right now most major markets in the USA have at least four competing cellular wireless providers, and four of these companies – Cingular, Sprint, T-Mobile, and Verizon – have national networks.[18]

Other wireless technologies
In this section, we briefly review several other types of wireless technology for providing communications services. These include: (1) fixed wireless, used for point-to-point communications; (2) wireless fidelity (Wi-Fi) and WiMAX, both of which are used primarily to link computers using a wireless network; and (3) satellite, which can be used for many different things, but for this discussion we will focus on its use as a broadband connection for Internet access and the provision of video.

Fixed wireless   In the past, ILECs used fixed-wireless networks mostly for wireless local loops (WLLs) when it was impossible to install cable to a remote location (e.g. very rural, swampy, or mountainous areas). These networks used microwave radio as their transmission medium. This application still applies, although fixed-wireless networks are also being used today as substitutes for coaxial and fibreoptic cable-based networks. A fixed-wireless network is capable of transmitting voice, data and video, the same as coaxial cable or fibre-based networks. However, most new fixed-wireless development is focused on data communications.

Cellular wireless systems and fixed-wireless systems both use radio spectrum. However, fixed-wireless systems require fixed antennae with narrowly focused beams and operate on a point-to-point basis. That is, an antenna at one location sends signals to an antenna at another specified location. Therefore, fixed wireless requires line of sight; that is, the two antennae must be able to transmit and receive without interference from buildings or other structures. This limits the distance over which fixed wireless can operate. Because of these limitations, fixed-wireless providers tend to focus on multi-tenant buildings as a potential customer base, making them more like a CLEC than a wireless provider.[19]

To encourage further development in fixed wireless, prices for network components (such as receivers and transmitters) must decline to a level that would allow fixed-wireless providers to compete effectively with current wireline offerings. That is, vendors must be willing to produce equipment on specification at sufficient scale to make it more economical for buyers. Given the beating that equipment vendors have taken recently in financing traditional equipment for the CLECs, this is unlikely to occur soon. Nevertheless, fixed wireless holds the promise of economically sustainable competition for wireline services because it has positive marginal costs and the service can be differentiated from traditional wireline service, primarily through mobility.

Wi-Fi and WiMAX   Wireless fidelity or Wi-Fi and WiMAX (short for wireless microwave access) both use the same fundamental technology – microwave radio – to transfer data wirelessly. Wi-Fi connects customers to each other and to the Internet without the restriction of wires, cables, or fixed connections; thus allowing consumers to change locations and to have full access to their files, office and network connections wherever they are.[20] In addition, Wi-Fi will easily extend an established wired network.[21] Like Wi-Fi, WiMAX is a standards-based wireless service that provides broadband connections over long distances and can be used for a number of applications, including 'last mile' broadband connections, cellular backhaul (the connection between the antenna and the switch which can be a distance away), and high-speed enterprise connectivity for businesses.[22] WiMAX can be used to transmit signal as far as 30 miles; however, on average, a WiMAX base-station installation will probably cover between three to five miles.[23]

What is the difference between Wi-Fi and WiMAX? They use different interoperability standards, operate at different speeds, and have different distance coverage. The fastest Wi-Fi connection is slower than the fastest WiMAX connection (currently 54 Mbps vs. 70 Mbps), which is comparable to the speed provided by a cable modem. However, the biggest difference between Wi-Fi and WiMAX is distance rather than speed. Wi-Fi usually operates in a much smaller area (a few hundred feet) than WiMAX (several miles). Moreover, WiMAX plans to license radio spectrum and to make the channels used to transmit data narrower, which means more data to more people using the same amount of radio spectrum. There are also plans to increase the distance customers can be from the base station.[24]

Wi-Fi and particularly WiMAX pose a serious threat to providers of DSL and cable modem services due to the potential flexibility they provide, and the fact that together they can completely supplant the wired networks. Like any other broadband technology, WiMAX can accommodate VoIP; for this reason, if WiMAX-compatible computers become common and VoIP technology continues to improve in quality, VoIP use could increase dramatically and wireline phone companies could be bypassed entirely. In addition, WiMAX has the potential to erase suburban and rural blackout areas where broadband Internet access currently does not exist. This is because WiMAX's last mile costs are probably far less than those of wireline and cable companies that do not find the provision of broadband service to remote locations economical.

Satellite Satellites are objects orbiting the earth used to transmit information via radio signals over long distances. Not long ago, telecommunications companies used satellites for long-distance calling when distances were so great that cables could not easily be placed, such as through oceans. Then, oceanic cables came into being and satellite, although still used, is not as important a transmission medium as it once was for long-distance telecommunications. However, this is not really the competitive satellite usage that interests us. Smaller satellites have become an integral part of our daily lives with services like DIRECTV and DISH Network for the provision of video and satellite broadband for the provision of two-way Internet access. Moreover, companies are advertising satellite communications for data, voice and Internet services.[25]

Satellite shares many features with the other wireless services discussed previously. Satellites require transmitters and receivers the same as other wireless systems. Spectrum can be reused, marginal costs vary with demand, although probably not in direct proportion, and the initial capital costs are high. Satellite competes primarily with cable in the video arena. However, satellite companies also provide broadband data services to consumers in rural areas who do not have access to DSL or cable modems. Although currently slower than DSL and cable in both the uplink and downlink for Internet connections, satellite can compete with those services. Latency problems make it even less suitable for voice transmission, although, as mentioned above, it has long been used for this purpose (e.g. for overseas calls) at a relatively high cost. Satellite is quite popular in Europe, supplanting cable, at least in the short run, for the provision of video services. We believe the satellite market can support at least one satellite video provider and a handful of satellite data providers in each area covered.

Structure and regulation of the industry

Industry structure

Based on the previous discussion, the economic incentives for consolidation in wireline and cable are so strong that competing wireline or cable carriers in the same operating areas are likely to merge or fail until all that remains is a single regional carrier having no direct competitors using the same technologies. Thus we would be surprised that if, in the long run, in any given geographic area, there would ever be more than one wireline provider and one cable provider.[26] Any entrant would face a brutal price war based on basic market dynamics. In the end, only one firm would survive. Currently, sufficient differentiation exists between cable and wireline offerings to make it unlikely that either one will drive the other out of business. Each has a core competency, video and data for cable and voice and data for wireline, but each can easily enter the other's space and compete if the prices in the other space become high enough to make entry profitable. Similarly, wireless and satellite carriers are sufficiently differentiated that the cable or wireline providers will not drive them out of business.

In the end then, the telecommunications industry will be characterized by intermodal competition among the surviving firms in each technology – wireline, cable, wireless and satellite. We see this phenomenon already as increasing numbers of wireline customers are dropping their second lines and replacing them with wireless or cable modems, and cable companies are competing fiercely with satellite video providers.[27] Wireline long distance companies are losing ground to 'anytime anywhere' packages offered by wireless companies. Besides, other telecommunications companies are buying up most of the surviving long-distance carriers (IXCs), thus effectively eliminating this segment of the wireline market. In a market characterized by intermodal competition, individual providers' prices may not be driven to short-run marginal cost, but neither will they be able to exercise significant market power.

At this point, it is interesting to consider moves by Verizon and SBC in the USA to provide their customers with fibre to the home or business, which we shall refer to by the common industry acronym FTTP (fibre to the premises).

FTTP allows a wireline company to provide voice, data and video services to its local customers at speeds significantly faster than cable or DSL.[28] In the past, telephone companies viewed FTTP as an expensive technology experiment and limited it to trials in showcase neighbourhoods to offer customers a glimpse of potential services in 'homes of the future'.

FTTP is now a reality. Verizon offers FTTP in certain serving areas under the name Fios, and claims that it is the 'latest in fiber-optic technology', delivering 'laser-generated pulses of light, riding on hair-thin strands of glass fiber, all the way to your front door. When Fios meets your computer, you can get broadband Internet up to 30 megabits per second'.[29] SBC unveiled plans for 'Lightspeed', its broadband project, in 2004. SBC plans to spend $4 billion over four years to reach 18 million households and ramp up from there. SBC also said that it planned to focus almost exclusively on affluent neighbourhoods. When SBC broke down its deployment plans by customer spending levels, it stated that 'Lightspeed would be available to 90 per cent of its "high-value" customers – those who spend $160 to $200 a month on telecom and entertainment services – and 70 per cent of its "medium-value" customers, who spend $110 to $160 a month'.[30]

Our technology-based model can predict the outcome of these developments. As things stand now, if VoIP becomes the norm, it is likely that cable will achieve technological dominance over wireline even in voice communications. Since both cable and wireline companies have zero short-run marginal costs, the price war scenario outlined above will develop, and the inferior technology will be driven from the market. If the wireline companies do not invest in FTTP, we think theirs will be the inferior technology. Therefore, improvements in VoIP could destroy the prospects for competition between cable and wireline providers for voice services. By rolling out FTTP, wireline companies may be attempting to establish a service that will technologically dominate the offerings of cable companies. Hence, FTTP initiatives being undertaken by both Verizon and SBC can be viewed as positioning for the great cable–wireline price war. We cannot guess who will win, but our model predicts that without product differentiation between the offerings, only one will survive.

Price-cap regulation
On a going forward basis, regulation must be consistent with the natural structure of the telecommunications industry outlined above. Treating a segment of the industry as a monopoly and regulating that segment as such will not have the expected consequences.[31] For example, asymmetric regulation of wireline companies due to an inappropriately narrow definition of their market could allow less cost-effective technologies to successfully substitute for wireline offerings. Regulators should not skew the market so that one technology has an unfair advantage over another, as discussed below.

Our model highlights important implications for price-cap regulation, the primary form of pricing regulation in the USA wireline industry today. Price caps are designed as a method of regulating a single firm that has no (effective) competitors. The first and last point to keep in mind is that where there is effective competition, the use of a price cap is both unnecessary and self-defeating. Furthermore, where there is no competition, either real or potential (i.e. where the market is uncontestable for the foreseeable future) we do see a role for price caps, and a corresponding role for regulators in setting and monitoring performance under those caps. Below, we discuss some practical aspects of implementing price caps for regulated companies, and then we turn to the issue of how to apply price caps when wireline companies provide both non-competitive and competitive services.

Practical issues in setting the price cap for regulated services   Rather than discuss the theory of price caps, our discussion focuses on the form of the cap adopted by the majority of regulators in the USA. The details of each plan vary among the states, over regions in the state, and even as applied to individual firms, but all plans set upper and lower limits on the extent to which prices for some or all services are allowed to vary. The lower limit is a price floor, which regulators impose to guard against the possibility that ILECs might attempt predatory pricing.

The upper limit, the price ceiling or cap, can take one of two forms: (1) a service specific cap (i.e. each service is specifically limited), or (2) a more flexible version where each service is bounded below (sometimes by zero) but the prices can rise freely as long as an index of the prices remains capped. Thus, if the cap rises 3 per cent, under the first scenario no price can rise by more than 3 per cent. Under the second approach, prices of one service could rise 10 per cent as long as the other prices of services included in the index fell enough to allow the entire bundle to comply with the overall cap. Quite often, the capped index is a revenue-weighted average of output price changes; as long as that index does not exceed allowed levels, companies are otherwise free to set their own prices.

Price-cap plans are usually determined as follows. First, hearings are held to rebalance prices or move prices closer to 'costs', the idea being to set initial prices close to what they would have been if the industry were competitive. Then services are assigned to baskets and caps are applied to indices of prices in the respective baskets. Often residential service is put in a basket of its own and the price is frozen or capped at current levels. Once initial prices are determined, the price cap for each basket increases or decreases according to a price-cap adjustment rule. The most famous of these is 'GDPPI − X'; that is, the price cap changes based on inflation (GDPPI) and X, which is usually some measure of productivity or relative productivity.[32]

Despite the seeming simplicity of price-cap regulation, a number of issues arise in implementation. First, the computation of price and productivity indices is fraught with controversy.[33] Though the theoretical underpinnings of the calculations were long ago put in place, in hearings each piece is subject to seemingly unending scrutiny. This is because some feel that the caps are too lax and allow the firm too high a profit, while others believe the caps are too tight and limit both entry and innovation. The former camp, which typically includes consumer groups, argues implicitly for a return to rate-of-return regulation and attacks the price-cap formula in order to lower prices.

Second, the formula requires that all inputs and outputs be taken into account, but usually only a subset of these inputs and outputs is included. This is often because regulatory commissions have no jurisdiction over some services and consequently cannot compel firms to collect and release certain data. Third, in deciding on the length of time over which the cap will apply, a tradeoff must be made between allocative and productive efficiency.[34] A short-duration cap is less effective in increasing productive or engineering efficiency; a long-duration cap is more effective in increasing productive efficiency. However, the shorter the duration of the cap, the better able the regulator is to prevent the firm from collecting monopoly profits and harming allocative efficiency. Conversely, a longer duration cap implies less regulatory control.

Price caps and competitive services   Where competition exists, price caps are simply too cumbersome to allow the market to function properly. In particular, a cap set too low discourages entry because it forces a new entrant to set similar prices. If this price is below competitive levels, the potential entrant cannot cover operating expenses much less startup and capital costs. A rational firm will therefore not enter. So entry is thwarted and an otherwise competitive market remains non-competitive. For example, in some states, regulators have frozen residential rates at their current levels, levels which are at or, as some have argued, below incremental cost, and allowed business rates to increase. The hope is that the increased prices on business services will help cover the costs on the residential services. Such pricing policies have encouraged entry on the business side but discouraged it on the residential side. Eventually, such a policy could leave a wireline firm that must serve both business and residential customers with insufficient revenues to stay in business. The firm would earn a normal return on the business side, but suffer a loss on the residential side.

Obviously, there will be a continued (and appropriate) demand for the regulation of wireline companies providing services that are currently deemed to be non-competitive. The central question for regulators then becomes: how should price caps be implemented when a wireline company produces both non-competitive services, such as local telephony in less populated regions of the country, as well as other services in urban areas subject to significant intermodal competition?

To address this issue, Jeffrey Bernstein and David Sappington, a former Chief Economist at the FCC (1999), have developed a price-cap formula that allows regulators to exclude competitive services from the cap, while still protecting consumers from an exercise of monopoly power. The truly innovative aspect of the Bernstein–Sappington method is that it allows regulators to set the appropriate price-cap adjustment factor (X), while circumventing a very thorny measurement issue: the measurement of input price and total factor productivity (TFP) growth specific to a particular wireline business. This measurement issue is important to address because there are joint and common costs among the various businesses, only some of which are regulated. With the Bernstein–Sappington method, regulators can calculate the appropriate price-cap adjustment factor based on aggregate productivity and price data; service-specific input prices and service-specific TFP growth data are not required. The method is simple: a price cap for the whole industry, including competitive services, is calculated in the usual way (i.e. GDPPI – X). From this we subtract an index of the change due to the competitive prices and divide the result by the proportion of revenues that are regulated.[35]

Recent industry history

Our model also explains many of the developments in the telecommunications industry during the late 1990s and early 2000s. Our model suggests that certain trends, such as entry into the provision of wireline broadband services by municipalities, may be economically non-viable while others may be profitable, such as specialization, product differentiation, and entry into the provision of services and content. We turn now to the specifics of these applications.

The telecom meltdown of the 1990s

An explanation of the meltdown of the 1990s follows simply from the technology-based model described above. Encouraged by the FCC's interpretation of the Telecommunications Act of 1996, CLECs entered the wireline market in droves in the USA based on the belief that the market would support a myriad of 'clone' wireline companies offering service through a combination of their own equipment and components leased from the incumbents.[36] However, the economics of the industry do not support this widespread view. As shown by the analysis above, only one wireline firm in an area can survive on its own merits.

Many small firms entered and by 2001 were mostly bankrupt. Some of these companies have reorganized repeatedly, but are now moribund and their equipment is idle and unpaid for. During the same time, the large wireline companies merged, forming even larger companies with greater economies of scale and scope.[37] Furthermore, some of these larger entities are acquiring IXCs, essentially removing IXCs from the market.[38] In contrast, during the same period, large numbers of wireless carriers took part in the FCC's spectrum auctions and entered the wireless market, and overall are thriving. The reason for the difference follows directly from the simple economics of our model: the wireline companies have very low or even zero short-run marginal costs. Therefore, cloned competitors cannot survive, except perhaps with government-mandated subsidies. Adjacent wireline companies may not compete, but may be able to reduce costs by merging, thus eliminating duplicate equipment. Wireless companies face positive marginal costs and have the ability to differentiate products. For this reason, they have a structure that need not produce a single survivor.

Inducing competition by regulating network access pricing

As a consequence of the FCC's attempt to jumpstart competition by unbundling the ILECs' networks and requiring that the ILECs' prices be set at their Total Element Long Run Incremental Cost (TELRIC), a great deal of attention has been devoted to two unbundling methods: *unbundled network element-platform* (UNE-P) and *unbundled network element-loop* (UNE-L). Under UNE-P, an entering CLEC would be able to lease switching capacity and the loop from a customer's premises to the wire centre from the ILEC. With UNE-L, the CLEC would have to provide its own switching. Under each approach, the ILECs' TELRIC prices are based on hypothetical cost models that have little if any validity; even if the models were accurate, it is unclear what the appropriate prices should be.

In order to remain in business, the CLEC must recover all of its costs; and these include its payments to the ILEC, as well as any of its own costs. Thus the CLEC's services necessarily cost the customer more than those of the ILEC, and there is certainly duplication from an economic point of view. Unless the CLEC provides a different service from the ILEC, it cannot survive. If it cannot provide a different service because it is competing using the same technology, then it is offering the same service at a higher price, and economics tells us that such a firm cannot survive.

Without regulations that provide CLECs with favourable but economically unjustified prices, terms and conditions of access to ILEC networks, the CLECs simply could not exist. In contrast, cable and wireless companies have developed and thrived over the same period without the help of the regulators. The reason they have done so well and the CLECs have not is a simple consequence of the technologies that they employ, as recognized by our model.

The continued maintenance of such an artificial and contrived environment has broader economic consequences. The extra cost of having CLECs in the market must necessarily be recovered either from ratepayers (through higher prices) or ILEC shareholders (through lower returns and/or bankruptcy). In turn, this inevitably puts the traditional wireline providers at a disadvantage relative to competitors using different technologies. If, for example, the extra costs are recovered from ratepayers, customers on the margin will move to alternative service providers who do not have the extra costs. On the one hand, as they do so the amount of fixed costs needed to be recovered from existing customers will increase, further driving away customers. As revenues fall, profit margins will be squeezed, making it difficult for the ILECs to invest in new or even replacement equipment. On the other hand, if these extra costs are not charged to ratepayers, ILECs' profit margins could decline, perhaps even below competitive levels. Investors will put their money elsewhere and, on the margin, investment in wireless and cable will appear relatively more attractive. Increased investment in cable and wireless may be appropriate for the market in any case, but market forces rather than asymmetric regulation should dictate the allocation of resources to competing technologies.

Municipalities in the broadband business

Recently, many municipalities have started buying some of the excess equipment and plant left over from the bankrupt CLECs and providing their own broadband and even telecommunications services rather than paying the ILEC for them. However, our technology-based model warns against this. First, if there is already a local broadband provider, the municipality will probably end up paying more for broadband than would have been the case if it had negotiated a deal with an incumbent for the services. Second, if the municipality intends to compete with the incumbent, there are only two possible outcomes: (1) the incumbent fails and the phone company becomes municipalized (as in the municipal provision of water supply, sewers and roads), or (2) the municipality fails and either goes out of business completely or is subsidized by tax revenues that could be better used elsewhere.

Where competition does not arise organically, rules should be instituted that aid the municipality in delivering services to customers who want them at a social cost that does not exceed the social benefit. These rules might entail improving the municipalities' bargaining positions with ILECs and other commercial providers of these services. For example, one could imagine a National Labour Relations type board that oversees the rules of negotiation between ILECs and public entities. But regulators should not develop rules that would subsidize or encourage inefficient entry.

The bankruptcy option for CLECs and ILECs

US bankruptcy laws provide two options for businesses. Chapter 11 allows reorganization, which implies that 'but-for' its debts the bankrupt entity is a concern that can pay for itself on a going forward basis. The firm is allowed to refinance its debt, write off some of it, or pay back some of it for a fraction of its original value. Chapter 7 is liquidation, a recognition that even a reprieve or forgiveness of some or all debt will be insufficient to make the bankrupt firm a going concern since it will never be able to cover its ongoing costs. This is the problem facing the CLECs in bankruptcy; viewed in light of the economic model discussed here, they will never be able to cover their ongoing costs because their very existence occasions a price war that favours the incumbent.

As discussed in the municipal broadband section, our technology-based model predicts that the incumbent firm has the cost advantage and will always win, perhaps not until after the ruinous effects of a price war for all concerned. In essence, our model predicts that Chapter 11 bankruptcies make little sense for CLECs; instead, they should be liquidated immediately and their equipment sold overseas where it is needed and will not cause additional market turmoil.

The problem of a bankrupt ILEC is another matter. It is reasonable to assume that a bankrupt ILEC will be a going concern and will be able to cover its operating costs. Therefore, for these companies, reorganization perhaps by sale to a CLEC with a better management team or a merger with an adjacent ILEC makes sense. Similarly, a bankrupt wireless company has equipment that can be used elsewhere, as well as valuable spectrum (except for that located in the most sparsely occupied areas or least-travelled areas). Accordingly, with qualifications, Chapter 11 reorganization for ILECs and wireless is an economically reasonable option.

The broadband mess

A number of companies including WorldCom, Enron Broadband, Qwest, 360Networks and PSINet attempted to become either broadband wholesalers or data-only carriers of high-capacity services.[39] They positioned themselves as 'carriers' carriers'; that is, they would carry the traffic generated by the traditional carriers on new high-speed fibre lines using the latest network management tools. Unfortunately, many firms entered this market segment in the USA, and a glut of capacity ensued, particularly in dense urban areas. In such areas, each duplicate network had the capacity to carry all of the forecasted demand many times over. Moreover, few of the new carriers had direct access to end users; therefore, they were simply wholesalers of identical services. As predicted by our model, a price war ensued forcing prices to zero and driving the carriers out of business.[40] Again, this scenario is the direct economic result of competition within a segment of the industry that has high capital costs and negligible short-run marginal costs. Surviving carriers appear to have been able to convince their customers that they are offering a differentiated product.

Structural separation is not the solution

Structural separation has been proposed both in the USA and elsewhere as a means to improve competition. Structural separation means splitting an ILEC into two independent entities, a wholesaler and a retailer. The retailer competes with other ILECs and has direct contact with the end-user customer. The wholesaler is anonymous and has no end-user contact except through the retailers, of whom there are many.

There are a number of problems with this approach. First, with intermodal competition, this intervention would appear to be unnecessary. Second, as in the electricity market, how can the retailer differentiate service: why would there ever be more than one retailer? Third, although splitting the company might allow more CLECs to survive, it would lose any synergies between the retail and wholesale unit and would insert an additional set of costs between the wholesale provider and the retailer. We are not convinced that more than one retailer could exist in the long term. At the same time, there is a risk that the additional costs put the wireline business at a disadvantage relative to wireless, satellite and cable competitors.[41]

Conclusions

Our simple model of the telecommunications industry fits the facts of recent history. It predicts the structure that seems to be emerging – one characterized by a few regional wireline carriers, none of whom compete with each other; a few regional cable companies, none of whom compete with each other; and a number of competing wireless and satellite companies that do compete with each other as well as competing with the wireline and cable companies. Much of the competitive discipline in the telecommunications industry will be intermodal, as in the transportation sector. Any attempt to raise prices will cause customers to migrate to substitute services. Thus, in most contexts, competition across technologies can be counted on to mitigate market power, and the role of regulation can be relatively limited and applied to those services that are currently non-competitive, such as local exchange services in relatively unpopulated areas.

Notes

1. The authors have benefited from discussions over the years on these issues with Larry Cole, Elaine Duncan, Aaron Edlin, Jeff Edwards, David Mandy, David Messerschmidt, David Salant, Timothy Tardiff, David Teece, Hal Varian, and Glenn Woroch. We also have benefited from having access to the outstanding reading list developed by David Sappington for his courses in regulation at the University of Florida. Patricia Cunkelman is thanked for her editorial and research assistance.
2. The local loop is the line from a telephone customer's premises – usually a circuit of two copper wires (a pair) – to the telephone company's nearest local switching centre (also called a wire centre or central office). The last portion of the local loop (from the terminal box, or pedestal, to the home) is a dedicated facility, as only the customer located at that site can use it. It is the same for cable TV.
3. The PSTN 'is the concatenation of the world's public circuit-switched telephone networks. … Originally a network of fixed-line analog telephone systems, the PSTN is now almost entirely digital, and now includes mobile as well as fixed telephones. The PSTN is largely governed by technical standards created by the ITU-T, and uses E.163/E.164 addresses (known

more commonly as telephone numbers) for addressing', *Wikipedia, the free encyclopedia*, s.v. 'Public Switched Telephone Network', <http://en.wikipedia.org/wiki/PSTN> (24 June 2005). In the USA the large ILECs, including Verizon and SBC, are the primary providers of ancillary services; CLECs also can provide these services, either by leasing capacity and components from the ILECs, building their own networks and interconnecting with the ILECs, or some combination of the two.

4. DSL technology is rapidly replacing traditional analogue technology. Concurrently, the large ILECs are undertaking major initiatives to replace the copper wire connecting their customers' homes to the local network with high-capacity fibreoptic cable. We defer our discussion of fibre to the customer's premises (FTTP) initiatives until later in the chapter.

5. Newer 'packet' switching equipment converts the call into a digital signal and then breaks it up into discrete units called packets before sending it over the network. Packets need not traverse the network using the same path and may arrive at the destination in a random order. However, each packet is addressed in sequence and assembled in order at the switching equipment nearest the destination. Then the call is routed back through another distribution network to the destination. Packet switching dominates data networks, like the Internet. However, packet switching in voice is still an emerging technology, as discussed further below.

6. The wires from all lines in the house go to this NID, which is where the responsibility of the phone company to maintain the network begins and its outside plant distribution network begins.

7. The telephone company's interoffice network links its central offices or switching centres together within that company's geographic boundaries. Calls outside that area travel over another company's interoffice network or a long-distance network.

8. When the network is already operating at full capacity, the short-run marginal cost is infinite.

9. This feature is what has allowed the development of DSL, which allows the simultaneous transmission of voice and data. The DSL modem and splitter connected to the existing phone line separate voice signals from high-speed data; thus a voice call and a DSL connection to the Internet can occur at the same time.

10. For example, signals degrade over distances on copper lines; hence the current network, with its existing equipment, cannot supply DSL beyond 18,000 feet from a switch. Even within 18,000 feet (6000 metres), copper can carry only so much information, the so-called Shannon limit. Clever engineers are working as we write to overcome these limitations. We note that DSL was the result of an earlier initiative to increase available capacity on copper wires. Copper-pair bonding, which simply means using many copper pairs to send a signal, may also increase the capacity of the PSTN.

11. Laffont et al. (1998) suggest requiring the ILEC to charge uniform prices. Under this rule, an entrant could survive by providing service in the low cost areas by undercutting the ILEC, who could not follow suit because it would have to lower prices to all its customers. We do not deny that this could happen if the costs of the entrant in the small area are below the average costs of the ILEC in its entire serving area. However, in that case, the entrant will take all the business there and become the new ILEC in that area. Instead of a few non-competing ILECs, the result will be many non-competing ILECs. Indeed, since the new entrant would be unregulated, the uniform pricing system would give the CLEC the incentive to acquire the ILEC or enter and completely replace it.

12. When cable companies first started providing Internet access, they were capable only of transferring data downstream, and customers had to send data upstream over their telephone lines. Many cable companies have now upgraded their networks with digital equipment and fibreoptic technology that allow two-way data transfers over cable. These cable companies set aside one cable channel for downstream data traffic and another to handle the upstream traffic from customers' homes.

13. Latency and bandwidth define the speed and capacity of a network.

14. Nevertheless, VoIP is growing in popularity. According to TechWeb News, cable VoIP subscribers increased from 50,000 in 2002/3 to 500,000 in 2003/4. See TechWeb News, 'Report: Cable VoIP Subscriptions Blasting Off', 2 February 2005, <http://www.techweb.com/wire/networking/59300576> (26 June 2005). According to Vonage, a VoIP company, it 'is currently

the largest VOIP provider in the US with over 634,000 subscribers as of the end of March, are adding over 20,000 per week, and well on their way to a million customers by the end of the year', Vonage Holding Corporation, 'Product Review', 18 May 2005, <http://www.vonage.com/corporate/press_reviews.php> (30 June 2005).

15. See FCC, *IP-Enabled Services; E911 Requirements for IP-Enabled Service Providers*, First Report and Order and Notice of Proposed Rulemaking, WC Docket Nos. 04-36, 05-196, FCC 05-116 (19 May 2005).

16. Cells get their name from their beehive-like structure. One can think of a set of cells as adjacent octagons, just like honey cells in a beehive. It is important to note that the interoffice or backbone network (the network that connects switching centres to other switching centres, IXCs, etc.) is very similar for wireline and wireless companies. Indeed wireless companies often lease the backbone facilities of traditional wireline companies rather than build their own. We note that no FCC regulation of rates, terms and conditions or interconnection agreements between carriers or their wireline competitors was necessary to bring about such leasing.

17. Only in the case of outmoded party lines are pairs subject to reuse.

18. Two other national networks, AT&T Wireless and Nextel have recently merged with Cingular and Sprint respectively.

19. Winstar Communications briefly had a very promising fixed-wireless service. After recovering from bankruptcy in 2001, it has restricted itself to providing services to governments. See CNN Money, 'Winstar files bankruptcy', 18 April 2001, <http://money.cnn.com/2001/04/18/companies/winstar/> (2 July 2005); see also Winstar, 'Government Solutions', <http://www.winstar.com/> (2 July 2005).

20. In technical terms, Wi-Fi is used generically when referring to any 802.11 network in the USA, which is an Institute of Electrical and Electronics Engineers (IEEE) standard for interoperability certification for wireless local area network (LAN) products. See *Webopedia*. s.v. Wi-Fi, <http://www.webopedia.com/TERM/W/Wi_Fi.html> (25 June 2005).

21. See Wi-Fi Alliance, 'Wireless vs Wired', <http://www.wi-fi.org/OpenSection/wireless_vs_wired.asp?TID=2> (25 June 2005).

22. WiMAX follows the IEEE 802.16 standard. See Intel, 'WiMAX – Broadband Wireless Access Technology', <http://www.intel.com/netcomms/technologies/wimax/> (25 June 2005).

23. See *Webopedia*. s.v. '802.16', <http://www.webopedia.com/TERM/8/802.16.html> (25 June 2005).

24. See Intel, 'WiMAX: Wireless Broadband for the World – An Interview with Jim Johnson', <http://www.intel.com/netcomms/columns/jimj105.htm>(25 June 2005).

25. See e.g. Encyberpedia Information Services, 'Broadband News Satellite Communications', <http://www.encyberpedia.com/satellites.htm> (26 June 2005).

26. Some CLECs might be able to differentiate their products enough to survive.

27. Second lines for Internet access are being replaced with cable and wireless services like Wi-Fi and WiMAX, and second lines used for voice are being replaced by wireless.

28. Although the Internet 'backbone' network is made up of fibreoptic cables, most customers connect to it through copper-based technologies like twisted pair, DSL, or a hybrid fibre-coaxial cable. These latter technologies have limited bandwidth and limited capacity to carry integrated voice, video and data services.

29. Verizon, 'About Fios', <http://www22.verizon.com/fiosforhome/channels/fios/root/about_fios.asp> (25 June 2005).

30. Leslie Cauley, 'Cable, phone companies duke it out for customers', *USA Today on the Web*, 22 May 2005, <http://www.usatoday.com/money/media/2005-05-22-telco-tv-cover-usat_x.htm> (26 June 2005).

31. See e.g. Viscusi et al. (2000).

32. The entire formula is $\% \ \Delta Output \ Prices = \% \Delta GDPPI - X$.

33. For a fuller discussion of the difficulty in setting price caps see Chapter 6.

34. Roughly speaking, allocative efficiency implies maximum consumer welfare as measured by consumer surplus. See Bigliaser and Riordan (2000).

35. Suppose that: (1) the price cap on overall output prices (C^*) is allowed to change such that $\dot{C}^* = \%\Delta GDPPI - X$ per year, and (2) the change in the output price index is $\alpha \dot{P}_r + (1 - \alpha)\dot{P}_c$, where α is the share of industry revenue due to the regulated services, $\dot{P}_c$ is the change in the

index of competitive prices, and $\dot{P}_r$ is the change in the index of regulated prices. Under the Bernstein–Sappington method, the rate of change in the price cap on regulated services is computed by solving these equations for $\dot{P}_r$. The formula for computing this change is $\dot{P}_r = (\dot{C}^* - (1-\alpha)\dot{P}_c)/\alpha$. Let us assume that the usual price cap would decrease 1 per cent annually and that regulated revenues account for 90 per cent of total revenues, while prices on competitive services are falling at 4 per cent. In that case, the cap on regulated prices falls by about two-thirds of a per cent per year, since $-0.067 \sim (0.01 - (1-0.9)(-0.04))/0.9$. This is not the full amount given by the traditional formula, but if the regulator sets the cap on regulated services more aggressively, the regulated company will not be able to cover its costs.

36. This belief was supported by some at the FCC, as reflected in the First Report and Order. See, 'In the Matter of Implementation of the Local Competition Provisions in the Telecommunications Act of 1996', *First Report and Order*, 11 FCC Rcd 15499 (1996).
37. NYNEX merged with Bell Atlantic, which in turn merged with GTE to form Verizon; SBC merged with Pacific Bell and then Ameritech.
38. SBC recently announced its acquisition of AT&T, followed shortly thereafter by Verizon's acquisition of MCI.
39. Once digitized, voice traffic is indistinguishable from data traffic.
40. For a list of bankruptcies, see *Converge! Network Digest*, Financial, 'A List of 67 Major Telecom Bankruptcies', <http://www.convergedigest.com/Mergers/financialarticle.asp?ID=4160> (1 July 2005).
41. See e.g. Viscusi et al. (2000).

Bibliography

Ai, C. and Sappington, D. (2002) 'The Impact of State Incentive Regulation on the U.S. Telecommunications Industry', *Journal of Regulatory Economics*, **22** (2), 133–60.

Armstrong, M. (1998) 'Network Interconnection in Telecommunications', *Economic Journal*, Royal Economic Society, **108** (448), 545–64.

Armstrong, M. (2002) 'The Theory of Access Pricing and Interconnection', in M. Cave, S. Majumdar and I. Vogelsang (eds), *Handbook of Telecommunications Economics*, Amsterdam: North-Holland Publishers.

Armstrong, M., Doyle, C. and Vickers, J. (1996) 'The Access Pricing Problem: A Synthesis', *Journal of Industrial Economics*, **44**, 131–50.

Baumol, W. and Sidak, G. (1994) 'The Pricing of Inputs Sold to Competitors', *The Yale Journal on Regulation*, **11** (1), 171–202.

Baumol, W., Ordover, J. and Willig, R. (1997) 'Parity Pricing and its Critics: A Necessary Condition for Efficiency in the Provision of Bottleneck Services to Competitors', *Yale Journal on Regulation*, **14** (1), 145–64.

Bernstein, J.I. and Sappington, D.E.M (1999) 'Setting the X Factor in Price Cap Regulation', *Journal of Regulatory Economics*, **16**, 5–25.

Biglaiser, G. and Riordan, M. (2000) 'Dynamics of Price Regulation', *Rand Journal of Economics*, **31** (4), 744–67.

Blackorby, C., Primont, D. and Russell, R. (1978) *Duality, Separability and Functional Structure: Theory and Economic Applications*, Amsterdam: North-Holland Publishers.

Cremer, J., Rey, P. and Tirole, J. (2000) 'Connectivity in the Commercial Internet', *Journal of Industrial Economics*, **48** (4), 433–72.

DeGraba, P. (2002) 'Central Office Bill and Keep as a Unified Inter-carrier Compensation Regime', *Yale Journal on Regulation*, **19** (1), 37–84.

Dnes, A. and Seaton, J. (1999) 'The Regulation of British Telecom: An Event Study', *Journal of Institutional and Theoretical Economics*, **155** (4), 610–16.

Economides, N. and White, L. (1995) 'Access and Interconnection Pricing: How Efficient is the "Efficient Component Pricing Rule"?', *The Antitrust Bulletin*, **40** (3), 557–79.

Gans, J. and King, S. (2000) 'Mobile Network Competition, Customer Ignorance and Fixed-to-Mobile Call Prices', *Information Economics and Policy*, **12** (4), 301–27.

Gans, J. and King, S. (2001) 'Using "Bill and Keep" Interconnect Arrangements to Soften Network Competition', *Economics Letters*, **71** (3), 413–20.

Kahn, A., Tardiff, T. and Weisman, D. (1999) 'The Telecommunications Act at Three Years: An Economic Evaluation of its Implementation by the Federal Communications Commission', *Information Economics and Policy*, **11** (4), 319–65.

Kahn, A. and Taylor, W. (1994) 'The Pricing of Inputs Sold to Competitors', *The Yale Journal on Regulation*, **11** (1), 225–40.

Kridel, D., Sappington, D. and Weisman, D. (1996) 'The Effects of Incentive Regulation in the Telecommunications Industry: A Survey', *Journal of Regulatory Economics*, **9** (3), 269–306.

Laffont, J., Rey, P. and Tirole, J. (1998) 'Network Competition: I. Overview and Non-discriminatory Pricing', *Rand Journal of Economics*, **29** (1), 1–37; 'Network Competition: II. Price Discrimination', *Rand Journal of Economics*, **29** (1), 38–56.

Laffont, J. and Tirole, J. (1994) 'Access Pricing and Competition', *European Economic Review*, **38** (9), 1673–710.

Laffont, J. and Tirole, J. (1996) 'Creating Competition through Interconnection: Theory and Practice', *Journal of Regulatory Economics*, **10** (3), 227–56.

Laffont, J. and Tirole, J. (1999) *Competition in Telecommunications*, Cambridge, MA: MIT Press.

Lewis, T. and Sappington, D. (1999) 'Access Pricing With Unregulated Downstream Competition', *Information Economics and Policy*, **11** (1), 73–100.

Oi, W.Y. (1971) 'A Disneyland Dilemma: Two-part Tariffs for a Mickey Mouse Monopoly', *The Quarterly Journal of Economics*, **85** (1), 77–96.

Sappington, D. and Weisman, D. (1996) *Designing Incentive Regulation for the Telecommunications Industry*, Cambridge, MA: MIT Press and AEI Press.

Shapiro, C. and Varian, H.R. (1999) *Information Rules: A Strategic Guide to the Network Economy*, Harvard, CT: Harvard Business School Press.

Shy, O. (2001) *The Economics of Network Industries*, Cambridge: Cambridge University Press.

Viscusi, W. Kip, Vernon, J.M. and Harrington, J. (2000) *Economics of Regulation and Antitrust*, 3rd edn, Cambridge, MA: MIT Press.

Woroch, Glenn A. (2002) 'Local Network Competition', in M. Cave, S. Majumdar and I. Vogelsang (eds), *Handbook of Telecommunications Economics*, Amsterdam: North-Holland/Elsevier Publishing.

Wright, J. (2002) 'Access Pricing Under Competition', *Journal of Industrial Economics*, **50** (3), 289–316.

15 The regulation of energy: issues and pitfalls
Colin Robinson and Eileen Marshall

Introduction

Almost always and almost everywhere the energy industries are regulated by governments. Of course, government involvement in market transactions is common, even in 'market economies': it often goes well beyond the establishment of essential market institutions (such as enforceable property rights, the maintenance of law and order and the provision of defence) that virtually everyone would agree is an appropriate function for government. Governments try to regulate markets, steering them in particular directions, which, they claim, are in accordance with the 'public good'.

Energy markets are among the most prone to government intervention. Energy, it is sometimes argued, is 'too important to be left to the market'. It is claimed, for example, that the energy industries have a significant environmental impact and that there are matters of strategy involved in energy supply, such as whether dependence on overseas sources of supply is desirable. This chapter examines the case for government involvement in energy markets and, where such involvement seems justified, the direction it can best take. First, however, it discusses what is meant by 'regulation'.

The meaning of 'regulation'

'Regulation' is not an activity exclusive to the state. In its broadest sense, regulation means the setting and enforcement of rules by some form of collective action. Such rules are an essential part of social and economic life, allowing individuals and organizations to deal with others in reasonable harmony. There is, however, an important distinction between voluntary and coercive regulation. Under voluntary regulation, in the energy industries as elsewhere, social norms and other rules of individual and business behaviour evolve through social and economic interaction, creating contracts and markets and, as time passes, adapt to changing circumstances: participants regulate themselves (though backed up by the rule of law, endorsed and maintained by government), and adjust the rules over time. By contrast, under coercive regulation, rules are imposed by governments on their citizens[1] and these rules are not naturally adaptive: they can be changed only by government action (Blundell and Robinson, 1999).

Regulation does not have to be only the domain of government, but the growth of government regulation in recent times[2] has meant that the term 'regulation' is now hardly ever applied to voluntary rule-setting, administration and enforcement.[3] Unless qualified, 'regulation' is generally understood to mean the setting of rules for others and their enforcement by governments and government-appointed regulators who aim to modify the outcome of voluntary transactions in markets. This chapter analyses regulation in that sense, as applied to energy markets, though it extends also to the creation of markets by regulators where such markets did not previously exist (as in the energy utilities). It discusses two distinct, though related, elements of energy regulation. First, there are 'energy policies' in which governments, for example, allocate exploration and production licences, control energy production, protect indigenous energy industries and try to modify the impact of energy activities on the environment. Second, there is regulation of the energy 'utilities' – efforts by governments or government-appointed energy regulators to set specific rules for the gas and electricity industries, relating for instance to the prices charged and the standards of service set by private companies (or sometimes by public corporations) and to bring new markets into existence. In the next section these various types of regulation are described. The following section then analyses why governments take these steps.

Types of government intervention in energy markets

Energy policies
Government energy policy measures can be categorized as follows.

Allocation of property rights in indigenous resources   Rights to explore for and produce indigenous primary energy resources such as oil, coal, natural gas and uranium are usually allocated by governments. Most countries make their awards by 'administrative discretion' – that is, a government department chooses which applicants should be licensed to exploit which areas – though a few countries, most notably the United States, allocate some of their resources by auctions that allocate licences to the highest bidders.[4] Whether rights are allocated by administrative discretion or by auctions can significantly affect the efficiency with which countries' resources are exploited, and may also influence their tax regimes (because award by administrative discretion, unlike auctions, does not collect resource 'rent').[5]

Depletion controls   Depletion controls are a device by which government or a government-appointed body regulates the rate at which indigenous reserves can be produced. In countries with indigenous energy resources, whatever their political systems, ranging from the United States to Norway to Russia and to the oil and gas producers of the Organization of Petroleum Exporting Countries (OPEC), governments more often than not intervene in the depletion decisions of private producers or operate production controls through the medium of state oil and gas companies.[6] The controls usually allow government to defer (or, more rarely accelerate) production and to influence the timing of the entry of new developments into production. Another form of control is 'repletion' – attempts by means of tax breaks, subsidies or administrative procedures to increase the total amount of a resource that is eventually recovered from an area.[7]

Protection of indigenous producers   When production of an indigenous energy resource is in decline, especially where the direct loss of many jobs seems likely, governments often act to protect the industry concerned. Attempts by West European governments, and particularly British governments of both major political parties, to protect their coal industries from the late 1950s to the 1990s, are an example (Gordon, 1987). Another form of protection has sheltered activities governments were anxious to promote, such as civil nuclear power from the 1950s onwards and 'renewable' forms of energy supply today.

Modifying environmental effects   Energy production, transportation and use all have effects on the natural environment, though there is controversy about the extent of those effects. Efforts to modify adverse environmental effects, especially to combat the apparent impact on global climate change of energy activities mainly because of carbon dioxide emissions, now constitute a major part of the energy policies of many developed countries.[8] Taxes on carbon, emissions trading schemes and the promotion of non-fossil fuels are all examples of actions which governments justify on 'environmental' grounds.

Regulation of energy utilities
Energy utilities – mainly gas and electricity companies – are also often supervised or controlled by governments. In the United States, for example, utility companies including gas and electricity suppliers have for many years had their rates of return regulated.[9] In Britain and many other West European countries, gas and electricity supply was for many years (and, in some cases, still is) in the hands of nationalized companies: in effect, gas and electricity were regulated directly by government through the boards of the state companies. Now that many European gas and electricity industries have been privatized, regulation has taken a different form: apart from the latest countries to have entered the EU, most other European Union countries now have regulators for these industries so that, instead of direct state control, government-appointed regulatory bodies supervise the companies. As privatization of utilities has spread around the world, utility regulation has spread also, so that many developing countries now have regulators specifically for their utility sectors (Parker, 2004).

At the beginning of the twenty-first century, therefore, energy regulation is a worldwide phenomenon. In many countries governments have wide-ranging

:rgy policies and increasingly they also have regulatory bodies to supervise gas and electricity utilities. What would justify intervention on such a scale?

Why regulate energy markets?

The reasons why governments regulate economic activities are invariably complex and are not necessarily consistent with the reasons economists would give to justify regulation. Economists tend to attribute intervention to attempts to correct market failures and governments often speak in market failure terms to justify their actions. However, references to these failures may sometimes be a cloak for other reasons for imposing regulation.

In practice, pressure group activity is clearly one reason why regulation of particular industries appears and is maintained. As public choice theorists have pointed out, interest groups have strong incentives to invest in lobbying vote-seeking governments because any gains are concentrated on their members, whereas losses tend to be dispersed over the population at large.[10] Moreover, there is severe information asymmetry in the sense that governments and regulatory bodies often have to rely on information from interest groups when making decisions and so are susceptible to the influence of such groups. It is true also that governments often rely on regulation rather than other instruments, such as taxation, because the costs are much less obvious to their citizens. Certainly, in the case of energy, there is no doubt that energy producers, trade unions, the scientific establishment, environmental groups and others have had powerful effects in shaping policies (Robinson, 1992, 2003).

If regulation is to a large extent the outcome of efforts by interest groups to impose their views on society through the medium of government, there is no reason to assume it improves welfare, even though carried out by government ostensibly for the benefit of the community. To discover whether regulation is or could be beneficial, the economic principles of regulation have to be examined. The standard basis for such an examination is to analyse the relevant market to determine whether or not it 'fails'. If it does, then means of correcting the failures through collective (usually government) action are sought.

In the discussion that follows we use the standard market failure approach as a starting point but with two major qualifications. First, there is the 'public choice critique' mentioned above, which points out the inconsistency of assuming, as mainstream economic theory does, that governments – intent on gaining and retaining power – will concentrate on policies that improve the welfare of their citizens as a whole (even if they know what such policies would be). In analysing market 'failures', we therefore draw attention, wherever appropriate, to the potential failings of government action to remedy those shortcomings. Second, there is the 'Austrian' critique which casts doubt on the notion of market failure, arguing that what neo-classical economists describe as 'failures' are merely departures from an idealized state of perfect competition that exists only in the minds of those economists (Kirzner, 1985, 1997). 'Failures' should not be treated as aberrations: they are an inherent part of all real-world markets and should be accepted as such. Austrians also argue that the perfectly competitive market model is incomplete and misleading because it concentrates on equilibrium and says virtually nothing about the *process* of competition which is essentially about the discovery of new ways of doing things by entrepreneurs.[11] This market process constantly reveals information that, according to the Austrians, cannot be gathered together by central planners because it is essentially decentralized. In the following discussion we therefore point out, in the appropriate places, where the Austrian approach can be revealing.

To make the discussion manageable, we divide it into two parts – first, 'energy policy' and second, 'utility regulation' (the rationale for specific regulation of the gas and electricity industries). For reasons of space we do not discuss methods of allocating licences to explore for and produce primary energy resources. Nor do we consider taxation of primary energy production, designed to extract natural resource rent, and taxation of transport fuels such as gasoline and diesel which exploits the inelasticity of demand for these fuels with respect to price.

Energy policies

'Failures' in energy markets
The underlying justification for the policies towards energy markets that exist in most countries is the idea that the interaction of producers and consumers in energy markets will, in one way or another, fail to produce outcomes that are in the public interest (Robinson, 1986, 1993, 2000, 2004). The adverse effects of these market interactions are, it is argued, sufficient to warrant corrective action by government. The main sources of alleged failure are, first, that markets do not provide adequate investment in security of energy supply because security has public good characteristics; second, that markets are myopic and do not foresee future price trends – in particular that they fail to anticipate the long-run rising trend of fossil fuel prices as scarcity increases and so suffer from short-termism in their investment programmes; third, that the external effects of energy production, delivery and use mean that markets will not yield acceptable environmental outcomes; and fourth, that markets fail to take into account the interests of future generations, either because they discount the future at too high a rate or because discounting is an inappropriate procedure to safeguard the interests of future generations. A fifth argument for intervention, discussed below under the heading of utility regulation, is that some energy markets are monopolistic and so government intervention is required to protect consumers from exploitation.

Analysing market failures

Achieving security of supply   One of the most common reasons governments use to justify energy policy measures is that energy markets, left to themselves, will not provide secure supplies for consumers. Governments often claim that energy is a 'strategic' good, that it is 'basic' to the functioning of society, and that its provision is too important to be left to markets. Those claims frequently lead to the argument that it is unwise to become dependent on overseas sources of energy because they may prove unreliable. Governments may therefore favour indigenous sources since, it is argued, they are more easily controlled and so are inherently more secure. For example, most documents on energy policy produced by the European Community give warnings about the possible insecurity of imported oil and gas and for many years such fears were behind the policies of individual governments which protected European domestic coal production.

Such arguments are unconvincing to many economists, but there is an economic rationale for government intervention to promote security of supply. It is that security has some characteristics of a 'public good' in that an individual or organization that invests in security provision is unlikely to be able to appropriate all the benefits of its action. For instance, an organization that invests in extra stocks of oil or in standby electrical generating equipment to protect against an interruption of supplies cannot avoid providing spillover benefits for others: first, because emergencies become less likely the more provision against them there is and second, because if an emergency does occur some of the pressure on supplies will be relieved by the organization's action. Thus the classic conditions apply in which investment in security will be less than optimal – if all the benefits could have been appropriated, there would have been more investment. So, the argument goes, the government should step in to compensate for the market failure. It could, for example, try to diversify sources of energy supply and energy technologies over and above what the market would do, thereby providing an economic justification for subsidizing a wide range of energy sources, not only coal, oil and gas but nuclear and renewables too.

The argument appears at first sight convincing but, on analysis, it seems much less so. First, there is the question of whether 'optimal' security is on offer. Optimality in this sense would result from a perfectly competitive market where all external effects had been internalized but, in the absence of such a market, how could optimal security be identified by a government? The idea that perfect policies can be discovered and implemented belongs more properly to 'Nirvana' economics (Demsetz, 1969) than to real-world choices. It can be argued that, since the market under-provides security compared with the ideal, the government should step in even if it cannot determine precisely what optimal security is because it knows that extra provision is justified. But the problem of government failure then arises. Governments have imperfect information and act in a fog of uncertainty (Downs, 1957). Not only do they lack information, even if they could see what would be in the 'public interest', they will not necessarily pursue it. It is naive to assume that politicians and civil servants are devoid of personal interests and simply aim at their perception of the public good (Tullock et al., 2000). Given that real-world governments are relatively poorly informed and are not simply disinterested servants of the public interest, a stream of unintended consequences tends to appear when they intervene.[12] For example, attempts at government security provision may crowd out private investment in security. One reason, familiar from other forms of regulation, is that when a government declares itself responsible for some activity, others naturally tend to opt out in the belief that government will provide. More generally, companies will often come to believe that governments with responsibilities for security will not allow markets to work in the event of an emergency: if they believe they will not be permitted to raise prices, the incentive to invest in security provision will be much diminished. Government action may then fail to enhance security or may even diminish it (Robinson, 2004; Marshall, 2005).

So the case for government intervention to improve security is by no means clear-cut. It is plain enough that, even though sellers have an incentive to provide security as one of the characteristics of their products, because that is what buyers want, they will not provide 'optimal' security in markets in the neoclassical sense. A very wise, fully-informed, far-sighted independent organization that acted purely on 'public interest' grounds might be able to bring about an improvement. But, given that intervention must rely on real-world governments rather than on Platonic Guardians, it is reasonable to be sceptical about its results. It is far from clear that imperfect security provided by government will be an improvement on imperfect security provided by energy markets.

Anticipating rising fossil fuel prices in the long run   One of the most deeply-engrained popular notions about non-renewable natural resources, such as the fossil fuels (oil, coal and natural gas), is that in the long run their extraction costs and prices will rise because, since they are finite, they will become increasingly scarce. So-called 'Ricardian scarcity' means that, as lower and lower quality[13] deposits of a natural resource come into production, marginal cost increases and so both costs and prices rise over time[14] (Tilton, 2003). The idea influences energy policies because, it is claimed, markets do not take a long enough view to recognize the increasing scarcity of coal, oil and natural gas. Government should therefore step in, using subsidies, tax breaks or direct action, to encourage the production of substitutes for fossil fuels: for example, it could promote nuclear power so that the resource base is increased beyond the fossil fuels or, as is the current fashion, it could favour 'renewable' forms of energy, such as wind or solar power,[15] that do not directly deplete the stock of fossil fuels. The rising price argument is also used to support depletion controls (see above) aimed at holding back production of indigenous resources for the long-term future when, it is assumed, they will be more valuable.

Economic theory may appear to support the rising price hypothesis but it is not so clear-cut, mainly because the relevant theory assumes complete information and abstracts from advances in technology. For example, it is not necessarily true that the lowest cost sources are exploited first. Because of imperfect knowledge, exploration sometimes reveals new sources that are lower cost than those already in production. Moreover, experience so far has shown that exploration constantly increases the quantity of known reserves, putting off the day when scarcity appears. New technology has in recent years reduced the costs of exploration and production and has brought into use resources previously considered uneconomic. New technology has also reduced the amounts of resources required per unit of production. Continued technological advance could conceivably make some resources worthless even though considerable quantities remain, because consumers have switched away from them: in that case, they will become less not more scarce.

In any case, the rising cost and price argument only states that they will *eventually* increase – not that they will do so in any given time period. Certainly the trend has not been upwards in recent times, though there have been periods, such as the 1970s and early 1980s, when fossil fuel prices (especially oil) rose substantially. Analysis of data (much from the United States) for well over a hundred years shows that real extraction costs, far from rising, have *fallen* substantially[16] and that prices have also tended to fall, though by less than costs. The reasons usually given for this declining cost trend are the technological advances mentioned above and, to a lesser extent, improvements in infrastructure and economies of scale (Barnett and Morse, 1963; Krautkraemer, 1998; Tilton, 2003). Estimates of the size of fossil fuel resources have constantly expanded because of exploration efforts and improvements in exploration technology.[17]

This empirical evidence should make one cautious about the view that governments should promote alternatives to fossil fuels when those alternatives cannot at present compete in the market. The result of such action may be to impose costs on energy consumers and taxpayers to deal with circumstances that do not come to pass. But there are also reasons of principle to question the case for intervention based on the prospect of rising long-run fossil fuel prices.

An underlying though often tacit assumption is that governments are better at forecasting long-run fossil fuel costs and prices than are markets. In practice, everyone has a poor record of predicting fossil fuel costs and price trends. But, given that market participants have a powerful profit incentive to make forecasts that are as accurate as possible, it is hard to believe they will be outdone by governments. Anticipating future prices is crucial for fossil fuel producers. If, for example, there is a trend towards increasing scarcity, that will tend to raise price expectations and the profit motive will induce private producers to hold back resources for the future: expectations of higher future prices will, other things equal, give suppliers an incentive to keep marginal units of their resource in the ground to be produced in the future when higher prices are expected. The supply response will bring forward the price increase to the present, inducing consumers to conserve their use of the resource and to switch to other resources that are less scarce. These responses will, no doubt, be 'imperfect' compared with the idealized competitive market, but at least they will be in the right direction – that is, consumption of an increasingly scarce resource will be reduced and of an increasingly abundant resource will be increased.[18] Moreover, diversification to non-fossil fuels will be encouraged by market forces. The intervention, or threat of intervention, by government may, however, as in the case of security of supply, displace private investment.

A more subtle case for intervention on rising price grounds does not rely on government's superiority as price-predictor. It uses the insurance principle – that no one knows what will happen to fossil fuel costs and prices but that, because they *might* increase substantially, the government should take out an insurance policy for the community as a whole by promoting the use of non-fossil fuels.[19] To calculate the size of the premium it would be worth paying would involve some heroic assumptions, for example about the probabilities of different future levels of fossil fuel prices, about the costs of the replacement fuels and about society's attitude to risk. A case could be made, on these grounds, for some support for fossil fuel replacements but of course the risk remains, as with any insurance policy, that significant costs are incurred against events that do not occur. Furthermore, it is possible in this case, as in those examined above, that there will be displacement of private investment by companies that, in the absence of government intervention, would have acted on the insurance principle, betting on 'long shots'.

Another problem in applying the insurance principle is that it is difficult to see what incentive governments have to spend money now on very long-term projects that are not obviously vote-catching. In this, as in other matters, governments in representative political systems are likely to be highly imperfect instruments when it comes to long-term decisions.

Safeguarding the environment   Arguments for regulating energy markets have concentrated increasingly on environmental externalities and, in particular in recent years, on the belief that the consumption of fossil fuels has adverse effects on global climate. A good example of the predominance of environmental considerations is the United Kingdom's February 2003 White Paper on energy policy (DTI, 2003), which says little about the policy concerns of its predecessors (Marshall and Robinson, 1984; Helm, 2003) but emphasizes the primacy of environmental issues in energy policy.

Markets will take into account environmental effects to the extent that those effects are of concern to producers and consumers. For example, if consumers become concerned about some environmental issue associated with energy supply, it will be profitable for producers to alter the characteristics of their products to meet consumer concerns and thereby to gain competitive advantage. Provided property rights are clear and are enforced by government, as they are or can be for many local environmental assets, owners will defend their rights against potential polluters as they would against other intruders and markets will work reasonably well. But where property rights do not exist or are difficult to establish, as in the case of the global environment, use of the environment will be free as far as a polluter is concerned, so there will be an external cost that is not fully taken into account by the market[20] and there will be a tendency to overuse the environment as a sink for wastes. In such cases, there is an argument for collective action to avoid over-use of the environment, where collective action includes both national government and international action.

It is widely believed that the emission of carbon dioxide from the combustion of fossil fuels is the most important such environmental issue at present. The argument is that individuals and organizations that burn fossil fuels have little incentive to reduce the emissions of carbon dioxide that ensue because they bear merely the private costs of their actions (the price of the fuel and associated costs): these private costs are less than the full social costs of those actions, including the adverse impact on world climate. Hence, the argument goes, the external costs should be incorporated directly or indirectly by government.

The case for government action to combat climate change is widely accepted, though a case against is made by a minority of scientists and economists (Robinson, 2004; Bradley, 2003). In essence the contrary case has three strands. First, there is a minority scientific view that a long-term trend to a warmer climate (the usual assumption about the impact of climate change) has not been established. There are doubts about the measurement of world temperatures and also about whether apparent recent warming is a trend or a cycle that will be reversed without intervention. If the cycle will naturally be reversed, intervention to moderate its warming phase might do more harm than good. There have also been criticisms of the projections of future warming made by the International Panel on Climate Change (IPCC)[21] (Castles and Henderson, 2003). Second, determining responsibility for any warming that has occurred is a difficult problem in multivariate analysis: it is not clear that carbon dioxide emissions are the main causal factor. Third, some economists question whether, if global warming is occurring, it will necessarily reduce world welfare. Some argue that increased carbon dioxide emissions and warmer temperatures will have beneficial effects. Others do not go so far but point out that, provided there are gainers as well as losers, it is very difficult to devise policies that will bring net benefits because interpersonal comparisons have to be made (Robinson, 2004).

There are also problems in determining what policies are appropriate if, despite the uncertainty, we act on the assumption that global warming is occurring. Programmes to reduce carbon dioxide emissions are likely to be extremely costly. One possible policy is to do nothing to reduce emissions, on the assumption that the least cost response is to let people adapt over time to a warmer climate.

If, however, the mainstream view is accepted, what policies would be appropriate? One is direct action by governments to promote energy sources that emit less carbon than fossil fuels. The two main candidates are nuclear fission power and renewable forms of energy, such as wind, solar, wave and hydro power. Most governments at present shy away from new nuclear power programmes, principally because of the potential adverse effects associated with nuclear fuel use and storage that make nuclear power unpopular with electorates, but many governments favour renewable sources such as wind and solar power. The British government, for example, is providing large subsidies for wind power in the hope of reaching a target of 10 per cent of electricity generated from renewables by 2010 and 20 per cent by 2020 (DTI, 2003; Simpson, 2004). Another form of direct government action is to try to persuade consumers to use less energy by subsidizing home insulation and other means of 'conservation'.

The problem with direct promotional action for particular fuels and with subsidized energy conservation is that it involves government in the difficult process of 'picking winners'. Bearing in mind the public choice and Austrian critiques of government action discussed earlier, the chances that it will succeed seem low. Governments, as explained above, are not disinterested servants of the public good: they are, for example, susceptible to the influence of pressure groups which are likely to be very influential in pushing their own interests when governments are known to be searching for technologies to support. Moreover, governments inevitably face the most serious problem of central planners – that they cannot gather together the information they need because it is essentially decentralized: the information that would otherwise have been produced by markets has been suppressed. Another approach, more appealing to most economists, is to apply standard microeconomic theory by introducing some general economic instrument that will take into account the externality and will then allow the market to adjust without being constrained by the views of the government about which energy sources are most acceptable and how much energy should be conserved (Marshall, 2005).

One such instrument would be a 'carbon tax' – a tax on fuel that varies according to the carbon emissions produced when the fuel is burned. Since the optimal tax cannot be calculated, the tax rate would have to be determined by government and so government failure would be involved in applying the economic principle: public choice theory suggests that the decision would be primarily political rather than economic. Another instrument, instead of directly putting a price on carbon by applying a tax, is a carbon trading scheme under which permits to emit specified amounts of carbon are allocated and trading of those permits encourages efficiency in reducing emissions; such a scheme would allow a price of carbon to emerge. Both carbon taxes and carbon trading schemes, in effect, mean dividing up the global environment to give 'pollution rights' to individual governments. There have been many experiments with such schemes and one was introduced by the European Union in January 2005 (Nicholson, 2005). Again there would be government failure involved in a carbon trading scheme because governments would not be acting simply to improve the welfare of their citizens: problems include setting and resetting the level of permits and their allocation.[22]

To summarize, there is a theoretical case for collective action where there appear to be particularly damaging environmental effects from energy production, distribution and use that cannot be reduced by the allocation of property rights. Global climate change may be an example though there is controversy about the details of the arguments usually presented and, as always with government and international action, there is the probability of government failure. As regards government failure in this case, a particular issue is that an organization with a very long view is required to deal with global environment problems. An interesting question is whether governments in representative political systems have such a long view. As explained in the previous section, they are likely to be generally reluctant to impose costs on voters for actions that will produce benefits only in the very long run during the administrations of distant successor governments.

Caring for future generations   An argument sometimes used is that governments should intervene in energy markets to safeguard the interests of future generations. It is claimed that the economic variable that links the present to the future – the discount rate – is deficient in providing for the interests of those generations. Proponents of this view sometimes go further and suggest that it is immoral to place a greater weight on present consumption than on future consumption, as discounting does. They would like to take specific actions, such as holding back a proportion of fossil fuel reserves for the benefit of our successors, for example by a depletion control policy (see above).

Placing a proper weight on the interests of distant generations – whose members have not yet been born and cannot therefore influence policies that may affect them – strikes a chord with most people. Yet identifying and implementing policies that would be beneficial to distant generations is fraught with problems. First, there is the question of what is meant by a 'distant generation'. Do we mean people who live in the second half of the twenty-first century? Or do we mean those who live in the twenty-fifth century? If the policy is to hold back some fossil fuel reserves for the future, there would presumably be an enormous difference in the amount we decide to hold back, depending on which generation is to be the beneficiary.

Second, there is the issue of whether measures such as holding back fossil fuel reserves would actually be advantageous to distant generations. These reserves are not 'lost' when they are produced; they are to a considerable extent transformed into capital equipment and technological advances that benefit our successors. For example, imagine what would have happened if 250 years ago our predecessors had decided to hold back for the twenty-first century a large part of Britain's coal reserves. Society today would have a lot of coal but would have forgone much of the capital stock and technological advance associated with the industrial and subsequent technological 'revolutions'. In material terms it would be much less prosperous. It is certainly quite possible that, far from increasing in value over the years, fossil fuels will turn out to be less valuable to distant generations than they are at present. They are scarce in the sense that they exist in limited quantities in the earth's crust but, in an economic sense, their scarcity might decline. Technological advance may, if it is allowed to happen, render the use of fossil fuels obsolete or at least less widespread than now.

It is as well to acknowledge that markets have many deficiencies when it comes to taking into account the interests of distant generations. But that is because of the sheer difficulty of the task of peering long distances into the future and deciding what would be best for our successors. Direct action aimed at helping them involves huge problems. Moreover, it invites extensive government failure. Governments do not have sufficient information for the action to have firm foundations and, even if they did, public choice theory raises doubts about their willingness to act in the 'public interest'. Open-ended commitments to benefit future generations would permit governments to take all manner of actions, whether or not genuinely directed at fulfilling those commitments, and the stream of unintended consequences is potentially massive.

Conclusions on the justifications for government intervention

The economic arguments for regulating energy markets in general, as set out above, are often used to justify government intervention. But, in assessing the effects of real-world energy policies, it should be recognized that they will be implemented by imperfect governments and imperfect regulatory bodies, lacking information and appropriate incentives, and so will have spillover effects on markets that are difficult to predict but may be adverse (for instance, because they reduce private investment that would otherwise have been forthcoming). The widespread, though usually implicit assumption that the results of government intervention will always and everywhere improve on what would otherwise

ie market outcome is therefore untenable. The results may be wel-
ng but, depending on circumstances, it is quite possible they will
:ducing.

Regulating gas and electricity utilities

A more promising field for government action appears to be the energy utilities
where one problem is that there are elements of 'natural monopoly' in the networks of pipes and wires that must be used to distribute the product.[23] If the
monopoly is genuinely 'natural', standard theory suggests that government
should intervene to protect consumers from possible exploitation by the sole
owner. But there are other reasons, such as attempting to promote competition,
why governments or government-appointed regulators might intervene in gas
and electricity markets.

As already mentioned, utility regulation by government agencies began in
the United States well over a hundred years ago. In Europe, because utilities
were often in the hands of central or local government, regulation came more
often directly from the relevant level of government. US regulation was generally based on controlling rates of return, which gave perverse incentives to
regulated companies to inflate their 'rate bases' to increase their total profits
(see below).[24] In more recent times, the pioneer in utility regulation has been
the UK which, when it privatized its utilities in the 1980s and 1990s, eschewed
US-style regulation because of its disincentive properties.[25] The UK model of
privatization and subsequent regulation has been exported all round the world,
though with variations according to local circumstances.[26]

Utility regulation in the UK, after privatization, had a number of novel features, examined below, which have now been copied to a greater or lesser extent
in many other countries.

Independent regulatory offices

Following privatization of the British utilities in the 1980s and 1990s,[27] a regulator was established for each of them who was appointed by the relevant
Secretary of State but was nevertheless independent of the political process because he or she had a set (renewable) term, usually five years. This independence
helped to give investors in the newly privatized utilities confidence that the industries would not be used to further the government's macroeconomic
objectives, as had happened under nationalization (Heald, 1980). The regulator
was able to establish an office and appoint his or her own staff. The original office for gas was the Office for Gas Supply (Ofgas) and for electricity the Office
of Electricity Regulation (Offer): in 2000 they were merged to form the Office
of Gas and Electricity Markets (Ofgem).

Measures were put in place to help ensure a transparent and relatively predict-
able regulatory system. First, the discretion of the regulators was constrained

by their general duties and powers set out in the relevant Acts of Parliament. Second, the regulated companies had a clear idea of the rules under which they would operate because each had a licence detailing their obligations and constraints. Third, appeals against regulators' decisions were to the Monopolies and Mergers Commission (now the Competition Commission) if they related to suggested licence modifications, including changes to the price control formula, and to the courts for certain other decisions.

Thus the regulatory regime sought to achieve what most economists consider to be the highly desirable separation of policy from regulation, and the day-to-day management of the utilities from both. Perhaps surprisingly, so far – 20 years after the privatization of gas and 16 years after electricity privatization – this separation has been maintained in practice.

Price regulation

Price-cap regulation was introduced in Britain when the first utility (British Telecommunications) was privatised in 1984, using an RPI – X formula in which RPI is the change in the retail price index and X is a term (usually a deduction) designed to increase efficiency by reducing the allowed price change to less than the change in the average retail price level in the economy.

RPI – X was designed to discourage profit being made from the exercise of monopoly power but to allow profit to be earned from improved efficiency. It fixes prices for a period ahead, usually five years for the 'natural monopoly' networks, giving the company an incentive to reduce costs, thus increasing profits, during that period. *Expected* increased efficiency over the period will be taken into account by the regulator and passed on to consumers by the initial level of X. When the price control comes to be reset, the company will keep any *unanticipated* gains made during the initial period including those due to greater than expected efficiency. The new information available by that time to the regulator will be taken into account when setting the next forward-looking level of X. Thus lower-than-anticipated costs in the initial period resulting from efforts by the company will result in lower prices to consumers in the next period.

Price-cap regulation is generally regarded as an improvement on 'rate of return' regulation, where, in the US, either the regulator or the regulated company can initiate a review at any time. The regulator audits the company's cost calculations and determines a 'fair' rate of return on capital employed: these data plus demand assumptions are then used to calculate total revenue requirements. Rate of return regulation can distort investment decisions, depending on the rate of return allowed by the regulator; it requires continuing supervision by the regulator of the company's assets and their use; and it provides no strong incentive to cut costs – indeed, it may encourage 'gold-plating' of investments (Averch and Johnson, 1962).

There are, however, dangers in applying price caps in circumstances other than those for which they were originally intended. The intention was to use them as a temporary means of controlling prices in the period before competition became established, being used permanently only in natural monopoly areas (Beesley and Littlechild, 1983). But it may well be that, because of pressure from international institutions, they are being used inappropriately in countries with little capacity to regulate (Parker, 2004). Even in Britain, its original home, whole industries, such as water in England and Wales, are being regulated permanently by a price cap without any attempt to distinguish between natural monopoly and potentially competitive sectors.

Another danger is that price caps revert over a period to rate of return regulation. The closer a regulator comes to accepting company estimates of future costs and then applying to them a cost of capital, and the shorter the period between price reviews, the closer the system will come to rate of return regulation and its claimed superior incentives will be lost.

Network separation

The conventional wisdom used to be that utilities are natural monopolies in their entireties: it then followed that regulators should attempt to control prices for the utility as a whole. The newer approach to utility regulation, however, aims to separate potentially competitive sectors of an industry from those that are genuinely naturally monopolistic, introducing competition to the former and, after an interim period of pro-competitive regulation designed to stimulate entry, regulating only the latter.

Separation of naturally monopolistic (network) activities from potentially competitive activities has been accomplished most successfully in the energy utilities in Britain, principally by the regulators themselves in combination with the competition authorities. The privatization schemes either failed to make any separation (gas) or made it only partially (electricity).[28] With the network separated and regulated as a natural monopoly, the remaining parts of the gas and electricity markets in the UK have been opened up to competition: all consumers have freedom of choice of supplier and there is no longer any regulation of retail prices.

The reason network separation is so crucial is that, without it, the prospects for introducing competition are poor and most research shows that it is the degree of market liberalization that is the prime determinant of the extent to which consumers benefit from privatization.[29] The network must be used by entrants to supply consumers and so, unless it is independently operated and the owner has no incentive to discriminate against entrants, new suppliers will not emerge, as the Monopolies and Mergers Commission (MMC) explained in its report on gas in 1993. Of the then British Gas, the MMC observed it was:

both a seller of gas, and owner of the transportation system which its competitors have no alternative but to use. In our view, this dual role gives rise to an inherent conflict of interest which makes it impossible to provide the necessary conditions for self-sustaining competition. (Monopolies and Mergers Commission, 1993, para 1.6)

Removing the statutory monopoly to supply consumers from an incumbent by privatization is not sufficient to ensure competition thrives. Without network separation and the market liberalization that then becomes possible, the gains from privatization are bound to be limited. The industry in question is likely to be governed by a regulator indefinitely.

Promoting competition

Perhaps the most fundamental component of the new regulatory regime was a move away from traditional price and profits regulation towards attempts to introduce competition into the utilities concerned. The intellectual foundation of traditional regulation had been, as in other microeconomic policy-making, to aim at achieving the results of perfect competition which, implicitly or explicitly, were regarded as an ideal outcome. The problem for the would-be regulator is that it is impossible to identify what the outcome of a competitive market would be without letting competition take place (Kirzner, 1997). Paradoxically, only with the perfect foresight associated with the perfect market could such a forecast be made. Consequently, the regulatory regime has no firm anchor, the regulator's objectives are unclear and uncertainty is generated for the regulated companies.

The new British system, as it evolved in the energy industries (Helm, 2003; Robinson, 2004) provides a different and firmer anchor. Instead of using the neoclassical ideal of perfect competition, its aim is closer to the Austrian idea of competition as a process of knowledge-creation and discovery (Hayek, 1948; Kirzner, 1997; Littlechild, 1978). This is beneficial to consumers because it promotes entrepreneurship and innovation, the gains from which are passed on to consumers because of marketplace rivalry. Rather than trying to guess at the outcome of a competitive market and then attempting to emulate it, the regulator attempts to start a competitive process. The regulator does not know where competition will lead, because that depends on the responses of entrepreneurs and consumers, but the process itself is assumed to be beneficial. It is the introduction of a competitive process that anchors the system.

It is unlikely that the British government itself was imbued with these intellectual ideas. But the results in some of the utilities were *as if* neo-Austrian economics was in the ascendant. The government was determined to avoid the deficiencies of US-style regulation and, by giving utility regulators duties to promote competition, it provided the regulators with incentives to start competitive processes.[30] Pro-competition duties, which encouraged the regulator to act in the consumer interest, also helped to avoid the problem of 'regulatory capture', under which regulators come to identify with producer interests (Stigler, 1971). Regulation thus had a different emphasis from what had been traditional. Instead of simply trying to control prices or profits, regulators could become proactive, taking the initiative to stimulate entry. Some regulators were more responsive than others.[31] In the British gas and electricity industries, in particular, there was a determined drive to introduce competition. Moreover, the regulators were encouraged by their duties to define natural monopoly areas narrowly. They stripped away activities that had previously been considered part of the network but were potentially competitive (such as meter provision, meter reading and storage), permitted competitive extensions to networks and generally minimized the area to which price regulation applied.

Conclusions on regulatory regimes

It would be wrong to give the impression that the main elements of the new regulatory systems, as originated in Britain and then transferred elsewhere, were all planned ex ante. The originators began with a view that competition is the best safeguard consumers can have, so all potentially competitive sectors should become actually competitive. From then on, regulators discovered what to do by learning from experience. Learning experiences were different in different utilities and some regulators were more active than others in promoting competition, so outcomes also differed. But the result, as far as the energy utilities are concerned, is a genuinely innovative form of regulation. The regulatory regime placed an emphasis on market entry and liberalization, leading to an open access transport network that entrants could use, and thus to the effective introduction of competition into the production and supply of gas and electricity.

Wholesale markets

A particularly difficult issue in liberalizing energy utilities is how to introduce competition into electricity generation. Generation is clearly a potentially competitive sector of the electricity market. Rivalry in generation should drive down costs and, provided retail markets are also competitive, rivalry in the supply of electricity should pass on those cost reductions to customers. Yet, in Britain, because of some unfortunate features of the privatization scheme, it took many years before competition in generation became established. There are lessons for other countries, some of which are following the original post-privatization scheme in England and Wales that has now been discarded.

The privatization scheme in England and Wales, which established two large fossil fuel generators, was not well suited to competition. Nevertheless, there was substantial entry to the industry once the previous government ban on the use of gas in power stations was lifted.[32] Many generators entered the industry with new natural gas-fired plant, under the 'dash for gas'. Despite the volume of entry, prices were little affected because of the way prices were set under the electricity pooling system (Robinson, 1996), almost invariably by the two big generators. Under a centralized pooling and despatch system through which virtually all wholesale electricity generated was bought and sold, the system operator was responsible for ranking in merit order generators' bid prices for 30-minute periods in order to meet the system operator's forecasts of electricity demand. All generators were paid the highest accepted bid, which set the system marginal price. The 'Pool' was carried over with some changes from the 'Merit Order' which had been operated by the Central Electricity Generating Board (CEGB) under state ownership.[33]

The Pool clearly acted to restrict competition. As a centralized system it was incompatible with a liberalized market and, as the regulator found, it quickly became very resistant to change. The extent to which it had kept up prices was revealed when it was replaced by the New Electricity Trading Arrangements (NETA) in 2001and wholesale prices in England and Wales fell about 40 per cent in the short term.[34]

The underlying idea behind NETA was to promote competition in generation (and thereby enhance competition in supply) by making the electricity wholesale market as close as possible to a normal commodity market (Marshall, 2003). The main obstacle to achieving that aim is that electricity markets must be balanced in real time: storage possibilities are very limited[35] so that, in any given time period, the amount demanded must be supplied. Thus market power is endemic in that, close to real time, both supply and demand curves for electricity tend to be very price inelastic.

NETA's solution was to establish a system in which the great bulk of electricity is traded and priced through forward, futures and short-term markets by bilateral trading among generators, suppliers, traders and customers. The forward and futures markets, developed by market participants rather than being imposed by government, allow contracts for electricity to be struck for several years ahead. Similarly, short-term power exchanges give participants the opportunity to 'fine tune' their contract positions close to the time when supply has developed. Thus decentralized, competitive markets operate for most of the electricity that is bought and sold.

However, close to real time, a centralized balancing mechanism operates under which the system operator[36] buys and sells electricity in order to balance the system. By the time the balancing mechanism opens for a trading period (initially one hour before real time in Britain) generators' and suppliers' contract positions will normally closely match their anticipated metered output and metered demand. But intervention by the grid operator is required to meet unanticipated changes on both the generation and demand sides. A feature of the regime is that, alongside generators' offers to supply extra electricity, large customers and suppliers can also bid in the balancing mechanism to reduce their consumption, thus helping the system operator balance supply and demand.

These new arrangements in Britain[37] do not eliminate the problem of market power in generation, but they confine it to a restricted part of the market under a clearly defined balancing system. Just as the electricity and gas regulator has minimized the natural monopoly sector of the two markets by introducing competition into peripheral areas of the networks (see above), it has stimulated competition in the wholesale electricity market to the extent that most wholesale electricity is not subject to utility-specific regulation. The system operator remains responsible for the physical balancing of the system but, as explained above, the supply of 'balancing' electricity is now a two-sided market with both generators and demand-side participants.[38]

Conclusions

Energy markets in most countries are regulated, to a greater or lesser extent. Energy regulation involves both the formulation of 'energy policies' and the regulation of gas and electricity utilities.

Energy policies in different countries have common features – for example, they are ostensibly designed to enhance security of energy supply, to anticipate future fossil fuel price trends, to avoid excessive environmental damage, and in some cases to safeguard the interests of distant generations. In all these cases, 'failures' in markets are the reasons usually given for government intervention. However, it is uncertain to what extent there have been real efforts to deal with market failures or whether these policies are primarily the outcome of lobbying by pressure groups. Moreover, examination of supposed failures and the likely consequences of intervention suggests that government attempts to deal with them will not necessarily lead to improvements in welfare.

Regulation of energy utilities has, in the past, often assumed that these utilities are natural monopolies in their entireties so that their prices or profits should be regulated. However, energy regulation in Britain, following privatization, has shown that gas and electricity markets are potentially competitive, except for the networks of pipes and wires. Once the regulator has introduced competition into the supply of the product for large and small consumers, its role reverts to the more traditional one of controlling the prices charged by the networks. British experience also shows that it is possible to deal with the apparently intractable problem of market power in electricity generation through the normal processes of a commodity market, using a very close-to-real-time balancing system which provides the necessary physical equation of supply and demand.

Notes

1. 'Imposition' does not necessarily imply a lack of consent. There may be a majority in favour of a new rule or, in a democratic system, a government may have received a mandate for the general direction of its regulatory actions.
2. Government regulation has grown to such an extent that, in many countries, attempts to curb

it have been made (OECD, 1998). An example of a body that is trying to avoid excessive regulation in the UK is the British Better Regulation Task Force. The BRTF's publications are listed on www.brtf.gov.uk.

3. In some professions (such as law, accountancy and medicine) there is a degree of self-regulation. Franchising might also be thought of as a form of self-regulation. However, non-government regulation is beyond the scope of this chapter.

4. Bids are not necessarily in cash. They can be in terms of the percentage royalties bidders agree to pay if their exploration is successful and they go into production.

5. The efficiency disadvantages of awards by administrative discretion disappear if the licences can subsequently be traded. A good analysis of the pros and cons of auctions and of why auctions were not used in the early days of British North Sea oil is in Dam (1976); see also Robinson and Morgan (1978) and Robinson (1981).

6. An exception is British offshore oil where, despite the presence of all the apparatus of depletion control, governments have been very reluctant to use those controls to influence production. See Robinson (1981).

7. The term was coined by the House of Commons Select Committee on Energy (1982), para 95.

8. In the 1980s and early 1990s, environmental policy concentrated on reducing sulphur emissions, particularly from power stations, which appeared to cause 'acid rain'.

9. The United States Interstate Commerce Commission was established in 1887, initially to control rail freight charges and passenger fares. For the history of US regulation see High (1991).

10. For an introduction to public choice theory see Tullock et al. (2000).

11. Friedrich Hayek (Hayek, 1948) is the originator of the idea of competition as a process of discovery; see also Kirzner (1985, 1997).

12. For example, in Britain protection of the indigenous coal industry from the late 1950s to the late 1980s had perverse effects on security. The monopoly power of the coal industry and its trade unions was enhanced, increasing the frequency of strike threats and actual strikes, requiring costly counteraction (such as holding very high coal stocks for power stations). In addition, the strikes themselves, especially the year-long miners' strike of 1984–85, were very costly to the economy; see Robinson and Marshall (1985).

13. 'Quality' can be lower for many reasons: for example, because a resource deposit is in a region which is inaccessible, because it lies very deep under the earth or under the sea, or because the inherent quality of the resource is poor (in the case of crude oil, for instance, because the oil is highly viscous and requires expensive refining).

14. The idea that the prices of non-renewable natural resources will rise over time is also consistent with the 'Hotelling rule' which is that the net prices (margins over cost) of producers of such resources will increase over time at a percentage rate equal to the rate at which they discount the future. If this equality does not apply, it pays producers to rearrange their production programmes so equality is achieved (Hotelling, 1931).

15. The British government's present fuel policy relies heavily on support for renewable forms of energy (DTI, 2003).

16. The classic study (Barnett and Morse, 1963), which showed that the real unit costs of extracting minerals had fallen nearly 80 per cent in the previous 90 years, has been confirmed in terms of the direction of change by many subsequent studies. Prices have not fallen as much as costs but there is little evidence of a rising trend (Krautkraemer, 1998). For example, the price of crude oil in real terms in late 2004, following a very big increase during the year, was significantly lower than in the last quarter of the nineteenth century (British Petroleum, 2004).

17. Considerable confusion is caused by the relatively small size of 'proved reserves', which denote only that proportion of the resource base that is known and can be economically extracted at current costs and prices. British Petroleum (2004) gives a definition of proved reserves. They are essentially the oil industry's working inventory of reserves which will be added to or depleted according to the prospective rate of return on exploration expenditure.

18. Experience in the 1970s and early 1980s is a good illustration of the adaptive capacity of energy markets. After a huge increase in crude oil prices starting in the early 1970s, which many

people argued presaged long-run scarcity, oil and other energy markets adjusted so that, within about ten years, by the early 1980s the world was awash with crude oil, prices were falling and OPEC was trying to cut production to hold up prices (Penrose, 1984).

19.   It is assumed that normal insurance markets would not be able to provide this kind of insurance and so the government should step in. This insurance principle is different from the crude 'precautionary principle' which is appealing to many environmentalists. Acting on the precautionary principle leads to a general presumption in favour of government action to deal with the many problems that might occur in the future rather than leaving those problems to be dealt with primarily by market forces (Robinson, 2000).

20.   Provided the environmental effect is of some concern to producers and consumers (see above), the market will take it into account to some extent.

21.   The IPCC is a joint subsidiary of the World Meteorological Organization and the United Nations Environment Programme which makes forecasts of climate change and its impact and proposes means of combating it. Its emissions scenarios are in IPCC (2000).

22.   Provided the permits are tradable, the initial allocation will not affect the efficiency of the scheme but there will be distributional implications (Coase, 1960).

23.   Monopolies that are 'natural' at a point in time need not remain so for ever. The presence of a profitable monopoly is an inducement to ingenious people to try to enter the market and so undermine the monopoly. Regulators need to be alert to the possibility of entry and to ensure that their actions do not discourage it.

24.   The seminal article on these perverse incentives is Averch and Johnson (1962).

25.   Much of the credit for the radical features of the British regulatory system is due to the late Professor Michael Beesley who was influential with the government when the system was devised and also played a major role in advising the new regulatory offices, especially in gas and electricity. Beesley (1997) sets out some of his thinking.

26.   This is not to suggest that proper account has always been taken of local conditions when applying the UK model: see for example Parker (2004).

27.   For a description of the privatizations in Britain, see Parker and Saal (2003).

28.   Government failure is a feature of the British privatization programme (Robinson, 1992, 2003). Despite the efforts of government advisers, nowhere was a clear division made between networks and potentially competitive sectors.

29.   Without market liberalization, there may well be gains in productive efficiency as companies enter the market for corporate control and so stock market pressures enhance their efficiency. But, unless consumers have choice of supplier, there is no automatic mechanism for passing on efficiency gains to consumers in terms of lower prices and better service standards.

30.   There was an accidental element in the inclusion of this duty in the relevant legislation (Robinson, 1994).

31.   There were some differences in the specification of the pro-competition duty. For example, the water regulator had a duty only to 'facilitate' rather than to promote competition.

32.   The electricity generators, in principle, had free choice of fuels from the time of privatization. In practice, for the first three years, up to 1993, the government insisted that the generators used large amounts of coal. Once these coal contracts were reduced the 'dash for gas' began.

33.   For example, under the Merit Order generating plants were ranked for despatch in terms of their costs; under the Pool the ranking was in terms of the prices they bid.

34.   NETA was introduced by the government on the basis of proposals by the regulator.

35.   Some electricity can be 'stored' in the form of 'pumped storage' schemes which allow water reservoirs to be filled and kept ready to generate electricity via hydroelectric schemes at very short notice.

36.   Originally National Grid Company but now National Grid Transco which is responsible for gas as well as electricity transmission.

37.   NETA was originally introduced for England and Wales but the Energy Act 2000 made provision for the arrangements to be extended to Scotland.

38.   Similar competitive arrangements have also been introduced into wholesale gas markets; see Yarrow (2002).

References

Averch, H.A. and Johnson, L.L. (1962) 'Behavior of the Firm under Regulatory Constraint', *American Economic Review*, **52** (5), 1052–69.

Barnett, H.J. and Morse, C. (1963) *Scarcity and Growth: The Economics of Natural Resource Scarcity*, Baltimore, MD: Johns Hopkins Press.

Beesley, M.E. (1997) *Privatisation, Regulation and Deregulation*, 2nd edn, London: Routledge.

Beesley, M.E. and Littlechild, S.C. (1983) 'Privatisation: Principles, Problems and Priorities', *Lloyds Bank Review*, 1–19.

Blundell, J. and Robinson, C. (1999) *Regulation Without the State*, Occasional Paper 109, London: Institute of Economic Affairs.

Bradley, Robert L. Jr (2003) *Climate Alarmism Reconsidered*, Hobart Paper 146, London: Institute of Economic Affairs.

British Petroleum (2004) *Statistical Review of World Energy*, London: BP.

Castles, I. and Henderson, D. (2003) 'Economics, Emissions Scenarios and the Work of the IPCC', *Energy and Environment*, **14** (4), 415–35.

Coase, R. (1960) 'The Problem of Social Cost', *Journal of Law and Economics*, **3** (1), October, 1–44.

Dam, K.W. (1976) *Oil Resources: Who Gets What How?*, Chicago: University of Chicago Press.

Demsetz, H. (1969) 'Information and Efficiency: Another Viewpoint', *Journal of Law and Economics*, **12** (1), 1–22.

Downs, A. (1957) *An Economic Theory of Democracy*, London: Harper and Row.

DTI (2003) *Our Energy Future – Creating a Low Carbon Economy*, Cm 5761, London: DTI.

Gordon, R.L.(1987) *World Coal: Economics, Policies and Prospects*, Cambridge: Cambridge University Press.

Hayek, F.A. (1948) 'The Meaning of Competition', in *Individualism and Economic Order*, London: George Routledge and Sons.

Heald, D (1980) 'The Economic and Financial Control of UK Nationalised Industries', *The Economic Journal*, June, 243–65.

Helm, D. (2003) *Energy, the State and the Market*, Oxford: Oxford University Press.

High, J. (ed.) (1991) *Regulation: Economic Theory and History*, East Lansing, MI: University of Michigan Press.

Hotelling, H. (1931) 'The Economics of Exhaustible Resources', *Journal of Political Economy*, **39** (2), 137–75.

House of Commons Select Committee on Energy (1982) *North Sea Oil Depletion Policy*, Third Report, Session 1981–82, para. 95, London: HMSO.

IPCC (2000) *Special Report on Emissions Scenarios*, Cambridge: Cambridge University Press.

Kirzner, I.M. (1985) *Discovery and the Capitalist Process*, Chicago, IL: University of Chicago Press.

Kirzner, I.M. (1997) *How Markets Work: Disequilibrium, Entrepreneurship and Discovery*, Hobart Paper 133, London: Institute of Economic Affairs.

Krautkraemer, Jeffrey A (1998) 'Nonrenewable Resource Scarcity', *Journal of Economic Literature*, **XXXVI**, December, 2065–107.

Littlechild, S.C. (1978) *The Fallacy of the Mixed Economy*, Hobart Paper 80, London: Institute of Economic Affairs, 2nd edn 1986.

Marshall, E.C. (2003) 'Electricity and Gas Regulation in Great Britain: The End of an

Era', in Lester C. Hunt, *Energy in a Competitive Market*, Cheltenham, UK and North-ampton, MA, USA: Edward Elgar.

Marshall, E.C. (2005) 'Energy Regulation and Competition after the White Paper', in Colin Robinson (ed.), *Governments, Competition and Utility Regulation*, Cheltenham, UK and Northampton, MA, USA: Edward Elgar.

Marshall, E.C and Robinson, C. (1984) *The Economics of Energy Self-sufficiency*, London: Heinemann Educational Books.

Monopolies and Mergers Commission (1993) *Gas and British Gas plc*, Cm 2314–17 (three volumes), August, London: MMC.

Nicholson, C.C. (2005) 'Emissions Trading: A Market Instrument for our Times', in C. Robinson (ed.), *Governments, Competition and Utility Regulation*, Cheltenham, UK and Northampton, MA, USA: Edward Elgar.

OECD (1998) 'Focus', *Public Management Gazette*, **8**, March, 1.

Parker, D. (2004) 'Privatisation and Regulation in Developing Countries', Beesley Lecture, December.

Parker, D. and Saal, D. (2003) *International Handbook on Privatization*, Cheltenham, UK and Northampton, MA, USA: Edward Elgar.

Penrose, E. (1984) 'OPEC and the World Oil Market', in David Hawdon (ed.), *The Energy Crisis: Ten Years After*, London: Croom Helm.

Robinson, C. (1981) 'The Errors of North Sea Policy', *Lloyds Bank Review*, July, 14–33.

Robinson, C. (1986) 'Depletion Control in Theory and Practice', *Zeitschrift fur Energie Wirtschaft*, **1**, 57–62.

Robinson, C. (1992) 'Privatising the British Energy Industries: The Lessons to be Learned', *Metroeconomica*, **43** (1–2), 103–29.

Robinson, C. (1993) *Energy Policy: Errors, Illusions and Market Realities*, London: Institute of Economic Affairs, Occasional Paper 90.

Robinson, C. (1994) 'Gas: What to Do After the MMC Verdict', in M.E. Beesley (ed.), *Regulating Utilities: The Way Forward*, Readings 4, London: Institute of Economic Affairs.

Robinson, C. (1996) 'Profit, Discovery and the Role of Entry: The Case of Electricity', in M.E. Beesley (ed.), *Regulating Utilities: A Time for Change?*, Readings 44, London: Institute of Economic Affairs.

Robinson, C. (2000) 'Energy Economists and Economic Liberalism', *The Energy Journal*, **21** (2), 1–22.

Robinson, C. (2003) 'Privatization: Analysing the Benefits', in D. Parker and D. Saal, *International Handbook on Privatization*, Cheltenham, UK and Northampton, MA, USA: Edward Elgar.

Robinson, C. (2004) 'Gas, Electricity and the Energy Review', in C. Robinson (ed.), *Successes and Failures in Regulating and Deregulating Utilities*, Cheltenham, UK and Northampton, MA, USA: Edward Elgar.

Robinson, C. and Marshall, E.C. (1985) *Can Coal be Saved?*, Hobart Paper 105, London: Institute of Economic Affairs.

Robinson, C. and Morgan, J. (1978) *North Sea Oil in the Future*, London: Macmillan.

Simpson, D. (2004) 'The Economic and Politics of Wind Power', Beesley Lecture, November.

Stigler, G.J. (1971) 'The Theory of Economic Regulation', *Bell Journal of Economics and Management*, **2** (1), Spring.

Tilton, J.E. (2003) *On Borrowed Time? Assessing the Threat of Mineral Depletion*, Washington, DC: Resources for the Future.

Tullock, G., Seldon, A. and Brady, G. (2000) *Government: Whose Obedient Servant?*, Readings 51, London: Institute of Economic Affairs.
Yarrow, G. (2002) 'The New Gas Trading Arrangements', in C. Robinson (ed.), *Utility Regulation and Competition Policy*, Cheltenham, UK and Northampton, MA, USA: Edward Elgar.

16 Economic regulation of transport: principles and experience

Ian Savage

Introduction

Transport represents a huge proportion of the world's economic activity. The Eno Foundation's annual *Transportation in America* compendium of statistics estimates that passenger transport represents 10 per cent of the United States's Gross Domestic Product, and freight transport another 6 per cent. With the inclusion of some closely related industries, transport probably accounts for about a fifth of all economic activity. Not surprisingly, this has made transport a major focus of government regulatory activity. In the United States the railways were one of the first industries to be regulated by the federal government, in 1887. In most, if not all, countries the government is not only a regulator, but also an important producer of transport services. At a minimum, government provides most of the roads, and it is common for buses, subways, railways, airlines, airports and ports to be in public ownership.

The regulation takes (at least) three forms. This chapter will deal with only one of these – the economic regulation of prices, output, entry and exit. Transport is also subject to regulation of product quality, most notably safety. For a review of the economics of transport safety and its regulation see Savage (2001). Transport is also subject to environmental regulation concerning damage to surrounding property and watersheds during the construction of new infrastructure, and the moderating of the risks of externalities caused during the transport of dangerous or hazardous cargo (for a review of the latter see Savage, 2003).

Characteristics of transport

There are a number of leading characteristics of transport that both engender the need for regulation, and present practical problems to the regulator. Probably the most important is that all forms of transport are dependent on extensive and expensive infrastructure, which is 'fixed' in both an economic and geographic sense. Roads, railway tracks, airports, waterway improvements, ports and pipelines require large amounts of capital to build. Moreover, the infrastructure only comes in lumpy increments, and each increment (a single-track railway line, a highway lane) can accommodate many users. Therefore, average total costs will fall over wide ranges of levels of demand. With the exception of markets with very high demand, where it is feasible for multiple infrastructure providers to

350

exist, there are natural monopolies in infrastructure provision. Consequently, there is the fear that the monopoly provider may charge prices that are high enough to produce excess profits and a decrease in social welfare, yet are not sufficient to encourage a rival firm to build a competitive infrastructure.

In transport economics, the cost conditions derived from large, lumpy, infrastructure are called economies of density. These economies are market specific, and do not arise simply because a firm serves many markets. Most analyses of transport costs have found limited economies of scale in firm size, that is to say economies due to the sheer scale of the organization (Braeutigam, 1999). Economies of density can also arise from the transport vehicles themselves. As soon as a bus company commits to running a 70-person capacity bus down a city street, an airline flies an Airbus A320 from New York to Chicago, or a container ship sails from Philadelphia to Rotterdam, the capital cost of the vehicle, staff costs and the majority of the fuel costs become a sunk fixed expense. The marginal cost of an additional passenger or container (up to the capacity of the vehicle) is close to zero. In relatively thin markets, these vehicle-level joint costs can constitute a natural monopoly even if infrastructure costs are not an issue (such as when there is vertical separation between infrastructure suppliers and vehicle operators).

As soon as a commercial firm has to recover vehicle and infrastructure costs, price has to exceed marginal cost. In setting prices, a complicating factor is that the common infrastructure and vehicles are shared by a wide variety of users with different price elasticities and willingness to pay. Business passengers sit next to leisure travellers on aeroplanes. Coal trains share the tracks with container traffic. Economists have long recommended that common costs can be recouped with the minimum of deadweight loss by price discrimination between users based on the marginal cost of serving them and their price elasticity (Ramsey, 1927). Price-inelastic consumers should pay a higher markup over marginal cost compared to price-elastic consumers. While allocatively efficient, such price discrimination infuriates consumers, especially if there are perceived distributional or equity concerns. While there may be few social objections to business airline passengers paying higher fares than leisure passengers, or shippers of bulk commodities paying higher rates than shippers of manufactured goods (albeit that those discriminated against will complain vociferously), the same is not true if commuters were asked to pay higher prices than those making discretionary trips at midday, or if transit riders in poorer neighbourhoods without access to a car had to pay more than the rider from an affluent neighbourhood with alternative options. In effect, Ramsey-style pricing discriminates in favour of optional journeys over necessary trips and in favour of those customers with a variety of transport options over those with few options.

Transport is also a network industry. People's residential location, workplace and leisure destinations are diverse. Industry, its suppliers and its customers form a complex web that expands across the world. Transport firms usually operate in multiple markets for reasons of economies of scope in production, and the desire of some customers to deal with one firm for their diverse transport needs. For these multi-market firms it is difficult to identify the costs or the revenues associated with a particular link in the network. Often there are implicit cross-subsidies between markets. Frequently these arise because prices are set by the network firm in a fairly uniform manner across markets, even though costs vary markedly. It is a standard result in economics that cross-subsidy results in a lower level of social welfare compared with when prices are tailored specifically for each market. However, the interconnectedness of revenues and cost between markets makes it difficult to substantiate the magnitude of the cross-subsidy.

Demand is differentiated not only spatially, but also by time-of-day and day-of-week. Transport demand tends to be heavily peaked. Highways are built with an eye to the demand at 5 in the evening, and there is a chronic overcapacity at 3 am. The need for urban transit buses is typically 50 per cent to 100 per cent higher in the peak periods than at midday. Containerized freight demand peaks in the autumn months. It is much more expensive to serve peak consumers than those who use off-peak service. However, traditionally the price differential between the peak and off-peak service has not reflected the difference in costs. In part this is because many of the customers in the peak are also off-peak users and their demand is interrelated. A commuter on a crowded train to downtown in the morning values the fact that the railway provides a reasonable service in the middle of the day in case circumstances dictate that he or she has to leave work early.

In summary, transport can be characterized by huge fixed infrastructure costs, joint costs in the form of vehicles, multiple users with different valuations of the service, network firms serving many different markets both geographically and by time of day, and prices that have little connection with the cost of provision.

The role of technological change

When viewed in a historical context, technology changes the relative advantages of different types, or 'modes', of transport and this in turn affects the need for regulation. Two centuries ago, legislators were worried about monopoly exploitation by canal companies. Then the advent of the railways led to the demise of the canals, and created concerns about railway monopolies. This concern then abated with the development of the internal combustion engine and the building of national networks of highways. Railways lost their monopoly power over passenger traffic and many (but not all) types of freight. Commercial aviation became regulated in an era when the technology was in its infancy, prices were high and the market was thin. The advent of the jet engine turned the aviation industry into a mass market where many firms can compete on certain city pairs. Widespread auto ownership in the 1950s meant that urban mass transit lost market share, and the market power that it may have enjoyed earlier in the century.

A problem emerges when the rigidities of the legal regulatory system lead to a continuance of regulation decades after technological change has blunted any monopolistic powers. Moreover, this continued regulation may financially harm the viability of the industry. For example, the United States Interstate Commerce Commission (ICC) refused to allow railways to abandon passenger service and freight service on secondary lines years after the ascendant highway and aviation industries had taken away most of the traffic. The financial burden of providing these loss-making services undermined the finances of railways and their ability to provide freight service on their main lines.

A roadmap for the regulator

How should a government decide on the appropriate regulatory regime (if any) for a particular transport mode? In Figure 16.1 is a roadmap showing a series of questions that a regulator should ask. This figure has been freely adapted and modified over the years since it was originally published by my colleague Ronald Braeutigam in 1989 (his paper also contains numerous references to the underlying theoretical literature).[1] In the remainder of this chapter, we will walk our way through the roadmap.

Is there a natural monopoly?

The initial question is whether there are natural monopoly conditions that might lead to possible market power. All transport modes involve some form of an expensive infrastructure and relatively low marginal costs associated with each user. Therefore, natural monopoly is a likely outcome except in two situations. The first occurs in some large markets where total demand is many times the minimum efficient scale of an individual firm. For example, due to high demand two competitive railways traverse western Canada even though the mountainous terrain makes infrastructure provision very expensive. In contrast, light traffic has resulted in only one transcontinental railway in Australia. Of course, the high cost of the infrastructure will mean that the total number of firms in a market will be quite limited, frequently just a duopoly. Depending on the conduct of these firms, this may or may not lead to regulatory concerns.

The other situation occurs when the provision of the infrastructure is naturally, or forcibly, separated from the actual operation of the service. Historically the providers of the highway infrastructure are separate entities from firms who provide bus, truck or taxicab services. Similarly, in the maritime and aviation industries, the operation of ports and airports has historically been separated from the shipping and airline companies. The operating firms pay relatively low

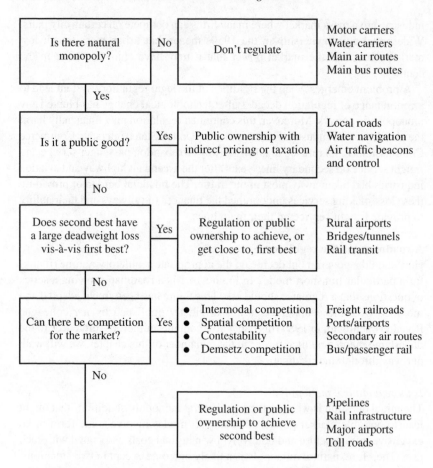

Figure 16.1   Road map showing a series of questions a regulator should ask

usage-dependent access fees in the form of licences, tolls and fuel taxes. Consequently, in the eyes of the operating companies, the infrastructure has been converted from a fixed to a variable cost. Provided that the operating companies do not have economies of scale in firm size, and that the markets are of sufficient size that the economies of density at the level of individual vehicles are unimportant, one might expect that there would be a highly competitive environment. This type of market would not need regulating. Examples are the trucking and maritime industries and heavily trafficked bus and airline routes. Taxicab service should also be competitive, albeit that regulation is often called for to control safety and to protect consumers from price gouging by cruising cabs. Of course, monopoly power remains with the infrastructure provider and it is therefore not surprising that roads, ports and airports are frequently provided by governmental or quasi-governmental organizations.

A recent development has been the forcible separation of previously vertically integrated state-owned railway companies into an infrastructure company (which remains in public hands or is regulated) and train operating companies. As described later in the chapter, rival firms can then bid for the rights to manage these train operating companies for a set period of time. While the European Union sees this as the future model throughout Europe, it has only been fully implemented in Great Britain and Sweden.

Is it a public good?

Assuming that it has been determined that a natural monopoly exists, the next step is to ask whether the mode has the characteristics of a public good. The definition of a classic public good is twofold. First, it must be difficult to exclude potential users and charge an access fee. Second, in non-congested situations, consumption must be non-rival, in the sense that one person's usage does not diminish the ability of others to consume. A prime example is the local road network where, unlike limited-access highways and bridges, it is difficult to charge a direct fee. Provision of navigational devices in the maritime industry and air traffic radio beacons and basic air traffic control services also have characteristics of public goods.

Not surprisingly, provision of all of these services usually resides in the public sector, occasionally with private entities providing management services. Typically they are indirectly financed through licence fees, fuel taxes, and sometimes from general tax revenues. However, that may change. Technological advances may eventually make it possible for direct pricing. For example, in Britain there has been a discussion that ultimately satellite-based vehicle location systems may permit collecting fees based on when and where a driver uses the system, rather than relying on licence fees and fuel taxes.

First-best versus second-best pricing?

For natural monopolies that are not public goods, prices can be charged directly to the user. The issue for a regulator then becomes, what price should be charged? Economic efficiency dictates that price should be equal to some concept of short-run or long-run marginal cost. This will obviously not generate the revenue necessary to cover the fixed infrastructure costs, except in cases where the price also includes the cost of a congestion externality, which is then used to finance capacity enhancements. At first best, the infrastructure would need to be funded either by some form of two-part or nonlinear tariff or from general tax revenues. The public funds for the latter incur a shadow value. The alternative is a second-best price equal to average total cost, which will be associated with a deadweight loss from users priced off the system. The deadweight loss is likely to be nontrivial as transport, with its large fixed costs and low marginal costs, is characterized by a large gap between marginal and average costs.

The crucial issue is the relative size of a potential deadweight loss from second-best pricing compared with the shadow value of the public funding necessary at first best. There are also subsidiary questions concerning the politics of pricing some users off the system, and whether a nonlinear tariff is practically or politically feasible. There are clearly some facilities where it is felt that it is politically inappropriate to charge a price that would deny mobility to some segments of the community. Examples might include bridges and tunnels to locations where there are no alternative routes, and provision of airport runways in remote locations where aviation is the only means of transport (such as airports in northern Canada and Alaska). In the case of urban mass transit, governments in many (most?) developed countries provide grants that cover the cost of new infrastructure construction and vehicle purchase. Users, often with the aid of additional subsidies, only have to pay for the cost of day-to-day operations. In this way, financially disadvantaged people are not priced out of access to jobs and denied basic mobility.

However, in other modes and markets where demand is more discretionary in nature, second-best pricing is more politically acceptable. Freight railways, pipelines, ports, urban airports and airlines are supposed to price so as to recover both their operating and capital costs. Intercity limited-access toll highways are frequently allowed to price at second best provided that there are parallel non-tolled highways which price-sensitive drivers can use. The task for the regulator is to ensure that these firms make enough surplus over operating costs to fund the infrastructure, but are not earning supernormal profits.

Traditional second-best regulation

Historically, at this point in the roadmap there would have been just two options: public ownership or regulation to constrain price to second best. In most parts of the world the period from 1945 until the mid-1980s was marked by nationalization of inherently commercial transport firms and implicit price setting by the government. In the United States provision remained largely in the hands of private firms, yet by 1940 most modes were regulated by government agencies.

Public ownership and economic regulation extended well beyond traditional natural monopolies (railways, pipelines, airports, ports) to included modes where competition was viable, such as maritime shipping, urban transit, taxis, aviation and trucking. Often these latter modes were regulated because other regulated modes argued that there should be a 'level playing field'. The railways argued in the 1930s that the newly emerged trucking industry should be regulated to prevent unfair competition. Similarly the urban transit industry argued that taxicabs should also be regulated to counter aggressive competition from jitneys (a hybrid of a taxi and a minibus) in the years after the First World War.

Irrespective of whether the government was directly dictating pricing and output by public ownership, or influencing it by regulatory commissions, there would appear to have been several common characteristics of the traditional regime.

The first feature is that regulators had a desire to directly influence prices and the structure of prices rather than indirectly affecting prices by controlling excessive profitability. While rate of return on capital regulation did exist for some transport modes (notably for oil pipelines in the United States), direct control over prices was more common. The basic motivation was to constrain perceived inequities from price discrimination. One of the famous lawsuits that prompted the regulation of the United States's railway industry dealt with agricultural shippers in Gilman, Illinois protesting that they had to pay a higher price to ship goods to New York than did similar shippers in Peoria, Illinois, which is located 100 miles further west on the same railway line. The cause of the differential was that the Peoria shippers were more price sensitive as they were located on a navigable river, which provided a competitive mode of transport.

Concerns about the fairness of the implicit allocation of common costs between users drew the regulator into the minutiae of the pricing schedule. The early regulators felt that it was their objective to reduce explicit price dispersion and to discourage a more subtle form of discrimination obtained by giving secret discounts or kickbacks to a subset of consumers. The form of price regulation adopted for the railways, and subsequently adopted in other modes, required firms to publish a list of their prices. To ensure that the prices applied to all consumers, firms were not allowed to offer discounts to select customers, and could not refuse to serve any customer willing to pay the price. The first of these effectively outlawed negotiations between transport firms and individual customers for bespoke contracts. The second, known as a 'common carrier obligation', was designed to stop a transport firm quoting a price but then deciding which customers it would allow to purchase at that price.

In practice, regulation went far beyond simply requiring a posting of prices. In a semi-judicial setting, aggrieved consumers could challenge a price increase, or protest about an existing price, on the basis that comparable consumers elsewhere were paying less. It became standard that the regulator had to approve any price changes. As one could imagine, the multiple combinations of commodity types and origins and destinations meant that a posted tariff could fill the equivalent of multiple telephone directories! The practical consideration of trying to organize such a tariff coupled with the regulators' concern about excessive price discrimination led to a more uniform set of pricing. In the extreme, there was a set rate per mile for a carload of a given commodity irrespective of the parts of the network utilized, or a standard formula was adopted for setting passenger fares.

The second feature of regulation was control over entry and exit. The common carrier obligation resulted in the necessity for firms to obtain regulatory approval for abandoning service in poor markets. This restricted the ability of firms to exit some of their markets, as the remaining customers in that market would complain to the regulator that they were to be denied service for which they would be willing to pay the (uniform) price. The converse of this was restriction on entry, or the granting of legal monopolies to publicly owned firms. Of course, this is not really an issue for modes that are natural monopolies. Entry controls became binding for more theoretically competitive modes that had become subject to regulation such as taxicabs, buses, trucking and aviation.

There is evidence that regulators used entry and exit controls to give preference to firms that provided a network of services, to allow maximum connectivity both in a geographic sense and by time-of-day and day-of-week. Network firms argued that entry would only occur on the best parts of the network ('skimming the cream' or 'cherry picking'), leading to lower prices in these markets, a diminished ability to cross-subsidize thinner parts of the network, and ultimately higher prices or a discontinuation of service in these thinner markets. Inherently, cross-subsidies between markets were not just tolerated, but actually encouraged by the regulator. There is a school of thought that the implicit cross-subsidization of thin markets from thick markets was part of the regulatory deal between network firms and the government, given in return for protection from competition in markets where more than one firm could possibly operate.

The questioning of traditional regulation

In the 1970s, a movement gained momentum that challenged the existing, all-pervasive, system of public ownership and regulation. The arguments of the challengers were basically fourfold.

The first was that standardized pricing and the resulting cross-subsidies were inherently bad and had led to poor resource allocation. Prices were 'too high' on parts of the network where high demand allowed extensive economies of density to be reaped, and 'too low' where lower demand allowed fewer economies of density. It was commonly claimed by critics in the 1970s that the uniform pricing system was supporting secondary airline and rail markets at the expense of the trunk routes. This can be seen as an ascendancy of those interests associated with the major or trunk routes, arguing that they had put up with poorer or more expensive service to cross-subsidize other markets that they did not use. One might also argue that the political power of the rural lobby had diminished.

This situation was made worse when exit controls forced network firms to continue to serve loss-making secondary services. In the extreme, the burden of these unremunerative services can threaten to undermine the viability of the network firms and endanger continuation of provision in the strong markets. In the case of the railways, technological change led to a general decline in passenger traffic and the diversion of local freight traffic from branch lines to trucks. Yet regulators required that many routes were kept open for years (decades?) longer than economics would suggest. In countries where the railways were publicly owned, huge public subsidies became common, and there were protracted public debates on discontinuing rural services. In the United States in 1970, the privately owned Penn Central Railroad, which represented a fifth of the industry and was a virtual monopolist in much of the populous Northeast of the country, declared bankruptcy, followed by other railways in the Midwest.

It is fair to say that the predictions of deregulation's proponents have proven to be true. Cross-subsidies have generally declined to the benefit of consumers in the busiest markets who have enjoyed lower prices or better service. However, fears that secondary services would disappear were misplaced. Alternative methods of service delivery have emerged that preserved service, such as the emergence of low cost, often non-union, firms using non-traditional technology. Examples include the development of commuter airlines flying small aircraft offering enhanced service from small airports to larger hub airports, and the emergence of 'shortline' railways, which took over operation of branch lines that were abandoned by the network carriers.

The second line of argument was that entry controls had led to the earning of rents that were then dissipated in the form of cost inefficiencies or excessive quality provision. In the airline and trucking industries, the number of firms had been fossilized at their equilibrium levels in the 1930s. However, both industries had witnessed enormous increases in demand over the following half a century, and had changed from infant industries to mature mainstream industries. Similarly, it is frequently argued that in many cities there are now 'too few' taxis to cater for an increased population. In markets where supply is artificially constrained, price can rise above an efficient level of costs. While it is possible in theory that owners of firms can thereby earn supernormal profits, it is generally the case that most transport firms made very modest returns during the period of regulation. (Although there is evidence of rents being earned by trucking firms and taxicab companies because they were able to sell their rights to be in the market, known as 'operating authorities' and 'medallions', respectively, to other firms for substantial prices.)

While regulation stopped the most blatant profit-seeking behaviour, it was unable to stop the appropriation of rents by organized labour. Transport was, and in many places still is, highly unionized. The ability of labour to strike and, in effect, halt commerce gave unions a strong position in negotiations. Firms also knew that the regulator would acquiesce to price increases to compensate for demonstrated increases in costs. Rose (1985) found evidence of rents earned by labour in the regulated trucking industry, which is quite remarkable as this is an industry that has few economies of scale or density, and has proven to be very competitive in the post-deregulation era. Not surprisingly, unionization of the trucking industry has dropped considerably in the United States since deregulation in 1980. In the airline industry, the regulation-era rents earned by labour have been eroded more slowly. Reports on the battles to remove these rents currently occupy the business pages (and the front pages) of the newspapers more than 25 years after airline deregulation in the United States, in 1978.

Proponents of deregulation were able to use comparisons of regulated and unregulated markets to support their contention that regulation had induced cost inefficiencies. For example, in the United States, regulation was applied at a federal level and the constitution limits regulation to services that cross state lines. In the larger states, such as Texas and California, there was an active intrastate air transport industry and these markets were more liberally regulated. Proponents of deregulation observed that the prices charged in these markets were considerably below those charged in interstate markets. Similarly, trucking rates for historically unregulated agricultural products were less than those for other commodities. Moreover, many shippers were finding it cheaper to operate their own trucking fleets to move their goods (known as 'private carriage' or 'own-account haulage') so as to avoid regulated prices.

Potential profits were also eroded by competition in product quality. Regulation was mainly concerned with price. Firms could only obtain a larger market share by providing a higher quality of service than their competitors. In the aviation industry, airlines competed by providing the latest models of aircraft, fancier in-flight amenities, and a larger number of daily flights. Increased service frequency is valued by consumers as it allows for more convenient departure times and less waiting around. However, demand is usually inelastic with respect to service frequency. Therefore, higher frequency depresses the average number of people per flight ('load factor') and increases the average cost per passenger. Longtime air travellers will have personal experience that quality has declined since deregulation as load factors have risen, the seats have been moved closer together, and full meals have been replaced by pretzels.

The third line of argument questioned the longstanding belief that regulation protected the nation from the disruption to mobility and the free flow of goods if a large network firm failed. The proponents of deregulation took the view that the bankruptcy and exit of inefficient or poorly run firms would not have disastrous long-run consequences. They argued that newly formed firms or existing competitors would take over the assets and continue to provide service. To a great extent this has proven to be the case. In the United States, Eastern Air Lines, Pan-American World Airways and Consolidated Freightways (the fifth-ranked general trucking firm) all ceased operation and exited the industry without merging with another firm, and were quickly forgotten. The national airlines of Switzerland and Belgium have ceased operation. However, there is still resistance in some quarters to such a Darwinian outcome. The United States government nationalized the bankrupt Penn Central system from 1973 to 1987; the New Zealand government renationalized the ailing Air New Zealand that it had privatized a few years previously; and in effect the British government took the bankrupt railway infrastructure company, Railtrack, back into the public sector. There is continued discussion in the United States about the desirability of providing a government guarantee for loans made to stave off the liquidation of major airlines.

Finally, proponents of deregulation argued that even a natural monopoly could be subject to market forces. Some of this competition may come from alternatives modes or neighbouring firms who provide consumers with imperfect substitutes. Alternatively, in some markets, discipline may be imposed by the threat of entry if monopoly rents are earned. In addition, an alternative regulatory structure emerged in the 1970s whereby rival firms compete for the rights to provide the monopoly service for a set period of time. The common characteristic is that market power may be limited even though it is unlikely that multiple firms would be competing in delivering the service to the consumer. The next part of this chapter considers four of these alternative market structures, all of which provide an affirmative answer to the question 'can there be competition *for* the market rather than *in* the market?'

Alternatives to traditional regulation

Intermodal competition
The first form of competition for the market arises from competition between modes. Even though a railway or a pipeline may be a natural monopolist in its own mode in a specific market, other modes may provide competition. Some of this competition only emerged after the Second World War as a result of technological change. Trucking now provides active competition to the railways for short-distance movements of all types of freight. It is also a competitor for non-bulk and high-value commodities over longer distances. When rivers and canals parallel railways or pipelines, there has always been strong barge competition for bulk commodities. It would be hard to argue that railway intercity passenger services have much market power nowadays given that the private automobile, commercial aviation and express bus services have captured a high market share. While these other modes are imperfect substitutes, in that they are either more expensive or slower, they do have the advantage that they are highly competitive. The traditional economic model of the dominant firm with a competitive fringe of firms is particularly suitable for analysing this type of competition. The model demonstrates that the exist-

ence of a competitive fringe greatly reduces the rents that can be extracted by a dominant firm.

Spatial competition

In some circumstances, a natural monopolist may face competition from firms in the same mode who operate in neighbouring markets. For example, if a port or airport started to charge outrageously high fees then traffic would move to neighbouring facilities. While users may find the alternative facility less convenient, some would be willing to switch if the differential in price became large enough. This rationale was used in the privatization of the Mexican state railways in the late 1990s. The state monopoly was split into seven regional vertically integrated companies. It was argued that any individual regional monopoly would not abuse its position as it would cause industry to relocate to other parts of the country, and importers and exporters would change their port of entry. (This is not to say that Mexican railways are completely unregulated. The government retains powers to intervene to resolve disputes over rates.) In Canada, rival railways have mandated access over each others' tracks for 30 kilometres around the junctions where they meet. Prices are kept in check because a shipper in this 30-kilometre zone, whose facility is only served by one firm, can request service from a second railway.

In a similar way, competition can occur between national networks. For traffic between North America and secondary cities in Europe and beyond, Lufthansa, the German national airline, provides competition through its Frankfurt hub to services provided by British Airways through London. Such competition relies on the ability of the airlines of one nation to have access to destinations in other countries. The liberalization of air travel in Europe initially focused on permitting 'open skies' access on international routes between member countries. The liberalization culminated in 1997 with the granting of rights for any European airline to operate domestic routes in any member country (known as 'cabotage'). It is frequently argued that more competition could be encouraged in the United States airline industry if foreigners were allowed to purchase domestic firms (there are currently limits on the proportion of foreign ownership), or if foreign airlines could start domestic services.

Contestability

An intellectual development in the 1970s called *contestability theory* (Baumol et al., 1982) had a considerable impact on the deregulation debate in transport, especially with regard to airlines. There are many secondary airline markets where there are only one or two firms providing service. The source of the natural monopoly is not economies of density due to the infrastructure, because airports are vertically separated – literally and figuratively – from the operation of the aircraft. The economies of density occur at the level of the aircraft itself.

There are also economies in 'station costs' because an airline wishing to start a service at an airport has to incur expenses such as providing ground handling staff and facilities, customer service staff, and local marketing. Often these expenses are the same whether an airline is offering two flights or ten flights a day.

Baumol et al. argued that under certain conditions the incumbent firms cannot extract monopoly, or duopoly, rents because there is always the threat that this may cause other firms to jump into the market. For example, United Airlines and Northwest Airlines would appear to be duopolists in the market for nonstop service between Chicago and Memphis. Baumol et al. would argue that regulation is not necessary because both firms know that raising the price above average cost would encourage, say, AirTran Airways to enter the market and initiate a price war. Much of the debate subsequent to deregulation is how applicable the theory has been, especially in thin markets, such as Chicago to Des Moines, Iowa.

The basic requirements for a contestable market are that potential entrants can replicate the costs of the incumbent firm(s), can turn up almost instantaneously when incumbents try to extract rents, and suffer no sunk entry or exit costs (because price is competed down to the operating cost of the incumbent firm(s) the entrant can never recoup any entry costs). There is no doubt that potential entrants have similar costs to incumbent firms as the technology is ubiquitous across firms. Also, relative to many industries, entry can occur quite quickly with a lag of perhaps three months. Consequently, proponents of contestability described aeroplanes as 'marginal cost with wings', implying that airlines could move their equipment quickly and costlessly from one market to another. While this is probably true to some extent, contestability has not proved the panacea that some, if not most, economists had argued in 1978.

In many airports in the United States, one or two airlines serve 85 per cent or more of the passengers. These are typically airports that an airline has selected as its hub airport. There is a debate among economists as to whether the observed higher prices at these airports are due to rent seeking or are merely a result of the higher quality service provided at major hubs. At these hub airports there is often competition on the major routes to other hubs, but monopolies on the feeder routes. Part of the explanation is that there really are sunk costs of entry. There are investments in station costs that cannot be recouped, marketing costs to advertise the new service and, what is more important, financial losses in the initial period of operation due to low initial load factors until people become aware of the new service. This is a deterrent to 'hit and run' entry as hypothesized by Baumol et al.

Not surprisingly, this has allowed incumbent airlines to protect their position and earn rents in certain markets. These are often known as 'fortress hubs'. In the United States this has been facilitated by the practice that airlines own or have long-term exclusive leases on gates. Other barriers to entry have included alleged predatory pricing against small new entrants to force them out and deter others, employing loyalty schemes such as frequent flier programmes to deter consumers from defecting to rival carriers, and offering discounts and kickbacks to travel agents and corporate travel arrangers to ensure that they book exclusively with the large incumbent firm.

Consequently, there is occasional lobbying by passengers at certain fortress hubs and users in secondary markets for a return of regulatory intervention. However, these concerns do not appear to attract widespread political support. Undoubtedly the increased inroads made by new entrant low-cost carriers into the market share of the incumbent 'legacy' carriers in the last decade, coupled with the poor financial performance of these latter firms, has blunted the protests. The North American experience has been repeated in Europe and increasingly in Asia. Indeed, there is an active debate worldwide about the continued existence of the large network airlines. Their future would appear to hinge on whether a sizeable number of consumers place a value on large airlines offering a network of services to numerous destinations, as compared with a fragmented industry with different firms serving different markets.

Demsetz competition
The final form of competition for the market has gained a lot of attention in recent years, especially in urban transport and rail passenger markets. In academic circles it is known as Demsetz competition, after its originator Harold Demsetz (1968). In the transport industries, it is more commonly referred to as competitive contracting, tendering or franchising. This model argues that even if there is a natural monopoly in provision, it is possible to hold an auction for the monopoly rights to serve the market. The rights are then re-auctioned sufficiently frequently so as to provide an incentive for the winning firm to provide high-quality service and to excise control over cost increases.

Demsetz competition has become common in the provision of urban bus services in developed countries. While one might imagine that actual competition, or contestability, should characterize urban bus services, this has not proved to be the case. Since 1986 the British bus industry has been completely deregulated excepting services in London. In practice, actual competition has occurred infrequently and typically has not been sustained. The thinness of most public transit markets nowadays in developed countries reduces the attractiveness to potential competitors due to economies of density at the level of the individual vehicle. In contrast, thick urban markets in many developing countries have witnessed active competition, especially when high unemployment encourages many owner-operated jitneys.

In London, events took a different course. The existing government operator, London Transport Buses, was split into a planning and marketing division and multiple operating divisions associated with the various garages. The operating divisions were then sold off to the private sector. They then competed among themselves and against other firms for the monopoly rights to operate individual routes for periods of three to five years. In general, this has been successful in that costs have fallen considerably, demand has increased, and there are multiple bidders for each contract despite consolidation in the industry. The London model has been adopted worldwide in the past 15 years, particularly in Australia, New Zealand, Argentina and Sweden. However, apart from San Diego and Denver there has been little movement in this direction in the United States.

A more recent application has been the privatization of passenger rail services. Typically, the former unified state railway is vertically separated into infrastructure and train-operating components. The infrastructure company typically remains publicly owned or is subject to regulation, while competitive contracts are issued for the provision of service over the infrastructure. Perhaps the most discussed example has been in Great Britain. The infrastructure remained with one company, Railtrack, which as described above had a rather checkered history, but the operation and marketing of passenger trains were split into an initial 25 franchises based on geography and type of service (local versus intercity). The franchises were then bid out for periods of seven to 15 years. Longer franchises were let in cases where more up-front investment was necessary. Some of these franchises were profitable and bidders had to indicate how much they would be willing to pay in the form of a concession fee. Others were loss-making and the bidders competed for who would need the least subsidy. The European Union already requires that all its member countries separate their publicly owned national railways into infrastructure companies and operating companies, and there are proposals that competition will be permitted in international and domestic markets and that new entrants must be charged the same infrastructure access fees as the incumbent operator. Currently, only Sweden has gone as far as Britain in terms of privatization. Countries such as France have established accounting separation between the infrastructure and operating companies, but there has not been any competition for service provision.

In theory, Demsetz competition can result in the elimination of monopoly rents by driving price down to average cost. The requirements for this to happen are that inputs are available to all bidders at prices determined in an open market, and that there are sufficient bidders so that collusion is unlikely. The first of these is usually not a problem. In Britain a series of leasing companies was established to own and lease railway rolling stock to operating companies. In urban transit there is an active second-hand market in vehicles, and the contracting agency always has the option of owning the vehicles itself and leasing them to successful bidders. The second requirement has become more of a problem. As Demsetz competition in passenger transport has spread around the world, market concentration has increased by the formation of a small number of multinational conglomerates who comprise the major bidders.

Unlike the other three alternatives which argue in favour of liberalized, or zero, regulation, Demsetz competition usually amounts to a greater amount of regulatory control compared with previous regulatory regimes. The contracting agency, which is typically governmental, is setting the terms of the contract on which the competitors bid. Usually this amounts to specification of the frequency of service, types of vehicles to be used, and the fares that will be charged. Especially in urban bus operations a common fare scale is used for all routes, and very little of the revenue is collected on the vehicle because most users purchase passes or multi-ride tickets from the central marketing agency. Demsetz competition is therefore all to do with costs, and the avoidance of inefficiencies. It is not surprising that Demsetz competition has been deployed in circumstances where a previously publicly owned operation was believed to have become inefficient. Demsetz competition allows the combination of the benefits of privatization with the continuance of public involvement either to moderate monopoly power or to meet other social goals, such as mitigating highway congestion or providing mobility to residents of disadvantaged neighbourhoods.

The continuation of second-best regulation
Ultimately the proponents of deregulation or alternative forms of regulation were largely successful. The United States and the United Kingdom were the pioneers in regulatory reform. In the United States there was complete deregulation of the airlines and trucking, in 1978 and 1980 respectively, and considerable liberalization of the regulation of the railways, primarily in 1980. Starting in the mid-1980s, Britain privatized the nationalized airports, airline, bus companies, ferries and railway. Other countries followed suit, notably New Zealand, Australia, Canada, Sweden, Chile and Argentina.

However, it would be wrong to assume that there has been a complete abandonment of economic regulation in transport. Regulation (or direct control when the companies are publicly owned) still persists where there is undeniable natural monopoly and market power, such as with pipelines, rail infrastructure, major airports which do not have close spatial competitors, toll highways, and for specific consumers who are 'captive' to a particular transport mode and company.

In the United States, the federal Surface Transportation Board can still take action where a railway is market dominant for specific flows, and price is greater than 80 per cent above average variable cost. Action is initiated on receipt of complaints from shippers. If regulation is called for, price is set on the principle of a 'constrained market price', which is defined as the theoretical price that an efficient new entrant would have to charge. This is calculated as the stand-alone cost of a competitor constructing and operating a rival route. This is really only applicable for certain markets for bulk commodities such as coal, grain, ores and some chemicals.

Regulatory reform of pipelines, perhaps the most archetypal natural monopoly, took a slightly different course in the United States. The explanation is that regulatory authority resides with a division of the federal Department of Energy rather than with a traditional transport regulatory body. Historically, liquid pipelines (i.e. pipelines for oil and oil products) were regulated by specifying a maximum rate of return on the replacement cost of assets. Starting in the early 1990s, this was replaced with price caps which stated that prices could only increase by an amount equal to the Producer Price Index on Finished Goods less one percentage point (PPI – 1%). The low inflation rate in the late 1990s meant that in some years prices had to be reduced! Not surprisingly, industry lobbying led to a revision of the formula to PPI – 0%, in 2001. But even in the pipeline industry there is evidence of regulatory reform. Studies have suggested that at least 70 per cent of traffic moves in markets where there are multiple pipelines or where there is competition from another mode such as barges. Consequently, pipeline companies can apply for an exemption from regulation in markets where there is evidence of actual or potential competition, or where pipeline companies and shippers have freely agreed on a price.

Paradoxically, in many countries there has been a need to establish new regulatory bodies to oversee former publicly owned companies that have been privatized. Explicit regulation has been necessary to supersede the former implicit regulation in public ownership. In many ways the cutting edge of innovative regulatory mechanisms has moved from the United States to the United Kingdom and other countries which have taken the most extreme amounts of privatization. For example, a new regulatory structure was necessary in Britain when three major airports near London were privatized under a single owner, BAA plc, in 1987. Landing fees and other charges were only allowed to increase by the retail (consumer) price index (RPI) less X percentage points, where X is set by the regulator and revised every five years. The RPI – X price-cap form of regulation has become very popular in Britain as many areas of the public sector have been privatized (see Rees and Vickers, 1995).

When Britain's railways were vertically separated and privatized in the mid-1990s, the government established an Office of the Rail Regulator whose mission was to oversee the prices paid by operating companies for access to the track, rather than regulating the prices paid by the ultimate consumer. The regulator was also charged with setting cost reduction goals for the infrastructure company and ensuring that these savings were passed on to the train operators. The final task was to ensure that the various train operators could obtain access to the infrastructure without discrimination. Certain post-privatization rail fares were regulated by another regulatory body using the RPI – X model, presumably because rail fares are politically sensitive, and in some commuting markets rail does have a sizeable market share.

A transport mode that has only recently come to the regulators' attention is the private toll highway. Traditionally most tolled facilities were operated by governmental or quasi-governmental bodies. More recently, private operation has been encouraged, sometimes as part of a public–private partnership. Private firms employ their own capital to build new facilities, and are then granted rights to collect tolls for a period of years. In some cases the road ultimately passes back to the public authority under a 'build, operate, transfer' (BOT) agreement.

The regulatory structure for toll roads varies. In France and Indonesia there is direct regulation. The operator has to apply to the government to change the tolls. In Spain, a price cap is employed where toll increases are tied to changes in the national price indices for steel, petroleum and labour. In the United States, toll highways in Virginia and California are or were regulated using rate of return regulation. In Illinois an existing tolled facility was recently leased to a private operator with a set schedule of the maximum allowable price for different years. In Britain, a new tolled facility that was built north of Birmingham is not subject to price regulation because it parallels a non-tolled, but congested, existing highway.

Conclusions

During the middle third of the twentieth century, competition had been eradicated from most transport markets. In many parts of the world, transport companies were taken into public ownership. Even the United States, with its strong tradition of private enterprise, heavily regulated most forms of transport. There has been a dramatic change in the past 25 years. Public ownership is receding. In some modes the possibility of direct competition or the potential for competition for the market has rolled back regulation. However, do not be fooled. Regulation is alive and well. The potential for market power remains due to economies of density in infrastructure provision and the operation of the vehicles. Moreover, as privatization has gained ground there has been a need to establish a whole new set of regulatory structures to replace the previous implicit regulation associated with public ownership.

Note

1. Ron and I have shared teaching duties for an undergraduate transport economics class for 15 years (at the time of writing), and we have both used variants of this roadmap in the class.

References

Baumol, W., Panzar, J. and Willig, R. (eds) (1982) *Contestable Markets and the Theory of Industrial Structure*, New York: Harcourt Brace Jovanich.
Braeutigam, Ronald R. (1989) 'Optimal Policies for Natural Monopolies', in R.

Schmalensee and R.D. Willig (eds), *Handbook of Industrial Organization*, vol. 2, Amsterdam: North Holland.

Braeutigam, Ronald R. (1999) 'Learning about Transport Costs', in J.A. Gómez-Ibáñez, W.B. Tye and C. Winston (eds), *Essays in Transportation Economics and Policy: A Handbook in Honor of John R. Meyer*, Washington, DC: Brookings Institution.

Demsetz, H. (1968) 'Why Regulate Utilities?', *Journal of Law and Economics*, **11** (1), 55–65.

Ramsey, F.P. (1927) 'A Contribution to the Theory of Taxation', *Economic Journal*, **37** (145), 47–61.

Rees, R. and Vickers, J. (1995), 'RPI – X Price-cap Regulation', in M. Bishop, J. Kay and C. Mayer (eds), *The Regulatory Challenge*, Oxford: Oxford University Press.

Rose, N.L. (1985) 'The Incidence of Regulatory Rents in the Motor Carrier Industry', *RAND Journal of Economics*, **16** (3), 299–318.

Savage, I. (2001) 'Transport Safety', in D.A. Hensher and K.J. Button (eds), *Handbook of Transport Systems and Traffic Control*, Amsterdam: Elsevier Science.

Savage, I. (2003) 'Safety', in D.A. Hensher and K.J. Button (eds), *Handbook of Transport and the Environment*, Amsterdam: Elsevier Science.

17 Regulation of water and sewerage services

Ian Byatt, Tony Ballance and Scott Reid

Introduction

Effective regulatory oversight of utilities begins by making appropriate decisions on industry structure, competition and regulation. Where it is feasible competition provides a spur to good service and efficient provision and there are therefore strong arguments for developing structures that facilitate it wherever possible. But should water services be treated like other utilities (i.e. energy and telecoms) in terms of how the sector should be organized, how competition should work and how it should be regulated (see for example Robinson, 1998)? Or are they a natural monopoly, in which the potential for competition between multiple suppliers for the same group of customers (i.e. competition in the market) is limited and hence some form of regulation is required to protect the customer interest?

In this chapter we examine these important questions by looking at two key themes in the regulation of water services: the regulation of *structure* and the regulation of *conduct.*

Consideration of the regulation of *structure* provides the necessary context for understanding the scope for competition *in* the market for water services and approaches to the regulation of industry structure. It also provides a framework for understanding the structure of costs in water services. We review the evidence on economies of scale and scope in water services, focusing on the situation in England and Wales. We then address the public oversight of the conduct of the water sector where competition is limited, in particular the need for and the role of a regulatory agency where there is private ownership of the assets, as is the case in England and Wales. We then consider the need for public oversight where there are other forms of private sector participation (PSP) (i.e. through contracts). We focus on the French model of water PSP and then broaden the discussion out to consider the likely requirements for regulation in other countries. We complete the picture by examining these issues in the context of public owned water services, as is the case in Scotland, where there is an independent regulatory body.

Regulation of industry structure

The importance of 'getting industry structure right' for water services lies in two related factors. First, the experience of history suggests that a laissez-faire approach to water services has not resulted in industry structures that are eco-

370

nomically or socially efficient. Second, policymakers have a public interest in an efficient structure for what are essential services and where, because of that essentiality, cross-subsidization is often a requirement to make service provision affordable.

The structure of costs in water services – economies of scale and scope
There are significant differences in the organization of water services worldwide, despite the production technology for those services being relatively well established and homogeneous.

At one extreme is the UK, where large vertically and horizontally integrated water and sewerage providers dominate the sector. At the other, and more common, extreme are the more fragmented municipal-based industry structures observed, for example, in Germany, France, Italy, the USA and Japan.

The evolution of these different industry structures reflects in part historical and geographical differences, but also competing views about the most appropriate model of organization for the production of water services. In England and Wales the reorganization of the sector in 1973 into ten regional water authorities was largely driven by a desire to see integrated river-basin management whereby a single entity where possible, should plan and control the uses of water in each river catchment. As such the reorganization was driven by factors broader than purely economic ones, although the assumption was that the industry was characterized by substantial economies of scale. With the implementation of the Water Framework Directive across the European Union, which will focus attention on issues of catchment management, these influences on sector structure may become more important more widely in Europe.

In this section, we examine in more detail the available evidence on the cost structure of water services to shed light on these debates and their implications for public oversight.

Some definitions   Water supply and sanitation services comprise the production of distinct multiple outputs, which could potentially be supplied by distinct markets. For example, the water supply process comprises: abstraction from underground sources and surface sources such as aquifers and rivers; storage (natural or artificial) in order to be able to maintain supplies during times of shortage (i.e. drought situations); treatment to remove natural and other pollutants; bulk transport before and/or after treatment; local storage (to cover diurnal variation in demand); and distribution via a network of mains to consumers.

There is also the customer interface retailing, which deals with connections, billing and payment systems. A simplified three-stage categorization of the production process might be bulk water supply, water transport and distribution, and retailing, as summarized in Table 17.1. A similar categorization of the production process for the wastewater sector also applies.

Table 17.1　The water supply chain

Supply chain		Components of supply system
Stage	Element	
1	Bulk water production/supply	• Raw water sources • Raw water trunk main • Water treatment plant
2	Trunk distribution	• Trunk main • Pumping station • Service reservoir
	Local distribution	• Local distribution system • Communication pipe
3	Retailing	• Meter and billing • Customer services

With multiple outputs, the key issues for efficient industry structure are the scale of operation and to what extent operations should be vertically and horizontally integrated. In simpler terms, how many independent suppliers should there be (within a defined market) and what services should they provide?

Baumol (1977) and Panzar and Willig (1977) provide important elements of the necessary conceptual framework for addressing these issues. A first concept, but by no means the most important, is that of *economies of scale*, which characterizes the relationship between unit costs and the scale of output. In the multi-product case this can be further refined in terms of *ray economies of scale*, which indicates how total costs vary when each output is varied in fixed proportions, and *product-specific economies of scale*, which measures how costs vary with changes in a specific output, holding the quantities of other outputs constant. Second, *economies of scope* exist where the joint production of outputs involves costs of production that are less than the sum of the production costs by separate specialized firms. Positive economies of scope can have two sources: the sharing across outputs of indivisible fixed costs (such as head office costs) that are not specific to each output or service, and cost complementarities in production activities, where the production of one output reduces the cost of producing the other output because of the ability to share inputs across production activities.

The presence of economies of scale in a multi-product firm need not imply lower total costs of production if *dis*economies of scope are also present. Equally, it can be efficient to operate under *dis*economies of scale, if the economies of scope from the production of multiple outputs are sufficiently large. Baumol (1977) shows that the appropriate test is whether costs are *sub-additive*;

that is, joint production by a single firm results in lower costs than independent production of the same outputs. Scale economies are neither necessary nor sufficient in determining the most efficient industry structure for water services. In practice, moreover, as discussed below and in Chapter 6, yardstick or comparative competition can be a valuable element in the regulation of conduct in water sectors and because of this there are benefits to preserving a sufficient number of comparators.

Measuring scale and scope economies in water services
The textbook model of the production process assumes that firms are free to adjust in the long run the level of all factor inputs to ensure that costs are minimized. For water services this formulation may be less than helpful for two reasons (see, for example, the discussion in Saal and Parker, 2000). First, the technology used in water services can be indivisible and associated with very long service lives. Second, managers do not have total influence over fixed factors, such as capital investment, as this is often determined or influenced by regulatory requirements. Legal obligations to meet quality standards or to connect customers to the network mean that capital, in particular, is a quasi-fixed input and this needs to be recognized when measuring scale and scope economies (see Stone and Webster Consultants, 2004a).

Evidence from England and Wales The consolidation of the water sector in England and Wales on the basis of better management of water services over a river basin provides important evidence on the extent of economies of scale and scope in water services. Recent work commissioned by the industry regulator for England and Wales, the Office of Water Services (OFWAT) provides the first systematic attempt in the post-privatization period to estimate scale and scope economies in this sector using a multiple output methodology (Stone and Webster Consultants, 2004a).

The 1945 Water Act encouraged the amalgamation of small municipal-based undertakings through self-organization in Britain (see Richardson, 2003).[1] By 1970, however, the industry was still relatively fragmented comprising 198 separate water supply undertakings (including 33 privately owned statutory water companies) and over 1300 publicly owned sewerage and sewage disposal authorities. The 1963 Water Resources Act had increased the centralization of planning with the creation of 29 river authorities with a range of water and waste disposal planning and licensing functions. The catalyst for consolidation of the operational undertakings was the work of the Central Water Advisory Committee, which was tasked in 1969 with examining the organization of water services in England and Wales. It was considered that water needed to be transferred between river basins, and that the planning of water resources should no longer be carried out by 29 separate authorities.

The Central Advisory Water Committee report (1971) laid the foundations for Integrated River Basin Management (IRBM) and provides the genesis for the ten Regional Water Authorities (RWAs) organized around major river catchments created in 1973. It also recommended an operational industry structure of about 50 water supply and sewerage undertakings to exploit available scale economies. However, the 1973 Act established the ten RWAs as multi-purpose bodies with responsibilities for water supply, sewage disposal, river management and planning and coordination functions.

The privatization legislation of 1989 transformed the RWAs into the privately owned water and sewerage companies (WaSCs), with the important exception that regulation of abstraction and the setting of quality standards were retained in the public sector (under the auspices of the Drinking Water Inspectorate and the National Rivers Authority, later absorbed into the Environment Agency). Thus the functions that had motivated the highly concentrated industry structure were not transferred to the privatized WaSCs, whose responsibilities were now solely operational. OFWAT was established at privatization as the economic regulator.

The privatization legislation also limited consolidation of the bigger companies (the ten WaSCs).[2] This reflects regulatory resistance to a reduction in the number of comparators, despite claims that significant cost savings could still be achieved through mergers (see for example Indepen and Accenture 2002).[3] The Competition Commission's report into the proposed take-over of Southern Water by Vivendi Water (now Veolia) in 2002 motivated OFWAT's commissioning of an investigation into scale economies in the England and Wales water industry.[4] The subsequent work – reported in Stone and Webster Consultants (2004a) – was extended to consider economies of scope and employed econometric methodologies to estimate models of industry costs over the period 1992–93 to 2002–03.

The main findings of the recent OFWAT study were as follows. First, there is clear evidence of scale economies for the smaller companies (interpreted here as companies serving populations below 400,000) with the average size water-only company characterized by constant returns to scale. Based on this study, the cost-minimizing scale for water supply undertakings is estimated to be around a population served of 650,000.[5] In contrast, the larger water and sewerage undertakings tend to be characterized by diseconomies of scale, which concurs with earlier evidence presented in Saal and Parker (2000). Similar findings have also been repeated in further work reported in Stone and Webster Consultants (2004b) using a similar methodology and Saal et al. (2004).[6]

On economies of scope the study provides mixed evidence about the horizontal integration of water and sewerage services. There is evidence of positive economies of scope from the integration of water and sewerage *production* activities, where there is the ability to share inputs across such similar activities, for example through the purchase of power for water and sewage treatment works. There may also be economies of scope through shared network management and common billing. However, the study provides no evidence that combining vertically integrated water and sewerage businesses yields economies overall. The diseconomies of scope seem to arise across the activities where the sharing of inputs is more limited, for example water production and sewerage connections, and sewage treatment and disposal and water connections.

The study also provides some support for the vertical integration of water supply. The cost savings are most evident for the smaller WoCs, with the management of network losses through leakage control appearing to have an important influence on these overall savings.

International evidence   International studies on water industry structure have tended to find similar results to the recent OFWAT studies on economies of scale.

Studies from the United States find evidence of 'u-shaped' cost functions for water supply. Kim (1985), Kim and Lee (1998) and Hayes (1987) present a range of evidence for different jurisdictions and time periods. A consistent finding is that economies of scale characterize the smaller firms that comprise the main part of the industry. Diseconomies of scale appear to characterize the largest firms. Average size firms tend to exhibit constant returns (though the average firms in these samples are significantly smaller than enterprises in the water industry in England and Wales), while most of these US studies find evidence of economies of scale for smaller-sized suppliers.

These findings are reiterated in the case of Italy by Fabbri and Fraquelli (2000), Garcia and Thomas (2001) for the Bordeaux region of France and Kim and Lee (1998) for Korea. Tynan and Kingdom (2005) review a range of international evidence and report that utilities, particularly those serving a population of 125,000 or less, could reduce operating costs per customer by increasing the scale of operation. Finally, Mizutani and Urakami (2001) present evidence for Japan, where the characteristics of the sample (in terms of the size distribution) are probably most similar to water supply in England and Wales. They also find evidence of diseconomies of scale and calculate the minimum efficient scale to be a population served of about 760,000. As highlighted above, this is comparable to the cost-minimizing scale for water-only undertakings in England and Wales, as calculated in the recent analysis for OFWAT.

Summary   The empirical evidence on water industry cost structures confirms that it is overly simplistic to regard water (and probably sanitation) as standard natural monopolies. Rather, the available evidence points to important trade-offs in the organization of water services. The most important trade-off – confirmed by engineering analyses at works level – is between the production (abstraction, treatment) and network functions. Economies of scale are most likely to lie in production activities (lower unit costs from larger sources and treatment works, for example), while diseconomies are fundamentally a function of distance and network size (Kim and Clarke, 1988; Garcia and Thomas, 2001).

Two important policy issues flow from this evidence. The first is whether an efficient operational configuration for water services needs to be matched by a similar pattern of independently owned and managed water service providers. In this respect the evidence is less clear-cut and the French concession system provides an example where operations are organized around municipal areas, while ownership and management are much more highly concentrated.[7]

The second relates to developing 'in market' competition. The available evidence reinforces the conclusion that the benefits of competition between competing producers (as opposed to competing retailers) are likely to be limited. An important consideration will be whether these benefits are able to offset the costs of forgoing the advantages of vertical integration of production and delivery.

Developing competition in water service markets
The scope for promoting competition in water services may be rather less than in other utility sectors, such as electricity and gas, where in many jurisdictions market reforms have now taken place. In part, this reflects the conditions necessary for sustaining competition in this particular network industry.

With water distribution and sewerage systems, barriers to entry due to the high level of sunk costs are generally considered to be substantial because of the frequent existence of spare capacity and the impracticality of multiple connections to individual premises.[8]

In utilities such as electricity and gas, competition has been facilitated through the separation of transmission and distribution systems from other components of the industry (either in terms of management, legal entity or ownership) and the introduction of competition in the upstream activities. This analogy begins, however, to break down when consideration is given to the ability to ring-fence the distribution network from upstream production processes. The clear-cut separation between resources (production) and distribution, which is the key to introducing competition in gas and electricity, does not exist to the same degree in the water sector. Small-scale localized supplies, as compared to supply by a large impounding reservoir and long-distance pipes, may make ring-fencing bulk supply from distribution difficult (and goes some way towards explaining the empirical findings on the benefits of vertical integration noted earlier).

While the scope for competition in the market may be limited, there is scope for facilitating competition in some areas, such as supplies to large industrial customers. Suppliers can be encouraged to consider outsourcing work where there are competitive markets for inputs. Where there is competition *for* the market, it is important to ensure that the industry is structured in such a way as to promote a high degree of competition for concessions of various kinds.

Is competition in bulk water supply possible?   Competition between multiple suppliers of bulk water on a large scale is constrained by a number of factors (see Ballance and Taylor, 2002). Bulk water supply is, like water distribution, highly capital intensive with many fixed assets having relatively long lives and few, if any, alternative uses. These large sunk costs create substantial barriers to entry for new suppliers. It is easier to provide for competition between smaller, localized sources.

Furthermore, high transportation costs for water relative to the cost of production, when compared to gas and electricity, mean that there are substantial locational monopolies for large-scale suppliers of bulk water. Even if a new entrant is able to construct a new reservoir and operate it more cheaply than an incumbent's existing facilities, it must be located sufficiently close to the final distribution point to ensure that these production cost advantages are not overwhelmed by additional transport costs.[9] Long-distance transport and distribution costs in the water sector are likely to account for the large proportion of total (average) costs, while, in comparison, in the electricity and gas sectors these costs are more likely to be a relatively small proportion of total (average) costs.

A third factor that is likely to constrain competition in bulk water supply is the rising cost nature of large increments to water resources. The least expensive water resources are developed first and as capacity is increased more expensive resources are commissioned.

Arrangements for introducing competition in bulk water supply must allow for a supplier of last resort, which is potentially far more complex for water than for other utilities. A significant element of the cost of supplying bulk water arises from the provision of water resources for exceptional droughts, which may occur once every 10–20 years, even in countries in Northern Europe, and maybe more frequently with climate change. If a new entrant is not required to provide standby supply for exceptional drought situations, this may place a substantial cost burden on an incumbent operator that is obliged to be the supplier of last resort.

There may be other problems restricting the scope for competition. First, the threat to water quality must be safeguarded if competition is to develop in the water sector. The entry of poorly treated water into a common main could cause contamination. Alternatively, there may be deterioration in perceived water quality even when water of the appropriate quality is input into a common main. Examples of this might be changes in water quality for industrial customers or changes in taste or water hardness for domestic customers. Finally, the unwinding of historic cross-subsidies in charging may cause consumer resistance to change.

Competition in retailing   It should, however, be possible to introduce competition in water services retailing, that is, the customer billing and payment function. Competition in this area is certainly the norm in a number of other utility industries, such as electricity and gas, in many countries where energy sector reforms have been adopted.

In terms of the practical separation of retailing from other functions in the water sector, there are examples of this type of separation taking place in locations as diverse as Serbia and Indonesia, although not linked to competition in retailing services. Often it has been linked to the establishment of municipal billing companies, which act as monopoly providers of billing services to a range of municipal service providers.

The scope for the development of competition in retailing will depend critically on the allocation of costs between those for providing wholesale water and the costs of providing retail services.

Summary   It is difficult to argue that the supply of water services in their entirety is a natural monopoly. There are clearly areas, such as retailing and supply to larger customers, where competition is possible, though the scale of the gains is not yet fully established. There is an argument for pursuing water sector reform to increase the scope for competitive forces both *in* the market and *for* the market.

There are doubts, however, about how far a model of competition in the market for water would be the widespread success that it has been for other utility sectors. Yet there are interesting developments in a number of jurisdictions. These include, perhaps most notably, the United Kingdom. The 1989 Water Act made provision for 'inset' appointments where a new supplier could be licensed within the area of an existing undertaker. This has been taken up in relation to large customers and has resulted in significant reductions in the charges they pay for bulk water. The recent Water Act of 2003 allows for common carriage to customers using in excess of 50 Ml/d per day, and the Water Services (Scotland) Act 2005 provides for competition in retailing for all business customers from 2008.

In Southern California, water 'wheeling' through bulk networks has been the subject of policy and legal debate since severe droughts in the late 1980s.[10] The scope for competition and water market liberalization in the European Union has also been the subject of recent investigation and policy debate (see for example WRc and Ecologic, 2002). The publication by the Commission of the European Communities (2003) is widely seen as an attempt within the EU to encourage greater harmonization (and hence reduce legal uncertainty and market distortions) within European water sectors, and to promote greater competition through the unbundling of vertically integrated water utilities. At the global level, the European Commission has advocated the incorporation of water services into the GATS regime for international trade in services, though liberalization is expected to take the form of competition *for* the market rather than *in* the market (see Stone and Webster Consultants, 2002, for an assessment). In Australia national competition policy arrangements provide for competitive entry.

As a result of the limited scope for competition *in* water and sanitation markets there is usually a need for a comprehensive framework for the regulation of the conduct of the sector, to which we now turn.

Regulation of conduct

The regulation of the conduct of a sector associated with considerable natural monopoly requires either regulation or competition *for* the market in the form of franchising – though franchises may not remove the need for regulation. Conduct regulation constrains a natural monopoly by rules covering areas such as quality, pricing and access. This requires an effective regulatory system.

The nature of the regulatory system, however, will very much depend on the type of private sector participation (PSP) in operation. We begin by discussing the case of England and Wales where the type of PSP resembles more closely that found in other sectors and hence the regulatory arrangements are more similar.

The regulation of water in the market economy – the case of England and Wales

In England and Wales where the ten publicly owned water authorities were privatized in 1989 and the independent water regulator OFWAT was established, the regulation of the conduct of the water companies is a major aspect of the industry's organizational framework.[11]

Responsibility for setting water quality and environmental standards has been distinguished from responsibility for setting price limits that allow companies to achieve these standards. In this way, ministers and their quality regulators are responsible for collective objectives, while the economic regulator is responsible for the individual objectives of customers.

Conduct is regulated by the economic regulator, OFWAT, and two quality regulators, the Drinking Water Inspectorate (DWI) and the Environment Agency (EA). Standards for water and wastewater quality are set by Ministers, following both national policies and European Union (EU) Directives. There are also regional and national customer service committees (WaterVoice). Some changes are planned for 2006, when OFWAT becomes the Water Services Regulation Authority (WSRA) governed by an executive board rather than an individual

Director General, and a Water Consumer Council for Water (CCWater) takes over from WaterVoice, but these changes are unlikely to have a significant effect on economic regulation.

The prime purpose of OFWAT is to ensure that companies properly carry out and can finance their functions, while protecting customers, promoting efficiency and facilitating competition.[12] Prices, but not profits, are controlled by a price-cap formula. The RPI – X regime applied to the other UK utilities has been modified into RPI +/– K, where K is a combination of the cost of higher water and environmental quality (Q) and the cost (allowing for increases in efficiency) of providing existing quality and better services to customers (X). K may be positive or negative, depending on the balance between the cost of higher water and environmental quality, and the ability of the companies to deliver water and dispose of wastewater more effectively and more efficiently.

Price limits are set for a period of five years, subject to annual adjustment in specific circumstances, such as a new legal objective. They cannot be altered in response to changes in circumstances within the control of the companies. With the exception of the Welsh company, Glas Cymru,[13] which now is a private-not-for-dividend company, they are all owned by private, often institutional, shareholders in the UK and abroad.

Although the price control regime was designed to regulate the outputs of the companies and the prices they can charge, there has, over the years, been a growing emphasis on the detailed measurement of costs, especially where new water quality and environmental obligations are concerned. This focus on input measurement with detailed costing imposes regulatory burdens, and can damage incentives to efficient behaviour. In a survey of water companies commissioned by OFWAT, SWC Consulting (2003) highlights these concerns in the context of capital investment.

Under this regime, there has been a substantial increase in investment to meet higher water and environmental quality and to improve service to customers. Very substantial improvements have been made to water services. Efficiency rose sharply following privatization as clear accountability was established for the governmental and regulatory bodies and effective use was made of comparative competition (though see Saal and Parker, 2000). As incremental quality improvements are becoming progressively more expensive, however, prices are now set to rise significantly (confirmed by an average 23 per cent real increase in prices determined by OFWAT for the 2005–10 period).

Linking the responsibilities of the different regulators has involved a structured dialogue. OFWAT devised a process involving the publication of open letters between Ministers, and an open and transparent dialogue with customers and other interested parties. This dialogue depends in turn on the collection, analysis and presentation of high quality information, most of which did not exist under nationalization.

Comparative competition has played a major role in achieving better perform-ance for customers and greater efficiency. The importance of comparative competition in water was recognized in the privatization legislation that provided for a compulsory reference to the Monopolies and Mergers (now the Competi-tion) Commission for all mergers of larger water companies: in judging a case, the Commission had to take account of its effect on the ability of OFWAT to make effective efficiency comparisons. A number of mergers of smaller com-panies have taken place, and in the case of some bigger ones, remedies had been agreed in the form of price reductions for customers. Some proposed mergers have been blocked.

Comparative competition has also involved good measurement, good analysis and good process. Guidelines for Regulatory Accounts are published and en-forced to ensure that the operations of the water utility are properly separated from any other activities. Key performance indicators have been specified, covering water quality, compliance with discharge standards and customer service. Comparable information, verified by independent reporters appointed by OFWAT, is collected from each company. The results are published, and the supporting information made publicly available. The measures have been used in price reviews to ensure that the regulated tariffs are set at levels which ensure that an efficient company could finance its operations, while putting pressure on less efficient ones to reduce their costs without, of course, reducing service to customers or companies failing their environmental obligations.

In setting price limits, comparative analysis has been used separately for (1) operating costs, (2) the costs of maintaining serviceability of the system to customers, (3) the costs of enhancing quality; and (4) relative customer perform-ance. Operating costs have been analysed econometrically. For enhancement costs a unit cost base has been used, where specified projects are costed by dif-ferent companies revealing their relative efficiency. Both methods have been used for capital maintenance. Good performance in customer service is rewarded in higher price limits and vice versa.

Privatization has provided powerful incentives for efficient capital markets, in equity and, increasingly, in bond markets. As a result of innovations, the cost of borrowing has fallen and companies have responded to the incentive to reduce the cost of capital by exploring optimal gearing, which has turned out to be much higher than expected. When, however, companies have large capital pro-grammes and are highly geared the need to maintain investment status for the bonds can add to the effective cost of capital. Privatization and regulation have driven substantial changes in how households and businesses pay for water services. Traditionally households and small businesses paid in relation to a property tax (rateable values) base. After privatization most, and now all new, households pay by meter. Existing customers have the right to opt for a meter and are doing so progressively. By the end of the decade, about one third of households will pay a volumetric charge. Metering has been extended to all businesses except where meter installation is difficult or expensive.

Extension of volumetric charging has been associated with significant reforms of tariffs. Cross-subsidies have been reduced. OFWAT has ensured a proper balance between the bills paid by households for measured and unmeasured consumption, resulting in significant savings by those paying volumetrically. Greater choice has resulted in wiser use of water as well as saving money. OFWAT has also acted to ensure that standing charges – for both household and business users – are kept down so that all users can exercise a proper economic choice.

Wastewater tariffs cover the costs of surface and highway drainage as well as the costs of collecting, treating and disposing of foul sewage. Customers who do not connect to the public network for surface drainage do not pay this element of charges. In principle, surface water charges should be related to the area drained, but this has been difficult fully to implement in practice. It has not proved practicable to charge highway users with the costs of draining roads.

Apart from England and Wales, private ownership of assets only occurs in very few places (e.g. Chile and parts of the USA) and as such the type of regulatory arrangements found here are not widely replicated. France has a highly developed system of franchising for water services, which is the most common form of PSP to be found around the world, and we will now discuss this.

Competition for the market and regulation – the case of PSP in France and lessons for elsewhere

The form of PSP most commonly found occurs through some form of contract with assets remaining in public (e.g. municipal) ownership and has its origins in France,[14] at that time driven by the need for financially starved municipalities to finance ambitious urbanization plans.

The large French companies (Veolia – previously Vivendi – and Suez) have been the world market leaders in the market for PSP in water. There are a variety of contract forms in France that are commonly used elsewhere in the world, the main ones being as follows.

Management contracts   There are two major forms of management contract in France. These are the *gérance* and *régie intéressée*. For both types, the contract's duration is typically around five years.

A *gérance* contract is a comprehensive operations and maintenance contract, where the private contractor provides all of the staff and expertise required to run a system, for a fixed fee. Under a *régie intéressée*, part or all of a contractor's payment is based on measurable results, which may relate to productivity or profits. The operator has responsibility only for operating the network, and no role in planning or undertaking capital investments or renewals.

Affermage contracts   The *affermage* contract (more commonly known as a lease) is the most common form of water sector delegation contract in France. The municipality or syndicate remains the owner of the assets and is responsible for financing capital expenditure and making investment decisions. The private operator is responsible for the operation of the system as well as asset maintenance, renewals and rehabilitation. The private operator is also likely to provide advice to the municipality on the need for new investment. The municipality may separately contract the private operator to implement capital investment decisions.

The private operator is remunerated directly by the consumer with a proportion paid to the municipality to cover its investment costs. The life of the *affermage* is usually of 10–15 years duration.

Concessions   Under a concession arrangement, the private operator is also responsible for financing new investment in the network and treatment facilities over the life of the contract, as well as operations and maintenance. The assets are, however, owned by the municipality. At the end of the contract, control over the utility's assets reverts to the municipality.

The concessionaire is remunerated directly by consumers and pays a portion of the amount collected back to the municipality to cover its expenses or any services provided by it. In practice, some investment may be undertaken directly by the municipality in order to benefit from government subsidies or cheaper finance. The life of a concession contract in France is now limited, by law, to a maximum of 20 years. Concession contracts signed before this limitation was introduced may run for longer periods, for example, as long as 30 or 50 years.

Contract-based approaches can be attractive to private operators because they reduce the risk associated with investment and the regulatory rules are embedded in an agreement between the two parties, which should make it more difficult for the public authority to change these rules in its own favour. There are, however, two issues of particular concern in relation to the contracting out of water services in relation to effective regulation and oversight, which we now discuss, using the French case as the reference point to make more general observations later.

Contract incompleteness and contract monitoring   A major problem associated with franchising is the presence of contract incompleteness. In the face of uncertainty about the future, a long-term contract of any description is likely to be incomplete. In network industries like utilities, where there are inevitable uncertainties about such critical elements as future investment needs and maintenance levels, the problem is significant.

In France, the regulatory regime is well adapted to dealing with this problem. Water sector PSP contracts (and other contracts with the private sector for the delivery of public services) are not treated in the same way as ordinary commercial contracts, but are governed by French public service law. Two core principles of French public service law are 'continuity of service' and 'continuing adaptation to circumstances' (see Shugart, 1998). If a company is in financial difficulty, for reasons which could not have been predicted, an extra payment can be claimed from the contracting municipality and this claim will be supported by the legal system. Unforeseen circumstances include legislation or policy decisions that impose additional costs on a private operator. Modifications can be made in the contractual terms as long as the private operator is appropriately remunerated. This provides the public authority with significant freedom in its decision-making authority, and significant protection for a private operator from bearing the financial burden of these decisions.

In France, however, the monitoring of the performance of private operators has been a weakness of its regulatory arrangements. Since 1995, private operators have been required under national legislation to produce annual performance reports to the contracting municipality regarding their performance. Dissatisfaction with both the level of compliance with this requirement and the quality of these reports has, however, recently led to a proposal to establish a national agency that would collect, publish and disseminate information on the comparative performance of water utilities in France, including both publicly and privately operated utilities.

Handling contract incompleteness and contract monitoring in other countries
The 'French regulatory model' is not easily transferable to other countries. Promises by public authorities of compensation in the event of loosely defined 'unforeseen circumstances' may lack credibility in some countries due to political reluctance to increase tariffs. Furthermore, legal systems in other countries may lack the impartiality and expertise necessary to adjudicate where disputes arise regarding this kind of commitment. Alternative mechanisms are often therefore required.

It may be difficult to deal with this problem of contractual incompleteness by simply trying to specify as much as possible in the contract (see Frontier Economics, 2003). Complete specification is simply not possible; some issue will eventually arise, most likely concerning tariffs, which will require either negotiation between the parties or some form of external decision-making. Formalized international arbitration, through bodies such as the International Chamber of Commerce, while impartial, is likely to suffer from a lack of expertise and it is also expensive.

An important role and rationale therefore emerges for a water sector supervisory agency of some kind (see Ballance and Taylor, 2003). It can support the ongoing effectiveness of a water sector PSP contract through adjudicating on those issues that cannot be fully addressed or specified in the contract, particularly tariffs, which simply cannot be pre-set for a 15 or 20 year period. It can have both the necessary expertise and the independence from government to make the requisite decisions and avoid this function being done through a process of obscure negotiation. Guasch (2004) points out that where there is weak public governance there has been a high incidence of contract renegotiation for water (and other utility) PSP contracts. A regulatory agency in such circumstances, however, would have a limited set of functions compared to say OFWAT in England and Wales, because of the very different nature of the arrangements.

A body can be established by legislation, which may have certain powers in relation to the formulation of regulatory rules and the approval of concession contracts, while other public authorities can have primary responsibility for negotiating and agreeing those contracts with private operators for the provision of water and sanitation services.

Under this approach, responsibility for monitoring the concession contract may be undertaken by the public authority, the regulatory body or both. The regulatory body may have some role in terms of acting as an appeals body when disputes between the public authority and the private operator arise.

This approach has been used where national (or regional) governments wish to exercise influence over municipal provision of water and sanitation services and related PSP contracts. Variations on this approach have been adopted in Portugal and are in the process of being adopted in Bulgaria and Indonesia.

There is, however, potential for conflict between the supervisory body and the public authority entering the PSP contract (e.g. a municipality) as well as a greater likelihood of conflicting or inconsistent rules being formulated. Foster (2002) points out that where this has been tried in Latin America (an 'Anglo-French hybrid') tensions have been created that can undermine the functioning of the model.

An interesting development in the context of regulation in the UK has been the establishment of the PPP Arbiter, whose main role is to advise on the fair price for the services provided by the three private sector infrastructure companies (Infracos). These companies will maintain, renew and upgrade London Underground's infrastructure under 30-year service contracts, under the new Tube Public Private Partnership (PPP). Previously the London Underground was publicly owned and operated. The levels of prices can be re-set at periodic reviews of the PPP contracts every 7½ years, when the Mayor of London and London Underground are able to re-specify what they require from the private sector, allowing flexibility in the changing needs of passengers. Extraordinary reviews can also be called in certain circumstances when the Arbiter will advise on possible adjustments to the payments made by London Underground to the Infracos. The Arbiter is also able to provide direction and guidance on any PPP contractual issues that London Underground and the infrastructure companies choose to refer to him.

Similar arrangements could be put in place for water PSP contracts, where the functions of the regulator are limited in scope, even if the functions that are exercised remain some of the more important ones (i.e. the resetting of prices).

For a supervisory agency to be effective, the contract must adequately acknowledge the agency's future role and specify the procedural mechanisms or triggers whereby it will be required to make decisions (e.g. resetting or re-basing tariffs). Otherwise, the actual responsibility of the supervisory authority for a particular issue is likely to be a further source of dispute.

An alternative means of resolving tariff disputes is the use of expert panels (see Shugart and Ballance, 2005) or external consultants to undertake periodic price reviews. This may be advantageous in situations where it is difficult to ensure that a regulatory agency is able to take crucial decisions in an independent way. An external source of expertise may save costs and achieve a sense of legitimacy that a regulatory agency cannot and also obtain the necessary expertise. A number of issues, however, need careful consideration, not least whether such decisions are advisory or binding in nature. If they are not binding, this can open up a further area for dispute.

Contract monitoring   Responsibility for the monitoring of a PSP contract can also be delegated to an agency, such as a specialist contract-monitoring unit established under the contract. This has been adopted in a number of PSP contracts internationally in recent years, including in Sofia, Bucharest, Manila and Jakarta. This agency can ensure that the private operator is meeting its obligations where additional mechanisms or institutions may be required. In particular, there may be a desire to make the monitoring process more impartial, particularly where its results have important implications for issues of contract compliance or performance-related payments.

Where performance-related incentives involving bonus payments to private operators are featured, so-called 'technical' auditors are often retained to provide impartial reports on the parameters impacting on these payments. Examples of management contracts where technical auditors have been retained include Amman (Jordan), Tripoli (Libya) and Dushanbe (Tajikistan).

Regulation of public utilities – the case of Scotland

The supervision of publicly owned utilities by a regulator offers an alternative to concession contracts when governments want to retain public operation as well as public ownership of water services. In such circumstances, it is worth considering the use of an independent regulatory body, which can analyse and supervise, as an intermediary between Ministers and suppliers. Scotland offers an example of how these arrangements can be, and are being, developed. They have already led to a considerable increase in the efficiency of the operations of the water services in Scotland. Similar arrangements are being developed in Northern Ireland.

Scottish Water is a public corporation, formed in 2002 from the three Scottish Water Authorities, owned by the Scottish Executive, the devolved government of Scotland. Under the Water Services (Scotland) Act 2005, Scottish Water is regulated by a Water Commission that is independent of ministers. (The Commission has taken over the work of the Water Commissioner, who had previously advised the Scottish Executive.) In November 2005, the Commission set price limits for Scottish Water, subject to appeal as is the case in England and Wales to the UK Competition Commission.

The Commission (and previously the Commissioner) is using all the comparative information collected by OFWAT to set price limits for Scotland that cover 'lowest reasonable overall costs'. Similar procedures have been devised to ensure that quality obligations are properly costed before being imposed by the Scottish Executive on Scottish Water. There is a transparent process, exposing the methodology used and involving consultation with all stakeholders before decisions are made. The performance of Scottish Water against these obligations and against standards of service for customers will be monitored by the Commission, jointly with the Scottish Drinking Water Quality Regulator and the Scottish Environmental Protection Agency (Water Industry Commissioner for Scotland, 2004 and 2005).

There are two major differences compared with the situation in England and Wales. First, because Scottish Water is financed from the Exchequer, its cost of capital is related to the cost of public borrowing and such borrowing is constrained by the UK public expenditure limits agreed for Scotland.

Second, the incentives facing management are rather different from those in England and Wales, because there are no capital market pressures for improvements in efficiency. To achieve the necessary hard budget constraints and comparable incentives for management, ministers, as owners, have said that they are ready to deny additional finance to Scottish Water where, owing to factors within management control, objectives have not been met and where greater efficiency has not been achieved. Customers cannot be expected to pay twice for the same outputs. The Scottish Executive may need to ensure that the pay – and bonuses – earned by managers are related to the achievement of customer and environmental standards and of greater efficiency in delivering them.

Notwithstanding the different incentives facing managers, the private sector has been used to good effect in Scotland. Scottish Water contracts out significant elements of its capital expenditure programme. Some of this was done (in the past) under UK Public Private Partnership (PPP) arrangements for a number of build–operate–transfer (BOT) type schemes for waste water treatment. There are nine PPP contracts presently in place.

In addition, Scottish Water Solutions was established in April 2002 for the purpose of delivering a large proportion (around 70 per cent) of Scottish Water's £1.8 billion capital investment programme. It was established as a joint venture limited company within a publicly owned organization, 51 per cent owned by

Scottish Water and 49 per cent split equally between two private consortia, the rationale being that a joint venture would eliminate incentives to companies to act in their own self-interests. Scottish Water Solutions is managing a number of major projects throughout Scotland. This illustrates that other types of competitive pressures can be used to help deliver a good deal for customers.

The Water Commission is engaged in working with the Scottish Executive to achieve the objectives outlined above, including the creation of a financial cushion that would be available to deal with adverse shocks outside management control without involving additional public expenditure. It will also advise the Scottish Executive on the incentives needed to ensure that minimum standards for customer and environmental services are met.

Conclusions

In this chapter we have examined two particular themes in the effective regulatory oversight of water, which involves making appropriate decisions on industry structure, competition and regulation.

First, we examined the regulation of *structure*; that is, the appropriate organization of the sector including the scope for the competitive provision of services *in* the market. Second, we examined the regulation of *conduct*; that is, where there is considerable natural monopoly power, what form should regulation take or alternatively what is the scope for competition *for* the market and in such circumstances is there a need for further regulatory mechanisms? Implicit in our analysis is that where it is feasible competition provides a spur to good service and efficient provision and there are therefore strong arguments for developing structures that facilitate it.

In terms of structure, the available evidence indicates that there are economies of scale in the operation of water services, but also that there may be diseconomies of scale beyond some point. The international evidence provides support for a 'u-shaped' cost function.

The empirical evidence on water industry cost structures also confirms that it is overly simplistic to regard water (and sanitation) as standard natural monopolies. There are important trade-offs in the organization of water services – that is, between the production (abstraction, treatment) and network functions. Economies of scale are most likely to lie in production activities (lower unit costs from larger sources and treatment works, for example), while diseconomies of scale are fundamentally a function of distance and network size.

Considerations other than economic ones might at times also influence industry structure. In the case of England and Wales, the reorganization of the sector in 1973 into ten regional water authorities was largely driven by a desire to see integrated river-basin management, whereby a single entity where possible should plan and control the uses of water in each river catchment. Similar pressures may be seen in Europe in the future with the implementation of the

Water Framework Directive, which will focus attention on issues of catchment management.

It is difficult to argue that water services in their entirety are natural monopolies. There are clearly areas, such as retailing and supply to larger customers, where competition is possible, though the scale of the gains is not yet fully established. Water sector reform could increase the scope for competitive forces both *in* the market and *for* the market. While there may be doubts whether competition in the market for water would be the widespread success that it has been for other utility sectors, there are interesting developments in a number of jurisdictions.

Turning to the examination of the regulation of conduct for the water sector, we focused our attention on the cases of England and Wales where there is an independent regulatory body (OFWAT) regulating privatized water utilities, of France where private sector participation (PSP) takes the form of contract and regulation is done primarily through contract (so-called 'regulation by contract'), and of Scotland where there is an independent body regulating a single publicly owned water utility.

Different approaches may be suitable for different circumstances. The regulatory models in England and Wales and France appear to have served their sectors well, despite being very different in many ways (see Ballance and Taylor, 2005; and Ballance, 2003). Regulatory models need to be tailored to the social and cultural circumstances of a country. Wholesale application of any one model to other jurisdictions is unlikely to succeed.

For the most part, where there is PSP it is usually in the form of contracts. As such, the England and Wales model is likely to have limited application. However, there are, as we have set out, features of the application of the French model that also make its application to other countries limited. These are associated with the legal system, the ability to deal with issues of contract incompleteness and the level of expertise required. The oft-cited public debate about whether, therefore, one should choose the 'English' or the 'French' model for regulation is misleading (see Ballance and Taylor, 2003). Where effective PSP contracts are desired (particularly deeper forms of PSP, such as concession and *affermage* contracts) there will be a need for the establishment of an effective institutional framework, particularly with respect to periodic tariff setting and contract monitoring. Consideration will need to be given to having a regulatory body but with far more limited powers than a traditional independent regulatory agency (such as OFWAT), like the PPP Arbiter for the London Underground in the UK, or indeed the use of expert panels for periodic tariff reviews.

The Scotland case is interesting in that in many jurisdictions the water sector is likely to remain under public ownership with a limited role for PSP. In such cases the Scottish model offers an example of the establishment of an independent regulatory body to ensure that the supplier delivers quality and customers standards in an efficient and acceptable way.

Notes
1. An additional pretext was the amalgamation of undertakings serving urban and rural areas, thereby providing greater opportunities for cross-subsidization.
2. The most significant changes are for Northumbrian Water, which merged in 1995 with the contiguous North East Water and the non-contiguous Essex and Suffolk Water in 2000.
3. OFWAT's resistance is well illustrated by the response to the Department of Trade and Industry's White Paper setting out proposals for inclusion in an Enterprise Bill:
    > OFWAT considers that the existing special provisions for dealing with mergers between water companies as set out in sections 32 to 36 of the 1991 Water Industry Act (WIA) should be preserved in the new merger regime. The 'public interest' test in these provisions expressly refers to the Director's need to be able to make comparisons in order to carry out his duties under the WIA. Due to the monopoly nature of the industry there is a need to retain comparative competition until such time as there is effective market competition even if ultimately it means that certain mergers have to be blocked. The current powers have been effective. (OFWAT, 2001)
4. The planned take-over of Southern Water by Vivendi Water received qualified approval from the Competition Commission (see Competition Commission, 2002), but was blocked by the Secretary of State for Trade and Industry, largely on the grounds of the detriment to comparative competition. The case was also noteworthy for OFWAT's consideration of the proposed remedy of Southern Water divesting their water supply operations in Hampshire to create a new comparator. Hampshire is a non-contiguous area within Southern Water's water supply area. This would have been the first instance of a reversal in the post-war trend towards consolidation, but the Competition Commission panel decided that the remedy of Vivendi divesting their stake in another water supply company (South Staffordshire Water) was preferable to the creation of a new company in Hampshire. One reason was that the divestiture of the Hampshire area would have exposed significant cross-subsidies within Southern's regionally averaged charges.
5. Strictly, this is the scale at which operating expenditure is minimized for the sample average undertaking.
6. These latter studies extend the previous analysis by examining the impact of scale on productivity growth in the post-privatization period. Saal et al. (2004), in particular, find that increasing scale has a negative impact on productivity growth.
7. There are also parallels with the debate in England and Wales about further consolidation in the sector on two fronts. First, the regulatory requirements for the maintenance of comparative data have meant that even with increased consolidation in ownership and management, sub-company comparisons of operational efficiency (based on operational area) provide an alternative that OFWAT itself has expressed a willingness to develop further, as part of its benchmarking exercise, when setting regulatory price caps. Second, the threat of take-over remains an important market discipline on management in England and Wales and for this reason there are benefits to regulation from retaining a certain fluidity in the structure of ownership (in effect a form of 'for market' competition).
8. Competition in telecommunications has ultimately also been constrained by the impracticality of multiple connections to a single residence. While multiple networks have been possible for trunk networks, the connection into individual premises (the so-called 'last mile') has remained a stubborn monopoly, though unbundling of local loops is now occurring.
9. OFWAT has calculated that in gas and electricity the indicative additional costs of transportation can be approximately 2.5–5 per cent per 100 km, while in water they are approximately 50 per cent.
10. For example, the Californian State Water Code was enacted in 1986. The so-called Wheeling Statutes are formally codified in Part 2, Chapter 11, Article 4 Joint Use of Capacity in Water Conveyance Facilities (sections 1810–14). Section 1810 stipulates the mandatory requirement

to allow access in return for fair compensation. In November 1998 San Diego County Water Authority (a retailer) started a legal challenge to the wheeling rates established by Metropolitan Water District (the network owner) to comply with statutory requirements. The case, after appeal, concluded in 2000 in favour of the network operator.

11. This section draws upon Byatt (2004).
12. The Water Act 2003 changes the primary duties to protecting the interests of the consumer through promoting effective competition where appropriate.
13. Glas Cymru is a limited company by guarantee with no equity shareholders that now wholly owns and controls Welsh Water (Dŵr Cymru), one of the ten water and sewerage undertakers. It was formed in 2001 to buy out Welsh Water from Western Power Distribution. The purchase was financed through bond issues. The majority of the operations conducted by Welsh Water have been contracted out. United Utilities and Kelda have been contracted to provide the bulk of the day-to-day water and sewage treatment operations and most site operations staff have transferred to the new contractors. Thames Water provides customer services.
14. In France private sector participation has been present since 1853 with the founding of Compagnie Générale des Eaux, which gained a water distribution concession in Lyon. Générale des Eaux gained further contracts in Nantes (1854), Paris (1860) and Nice (1864). Following the establishment of Générale des Eaux, Eaux de Banlieue was established in 1867 and Lyonnaise des Eaux in 1880.

References

Ballance, A. (2003) *The Privatisation of the Water Industry in England & Wales – Success or Failure and Future Direction*, London: Stone and Webster Consultants.

Ballance, A. and Taylor, A. (2002) 'Competition in the Water Market: A Review of the Issues', *Water*, **21**.

Ballance, A. and Taylor, A. (2003) 'Regulation of Private Sector Participation in Water: The Myth of Clear Cut Choices', *Water*, **21**.

Ballance, A. and Taylor, A. (2005) *Competition and Economic Regulation in Water: The Future of the European Water Industry*, London: International Water Association.

Baumol, W. (1977) 'On the Proper Tests for Natural Monopoly in a Multiproduct Industry', *The American Economic Review*, **67**, 809–22.

Byatt, I. (2004) 'Managing Water for the Future: The Case of England and Wales', in J. Trottier and P. Slack (eds), *Managing Water Resources, Past and Present: The Linacre Lectures 2002*, Oxford: Oxford University Press.

Central Advisory Water Committee (1971) *The Future Management of Water in England and Wales: A Report by the Central Advisory Water Committee*, London: Central Advisory Water Committee.

Commission of the European Communities (2003) *Green Paper on Services of General Interest*, COM (2003) 270 Final, Brussels: European Commission.

Competition Commission (2002) *Vivendi Water UK PLC and First Aqua (JVCo) Limited: A Report on the Proposed Merger*, London: Competition Commission.

Fabbri, P. and Fraquelli, G. (2000) 'Cost and Structure of Technology in Italian Water Industry', *Empirica*, **27**, 65–82.

Foster, V. (2002) 'Ten Years of Water Service Reform in Latin America: Towards an Anglo-French Model', in P. Seidenstat, D. Haarmeyer and S. Hakim (eds), *Reinventing Water and Wastewater Systems – Global Lessons for Improving Water Management*, New Jersey: John Wiley & Son Inc.

Frontier Economics (2003) 'Water Under the Bridge', *Frontier Economics Bulletin*, April 2003.

Garcia, S. and Thomas, A. (2001) 'The Structure of Municipal Water Supply Costs: Application to a Panel of French Local Communities', *Journal of Productivity Analysis*, **16**, 5–29.

Guasch, J.L. (2004) 'Granting and Renegotiating Infrastructure Concessions: Doing It Right, Vol. 1 of 1', *WBI Development Studies (Report No. 28816)*, Washington, DC: World Bank.

Hayes, K. (1987) 'Cost Structure of the Water Industry', *Applied Economics*, **19**, 417–25.

Indepen and Accenture (2002) *Water Merger Policy: Time for Review*, London: Indepen and Accenture.

Kim, E. and Lee, H. (1998) 'Spatial Integration of Urban Water Services and Economies of Scale', *Review of Urban and Regional Development Studies*, **10**, 3–18.

Kim, H.Y. (1985) 'Economies of Scale in Multiproduct Firms: An Empirical Analysis', *Economica*, **54**, 185–206.

Kim, H.Y. and Clarke, R. (1988) 'Economies of Scale and Scope in Water Supply', *Regional Science and Urban Economics*, **18**, 479–502.

Mizutani, F. and Urakami, T. (2001) 'Identifying Network Density and Scale Economies for Japanese Water Supply Organisations', *Papers in Regional Science*, **80**, 211–30.

OFWAT (2001) 'Productivity and Enterprise – a World Class Competition Regime', *Response to the DTI White Paper*, October 2001, Birmingham: Office of Water Services.

Panzar, J.C. and Willig, R.D. (1977) 'Economies of Scale in Multi-output Production', *Quarterly Journal of Economics*, **91**, 481–93.

Richardson, H.J. (2003) 'The Water Industry in England and Wales: Constantly Changing Development over the Past Half Century', *Water Intelligence Online*, 1–11.

Robinson, C. (1998) 'A "crisis" in Water: The Wrong Sort of Privatisation', in J. Morris (ed.), *The Crisis in Water*, London, Institute of Economic Affairs.

Saal, D. and Parker, D. (2000) 'The Impact of Privatisation and Regulation on the Water Industry in England and Wales: A Translog Cost Function Approach', *Managerial and Decision Economics*, **21**, 253–68.

Saal, D., Parker, D. and Weyman-Jones, T. (2004) 'Determining the Contribution of Technical, Efficiency, and Scale Change to Productivity Growth in the Privatised English and Welsh Water and Sewerage Industry: 1985–2000', *Aston Business School Working Paper RP0433*, Birmingham: Aston University.

Shugart, C. (1998) 'Regulation by Contract and Municipal Services: The Problem of Contractual Incompleteness', PhD, Harvard University (Graduate School of Arts and Sciences).

Shugart, C. and Ballance, A. (2005) *Expert Panels: The Future for Public Utility Regulation?*, Washington, DC: World Bank 2005 (http://rru.worldbank.org/Discussions/topics/topic66.aspx).

Stone and Webster Consultants (2002) 'GATS and the Liberalisation of Water Supply Services', in *Final Report to Gesellschaft fuer Technische Zusammenarbeit (GTZ)*, August 2002, Bonn: GTZ.

Stone and Webster Consultants (2004a) 'Investigation into Evidence for Economies of Scale in the Water and Sewerage Industry in England and Wales', in *Final Report to Office of Water Services*, January 2004, Birmingham: OFWAT.

Stone and Webster Consultants (2004b) 'An Investigation into OPEX Productivity Trends and Causes in the Water Industry in England & Wales – 1992–93 to 2002–03', in *Final Report to Office of Water Services*, May 2004, Birmingham: OFWAT.

SWC Consulting (2003) 'Ofwat Study into the Effects of Regulatory Policy on Company Investment Decision-making', in *Final Report to OFWAT*, March 2003, Birmingham, OFWAT.

Tynan, N. and Kingdom, W. (2005) 'Optimal Size for Utilities? Returns to Scale in Water:

Evidence from Benchmarking', *Public Policy for the Private Sector*, January, Note Number 283.

Water Industry Commissioner for Scotland (2004) *Our Work in Regulating the Scottish Water Industry – Volume 3: The Calculation of Prices*, Stirling: Water Industry Commissioner.

Water Industry Commissioner for Scotland (WICS) (2005) *The Strategic Review of Charges: Draft Determinations Volumes 1 to 7*, Glasgow: Water Industry Commissioner, June.

WRc and Ecologic (2002) *Study on the Application of the Competition Rules to the Water Sector in the European Community*, Prepared by WRc and Ecologic for the European Commission – Competition Directorate General, December 2002, Swindon: WRc Plc.

Index